British School of Archaeology
in Jerusalem

Monograph Series

I

THE RED TOWER

(al-Burj al-Ahmar)

Settlement in the Plain of Sharon
at the Time of the Crusaders and Mamluks

A.D. 1099–1516

by

DENYS PRINGLE

With Contributions by Judith Cartledge,
John Hanbury-Tenison, Richard Hubbard, Joyce McKay,
Yaakov Meshorer and Donald S. Richards
and Survey Drawings
by Peter Leach

BRITISH SCHOOL OF ARCHAEOLOGY IN JERUSALEM
LONDON 1986

British School of Archaeology in Jerusalem Monograph Series No. 1

Published by the British School of Archaeology in Jerusalem,
c/o The British Academy, 20–21 Cornwall Terrace, London NW1 4QP

BRITISH LIBRARY CATALOGUING IN PUBLICATION DATA
Pringle, Reginald Denys
    The Red Tower (al-Burj al-Ahmar)
    1. ISBN
    2.
    I. Title. II. Series.

    ISBN 0 9500542 6 7

Computer typeset by SB Datagraphics
Printed in Great Britain by Spottiswoode Ballantyne Printers Ltd

CONTENTS

LIST OF FIGURES

LIST OF PLATES

INTRODUCTION

Studies of rural settlement in Palestine at the time of the Crusades have invariably tended to approach the subject from the standpoint of the Franks' own colonization and exploitation of the land and its people (e.g. Cahen 1951; Prawer 1980, 102–214; Benvenisti 1970, 211–270). Since most of the documentary evidence on which such studies are based comes from Frankish sources this perspective may indeed seem inescapable. Yet estimates of rural population size and density, however they may differ when it comes to actual numbers, all agree on one thing: that the Frankish population in the countryside was numerically insignificant compared to the population of native Syrian peasantry (Benvenisti 1970, 18–19). Historians of settlement are therefore faced with the considerable handicap that even in a period of relatively abundant documentation, compared that is to any other two centuries in Palestine between the 6th and the 16th century, most of the evidence relates only to a minority of the population.

In northern and western Europe, it has often been possible to offset imbalances of this kind in the written record by combining documentary research with archaeological excavation and survey (see for instance, Comba 1983; CNRS 1979; Sawyer (ed.) 1976). In Syria and Palestine, however, such little archaeological work as has been undertaken on the period of the Crusader occupation has tended to reinforce rather than lessen the bias of the written records, since it has usually concentrated on Crusader monuments alone and ignored all other aspects of medieval rural settlement.

In 1983, therefore, the British School of Archaeology in Jerusalem undertook a project of excavation and survey centred on the Red Tower (al-Burj al-Ahmar), a Crusader castle in the Sharon Plain. The main purpose of this study was to attempt to make good some of the deficiencies in our archaeological record for a particular area of countryside in the Crusader and Mamluk periods. More generally it was intended to test whether by combining the more traditional methods of documentary research with archaeological excavation and survey, it might be possible to approach the question of rural settlement at the time of the Crusaders and Mamluks from a rather different viewpoint than hitherto. If the result of such an experiment is to raise more questions than it answers, then it will at least have demonstrated the incompleteness of our present knowledge and, perhaps, some avenues for future research.

The scale of the research project was, as always, limited both by time and by funds. These restraints, however, can also be seen as an advantage, since they mean that the results, however imperfect or provisional they may have to be, will at least appear in print earlier than would otherwise be the case. The area selected for survey comprises the central part of the Sharon Plain and the western edge of the adjoining hills of Samaria. It is conveniently defined by the borders of the 1:50,000 series map, Sheet 5-III (Nathanya), and represents a rectangular block of territory 20 km. (N–S) by some 25 km. (E–W), bounded on the west by the sea. In the Roman, Byzantine and medieval periods the area contained no major towns or cities.

The time-scale of the survey was limited to the period of Crusader and Mamluk control of the area, that is to say from 1099 until 1516 when Palestine became subject to the Ottomans. Concentrating on so narrow a time-period might normally be counted a weakness in archaeological survey, as indeed would our concentration on known settlement sites rather than on random or comprehensive coverage of the entire survey area (cf. Cherry 1983). Compensation for such shortcomings, however, was provided in this case by drawing on the results of other multi-period archaeological surveys which have already been conducted over all or part of the same area. These include: the archive and sherd collection of the Government of Palestine's Department of Antiquities, assembled between 1918 and 1948 and housed in the Palestine Archaeological (Rockefeller) Museum in Jerusalem (inspected by kind permission of the Israel Dept. of Antiquities); the Archaeological Survey of Israel, whose sherding activities have also covered the whole of our area and whose report on the emergency West Bank Survey of 1967–68 is also available in print (Kochavi (ed.) 1972); the ʿEmeq Hefer Regional Survey, a multi-period archaeological survey covering the area surrounding the valley of the Nahr Iskandaruna (information kindly supplied by Mr. Y. Porath and Prof. S. Paley); and the Apollonia–Arsuf Survey, which covers the territory of Arsuf and impinges on the southern part of our survey area (information kindly supplied by Mr. I. Roll). When combined with our own survey of selected sites carried out in 1983, therefore, it may be said that archaeological survey of the area has been reasonably comprehensive, though arguably of uneven quality and intensity.

The "area survey" was accompanied by excavation at the Red Tower (al-Burj al-Ahmar), a small Crusader castle situated in the centre of the plain and of the survey area. The immediate purpose of this excavation was, first, to find out more about the nature of the castle and its sequence of construction and occupation; and secondly, to help define a ceramic sequence with which to date medieval occupation at other sites in the region identified by surface sherding. This particular site was selected because it was reasonably well documented and therefore likely to produce dated groups of finds; also because it seemed likely (as indeed proved to be so) that these objectives could be met with only limited excavation by a small team of volunteers.

The results of the survey, the excavation and the analysis of the finds from the latter form the basis for the following three parts of this volume. The project was sponsored by the British School of Archaeology in Jerusalem, with additional support from the British Academy, the Society of Antiquaries of London, the Palestine Exploration Fund and the European Science Foundation.* I am especially grateful to the Director of the Israel Department of Antiquities, Mr. A. Eitan, for granting the British School permission to excavate the site and to carry out the associated survey; and to the Department's local representative, Mr. Y. Porath, for his considerable assistance and practical advice.

The excavation was carried out between 5 July and 20 August 1983 by a team of up to 12 volunteers from the U.K., Canada, U.S.A. and Eire under my direction. Survey work was carried out by Mr. Peter Leach and the finds department was run by Miss Hannah Arnup. Josephine Bateson, Elizabeth Harvie, Andrew Peterson and Elizabeth Yarwood acted as site-assistants. A first-aid box was generously donated by the Venerable Order of St. John of Jerusalem, whose predecessors once occupied the site; and survey equipment was loaned us by the Hebrew Union College, Jerusalem. Accommodation was provided in local school buildings through the generosity of the Regional Council of ʿEmeq Hefer, and meals at the near-by Ruppin Agricultural Institute.

Both of these facilities were shared with the American teams excavating near-by at Tell Hefer and Mikhmoret through the kindness of Prof. S. Paley (State University of New York, Buffalo) and his colleagues.

Most of the area survey was carried out in November 1983 by Peter Leach and myself, at times assisted by Mr. Abdul Jawad Abbasi. Our task was made easier by information and practical assistance provided by S. Dar, Y. Minsker, Y. Porath and R. Reich. For permission to consult and reproduce items from the archaeological records of the Department of Antiquities of the Government of Palestine (1918–48) I am grateful to the Director of the Israel Department of Antiquities and to members of his staff, particularly Mrs. Ayala Zusman, Mr. Ronnie Reich and Mr. Benjamin Sass. For permission to inspect pottery collected in the Archaeological Survey of 1967–68, I am also grateful to Z. Yeivin and Y. Porath. A soil map of the Nathanya area was kindly made available to me by the Israel Department of Agriculture in Tel-Aviv. Access to the K. A. C. Creswell Archive in Oxford was kindly afforded by Dr. James Allan of the Ashmolean Museum, Department of Eastern Art.

The excavation and survey drawings are the work of Mr. Peter Leach, while those of small finds are mostly that of Miss Macia de Renzy-Martin. For permission to reproduce certain photographs I am grateful to the Israel Department of Antiquities and the Ashmolean Museum, Oxford.

Finally, in preparing the text I am grateful for having been able to draw on the expertise of a number of colleagues, including Prof. D. Barag (Jerusalem), Prof. J. Carswell (Chicago), Prof. H. E. Mayer (Kiel), Dr. Helen Philon (Athens), Prof. J. S. C. Riley-Smith (London) and Prof. Yoram Tsafrir (Jerusalem). The remaining errors of fact or judgement are my own responsibility. I completed the text while holding a Fellowship at Dumbarton Oaks, Washington D.C.

Dumbarton Oaks
June 1985

* The archaeological material and topographical data presented in this publication have been collected in part with the financial support of the European Science Foundation through its research programme in the historical geography of the Byzantine Empire. This programme, whose initial period of financing by the ESF ran from 1979 to 1983, is designed to make an inventory of certain cities, towns and other remains of the Byzantine Empire which are in danger of disappearing. The Additional Activity in Byzantine Studies of the ESF is co-ordinated by an organizing committee which includes Byzantine scholars from several European countries. It is directed by Prof. H. Ahrweiler. The following organizations contributed to the financing of the Additional Activity in Byzantine Studies of the ESF: Österreichische Akademie der Wissenschaften, Fonds National de la Recherche Scientifique/National Fonds voor Wetenschappelijk Onderzoek of Belgium, Statens Humanistiske Forskningsråd of Denmark, Centre National de la Recherche Scientifique of France, Deutsche Forschungsgemeinschaft, National Hellenic Research Foundation of Greece, Royal Irish Academy, Consiglio Nazionale delle Ricerche of Italy, Nederlandse Organisatie voor Zuiver-Wetenschappelijk Onderzoek, British Academy, Savet Zajednica za Nauka Jugoslavije.

PART ONE

Medieval Settlement in the Sharon Plain and Adjacent Hills

I. THE PATTERN OF MEDIEVAL SETTLEMENT

1. NATIVE SETTLEMENT

The Sharon Plain represents that part of coastal Palestine some 16 km. wide which extends 50 km. north and south between the Nahr az-Zarqa (Nahal Taninim or Crocodile River) and the Nahr al-ʿAuja (Nahal Yarqon) (see Abel 1933(1), 94–98, 414–416; Orni and Efrat 1980, 35–49; and particularly for what follows, Karmon 1961). It represents, in fact, less a plain than a series of distinct low-lying topographical belts, running in roughly parallel sequence between the sea and the mountains of Samaria. The part of the Sharon chosen for study here, an east–west slice 20 km. wide through the centre of the area, is fairly typical of the area as a whole.

The western belt of the Sharon comprises three parallel ridges of *kurkar*, a marine sandstone formation, the western one forming the present sea cliffs, 30–40 m. high and mostly covered by dune sand, and the eastern one 4 km. inland, between 40 and 60 m. high and covered by red sands known as *hamra*.

The central belt, between 4·5 and 13 km. from the sea, comprises low rolling hills of *hamra*, up to 50 or 60 m. above sea level. This land is unsuitable for arable cultivation; today it is used mostly for orchards, but in antiquity was covered by dense woodland, remains of which persisted until the late 19th century (Conder 1875, 92). In the north of our area, the *hamra* is cut by the valley of the Nahr Iskandaruna (Nahal Alexander) and in the south it contains the basin of the Nahr al-Faliq (Nahal Poleg). Both these rivers, however, have to pass through the *kurkar* ridge in order to reach the sea. The constriction of their mouths at various times in history has thus often led to flooding and the formation of swamps about their lower courses.

The eastern belt represents a lower trough, 2–6 km. wide, lying between the hamratic soils and the mountains. In our area it is drained north and north-west by tributaries of the Nahr Iskandaruna. The land contains good alluvial material, suitable for arable cultivation though prone to flooding in the winter.

Finally comes the hill country, rising in our area as high as 400 m. To the north of the Wadi Nablus (Wadi ash-Shaʿir or Nahal Shechem), which cuts through them from east to west, the hills are formed of alternating hard limestone and soft chalk, allowing for softly moulded contours and wide valleys. To the south the limestone is consistently harder, producing a more rugged terrain.

The earliest human colonists in the Sharon, from the third millennium B.C. (Early Bronze Age I) onwards, seem to have favoured its eastern margins and river basins for establishing their settlements. Two lines of tells flank the eastern belt on either side, occupying sites on the edge of the *hamra* and limestone respectively (Karmon 1961, 52–53; Gophna and Kokhavi 1966). This alluvial area also represents the easiest natural line of communications in the Sharon, running north and south, and was thus chosen in ancient and more recent times as the route for the so-called "Way of the Sea" or *Via Maris*, linking Egypt with the Fertile Crescent (Orni and Efrat 1980, 355, 359). In the lower valley of the Iskandaruna, where the river breaches the east *kurkar* ridge, activity is attested from the Chalcolithic period (fourth millennium B.C) at Kh. Madd ad-Dair (1413. 1968) on the south bank and from Middle Bronze Age IIA at Tall al-Ifshar (Tel Hefer: 1415.1976) on the north (Paley and Porath 1979; 1980; 1982; Paley, Porath and Stieglitz 1982; cf. Gophna and Kokhavi 1966). There is no evidence in these periods, however, for any penetration of the forested *hamra*.

In the Roman and Byzantine periods (37 B.C.–A.D. 636), the pattern of settlement altered dramatically. By the end of that period an even spread of settlements covered the Sharon Plain and penetrated the woodlands of the *hamra* (see Fig. 1). The lower courses of the Nahr Iskandaruna and Nahr al-Faliq were drained by artificial channels cut through the *kurkar* ridges, hence the medieval name of *Flum de Rochetaillée* subsequently given to the latter; and paved roads and new bridges allowed for a system of communications less dependent on natural conditions. It seems likely, however, that the principal north–south route remained the *Via Maris*, following the eastern belt, while a coastal road from *Caesarea* to *Joppe* (Jaffa) probably followed the line of the second *kurkar* ridge (cf. Avi-Yonah 1940, 42; Karmon 1961, 53–57; fig. 2). A road from *Antipatris* (Ras al-ʿAin) to *Caesarea* branched north-west from the eastern route at Qalansuwa, to cross the Nahr Iskandaruna near the site of the bridge called in Ottoman times al-Jisr al-Maktaba, proceeding thence towards Hadera (Dar and Applebaum 1973); the fact that this road crossed the marshy lower flood plain of the river provides,

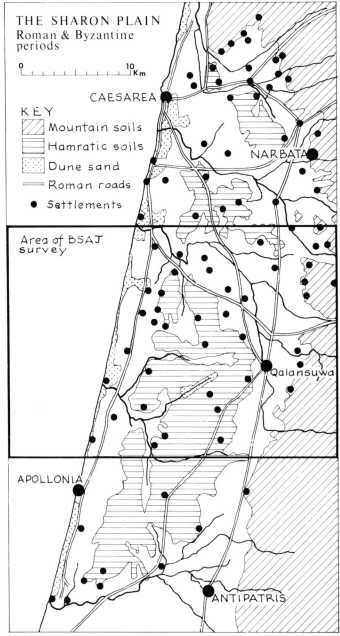

Fig. 1. Map of the Sharon Plain in the Roman period (after Karmon 1961; and Dar and Applebaum 1973).

incidentally, corroborative evidence that the marshes had been drained. Near the site of the modern village called Burgata (1463.1924), this road was met by another from *Neapolis* (Nablus), which may then have continued north-west to a lower crossing point of the river at Muwailha on the line of the inland *kurkar* ridge between Kh. Madd ad-Dair and Tall al-Ifshar (Avi-Yonah 1940, 14 and map (no. 19); Karmon 1961, 56–57; Dar and Applebaum 1973, 97; fig. 2).

The expansion of settlement in the Roman and Byzantine periods was doubtless made possible by the relatively stable conditions prevailing and was encouraged by the urban and overseas markets and sources of investment opened up to agriculture in the region by the development of Caesarea, both as a port (from 13/12 B.C.) and (after A.D. 44) as provincial capital of *Judaea* and later of *Palaestina Prima* (cf. Avi-Yonah 1958).

Evidence gathered by the ᶜEmeq Hefer and Apollonia–Arsuf Surveys indicates that the Muslim conquest brought about no immediate change in the settlement pattern of the Sharon (information kindly supplied by Y. Porath, S. Dar and I. Roll; cf. Roll and Ayalon 1981, 124). Yet comparison of the distribution of settlements in the Roman–Byzantine period (Fig. 1) with that in the 12th and 13th centuries (Figs. 2–3) shows that profound changes had occurred by the time of the First Crusade. In 1961, Professor Karmon estimated that the number of settlements in the western and central parts of the Sharon Plain had fallen by more than two-thirds during these five centuries (from 58 to 17), while in the eastern area the number had remained stable (35 in both periods) (1961, 58; cf. Ashtor 1976, 54). The evidence from the more recent surveys will no doubt enable these figures, and perhaps their implications, to be nuanced somewhat, though it seems unlikely that it will alter very significantly this observed overall trend. More valuable will be the evidence that the surveys provide for dating the stages by which the transformation took place. For the time being, however, some general observations will have to suffice.

First, it needs to be remembered that the changes indicated above relate only to numbers of settlements and not to their size. Indeed, the population of Palestine may already have been declining from the 7th century, though this would not necessarily have resulted immediately in the abandonment of settlements. Secondly, the argument that the incoming Muslim Arabs neglected the Roman agricultural installations, in particular systems of irrigation, drainage and terracing, thereby causing irreversible soil-erosion, the formation of swamps and sand dunes and a consequent dwindling of settlement can no longer be sustained in so crude a formulation (cf. Reifenberg 1955; Benvenisti 1970, 263; Ashtor 1976, 58–60). The first four centuries of the Hijira now appear, on the contrary, to have been a period of technological innovation in the Islamic world as a whole, with new crops introduced from the Far East enabling a small revolution in Near Eastern farming methods to take place. Agricultural decline would seem to have begun only after c.1100 and to judge from the ·achievements of the earlier centuries it cannot have been a result purely of ignorance (Watson 1981; 1983). That agricultural installations over much of Palestine fell into decay at some stage after the Byzantine period and before the First World War is clear from archaeological observations made in modern times (cf. Guy 1954; Reifenberg 1951; Rim 1951; Shaw and Pharaon 1941; Ashtor 1976, 45–66). The archaeological evidence for abandonment, however, will have to be systematically collected and analysed before any definitive historical conclusions may be drawn about its causes, chronology and implications. Such information as there is suggests that, as in Transjordan (cf. Sauer 1982, 332–333), the

process of depopulation and abandonment had already begun in the 7th century but accelerated markedly in the mid-8th century at the time of the seizure of caliphal power by the Abbasid dynasty and the shift of the centre of government from Damascus to Baghdad (Tsafrir 1984).

Three particular factors may be identified as causing the abandonment of so high a proportion of the villages of the western Sharon between c.750 and the advent of the Crusaders. First, one effect of the Muslim invasion had been to cut Syria and Palestine off from the Mediterranean markets that their agricultural produce had formerly reached. Although Caesarea and Arsuf continued to serve as ports throughout the early Muslim period, they operated on a more restricted and localized scale than under the Byzantine regime (Ashtor 1970a, 168–172; 1970b; Kennedy (H) 1985, 23); and archaeology has shown how their occupied areas had shrunk by the 12th century (Reifenberg 1951; Frova, Avi-Yonah and Negev 1975; Roll and Ayalon 1982). The diminished demand for cash crops, such as corn, oil and wine, would eventually have encouraged a retreat from secondary lands such as the *hamra* and some mountain soils that had been brought under cultivation only in the Roman–Byzantine period (on wine-production on the *hamra*, see Roll and Ayalon 1981). Failure to maintain Roman terracing in the latter areas and to keep open the river mouths in the former would have caused soil-erosion in the hills and flooding in the lower river valleys, making the process of abandonment, once started, more difficult—and in some cases impossible—to reverse (cf. Guy 1954; Vita-Finzi 1969, 83). Roman harbour works, like those at Caesarea, also contributed significantly to the formation of dunes (Rim 1951, 38–40). In the eastern Sharon Plain, however, despite the problems of intermittent flooding, increased colluviation would have produced excellent valley soils for cultivation (see Vita-Finzi 1969, 116–120); and the reduced dependence on cash crops for export may also have contributed towards a diversification in farming methods. Settlements placed on the higher land, either side of the eastern plain and overlooking the valleys leading down from the hills, would have been ideally situated to benefit from these conditions (cf. Ashtor 1976, 54).

The second and third factors concern security and communications. In the 9th and early 10th centuries, the coast of Palestine became in effect a fortified frontier, with Muslim war fleets based at Tyre and Acre, and a system of fortified towns or *ribāṭāt*, including Caesarea and Arsuf, interspersed with watch-towers, strung out along the coast as a guard against Byzantine raiding (Elʿad 1982; cf. Ashtor 1970ab). A stone-built watch-tower, 8 m. square with walls at least 1 m. thick, has been excavated at Minat Abu Zabura (Mikhmoret: 137.201),

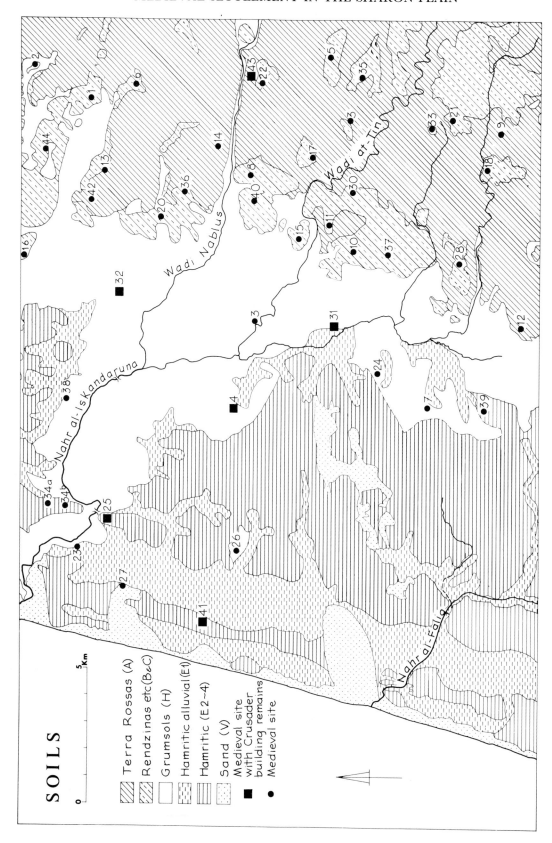

Fig. 2. Map of the Central Sharon, showing the relationship of medieval settlement to soils (Information on soils by courtesy of the Israel Ministry of Agriculture, Tel Aviv).

SOILS

◫	Terra Rossas (A)
◩	Rendzinas etc (B&C)
▢	Grumsols (H)
▨	Hamritic alluvial (Et)
▥	Hamritic (E2–4)
░	Sand (V)
■	Medieval site with Crusader building remains
●	Medieval site

0   5 Km

overlooking a small natural harbour just north of the mouth of the Nahr Iskandaruna; pottery and coins suggest that this was in use in the 10th and 11th centuries (Paley, Porath and Stieglitz 1982, 260–261; pl. 43c). Another tower is also known further south, overlooking what was once probably another landing point at the mouth of the Nahr al-Faliq (134.185).

In the eastern Sharon, however, conditions were different. In 715/7 Ramla became the capital of the *jund Filasṭin* (see Honigman 1936). The *Kitāb al-masālik wa'l-mamālik* of Ibn Khurradādhbih (*c*.820/5–*c*.911) describes the principal road from Damascus to Cairo as passing from Lajjun to Qaqun, Qalansuwa, al-ʿAuja (Ras al-ʿAin), and thence to Ramla, following the line of the traditional *Via Maris* (Hartmann 1910, 674–679). The villages of the eastern Sharon were thus able to benefit from being located next to one of the principal highways of Muslim Syria, while their distance from the coast and, in many cases, hill-top sites gave them additional security.

None the less, insecurity also affected the inland regions of Palestine. This was particularly so in the century and a half immediately preceding the First Crusade. For a brief time in the late 10th century the area represented a war zone between the Byzantine empire and the Fatimids of Egypt, and then through most of the 11th century between the Fatimids and the Seljuk Turks (Prawer 1975(1), 89–120; Runciman 1954(1), 29–37, 75–79). Historians, both of medieval Islam and of the Crusades, have perhaps been over-ready to attribute the flight of Muslim peasants and the creation of *terrae uastatae* in Palestine to the advent of the Crusading armies (cf. Watson 1983, 144; Prawer 1975(1), 507). The eleven villages in Galilee given by Tancred to the Abbey of Mount Tabor in 1101, however, which "devastated in time of war are no longer populated by any inhabitants" (*Cart. des Hosp.* (2), 898, "Chartes du Mont Tabor", no. 1: *casalia . . . que nunc, bellorum tempestate uastate, nullo coluntur inhabitatore*), seem more likely to have been deserted well before the Franks arrived on the scene. Archaeological evidence has shown that a new quarter of the town of Capernaum on the Sea of Galilee which developed in the first half of the 7th century was abandoned during the 10th (Tzaferis 1983b), though other parts of the site were later reoccupied (Loffreda 1983, 372); and excavations in Tiberias have shown that the city's southern quarter of Hamma came to be abandoned in the first half of the 11th century (Oren 1971). In the central Sharon Plain, the now-lost village of Kafr Sallam (site 19), which was described by al-Muqaddasī (*c*.985) as populous and possessing a Friday mosque, was deserted by 1065, when German pilgrims took refuge behind its walls in the face of an attack by local ruffians (see below, pp. 33–34).

It seems reasonable to assume that the village settlements documented in the central Sharon by written sources or archaeology in the 12th and 13th centuries represented native settlements, even where, as at Qaqun and Qalansuwa, we know that they also contained some Frankish inhabitants. Although it is unlikely to be complete, the map showing the distribution of villages (*casalia*) in this period may therefore be regarded as providing a fairly representative picture of the pattern of native settlement at the time of the Crusades (see Fig. 3). Only two of these sites, Dair ʿIsfin (7) and Kefar Vitken (Kerem) (23) are documented only in the Mamluk period.

In the western belt the coastal route, passing at times along the sea shore, at times along the second *kurkar* ridge, still seems to have been in use in the 12th century. The army of King Richard I proceeding south from Acre in 1191 followed the shore line as far as the *Flum Mort* (Nahr al-Mafjir), but then struck inland until it reached Arsuf because the beach was strewn with rocks (Ambroise, lines 6043f.; *Itin. Ric.*, IV, 15 (ed. Stubbs, 257); cf. Prawer 1975(2), 81; Karmon 1961, 48–49). The construction of a castle at Madd ad-Dair (*Mont-didier*) (25) and the name *Flum de Mondidier* given to the Nahr Iskandaruna by a chronicler describing Frederick II's progress south in 1229 (*Eracles*, XXXIII, 7: *RHC Occ* (2), 373) suggest that the Roman bridge still existed or was rebuilt at this point. Madd ad-Dair is described as a village in 1135, and pottery finds also suggest medieval occupation at (Kh.) Shaikh Muhammad (34) on the opposite bank and at Mujahid Shaikha (27). Possibly the harbour at Minat Abu Zabura was also used in this period. South of Madd ad-Dair, the village of al-Maghair (26) occupied a small area of relatively fertile soil on the line of the same *kurkar* ridge. In 1135, its appurtenances included "woods, pastures and waters", suggesting an economy including livestock and timber products, as well as tillage. West of it stood the Castle of Roger the Lombard (41).

Al-Maghair lies on the western edge of the *hamra*, which, it appears, was still heavily wooded in the 12th century possibly as far north as the Nahr Iskandaruna. In September 1191, Richard I's army entered the forest soon after crossing the *Flum Salé* (Ambroise, lines 6075f.; cf. *Itin. Ric.*, IV, 16 (ed. Stubbs, 259)). Saladin, shadowing the Crusading army on its eastern flank, crossed the river (*Nahr al-Qasab*, "River of Reeds") further inland and pitched camp on a hill in the woods near a place called *Dayr al-Rāhab* (Bahāʾ al-Dīn, 286–287). The identification of this is uncertain (cf. Prawer 1975(2), 81 n. 12), though it seems possible that it would have been on the eastern edge of the *hamra*. It took the Crusaders a day to cross the forest, known to them as the "Forest of Arsur" (Ambroise, lines 6100–6111; *Itin. Ric.*, IV, 16 (ed. Stubbs, 259); cf. Röhricht, *Karten*, no. 16

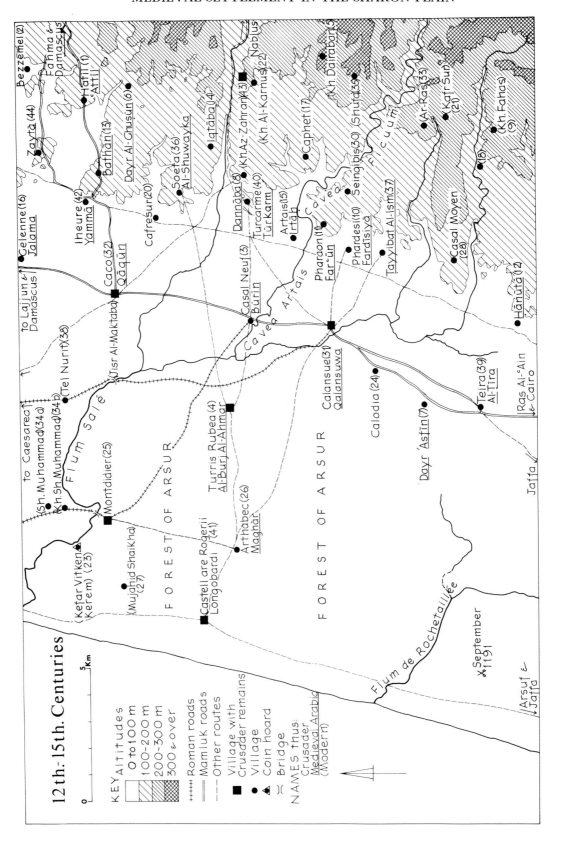

Fig. 3. Map of the Central Sharon in the 12th to 15th centuries (note that all sites except nos. 7 and 23 were occupied or recorded in the Crusader period).

(*Foresta de Arsura*); Prawer 1975(2), 81. It was in these same woods that Sultan Baybars went hunting in 1265 while waiting for suitable timber to arrive for making the siege-engines for his attack on Caesarea (al-Maqrīzī (1, 2), 6). To the south, the woodland thinned out around the valley of the Nahr al-Faliq (*Flum de Rochetaillée*), and it was in the plain south of this that Richard won his first decisive victory over Saladin in the field (Ambroise, lines 6125–6734; *Itin. Ric.*, IV, 17– 20 (ed. Stubbs, 260–277); Prawer 1975(2), 81–82). No medieval sites are documented in the *hamra* area, save for al-Maghair (26) on its western flank and the Red Tower (4) and others on its eastern.

Most of the documented medieval sites in our area lie in the eastern Sharon and adjacent hill country. On the western side of the eastern belt, a row of sites lined the edge of the *hamra*. They included, from north to south, the Red Tower (4), Qalansuwa (31), Kiludiya (24), perhaps Dair ʿIsfin (7), and at-Tira (39). In the plain itself lay Jalama (16), Qaqun (32) and Burin (3), with Tel Nurit (38) in the lower valley of the Nahr Iskandaruna. On the east side of the plain the villages sited at altitudes of between 60 and 200 m. and overlooking it or the valleys leading into it included Bait Sama (2), Zaita (44), Yamma (42), Kh. Ibthan (13), ʿAttil (1), Dair al-Ghusun (6), Kafr Sibb (20), Shuwaika (36), Iqtaba (14), Dannaba (8), Tulkarm (40), Irtah (15), Kh. Kaffa (17), Farʿun (11), Kh. Nisf Jubail (deserted) (30), Fardisiya (10), at-Taiyiba (37), al-Majdal (28) and Hanuta (12). While these villages were well placed to make use of the alluvial valley soils below them, it may also be noted that all but one of them are sited on chalky grey-brown *rendzina* soils, the exception being Iqtaba, situated on the *terra rossa* which thinly covers the higher limestone hill slopes. Orchards, gardens and some cereal cultivation would therefore have been possible in their immediate surroundings, with terraced olives and pastureland for sheep and goats available on the hill slopes beyond. A series of water mills is also recorded in the Wadi at-Tin (*cauea Ficuum*, "Valley of the Figs") between Kh. Kaffa and Kh. Nisf Jubail (*Cart. des Hosp.* (2) 65, no. 1251).

The principal route of communication in the Sharon ran, as in Roman and early Islamic times, from north to south down the eastern belt. This was joined by the road from Nablus at Burin or perhaps at Qalansuwa. It is uncertain, however, whether the road to Caesarea, which in Roman times had branched north-west from this route at Qalansuwa, crossing the Nahr Iskandaruna at the Jisr al-Maktaba (1466.1961), was still in operation in the 12th century. No medieval settlements are recorded on its course in this area, except perhaps Kafr Sallam; but this site was, as we have seen, already abandoned by 1065. The Jisr al-Maktaba itself was destroyed by flood waters before 1939 (J. Ory, *PAM*,

9.10.1939); but a description of its appearance in the 1870s suggests that it was essentially a Turkish structure (Conder and Kitchener 1881(2), 194; cf. Palestine 1929, 49; 1948, 56). It seems quite possible, therefore, that the principal road from Caesarea to Nablus or Ramla in the 12th century passed by way of Qaqun, thereby avoiding any major crossing of the river or its marshes (cf. Karmon 1961, 58). That Qaqun occupied a cross-roads of some importance early in the century is indicated by the rallying of troops there from Tiberias, Acre, Caesarea and Jerusalem by the Regent and the Patriarch in 1123, to march against the Egyptian forces attacking Jaffa (see below, pp. 14 and 60).

It also seems possible that the road between Burin and the bridge at Kh. Madd ad-Dair was still in use in the 12th century. This may have been the route followed by Saladin in 1191. It would also, however, have put in communication the lands belonging to the abbey of St. Mary Latin at Madd ad-Dair, the Red Tower and Qaqun. A description of these in 1248 gives an impression, at least, of the diverse rural economies practicable on the monks' estates, which would have extended around the basin of the Nahr Iskandaruna from the *kurkar* ridge in the west to the edges of the *hamra* and limestone in the east. They included, "woods, wastes, plains, mountains, pastures, cultivated and uncultivated (arable) lands, waters and water channels" (*Cart. des Hosp.* (2), 673–675, no. 2482). The existence of woods and wastelands may explain in part the high proportion of pig bones recovered from the 13th-century phase at the Red Tower (see below pp. 178– 180).

In 1131, lands in the territory of Qaqun and Kafr Sallam included arable lands and lands in the marshes extending as far as the river, though the latter could not apparently be relied upon. When Walter I, Lord of Caesarea, gave four carrucates of the marshy land to the Hospital at that date, he therefore undertook to replace them with as much land in the drier "sandy region" (*in Sabulone*, presumably the *hamra* rather than the dunes) as would fully compensate for them if they should prove deficient. This suggests that so long as it was possible to keep them well drained, these damper alluvial soils were considerably more productive than the sandy ones (*Cart. des Hosp.* (1), 84, no. 94; cf. Prawer 1980, 194). Indeed, the pilgrim Theodoric describes Qaqun in 1172 as situated *in fertilissima terra* (XXXIX: ed. Bulst, 43; ed. Tobler, 89). But the liability of the area to flooding is also evoked by the accounts of the Crusading expedition against the Mamluks holding the castle of Qaqun in late November 1271, when it is described as surrounded by "ditches full of water" (Templar of Tyre, 200–201).

A second group of hill villages is found further up into the mountains south-east of Tulkarm. These lie between 200 and 350 m. above sea level and like the lower group they mostly occupy *rendzina* soils. They include Kh. az-Zahran (43), Kh. al-Karnus (22), Kh. Dairaban (5), Shufa (35), ar-Ras (33), Kh. Kafr Sur (21), Kh. Fahas (9) and Site 18 near Kafr Jammal. None of these sites is mentioned in Crusader documentary sources, though surface finds of pottery indicate 12th- and 13th-century occupation. Their inaccessibility and relative poverty compared to the larger settlements nearer the plain may have meant that these villages were not so readily given, sold or exchanged by Frankish landowners, and thus failed to be mentioned in the charters that are our primary source of documentary evidence for village life in this period. But it should also be stressed that the survival of this evidence is extremely patchy; it relates almost exclusively to ecclesiastical holdings and even among these there are notable gaps.

2. CRUSADER COLONIZATION (A.D. 1099–1265)

SOCIAL AND MILITARY ASPECTS

It has been argued above that the pattern of village sites documented by archaeological and written sources in our area in the 12th and 13th centuries would have corresponded closely with the distribution of native Arab settlement at the time of the Crusader conquest. We do not know how many villages were abandoned on the approach of the Crusading armies, nor how many were subsequently repopulated. But it seems unlikely that either of these possible factors would greatly have affected the overall pattern except in minor details.

During the period of Crusader occupation, the rural population throughout the Latin Kingdom of Jerusalem remained essentially one composed of native Muslims and oriental Christians, with some smaller regional groupings of Jews and Samaritans (see Prawer 1980, 201–214; Smail 1956, 40–57; on village administration, see Riley-Smith 1972, 9–15). Over the top of this sub-stratum of peasant villages, however, there was imposed a hierarchy of settlements in which the Frankish element was more strongly represented. These settlements would have included, from bottom to top: castles and a handful of rural religious houses; small towns, including some "new towns" composed almost entirely of Latin settlers; and larger towns and cities (cf. Benvenisti 1970, 17–21, and *passim*; Smail 1956, 57–62).

The central Sharon contains no major towns. It covers, in effect, the southern part of the territory of Caesarea, which, after the city fell in May 1101, became by 1110 a lordship granted to Eustace Garnier. Apart from a four-year period from July/August 1187 to September 1191 when it was held by Saladin, the lordship was to remain in the hands of the Garnier family until 1265, when it was taken by the Mamluks

(La Monte 1947; Hazard 1975, 93–100). To the south lay the lordship of Arsuf, to which Hanuta, al-Majdal and perhaps at-Tira on our map belonged. The boundary with the lordship of Nablus probably corresponded roughly with the eastern edge of our map (cf. Beyer 1936, 3–15). After 1187, however, Nablus was never again in Crusader possession, and until 1265 this boundary represented the frontier between Frankish- and Muslim-held territories (cf. Prawer 1975(2), 207, 285; maps VII–VIII; Prawer and Benvenisti 1970).

From the first decade of the 12th century and throughout the period of Frankish occupation we find numerous references to grants of land, in some cases amounting to entire villages, made in the area by the lords of Caesarea to their knights and vassals. The instances are detailed, site by site, in the following Gazetteer (see also Beyer 1936). Most of our evidence for land-ownership, however, comes from ecclesiastical archives and is therefore concerned with lands which at some time or other came into the possession of religious houses, including the military orders. It is therefore important to stress that despite the relative preponderance of information relating to ecclesiastical ownership, most of the land in this area is more likely to have been held in the 12th and 13th centuries by secular tenants of the lords of Caesarea. But as has been mentioned already, relatively little evidence survives compared to what must once have existed.

Among the ecclesiastical owners of land in the area, the Archbishop of Caesarea is recorded in possession of Burin (3) in 1253. The Benedictines of St. Mary Latin possessed Madd ad-Dair (25) by 1123, the Red Tower (4) by then or by 1149/54 and certainly by 1158, and land in Qaqun by the latter date. By 1236, they were leasing Madd ad-Dair and the Red Tower to the Templars. The Templars may also possibly have had a commandery in Qaqun in 1187, but the evidence for this is suspect. The largest documented ecclesiastical land-owner in the area, however, was the Hospital of St. John. The Hospitallers received property in Qaqun before September 1110 (to which later additions were made), the whole of Qalansuwa (31) in 1128, land in Kafr Sallam (19) by 1131, al-Maghair (26) by 1135, Kiludiya (24) by 1153, al-Majdal (28) by 1176, Tulkarm (40) in 1212; and from 1248 they were leasing Madd ad-Dair and the Red Tower from the Abbey of St. Mary Latin.

Ownership of land, however, does not necessarily imply physical occupation of it. The written sources provide little direct evidence for the settlement of Franks in our area. A more useful indication of the extent of Frankish settlement is provided, however, by castles and other architectural remains left by them. Six, or possibly seven sites are attested with evidence of Frankish buildings. The earliest appears to have been the castle of *Malu(a)e*, built by King Baldwin I (1100–

18). Unfortunately its precise position has yet to be determined, though it was possibly situated somewhere near Qaqun, on or near the road from Caesarea to Nablus. The castle of Qaqun itself existed by 1123, though the tower which dominates the site may have undergone some modification later in the 12th or 13th century. Madd ad-Dair was given to the Benedictines by 1123, and it seems likely that the tower there was built by a previous tenant. Similarly, the Red Tower, which is first recorded as the "Tower of Latina" in 1158, also seems likely to have been constructed before the Benedictines gained possession of it, that is by 1149/54 or possibly even by 1123. The Castle of Roger the Lombard (41) is attested in 1135. And the complex of buildings at Qalansuwa, although not having quite the character of a castle, would probably have been constructed by the Hospitallers between 1128 and 1187; it includes a tower, however, which may possibly represent part of an earlier work of fortification. Finally, pieces of diagonally tooled masonry at Kh. az-Zahran (43) could betray the former existence of a Crusader building, perhaps a tower overlooking the lower course of the Wadi Nablus.

The dating evidence, such as it is (for detailed discussions of individual buildings, see the Gazetteer and, for the Red Tower, Part Two below), thus suggests that most if not all of the castles or towers in this area had their origins sometime in the first three decades of the 12th century. Other considerations not only support this dating but also suggest the likely historical context for their construction in the early phase of Frankish conquest and colonization of the region. Like the Norman conquest and settlement of England, the extension of Frankish control over the countryside of Palestine was typified in its early phases by the granting of landed fiefs in return for military services (see Prawer 1980, 9–15; Riley-Smith 1983) and by the construction of castles to reinforce seigneurial, and hence royal, authority over the subject population (cf. Deschamps 1939, 5–24; Smail 1956, 60–62). A similar pattern of castle-building enforcing a social and administrative structure based on personal military obligations had been developing in northern France from the beginning of the 11th century (see Fournier 1978, 100–135; Le Maho 1976), and this no doubt formed a model that was applied by the Normans in England from 1066 onwards (Brown 1976, 40–51) and apparently by the Crusaders in Palestine in the early 12th century.

The castle's functions were thus not always, if ever, exclusively military. Leaving aside *Malu(a)e* and Kh. az-Zahran, about which we have insufficient evidence, each of the remaining four castles in our area, and perhaps the tower at Qalansuwa as well, would seem in origin to have been a seigneurial centre dependent in some way or other on the lord of Caesarea. We have evidence at Qaqun of certain unnamed knights of Caesarea possessing lands there before 1110; and other references to knights holding properties in the village occur throughout the 12th century. In 1131, 1135 and 1175 there is mention of a viscount, implying the existence of a burgess court governing the affairs of the local Latin inhabitants. Another officer of the lord of Caesarea, a dragoman mentioned in 1135, would have dealt with judicial matters affecting the local Syrian population (cf. Riley-Smith 1972, 15–19). In the 12th century, and presumably in the 13th, Qaqun would thus have represented a centre from which the lord of Caesarea, through his appointed officers, was able to administer the southern part of his lordship. It seems probable, however, that the castle of Qaqun also played its part in securing the lord's authority in the region, by serving as the residence of the viscount or castellan and of his entourage (cf. Prawer 1980, 256, 264, 271, 274, 279); and that many of the knights who held lands or rents in Qaqun would have formed part of the military establishment, the *milites castri*, of the place (cf. Fournier 1978, 114–119).

The Castle of Roger the Lombard (41) appears by its name to be a clear instance of a castle being held by a knight. Unfortunately we know nothing more about the owner, save that a man of the same name is mentioned in Jerusalem in 1129. If he or his family were not immigrants from the time of the First Crusade, he may perhaps have been part of the Italian contingent that helped capture Caesarea in 1101. In either case, in 1135, Roger would presumably have been holding the castle from the lord of Caesarea.

Madd ad-Dair and the Red Tower also seem likely to have been held in the first instance by knights of the lord of Caesarea. The first was subsequently granted to St. Mary Latin by Eustace Garnier (d. 1123), the second perhaps by Eustace or by his successor Walter I (d. 1149/54). Up to 1128 Qalansuwa was held by a knight, Geoffrey (or Godfrey) of Flujeac, as a rear-fief of the lord of Baisan, who in turn held it of the lord of Caesarea. It may be that the tower surviving at Qalansuwa belongs to this early phase of "feudal" possession, though its dating is far from certain.

From the earliest period of the development of the lordship of Caesarea, therefore, and in the case of Qaqun throughout the 12th century at least, we can see castles being used to enforce the lord of Caesarea's authority over his seigneury. But what of the military functions of these castles? In many respects the military functions of medieval castles in the West and of those built by Westerners in the East represented a reinforcement in earth, wood or stone of the military organization of society. Castle walls helped to protect the ruling elements of medieval society against unrest at home as much as from threats from outside.

Castles might therefore be sited so as to protect the internal communications within a territory, in particular to guard the security of roads or bridges (cf. Fournier 1978, 161–168). The 12th-century castle at *le Destroit* (Kh. Dustray: 145.234), for instance, was built by the Templars in the northern part of the lordship of Caesarea to protect travellers against attacks by robbers at a point where the road from Acre to Caesarea passed through a narrow defile (Deschamps 1939, 23–24; Johns 1947, 15–16, 94–98; figs. 6 and 38). Kh. az-Zahran and *Malu(a)e* could also perhaps fall into this category; and the siting of Roger the Lombard's castle on the coast road may have been intended in part to ensure its security. Castles, however, could not close frontiers or physically block possible invasion routes against a determined foreign army. In such circumstances the most that their builders could hope them to achieve was to serve as bases for mobile garrisons, prepared to meet the enemy in the field; or, if the field army lost the day, to act as refuges in which the survivors and the civilian population of the area might endure the enemy's occupation of the surrounding area until help should arrive (cf. Smail 1956, 204–215; 1973, 89–91). For a combination of reasons therefore, castles were often concentrated in areas and periods of heightened insecurity. In western Europe one may note, for example, the concentration of 11th- and 12th-century castles on the borders of Normandy and the Vexin (Fournier 1978, 159; cf. 158–160) or in the Marches between England and Wales (Renn 1968, 14; map D). In the 12th century, the Sharon Plain would have been at its least secure for a prolonged period in the early years of the century. Jaffa was taken by the Franks in 1100, and Arsuf and Caesarea in 1101. Ascalon, however, remained in Egyptian hands until 1153; and it was possible for the Muslims from this springboard to launch raids as far north as Jaffa in 1123 and al-Bira north of Jerusalem in 1124. In 1123 the castle of Qaqun served as the base from which Eustace Garnier, as Constable and Regent of the Kingdom, together with the Patriarch Warmund, launched the counter attack which resulted in the defeat of the invaders at Yibna. Not until the reign of Fulk of Anjou (1131–43) was the threat from Ascalon significantly reduced by the construction of a ring of Crusader fortresses about it (cf. Prawer 1975(1), 328–330; map XIV; Smail 1956, 211–213).

The purely military value of the castles of the Sharon plain, never very great, would therefore have been reduced to insignificance by around 1140. Their failure to develop, however, was also influenced by other factors. Principal among these was the lack of interest shown by the Franks in Palestine for colonizing the land. In general, the owners of rural property, including those holding land for military service, were content to derive revenues from them without actually residing on them (cf. Prawer 1980, 148–156; Smail 1956, 59). The reason was principally lack of numbers, which caused most Franks to stay together within the safety of the major towns. In our area it seems unlikely that there would have been any significant settlement of Franks outside the fortified sites enumerated above. Latin church buildings, which in Europe serve not only as an indicator of settlement distribution to historians but were also used in the 12th and 13th centuries as instruments for the colonization of new lands (Heck 1975), are unrecorded in our area except at Qaqun, though it seems quite possible that one would also have existed at Qalansuwa. For a combination of reasons, therefore, the somewhat optimistic early phase of land-distribution and castle-building was replaced from *c.* 1120 onwards by a second, perhaps more realistic phase, in which not only village lands but castles too were relinquished by their feudal tenants and granted to religious houses or military orders.

We can only guess the use to which the Benedictines of St. Mary Latin put the castles of Madd ad-Dair and the Red Tower after they came into their possession. There is no evidence that they ever established priories at these sites. Possibly the castles were used as administrative centres and residences by the stewards or dragomans appointed by the monks to administer their estates; possibly they were temporarily abandoned; or possibly they were leased to others who could find a military use for them. It might have been in this way that the Templars gained occupancy of the two sites, for which in 1236 they were paying rent to the abbey. The excavations at the Red Tower unfortunately shed little light on this particular period. They show, however, that the castle's tower was reoccupied after the Third Crusade and was tidied up and perhaps refurbished later in the 13th century, just before it was destroyed by the Mamluks. The arrow-slits in the tower at Qaqun, whose closest parallels are those in the 13th-century walls of Caesarea, could also suggest that this castle too was refurbished after it had been won back from Saladin. At this time Qaqun would have been very near the edge of Crusader-held territory.

We have no evidence for the later history of the Castle of Roger the Lombard, though it is still possible that excavations may one day provide some clues. At Qalansuwa, the complex of buildings constructed during the 12th century has more the character of a collection of administrative and agricultural buildings connected with the Hospitallers' running of their estates in the region than of a fortified castle (see below). It also appears, however, that a Frankish settlement including knights and burgesses with their own court developed there in the 12th century, perhaps initially under Hospitaller patronage but later independent of it. In

1166 the reference to a knight and to a viscount of Qalansuwa in the court of the lord of Caesarea indicates that the Hospitallers' rights over the place were not exclusive.

Only in Qalansuwa and Qaqun therefore does there appear to have been any significant settlement of Latins in the 12th century, giving them perhaps the status of small towns rather than villages. Their character in the 13th century is harder to assess because of the paucity of evidence. It may be noted, however, that John of Ibelin mentions neither of them in his list of burgess courts in the kingdom, though this list was evidently not entirely comprehensive (*Livre*, CCLXX: *RHC Lois* (1), 419–421).

ARCHITECTURE

Three of the castles in the central Sharon of which we have surviving remains, the Red Tower, Madd ad-Dair and Qaqun, were dominated by a large tower-keep or *donjon*. Excavations have shown that the Red Tower, measuring 19.7 × 15.5 m., was also surrounded by an outer wall, almost 2 m. thick, enclosing an area about 60 m. square (see Figs. 33–34). The towers at Madd ad-Dair and Qaqun were of comparable size (c.12.5 × c.16 m.; and 14.5 × 17.6 m. respectively); it seems likely that they too would have had outworks, though no trace of these now remains (see Figs. 9, 15–16).

Towers of this kind clearly represented more than simple refuges, even though, as events at al-Bira proved in 1124, they could be used as such when the need arose (cf. Pringle 1985a, 151). In the Red Tower, the ground floor, badly lit and partly below ground, was probably used only for storage. The first floor, however, was evidently a living area, as the excavated fragments from its mosaic floor and painted wall plaster illustrate. At Qaqun, the ground floor does not appear to have had any window openings at all; while the first floor was, on the contrary, lit by arrow-slits set in wide casemates, which also served a defensive purpose (Fig. 17). Below the tower was a cistern supplied with rain water from the roof by means of a ceramic pipe built into the wall.

Towers such as these, combining both residential and defensive functions and set within larger fortified enclosures had developed in northern France in the late 10th and early 11th centuries (de Bouard 1974; Brown 1976, 24–26; Deyres 1969); and during the 11th to 13th centuries scores of them, more or less refined and of differing sizes and shapes, were built throughout the countrysides of northern France (cf. Châtelain 1973; Finó 1970, 170–177, 223–224; Fournier 1978, 80–90) and England (cf. Brown 1976, 65–81; Héliot 1969; 1974; Renn 1968, *passim*). It seems likely, therefore, that the type of castle combining a tower-keep and a fortified enclosure, or bailey, for which there is no obvious

Byzantine or Islamic prototype (cf. Pringle 1981(1), 155, 170), was a Frankish introduction to the area. This likelihood is reinforced by the recent observation that one of the earliest defensive works constructed by the Franks in the East, at Anavarza in Cilicia, consisted of adding a massive *donjon* to an already existing fortified enclosure (Edwards 1984).

The tower-keeps built by the Franks in the Kingdom of Jerusalem and in the northern Crusader states, however, differed in certain respects from those built in the West (cf. Smail 1956, 226–230; 1973, 98). Excepting Montfort (1226–), whose keep is D-shaped (Dean 1927, fig. 4), they are invariably rectangular in plan, and in size they rarely attain more than 20 m. in length, breadth or height. Whereas the tower-keep built at Rochester in Kent from 1127 onwards was 21.35 m. square and over 34 m. high, with four floors (Brown 1976, 67–69; figs. 28–29; Renn 1968, 299–303; figs. 65–66; pl. XL), among Crusader *donjons* it is unusual to find more than two floors, though the lower one might sometimes be raised on a scarped rock plinth as at Kh. Dustray (145.234: Conder and Kitchener 1881(1), 288, 309–310; Johns 1947, 15–16, 94–98; figs. 6 and 38) and the Castle of Figs (*Castrum Ficuum*, 141.094: Kloner 1983), or built up over a cistern as at Jubail (Deschamps 1973, 203–215) and Montfort (Dean 1927; Benvenisti 1977). At Beaufort Castle, the keep, dating from 1139, measured only about 13 × 12.3 m. and stood 13 m. high with walls 2.8 m. thick; it too had only two floors with an entrance initially at ground level (Deschamps 1934, 204–206). Another point of difference between Crusader and Western keeps is that the former are usually vaulted throughout, though in northern Syria at Qal'at Yahmur (see below) and Tukla (Deschamps 1973, 327–328) they also have intermediary mezzanine floors of wood; in the West, however, the upper floors are more usually of timber. Lastly, whereas in the West the principal entrance to a tower-keep is almost invariably at first-floor level and is often protected by a fore-building, in the Crusader East it is more often at ground level (Pringle 1983a, 170).

While keeping in mind the north-west European affiliations of the Crusader *donjon* or tower-keep, therefore, parallels for the three represented in the central Sharon are probably best sought among local Crusader examples. In the Red Tower and Madd ad-Dair, the basement of the *donjon* consisted of two barrel-vaults side by side; at the Red Tower these were arranged length-wise with respect to the plan of the tower, and at Madd ad-Dair breadth-wise. The latter may be compared with the tower at al-Bira, which is not only of roughly the same size (c.16 × c.14 m.) but also of comparable date, having been built by the canons of the Holy Sepulchre before 1124. This tower stood at the centre of a rectangular enclosure, measuring some

60 × 45 m., which was subsequently covered, at least in part, by barrel- and groin-vaults (Pringle 1985a, 151–157; figs. 3–6).

Qalᶜat Yahmur (*Castrum Rubrum*) in the County of Tripoli may be taken as the "type site" for this simple kind of keep-and-bailey castle (see Lawrence 1936(1), 33–34; figs. 30–33; Deschamps 1934, 56–57; fig. 11; 1973, 317–319; pl. LXXIXa). It has been suggested that this was the castle of the Wadi Ibn Ahmar that was temporarily seized from the Franks in 1137. Otherwise the first reference to it is in 1177, when Raymond III,

Count of Tripoli, conceded it to the Hospitallers; up till then it had apparently been held from him by Raymond of Montolif, to whom the Hospitallers paid 400 bezants in compensation the following year (*Cart. des Hosp.* (1), 353–354, no. 519; 371–372, no. 549; *RRH*, 146, no. 549; *Ad*, 35, no. 562a; cf. Deschamps 1973, 317).

The tower measures 16·2 (N–S) × 14·1 m. (E–W), with walls 1·8–2·2 m. thick, and stands about 12 m. high (see Fig. 4). The ground floor, entered by a doorway in the east wall, is enclosed by four bays of groin-vaults, springing from a central pier 2 m. square. The first floor

QALᶜAT YAHMUR

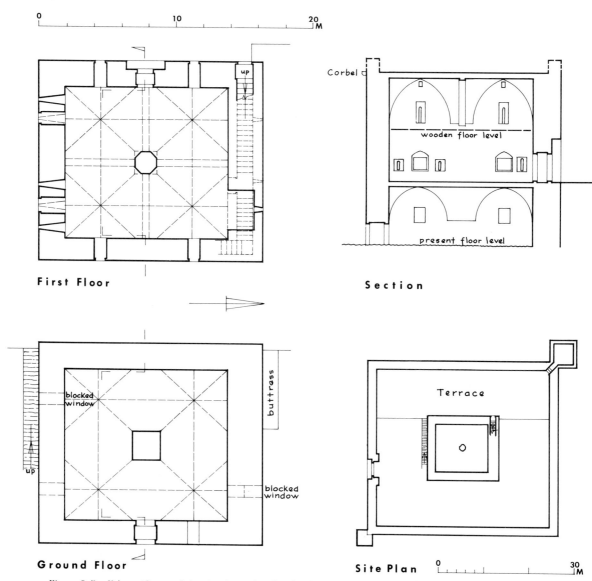

First Floor

Section

Ground Floor

Site Plan

Fig. 4. Qal'at Yahmur (Castrum Rubeum): plans and section of castle (based on Lawrence 1936; and author's field notes, 1984).

Pl. I. Qal'at Yahmur (Castrum Rubeum): First-floor entrance to medieval castle keep (photo. author).

stair from inside the first-floor room; a closer examination of the building would be necessary, however, to resolve this apparent difficulty. At a point some 3·5 m. above the first-floor level, the stair reaches a landing from which a door opened on to what formerly would have been a wooden mezzanine floor (see Pl. II). This floor level has retained its original arrow-slits, two in each wall. The same stair then continues to the terrace roof, after making a turn to the right. Nothing now remains of the parapet or crenellations of the tower, save for a pair of corbels that once supported a machicolation above the east ground-floor door.

The outer enceinte of Qal'at Yahmur measures overall some 37 × 42 m., with walls 1·90 m. thick. A solid corner turret, about 3·65 m. square, attached to the south-east corner, probably once supported a corbelled tower, such as still exists on the north-west. Both of these appear to be later additions. The south-eastern one, however, built of large smooth ashlar similar to that of

Pl. II. Qal'at Yahmur (Castrum Rubeum): Interior of keep at first-floor level looking NE. Note doorway in N wall leading from staircase to level of former mezzanine floor (photo. author).

has its own door (Pl. I), now approached from a vaulted terrace built between the tower and the outer wall of the castle (as at al-Bira); it is rectangular and set back in a pointed-arched recess. The first floor is also groin-vaulted, the vaults springing from a central octagonal pier and the bays separated from one another by transverse arches springing from rounded corbels (Pl. II). Two types of window are found, splayed arrow-slits narrowing from 0·65 m. inside to 0·07 m. on the outside, and broader rectangular openings; the latter appear to be later insertions, replacing in most cases earlier arrow-slits. The greatest concentration of these early embrasures would therefore have been on the south, facing the principal outer gateway of the castle.

A stair covered by a rising pointed barrel-vault leads up within the thickness of the north wall of the tower. At present it is entered through a rectangular door directly from the terrace. Since this arrangement means that there is no direct internal communication between any of the floors of the tower, it may be wondered whether there was not originally some form of direct access to the

the outer wall itself, may perhaps be earlier than the other; its principal function would have been to flank the main south gate of the castle. This itself is an original Crusader feature, comparable, as T. E. Lawrence observed, to the north town gate at Tartus. It is rectangular in profile, 2·10 m. wide, and recessed 0·87 m. behind a pointed arch and a row of four machicolations. A triple-armed cross (now mutilated) in a mandorla is carved in low relief on one of the blocks above the lintel.

Another Crusader tower with vaulting springing from a central pier is Qaqun. The most impressive example of this type, however, is the massive *donjon* at Sahyun (now renamed Qal°at Salah ad-Din) (see Pl. III and Fig. 5). This tower represents simply the largest of a

Pl. III. Qal°at Sahyun: Crusader keep inserted into E wall, from NE (photo. author).

number of towers added by the Crusaders to an originally Byzantine castle between 1108 and 1132. The *donjon* is 24·5 m. square, and stands 22 m. high with walls 4·4–5·4 m. thick. It forms a key element in the Crusaders'

strengthening of the exposed east wall of the castle, its own east face representing a vertical continuation of the rock-cut chasm which detaches the fortress's site from its parent rock (Deschamps 1973, 239–240; pl. XXI). Nearer in size to the towers at Qaqun and Qal°at Yahmur is the tower that formed the south-west corner of the faubourg defences at Pilgrims' Castle (°Atlit), dating presumably from the same time as the castle itself sometime after 1218. This measures 14·1 × 11·7 m., roughly the same dimensions as Kh. Dustray (Johns 1947, 81–85; fig. 29). Although these major towers at Sahyun and Pilgrims' Castle formed part of much larger military works, they were none the less self-contained defensive units with only a single entrance and no other communication with the curtain walls adjoining them. Both could also probably have served as residential quarters in times of peace.

The type of small castle with a rectangular tower-keep standing at the centre of a rectangular enclosure is also found at Jubail in the County of Tripoli, where the *donjon* (22 × 18 m., and 21 m. high) was built from 1104 onwards within a somewhat irregular though roughly rectangular enceinte, measuring overall some 48·5 × 46 m. (Deschamps 1973, 203–215). In the 12th-century Castle of Figs (*Castrum Ficuum*), south-west of Hebron, the keep was some 20 m. square and surrounded by an outer wall about 52 × 45 m. (Kloner 1983). And at Smar Jubail, also in the County of Tripoli, an undated Frankish castle recorded by P. Deschamps comprises a central keep (15 × 13·5 m.) set in an irregular enceinte on the edge of a cliff, about 50 × 46 m. in overall size (1973, 302–303; pl. LXIV). A number of other examples are known in the Judaean and Samaritan hills around Jerusalem and Nablus, but have yet to be properly recorded; these can only date to the 12th century.

The Castle of Roger the Lombard (°Umm Khalid) seems to have differed in a number of respects from those of Madd ad-Dair, the Red Tower and Qaqun, illustrating the point that despite the similarity between those three there was no standard type of Crusader castle. Here there appears to have been no tower-keep (see Fig. 19). Our evidence for reconstructing the castle is based on a plan and descriptions of the south range of the building made in or before 1946, since when it has been completely destroyed. The available evidence suggests that the castle consisted of a rectangular complex, perhaps some 33 m. or more square, with vaulted ranges of buildings set about a central open courtyard. Apart from a solid turret, 3·5 m. square, at its south-east corner and a number of embrasures in its south wall, the building does not appear to have been heavily defended. The south wall, which seems to have been an external wall, even contained a small doorway. Indeed, the complex has much in common with the

SAHYUN ~
Donjon

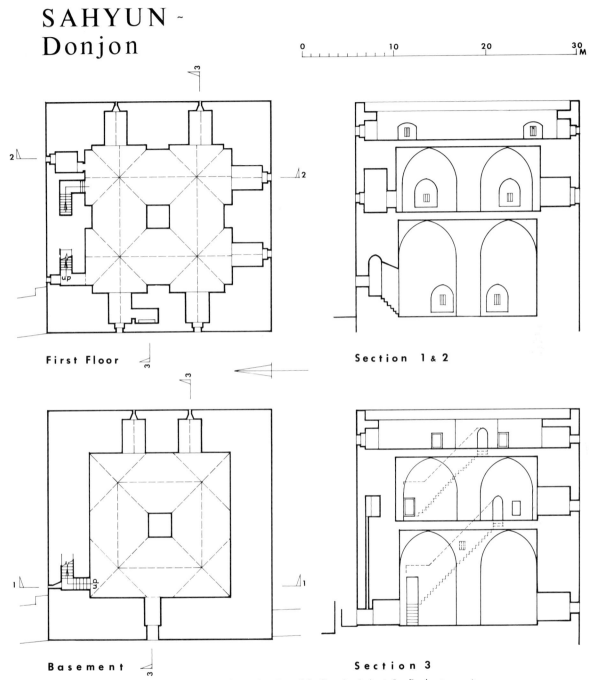

Fig. 5. Sahyun (Saone): plans and sections of the Crusader donjon (after Deschamps 1973).

semi-fortified "manor houses" or estate centres that were built in the 12th century in the area around Jerusalem. Examples include ar-Ram, al-Qubaiba, Kh. ʿIqbala (*Aqua Bella*), Jifna and Burj Bardawil, among others (Benvenisti 1970, 232–245; 1982, 147; figs. 16–18; Pringle 1983a). The building surviving at Kh. Bir Zait (1682.1535), north-west of Ramallah, illustrates the

type and forms a point of comparison for ʿUmm Khalid (Fig. 6). This structure measured some 35 m. (E–W) × 37 m. (N–S), with barrel-vaulted ranges enclosing three sides of a central open courtyard. As at Kh. ʿIqbala, the north side may have been enclosed simply by a wall containing the principal gateway. In the courtyard was a cistern. By an odd coincidence, the south-eastern

Kh. BIR ZAIT

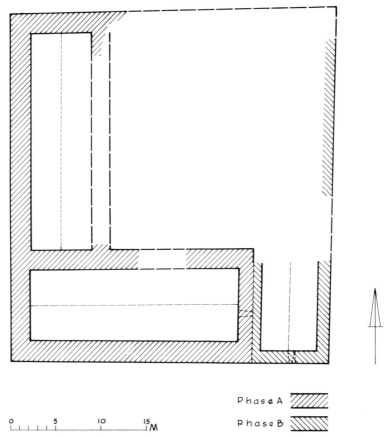

Phase A

Phase B

0   5   10   15 M

Fig. 6. Khirbat Bir Zait: plan of the Frankish "manor house" (BSAJ Survey 1982).

chamber at Kh. Bir Zait, like that at 'Umm Khalid, has at times given the impression of being the base for a tower; in fact it appears more likely that it represents simply the southern surviving part of the east range (cf. Benvenisti 1970, 237; Gúerin 1868(3), 34; de Vaux 1946, 262; Abel 1928, 50–51; Conder and Kitchener 1881(2), 329; Kallai, in Kochavi (ed.) 1972, 173–174, no. 72; D. C. Baramki, *PAM*, 15.7.1947).

The economic and administrative functions served by buildings of this kind and by the smaller types of keep-and-bailey castle described above may often have been identical. This is almost certain to have been the case with the castle at al-Bira (*Magna Mahumeria*) and the "manor house" at al-Qubaiba (*Parua Mahumeria*), both of which would have served as residences, courts and storehouses for the stewards appointed by the canons of the Holy Sepulchre to run their "new towns" founded in these two locations (cf. Pringle 1983a, 172–174; 1985a, 157). The differences in their design may perhaps result from al-Bira having been founded earlier than al-

Qubaiba, in a period (and geographical area) of greater insecurity. It successfully withstood a siege in 1124, as we have seen. Semi-fortified or "lightly defended" rural dwellings, however are also found in the West throughout the Middle Ages; and whether more emphasis was placed on defensibility or amenity, including ease of access and domestic comfort, may sometimes have reflected more the mentality of the builder than his actual needs of either (cf. Brown 1976, 16–18; Fixot 1974, 283). The fact that the lightly defended building at 'Umm Khalid is described in 1135 as a "castle" (*castellare* or *castellaris*), while the "castle" at al-Bira is called merely a "court" (*curia*) in 12th-century sources, illustrates the danger in trying to impose standard interpretations on structures classified by architectural form alone.

Finally, at Qalansuwa a large complex of buildings has been recorded, dating from the 12th century. The earliest of these, as we have tentatively suggested above, may have been a tower 12 m. square sited just west of the others. The largest building, however, is a rectangular structure, 16·5 m. wide and 28–30 m. long, that we have described as a "hall". This comprises an undercroft, vaulted with eight bays of groin-vaults springing from three rectangular piers, above which there would probably have a first-floor hall vaulted in a similar fashion, but perhaps with columns in place of piers. Although strongly built and imposing in appearance with a first-floor entrance, this was evidently not a strictly military building. The basement, for instance, had at least two doors in its outer walls and probably a splayed lancet window in each of the other bays; and while these could probably have been used as arrow-slits, no other defensive embrasures are recorded in the building. The other buildings at Qalansuwa seem to represent ranges of vaulted store rooms, set about an open central courtyard, of which the "hall" occupied the east side. No trace of fortifications exists, though this does not mean that evidence for them may not some day come to light.

This complex has the general character of a group of buildings such as one might expect to find set around the *basse-cour* of a monastic house or a castle, though without any fortified enceinte. An analogy from the Latin East may be suggested in the outer ward of the Templars' castle at Tartus, constructed around their earlier *donjon*

by 1212 (Enlart 1925(2), 427–430; pls. 174–183; Deschamps 1973, 287–292; Rey 1871, 69–83; pl. XX). Here the walls of the heavily fortified circuit extend in a semi-circle on the eastern landward side; they are lined on their inner face by rows of vaulted store-rooms. On the west, by the sea, stood the tower-keep surrounded by an apron-wall and glacis; on the north-east was the church; and on the north a first-floor hall. The latter dates from the 13th century and is larger and more elaborate than the hall at Qalansuwa. It measures internally 44 × 15 m., and was vaulted with twelve bays of rib-vaults, carried on granite columns. Its function, however, as residential accommodation for the Templar knights, and the function of the store-buildings may have been similar to those of the corresponding Hospitaller structures at Qalansuwa. The importance of Qalansuwa to the Hospital, however, seems always to have been economic rather than military. It seems quite probable that the buildings recorded here were used by them in the 12th century and possibly in the 13th as part of an administration and collection centre for exploiting their estates in the region. This may even have attained the status of a commandery, though direct evidence is lacking (cf. Riley-Smith 1967, 429 n. 4). Remains of a more modest example of a local Hospitaller collection centre, comprising no more than a rectangular tower

QULA

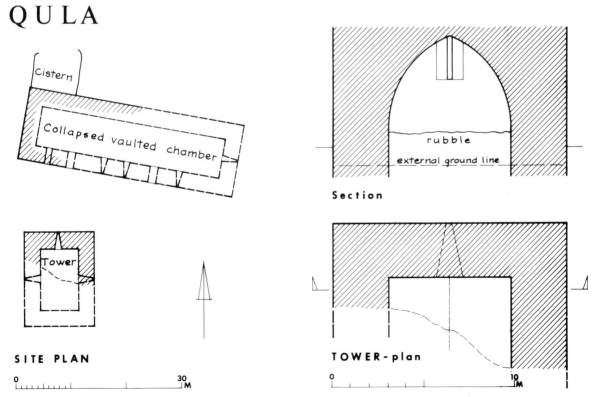

Fig. 7. Qula (Cola): plan of Crusader tower and vaulted building (after Benvenisti 1970; and BSAJ Survey 1983).

(13 × 17 m.) and an adjoining barrel-vaulted structure, can still be seen south-east of Qalansuwa at Qula (146.160); this property was acquired by the Hospitallers in 1181 (*Cart. des Hosp.* (1), 412–414, nos. 603 and 606; *RRH*, 162, no. 611; Benvenisti 1970, 227–229, 276; Conder and Kitchener 1881(2), 297, 358; Guérin 1874(2), 390–391; Langé 1965, 94, 182; fig. 43; Riley-Smith 1967, 69, 135, 427 n. 2, 457).

3. THE MAMLUK RECONQUEST (A.D. 1265–1516)

Caesarea fell to Sultan Baybars early in 1265, the fortified town on 27 February and the citadel on 5 March. Its fortifications were then systematically destroyed (Ibn al-Furāt (2), 70–72; al-Maqrīzī (1, 2), 7–8; Riley-Smith 1971, 205–206; Prawer 1975(2), 462–464). After raiding the faubourg of Pilgrims' Castle (ᶜAtlit), the Sultan next turned his attention to Arsuf. Here the citadel surrendered to him soon after the

faubourg had fallen, on 30 April; the fortifications of both were then demolished (Ibn al-Furāt (2), 73–78; al-Maqrīzī (1, 2), 8–10; Riley-Smith 1971, 207–208; Prawer 1975(2), 467–469). Although Pilgrims' Castle was to remain in Frankish hands until after the fall of Acre in 1291, Baybars's conquests of 1265 gave the Mamluks effective control of the Sharon Plain up to the Wadi az-Zarqa.

The effects of the conquest were also felt in the countryside. One of Baybars's first acts after capturing the two principal Frankish strongholds of the region was to prepare a land survey detailing the revenues of their territories. Although the surveys themselves do not survive, the certificate by which Baybars granted certain of these lands to some sixty of his amirs in freehold tenure is recorded by Ibn al-Furāt ((2), 78–82) and al-Maqrīzī ((1,2), 10–15; cf. Irwin 1977, 65–67). The identification of the villages mentioned in these texts has been discussed by, amongst others, Ch. Clermont-Ganneau (1888(2), 56–57), Father F.-M.

Table 1. Summary of evidence for settlement in the central Sharon in the Mamluk period (1265–1516)

Site no.	Site name	1265	Pottery	Buildings	Coins	Other refs.
1	ᶜAttil	●				
3	Burin	●	●			
4	Burj al-Ahmar	●	●	●	●	
6	Dair al-Ghusun	●				
7	Dair ᶜIsfin					●
8	Dannaba	●				
9	Kh. Fahas		●			
10	Fardisiya	●	●			
11	Farᶜun	●				
12	Hanuta	●	●			
13	Kh. Ibthan	●				
14	Iqtaba	●				
15	Irtah	●				
16	Kh. al-Jalama	●	●			
17	Kh. Kaffa		●			
18	Kafr Jammal		●			
20	Kh. Kafr Sibb		●			
21	Kh. Kafr Sur		○			
23	Kefar Vitken (Kerem)				●	
28	al-Majdal		●			
31	Qalansuwa	●		●		
32	Qaqun	○	●	●		●
33	ar-Ras		○			
36	Shuwaika	●				
37	at-Taiyiba	●	○			
38	at-Tira					●
39	Tulkarm	●				
41	Yamma	●				
42	Kh. az-Zahran		●			
43	Zaita	●				

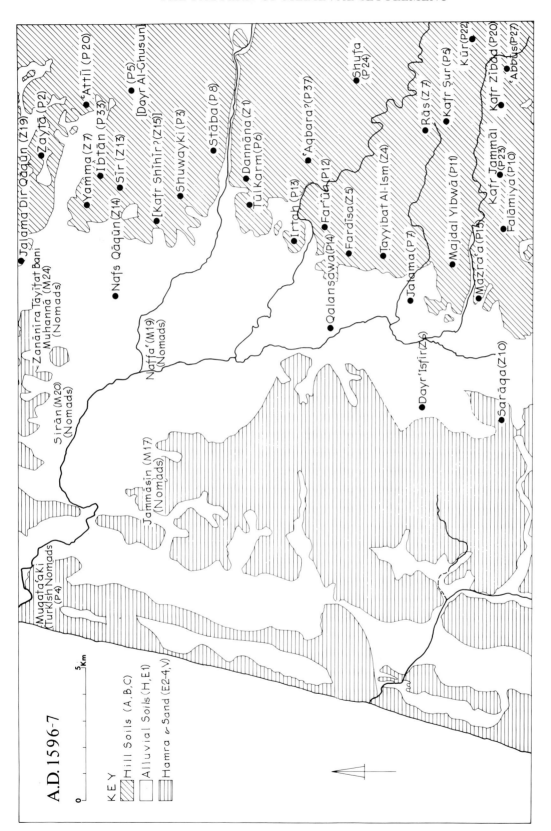

Fig. 8. *Map of the Central Sharon, A. D. 1596/7, showing relation of settlement to soils (settlement information after Hütteroth and Abdulfattah 1977; soil information by courtesy of the Israel Ministry of Agriculture, Tel Aviv).*

Abel (1940) and more recently J. S. C. Riley-Smith, the latter using a more authoritative edition of the text of Ibn al-Furāt than was available before (1971, 208–210). While the list evidently does not represent a complete documentation of all the sites occupied in 1265, it does nevertheless form an important source of information for determining the distribution of village settlements in the 13th century, with implications for both the Frankish and Mamluk periods of administration.

A second source is archaeology. The excavations at the Red Tower have helped to refine the regional dating of certain types of glazed ware attributable to the late 13th century onwards; and the distribution of a number of such wares is set out in Tables 1 and 4. The dating of medieval pottery types in Palestine, however, is as yet rarely precise enough to give any detailed indication of the likely periods of occupation and abandonment of sites except within very broad limits. Secondly, the sherding of sites in our area has not been as comprehensive as one could wish; many sites will therefore have escaped the net. And thirdly, the presence of surface sherds does not usually give much indication of the nature of occupation at a site. In the present state of research, therefore, the information contained in Table 4 is probably more useful for illustrating the traded distributions of certain wares than in giving a reliable picture of settlement in Mamluk times.

Sites occupied during the Mamluk period that have been documented by written or archaeological means are listed in Table 1. The list, however, is far from being a complete record and it would probably be unwarranted to attempt to draw any general conclusions from it. Research on the archaeological and documentary sources relating to the countryside of Palestine in Mamluk times remains a desideratum. Fortunately, however, there is another source which, though dating from the end of the 16th century, does at least allow some of the general changes in the settlement pattern of the region that would have taken place during the Mamluk period to be investigated. This is the Ottoman taxation survey of 1596/7 of which the registers (daftar-i mufaṣṣal) relating to Palestine, Transjordan and southern Syria have now been conveniently analysed by W. Hütteroth and K. Abdulfattah (1977).

By comparing the map of settlements documented in the 12th and 13th centuries (Figs. 2–3) with that showing the distribution of villages assessed for tax in 1596/7 (Fig. 8), it may be seen that the principal change to have taken place during the intervening 300 years was the abandonment of the western kurkar ridges and the hamra by settled life and its replacement by bands of nomadic tribesmen. This was accompanied by a reduction in settlement on the western edge of the eastern alluvial soils; but in the limestone region the pattern of settled life appears to have remained relatively stable (cf. Hütteroth 1975, 6). These data may be conveniently summarized in the form of a table (see Table 2).

The beginning of this shift of settled life away from the western Sharon may be seen already at the time of Baybars and may, in part, have been simply a continuation of the process of abandoning the less fertile hamra soils that had been so marked between Abbasid times and the 12th century. It may be noted that among the villages given by Baybars to his amirs only two, al-Sayr al-Fawqa/al-Sufra (141.205: Abel 1940, 42, no. 24; Riley-Smith 1971, 210, no. 29) and Barwayka/Barnikiya appear to lie near the coast; and of these, the latter may well represent the inland site of Kh. Ibraika (145.178) just south of Hanuta as Abel formerly proposed (1940, 42, no. 32) rather than Buraika (148.218: cf. Riley-Smith 1971, 209, no. 7); it may be noted that it comes in the list between Kasfā and Ḥānūtā, both of which lay in the territory of Arsuf.

The almost total omission of lands in the western Sharon from Baybars's grants, however, may also have been a matter of policy. To Baybars has been attributed the establishment of a policy also pursued by later Mamluk rulers of destroying not only all Frankish fortifications in the coastal plain but settled life itself, and of peopling the area with tribes of nomadic Turks, Mongols and Kurds so as to disincline the Franks from ever attempting to colonize it again (Ayalon 1965, 7–12). It was Baybars who destroyed Caesarea and Arsuf. In the same year (1265) he took the Frankish castle of Surie/Sumerie (Templar of Tyre, 171), possibly to be identified with Kh. ash-Shaumariya (Castellum Feniculi, 141.215), near the mouth of the Nahr az-Zarqa (Prawer 1975(2), 465 n. 34); and he destroyed the castle of al-

Table 2.   Changes in settlement distribution in the central Sharon between the 12th/13th centuries and 1596/7

No. of settlements in:	W. Belt and Hamra	E. edge of Hamra	E. plain	Foothills	Hills
12th–13th c.	5	5	4	18	8
1596/7	(Nomads)	3	3	17	8

Mallūḥa (Ibn al-Furāt (2), 72), which seems likely to be the *Turris Salinarum* (Burj al-Malih, 141.215), sited nearby (Prawer 1975(2), 465; Palestine 1948, 46; Israel 1964, 1403). The destruction of the castle, though not the village, of the Red Tower (al-Burj al-Ahmar) can also most probably be assigned to 1265 or soon after (see below, p. 128).

While destroying the castles that might have given the Franks a foothold on the coastline, Baybars also built up the inland defences. In the central Sharon, the principal Mamluk stronghold was Qaqun, which he refortified in 1266 (see Gazetteer). Qaqun, the objective of an unsuccessful Crusading expedition in 1271, became under the Mamluks the administrative centre for the whole Sharon Plain from the Nahr al-ʿAuja to the Nahr az-Zarqa (cf. Avi-Yonah 1970) and also gave its name to the plain itself (cf. Jaussen and Abel 1923, 85).

A second factor to affect settlement in the Sharon in Mamluk times was the revival of the *Via Maris* route, linking Cairo and Damascus. This road is described by Khalīl al-Ẓāhiri (d. 1468) as passing from Gaza to Jibnin (?), Baidaras, Lydda, al-ʿAuja (Ras al-ʿAin), at-Tira, Qaqun, Fahma, Jinin, Zirʿin, ʿAin Jalut, Baisan, Irbid and so to Damascus (Quatremère 1837 (2, 2), 91, n. 34; cf. Hartmann 1910, 686–693; 1913; Avi-Yonah 1970). The triple-arched bridge, 15 m. wide, which crosses the Nahr Musrara at Jindas just north of Lydda, was constructed by Baybars in March 1273/A.H. 671 (Clermont-Ganneau 1896(2), 110–118; Guy 1954, 79–87; pls. 5–8); and Baybars was also probably responsible for the similar one at Yibna (Clermont-Ganneau 1896(2), 181–182). The construction of a cistern at Qalansuwa in 1336 by the cup-bearer Qūsūn al-Nāṣiri (see Appendix 2, pp. 81–82, no. 8) may also have been connected with the operation of this road. At Qaqun, a large caravanserai was built by ʿAlam al-Din Sanjar Jawli (d. 1345); this was probably sited on the west side of the village, where the *Maqam al-Jawili* and a well could still be seen in the 1940s. It was apparently still in operation as a toll-station at the end of the 16th century (Hütteroth and Abdulfattah 1977, fig. 9).

The survey of 1596/7 may also be used to present a picture of rural settlement in the central Sharon after the end of the Mamluk period. As has been mentioned above, the survey indicates that the heaviest concentration of settlements was in the foothills on the edge of the plain. The villages in this area, however, appear not only more numerous than those in the other regions; they were also more populous and more prosperous. Their average population was about 213 inhabitants, contrasting with 105 in the plain and 127 in the hills; and the average level of taxation paid per village may be estimated at 11,405 *aqja*, contrasting with figures of 9,261 in the plain and 7,011 in the hills (see Table 3).

The reason why the foothills were able to support a larger and more thriving population than the other regions is made clear by the taxation returns which record the amounts of tax levied on different agricultural products (Table 3). Since these assessments were based for the most part on set proportions of the products harvested each year, one may extrapolate from the figures given the approximate value of different products for each village included in the survey. The results are illuminating. In the villages of the plain, arable farming of wheat, barley and summer crops, represented some 87% of village income derived from agriculture, while fruits, olives, goats and bees (products of wastes or lands less suitable for arable cultivation) made up the remaining 13%. In the hill villages, this pattern was reversed, 61% being represented by fruit, olives, goats and bees, while only 39% came from corn and summer crops. The villages of the foothills, however, show a more balanced agrarian economy, with corn and summer crops representing 62% and other products 38%. These differences can be illustrated more tellingly by comparing the relative proportions of just two products, wheat and olives, the two staples of village diet. In the plain they represented 51% and 7% respectively; in the hills, 25% and 48%; while in the foothills the figures are 37% and 26%.

It seems therefore that the principal reason for the higher carrying capacity of the foothill region of the eastern Sharon in the late 16th century, as no doubt in earlier periods too, was the ability of the people settled there to make use of the arable lands available in the eastern plain and in the lower stream valleys for corn and summer crops, the *rendzina* soils of the lower hill slopes for fruit, olives and some garden and corn crops, and the high waste lands for grazing and bee-keeping.

In the western zones the taxation paid by the nomadic tribes was not assessed directly on the basis of agricultural production; thus the survey tells us little about their economies. It may be noted, however, that one tribe, the Jammāsīn, paid a special levy on their water buffalo, indicating one particular use to which the marshes of the Nahr Iskandaruna were put at this time; and in the same period a significant increase in the proportion of cattle to sheep/goat bones is recorded by the excavations at al-Burj al-Ahmar. It is also likely that a number of the *mazraʾa*, or isolated arable lands, most of which would have belonged to villages of the hills but which cannot be located on the ground (cf. Hütteroth and Abdulfattah 1977, 78–79), would have been in this area. In the late 19th century several hill villages made use of small seasonal settlements in the plain for summer grazing or for winter and spring cropping (Amiran 1953, 199–201; fig. 5). Many of these, including Khirbat Bait Lid (= al-Maghair, site 26), were themselves former villages. The occupation of

Table 3.   Summary of data from the Ottoman survey of 1596/7 relating to the central Sharon

	Pop.	Total Tax	Relative % values of agricultural products:							Refs.
			Wheat	Barley	Summer crops	Olives	Fruit	Goats and Bees	Buffalo	
Nomadic tribes (W. Zone):										
Muqata°aki	190	1,400						100·00		137, P4
Jammāsin	172	6,060						6·17	93·83	138, M1
Zanānira	45	500								138, M2
Sirān	187	1,000								138, M2
Naffa°	50	500								138, M1
Averages	129	1,892	—	—	—	—	—	22·18	77·82	
E. Alluvial Zone:										
Nafs Qāqūn	99	16,590	46·25	8·14	35·83			9·77		138, Z14
Jalama	95	4,470	53·21	12·25	28·19	4·08		3·27		139, P7
Qalansawa	145	11,342	53·18	11·70	28·10	3·90		3·12		139, P14
Dayr °Isfir	152	7,500	52·46	7·39	4·43	30·79		4·93		141, Z6
Jalama dir Qāqūn	35	10,000	56·11	24·04	10·32	4·51		5·01		160, Z19
Sarāqa	103	5,665	48·24	9·71	19·41	16·18		6·47		141, Z10
Averages	105	9,261	50·91	12·60	23·42	6·78	—	6·47	—	
W. Edge of Hills:										
Zaytā	490	?	65·85	6·63	15·91	8·97		2·65		137, P2
Yamma	95	14,000	48·20	15·09	13·58	13·83		9·30		138, Z7
°Attil	295	14,872	46·38	10·21	12·25	23·82		7·35		126, P20
Ibtān	NIL	7,200	29·73	3·49	23·73	29·08		13·96		127, P33
Sir	10	8,842	26·20	36·90	18·45	6·15		12·30		138, Z13
Dayr al-Ghusun	—	—	—	No data available		—	—	—	—	—
Kafr Shihir	85	18,000	41·08	10·13	26·04	14·27		8·49		138, Z15
Shuwayki	505	23,250	36·60	9·02	12·93	27·71		13·74		137, P3
Stāba	105	4,100	38·90	13·70	13·15	11·42		22·83		137, P8
Dannāba	83	7,970	31·18	12·55	18·63	20·91		16·73		138, Z1
Tūlkarm	880	21,600	21·98	5·81	4·74	50·96		16·51		137, P6
Irtah	215	8,842	35·88	15·79	37·90	7·48		2·95		139, P13
°Aqbara	128	5,692	53·67	14·17	1·51	3·94	1·51	25·20		127, P37
Far°ūn	115	3,837	57·10	6·70			13·86	22·34		139, P12
Fardisa	67	5,000	33·09	11·03	17·65	22·06		16·18		141, Z5
Tayyibat al-Ism	255	19,800	20·78	12·47	23·42	34·15		9·17		141, Z4
Majdal Yibwa	235	13,050	26·39	4·21	13·20	42·15		14·05		139, P11
Mazra'a	60	6,424	35·70	12·96	13·84	31·72		5·77		140, P15
Averages	213	11,405	37·03	9·62	15·29	26·06	0·31	11·67	—	

Table 3. (*cont.*)

	Pop.	Total Tax	Relative % values of agricultural products:							Refs.
			Wheat	Barley	Summer crops	Olives	Fruit	Goats and Bees	Buffalo	
Hills:										
Shufa	40	3,202	48·63	8·56	17·12	14·27		11·42		126, P24
Rās	125	6,600	34·19	8·03	11·24	26·75		19·80		141, Z7
Kafr Ṣur	110	6,100	11·60	8·17	6·37	40·85		33·01		139, P5
Kūr	167	4,000	12·51	4·40	5·28	66·06		11·74		140, P22
Falāmiya	130	9,862	16·13	2·84	3·41	66·26		11·36		139, P10
Kafr Jammāl	98	11,074	23·54	5·53	5·53	59·87		5·53		140, P23
Kafr Zibād	250	10,280	38·87	8·21	16·42	27·37		9·12		140, P20
'Abbūs	95	4,974	33·13	5·83	4·67	48·60		7·78		140, P27
Averages	127	7,011	24·53	6·05	8·10	48·22	—	13·10	—	

All data are taken from Hütteroth and Abdulfattah 1977.

Population: Estimates assume an average family size of 5, to which the figure for unmarried men is added (Hütteroth and Abdulfattah 1977, 36–37). In our survey area, the entire population was classed as Muslim, except for seven families of Christians at Zaytā (P2).

Total tax: This includes all taxes (except *waqf*) and is expressed, like all the taxation figures in the *daftars* in *aqja*.

Relative % values of agricultural products: The rates of taxation of agricultural products varied according to the product and the locality. In order to obtain a nearer approximation to the pre-taxation values of the various products, the tax figures were therefore multiplied by the known or assumed tax rate (see Hütteroth and Abdulfattah 1977, 76–85). *Summer crops*: include summer vegetables, such as beans and melons, as well as *dura*. *Olives*: include both fruit and oil. *Fruit*: includes all tree-grown fruit crops. *Buffalo*: these are water buffalo, taxed apparently for their yield of milk and meat.

Refs.: All references are to page number (in Hütteroth and Abdulfattah 1977), followed by the fiscal unit number given in the *daftar*.

the Red Tower (al-Burj al-Ahmar) after *c.*1390 may also have been of this type.

One further point may be noted. By 1596/7, the largest village in the central Sharon was no longer Qaqun, the administrative centre since the time of Baybars and still at this time a market and centre of a *nāḥiya* (Hütteroth and Abdulfattah 1977, 88; fig. 8). The estimated population of Tulkarm now outnumbered that of Qaqun by 880 to 99, and its taxation total was a third as much again. Even before the arrival of the railway at the end of the 19th century therefore Tulkarm's position at the mouth of the Wadi Nablus seems to have given it an important advantage over the other settlements of the region.

II. GAZETTEER OF SITES OCCUPIED BETWEEN 1099 AND 1516

The following 44 sites are documented by archaeological or written evidence (or both) as having been occupied at some time or other between 1099 and 1516, the period of Crusader and Mamluk occupation of the Sharon Plain. Their locations are indicated in Figs. 2 and 3. Throughout the Gazetteer, sites are normally listed and referred to by their modern Arabic names, which in many cases correspond with both the medieval Arabic and medieval Crusader name. Modern Hebrew names are given for Sites 23 and 38, where there is no Arabic equivalent. Alternative names and variants of names occurring in documentary sources are indicated as follows:

Cr.   = Crusader (French or Latin)
Med. Ar. = Medieval Arabic
Hebr.   = Modern Hebrew

The eight-figure references at the head of each entry serve to locate the site (or its central point) to within a 100 m. square of the Palestine (or Israel) Grid. The altitudes relate to the highest part of each site above mean sea level, rounded down to the nearest 10 m.

1. ʿATTIL   1570.1974, alt. 110 m.
Cr. Hatil; Med. Ar. ʿAttil

Certain rents in *Hatil* formed part of the fief of the *scribanus* John that was granted, in February 1200/1, to his nephew Soquerius by Aymar, Lord of Caesarea (*Cod. Dipl.* (1), 288–289, no. 9: *RRH*, 205, no. 768; cf. Riley-Smith 1972, 25). In 1265, Baybars granted the whole territory of ʿAttil to the atabek Fāris al-Dīn Uqṭāy al-Ṣāliḥī (Ibn al-Furāt (2), 80; al-Maqrīzī (1, 2), 13).

Early occupation of the village site is attested by rock-cut cisterns and caves, a cylindrical masonry-lined well (Bir al-Butma), fragments of mosaic, column-drums and capitals. A group of marble and granite columns forming part of a house a short distance north-west of the mosque, however, came according to local people from Caesarea; this possibly throws into doubt the reported identification of remains of a church at ʿAttil in 1977 (Haufani 1977; cf. Bagatti 1979, 135). Just east of these columns stands a domed 19th-century building, some 10 m. square. Much of the central part of the village is now in ruins.

The present mosque, though containing reused building material, appears to be of no great antiquity. North of the village, the wely of al-Masyad is reported to have "foundations of ancient appearance" (*PAM*,

17.8.1922). Another wely, with a dome, stands south-west of the village next to the approach road.

Visited 22.11.1983.

Bibliography:
Cod. Dipl. (1), 288–289, no. 9 (1200/1); Ibn al-Furāt (2), 80; al-Maqrīzī (1, 2), 13; *RRH*, 205, no. 768 (1200/1).

Abel 1940, 40, no. 1; Bagatti 1979, 135; Beyer 1936, 38; Conder and Kitchener 1881(2), 151; Guérin 1874(2), 345; Haufani 1977; Palestine 1929, 12; 1948, 57; Rey 1883, 422; Riley-Smith 1971, 209, no. 4; Röhricht 1887, 248.

2. KHIRBAT BAIT SAMA   1582.1994, alt. 100 m.
Cr. Bezzemel

Some rents in *Bezzemel* belonged to the fief of the *scribanus* John that passed with the scribanage to his nephew Soquerius in February 1200/1 (*Cod. Dipl.* (1), 288–289, no. 9; *RRH*, 205, no. 768).

The site occupies a low natural mound in the centre of an alluvial depression, now given over to fruit and vegetable growing with olives on the rocky higher ground beyond. The mound is covered with remains of buildings and rectilinear terrace enclosures, built of reused ashlars. Although no buildings survive intact, early occupation is attested by rock-cut tombs and cisterns, columns, capitals and other architectural fragments seen there earlier this century. In 1922, a cylindrical well (d. 2·5 m.) lined with fine ashlar masonry was uncovered, and near-by a floor of white mosaic (*PAM*, 16.8.1922).

Quantities of Byzantine pottery litter the site and the area around. Most of the medieval pottery, including types from the 9th to the 13th century, was concentrated on the southern end of the higher central part of the mound.

Visited 18.11.1983

Bibliography:
Cod. Dipl. (1), 288–289, no 9; *RRH*, 205, no. 768 (1200/1).

Beyer 1936, 37–38; Conder and Kitchener 1881(2), 196; Gophna and Porat 1972, 212, no. 40; Palestine 1929, 76; 1948, 57; Rey 1883, 418.

3. KHIRBAT BURIN   1487.1909, alt. 30 m.
Cr. Burin, Buria, Casal Neuf; Med. Ar. Būrīn

A certain Hugh of Burin (or Buria) witnessed two charters of the Lady of Caesarea in February 1207 (*RRH*, 220, nos. 818–819). The site should probably be identified with *Casal neuf*, which in December 1253 belonged to the Archbishop of Caesarea and formed with Tulkarm the southern boundary of the lands of *Cafresur* (Kafr Sibb) (*Cart. des Hosp.* (2), 749–750, no. 2661; *RRH*, 319, no. 1210). This name would seem to imply that Burin had been repopulated in Frankish times after a period of abandonment. To judge by the pottery evidence from the site (see Table 4), however, such a period could not have lasted for long, for material from all periods is represented. In 1265, Baybars divided the territory of Burin between two of his amirs (Ibn al-Furāt (2), 81; al-Maqrīzī (1, 2), 13).

Today the site is unoccupied and is represented only by a low artificial mound on the northern edge of a tributary of the Nahr Iskandaruna. In 1926, the new motor road constructed from Tulkarm to the coast passed over the northern part of this mound and in the cutting, which in places was as much as 1·20 m. deep, a number of stone blocks and a column-base were unearthed (P. L. O. Guy, *PAM*, 1926). Eight years later, the road surface was lowered by a further 1·50 m. over a length of about 70 m. where it crossed the mound. During the course of this work "hundreds" of stones were dug out, including an ionic capital and two column bases, together with medieval pottery, some of it glazed (N. Makhouly, *PAM*, 19.11.1934).

The greater and highest part of the mound, which rises to some 7–8 m. above the surrounding land surface, lies south of the modern road. Its surface is covered by a series of retaining walls, which give it a somewhat rectangular outline. In the cutting for the ditch on the west side of the road to Qalansuwa, which impinges on the east side of the mound, a mosaic floor composed of white tesserae (3 × 3 × 4 cm.) was noted in November 1982. Traces of walling are also to be seen in the animal burrows and military trenches (from 1947–48) which have disturbed the top of the mound itself. Another result of this disturbance has been to throw up a large quantity of pottery, including Roman and Byzantine, glazed and unglazed early Islamic wares including types of the 9th to 11th century, and a range of medieval types from the 12th to the 14th century and possibly later. The only coin recovered was a Palestine 5 mils of 1946.

Visited 18.11.82, 16.11.83.

Bibliography:
Cart. des Hosp. (2), 749–450, no. 2661 (1253); Ibn al-Furāt (2), 81; al-Maqrīzī (1, 2), 13; *RRH*, 319, no. 1210 (1253).

Abel 1940, 41, no. 10; Bagatti 1979, 134; Beyer 1936, 40; Conder and Kitchener 1881(2), 178; Guérin 1874(2), 349–350; Israel 1964, 1411; Palestine 1929, 25; 1948, 57; Riley-Smith 1971, 209, no. 10; Röhricht 1887, 251.

4. AL-BURJ AL-AHMAR,   1455.1917, alt. 40 m.
KHIRBAT AL-BURJ AL-ᶜATUT
Cr. *Turris Latinae, Turriclee, Tourre-Rouge, Turris Rubea*;
Med. Ar. *al-Burj al-Aḥmar*; Hebr. Ḥ. *Burgata*; Eng. *The Red Tower.*

See Parts Two and Three below (pp. 83–194).

5. KHIRBAT DAIRABAN   1586.1881, alt. 350 m.
A piece of turquoise-glazed Raqqa pottery was picked up on this site during the 1967–68 Survey.

Not visited.

Bibliography:
Gophna and Porat 1972, 220, no. 110; Palestine 1929, 29; 1948, 62.

6. DAIR AL-GHUSUN   1575.1955, alt. 190 m.
Med. Ar. *Dayr al-Ghuṣūn, Dayr al-ᶜUṣfūr*
In 1265, the whole of Dair al-Ghusun was granted by Baybars to the amir Badr al-Dīn Muḥammad Bī.

Visited 22.11.1983.

Bibliography:
Ibn al-Furāt (2), 81; al-Maqrīzī (1, 2), 14.

Abel 1940, 41, no. 16; Beyer 1936, 38; Conder and Kitchener 1881(2), 152; Guérin 1874(2), 345; Riley-Smith 1971, 209, no. 12.

7. DAIR ᶜISFIN   1456.1843, alt. 70 m.
Med. Ar. *Dayr ᶜAsfin*
Dair ᶜIsfin may perhaps be identified with *Theraspis* of the 6th-century Madaba mosaic map (Avi-Yonah 1940, 15; 1976, 101). On an Arabic inscription in the *ḥaram* in Hebron, the village is listed as containing *waqf* property of the mosque; unfortunately this text cannot be precisely dated, though if it is not itself of Mamluk date, it seems likely at least to relate to endowments made by Mamluk sultans (Jaussen and Abel 1923, 85, 94).

The site is now totally abandoned and obliterated.

Not visited.

Bibliography:
Conder and Kitchener 1881(2), 179; Israel 1964, 1412; Jaussen and Abel 1923, 85, 94, Palestine 1948, 62.

8. DANNABA   1542.1911, alt. 120 m.
Med. Ar. *Dannāba*
In 1265, Baybars divided Dannaba between al-Malik al-Mujāhid Sayf al-Dīn Ishāq, Lord of al-Jazīra, and al-Malik al-Muẓaffar, Lord of Sinjar.

Not visited.

Bibliography:
Ibn al-Furāt (2), 81; al-Maqrīzī (1, 2), 14.

Abel 1940, 41, no. 15; Beyer 1936, 39; Conder and Kitchener 1881(2), 159; Gophna and Porat 1972, 218, no. 87; Guérin 1874(2), 355; Riley-Smith 1971, 209, no. 13.

9. KHIRBAT FAHAS 1558.1815, alt. 260 m.

The official lists of the Antiquities Department mention a watch-tower of unspecified date. Pottery from the 1967–68 Survey includes a piece of glazed slip-painted ware.

Not visited.

Bibliography:
Gophna and Porat 1972, 226, no. 161; Palestine 1929, 93; 1948, 63.

10. FARDISIYA 1515.1871, alt. 90 m.
 Cr. *Phardesi*; Med. Ar. *Fardisiyā(Afrādnasīfa)*

Fardisiya is mentioned only once in Crusading sources when, in February 1207/8, its lands were said to mark the southern boundary of those of *Pharaon* (Farʿun) and *Seingibis* (Kh. Nisf Jubail). At this time the village belonged to a knight called Grémont (*dominus Gormundus*) (*Cart. des Hosp.* (2), 65, no. 1251; *RRH*, 220, no. 819), who may possibly be identified with a lord of Baisan of that name appearing in charters between 1198 and 1220 (cf. Beyer 1936, 39; La Monte and Downs 1950, 66). In 1265, Baybars granted the whole of Fardisiya to the amir Sayf al-Dīn Baydaghān al-Ruknī (Ibn al-Furāt (2), 82; al-Maqrīzī (1, 2), 15).

The village formerly occupied the saddle of a promontory overlooking the coastal plain. Most of the old buildings have now been abandoned for several years, and the area is currently being redeveloped as a residential extension to Taiyiba. The only surviving building of any antiquity is the *maqam* of Shaykh Mūsa, a small rectangular building with a pendentive dome and a wide pointed-arched opening on the north; the east and west windows have ogival heads formed by the juxtaposition of pairs of rounded corbels.

Pottery from the south and east areas of the site includes a range of 12th- to 13th-century and later types. Visited 18.11.1983.

Bibliography:
Cart. des Hosp. (2), 65, no. 1251 (1207/8); Ibn al-Furāt (2), 82; al-Maqrīzī (1, 2), 15; *RRH*, 220, no. 819 (1207/8).

Abel 1940, 42, no. 34; Beyer 1936, 39, 57; Clermont-Ganneau 1888(1), 334–337; Conder and Kitchener 1881(2), 164; Guérin 1874(2), 352; Prutz 1881, 175; Rey 1883, 423; Riley-Smith 1971, 209, no. 15; Röhricht 1887, 246.

11. FARʿUN 1526.1881, alt. 150 m.
 Cr. *Pharaon*; Med. Ar. *Farʿūn*

Certain rents in *Pharaon* formed part of the fief belonging to the office of *scribanus*, granted in February 1200/1 to Soquerius by Aymar, Lord of Caesarea (*Cod. Dipl.* (1), 288–289, no. 9; *RRH*, 205, no. 768). In February 1207/8, Aymar's wife Juliana granted both *Pharaon* and *Seingibis* to the Order of St. John. On the east these lands were bounded by the *Cauea ficuum* (Wadi at-Tin), its mills (*Petra Molarum*) and the lands of *Caphet* (Kh. Kaffa), to the south by the lands of *Phardesi* (Fardisiya), to the west by *Calanchun* (Qalansuwa) and to the north by the *Cauea Artais*, or lower course of the Wadi at-Tin which evidently marked the boundary with the lands of Irtah (*Cart. des Hosp.* (2), 65, no. 1251; *RRH*, 220, no. 819). In 1265, the lands of Farʿun were divided between two of Baybars's amirs (Ibn al-Furāt (2), 81; al-Maqrīzī (1, 2), 14).

Not visited.

Bibliography:
Cart. des Hosp. (2), 65, no. 1251 (1207/8); *Cod. Dipl.* (1), 288–289, no. 9; Ibn al-Furāt (2), 81; al-Maqrīzī (1, 2), 14; *RRH*, 205, no. 768 (1200/1); 220, no. 819 (1207/8).

Abel 1940, 41, no. 21; Bagatti 1979, 133; Beyer 1936, 38–39; Clermont-Ganneau 1888(1), 334–337; Conder 1889b, 202; Conder and Kitchener 1881(2), 164; Guérin 1874(2), 352; Meistermann 1936, 469; Prutz 1881, 167, 175; Rey 1883, 423; Riley-Smith 1971, 209, no. 14; Röhricht 1887, 246.

12. KHIRBAT HANUTA 1485.1807, alt. 90 m.
 Med. Ar. *Ḥānūtā*; Hebr. *Ḥ. Ḥanut*

In 1265, Baybars granted the amir ʿAlam al-Dīn Sanjar half of Hanuta. This village lay in the territory of Arsuf (Ibn al-Furāt (2), 82; al-Maqrīzī (1, 2), 15).

The site of Ḥanuta, lying on the eastern edge of the coastal plain overlooking at-Tira, is now almost completely obliterated and planted with cypress and fir. A new road cuts east–west through it. To the south are rock-cut cisterns and tombs, with a scatter of Byzantine coarse pottery becoming denser nearer the road. On the north side cisterns and a scatter of Byzantine pottery extend up to 200 m. from the road. The surface finds also include debris from a glass-furnace and sherds of medieval pottery of the 12th to 13th centuries and after.

Visited 17.11.1983.

Bibliography:
Ibn al-Furāt (2), 82; al-Maqrīzī (1, 2), 15.

Abel 1940, 42, no. 33; Beyer 1951, 179; Israel 1964, 1412; Palestine 1948, 62; Riley-Smith 1971, 209, no. 17.

13. KHIRBAT IBTHAN 1542.1967, alt. 160 m.
 Med. Ar. *Bathān*

In 1265, Baybars granted all of *Bathān* to the amir ʿAlam al-Dīn Sanjar al-Ḥalabī al-Ṣāliḥī (Ibn al-Furāt (2), 81; al-Maqrīzī (1, 2). 13).

The medieval village seems more likely to correspond with the hill-top *khirba* of the same name than with the present village just north of it. Here the Survey of Western Palestine noted traces of ruins and a well. The site is now inaccessible.

Not visited.

Bibliography:

Ibn al-Furāt (2), 81; al-Maqrīzī (1, 2), 13.

Abel 1940, 41, no. 9; Beyer 1936, 38; Conder and Kitchener 1881(2), 196; Palestine 1929, 107; 1948, 57; Riley-Smith 1971, 209, no. 8.

14. IQTABA   1553.1924, alt. 170 m.
Med. Ar. *Iqtāba, Sabāhiyā*

In 1265, Baybars granted Iqtaba to the amir ᶜAlam al-Dīn Ṭardaj al-Amadī (Ibn al-Furāt (2), 81; al-Maqrīzī (1, 2), 14).

V. Guérin noted ancient cisterns at the site in the 1870s. Today it is occupied by a small village.

Not visited.

Bibliography:

Ibn al-Furāt (2), 81; al-Maqrīzī (1, 2), 14.

Abel 1940, 41, no. 22; Beyer 1936, 48; 1951, 281; Conder and Kitchener 1881(2), 185; Guérin 1874(2), 354; Riley-Smith 1971, 210, no. 27.

15. IRTAH   1518.1892, alt. 80 m.
Cr. *Artais*; Med. Ar. *Irtāḥ*

The valley of *Artais* is referred to in 1207/8 as defining the northern boundary of the lands of *Pharaon* and *Seingibis* (*RRH*, 220, no. 819). In 1265, the village was divided between two of Baybars's amirs (Ibn al-Furāt (2), 81; al-Maqrīzī (1, 2), 14).

Occupation in Byzantine and early Islamic times is attested by pottery, column-drums and capitals, rock-cut tombs, cisterns and troughs, and by a masonry tank (*c.* 3 × 14 m.) surviving south-west of the village.

Some 30 m. south-west of this tank stands the *maqam* of Nabī Yaᶜqūb. The building consists of two domed chambers, each roughly square in plan and with a *miḥrāb* in the south wall; they are entered through separate pointed-arched doors from a courtyard on the north (Pl. IV). The dome of the eastern chamber rests externally on an octagonal socle; inside it is carried on arched squinches, with a blind arch on each of the other four sides. The western dome is squatter and without socle or squinches. An inscribed column was noted on the east side of its entrance in 1941 (see below, Appendix 2, no. 7). S. A. S. Husseini also records,

> "Inside the chamber near the middle of the south wall there is a small marble base hollowed out and open[-ing] into a ... vaulted tomb chamber [underneath], which is entered from outside through a square built opening. This

vault is built of good masonry with its axis south–north. At a later date ... the vault was partition[ed] by a cross wall having a straight-sided entrance curved at the top communicating into the so-formed inner chamber. Along the south side of the inner chamber a tomb is built apparently of rough stones covered with a thick coat of plaster. At the east and west ends of the tomb stands a stone post" (*PAM*, 29.6.1941).

As Husseini and others have noted, the *maqam* appears to have been built over the remains of an earlier building, to which probably belong the vaulted lower chamber and six courses of drafted masonry (consistently 0·585 m. high, and up to 2·75 m. long) surviving *in situ* at the base of its south wall (see Pl. V). The date of this building is likely to be Roman or Byzantine, though its function is uncertain.

Visited 23.2.1982.

Bibliography:

Cart. des Hosp. (2), 65, no. 1251 (1207/8); Ibn al-Furāt (2), 81; al-Maqrīzī (1, 2), 14; *RRH*, 220, 819 (1207/8).

Abel 1940, 42, no. 25; Beyer 1936, 39; Clermont-Ganneau 1888(1), 334–337; Conder 1890, 31; Conder and Kitchener 1881(2), 164; Gophna and Porat 1972, 220, no. 108; Guérin 1874(2), 352; Palestine 1929, 44; 1948, 62; Prutz 1881, 175; Riley-Smith 1971, 209, no. 19; Röhricht 1887, 246.

16. KHIRBAT AL-JALAMA   1511.1999, alt. 50 m.
Cr. *Gelenne*; Med. Ar. *Jalama*; Hebr. *Ḥ. Gelon*

In February 1200/1 the fief granted to the *scribanus* Soquerius included some rents in *Gelenne*. At this time the village is described as having formerly belonged to the lords of Caesarea, but its new owner is not identified. (*Cod. Dipl.* (1), 288–289, no. 9; *RRH*, 205, no. 768). In 1265, the village was divided between three of Baybars's amirs (Ibn al-Furāt (2), 81; al-Maqrīzī (1, 2), 13–14).

The site occupies a rounded hillock on the eastern edge of the coastal plain. In the 1870s, the Survey of Western Palestine noted walls and foundations, much weathered and of ancient appearance, and among the ruins a small domed building (Conder and Kitchener 1881(2), 197). This was evidently the *maqam* of Shaykh Masṣūd. Later accounts describe this as built of ancient materials, including column-drums, with a dome constructed on squinches and a *miḥrāb* in the south wall (*PAM*, 24.8.1922; D. C. Baramki, *PAM*, 14.7.1943).

The site is now covered by the settlement of Lahavot Haviva. Pottery from the south and east slopes include Byzantine and some early Islamic course wares, as well as medieval wares of the later 13th century.

Visited 16.11.1983.

Bibliography:

Cod. Dipl. (1), 288–289, no. 9 (1200/1); Ibn al-Furāt (2), 81; al-Maqrīzī (1, 2), 13–14; *RRH*, 205, no. 768 (1200/1).

Pl. IV. *Irtah (site 15): Maqam of Nabi Ya'qūb from NE (photo. author).*

Pl. V. *Irtah (site 15): Maqam of Nabi Ya'qūb from S, showing early masonry at base of wall (photo. author).*

Abel 1940, 41, no. 12; Beyer 1936, 38; Conder and Kitchener 1881(2), 197; Israel 1964, 1411; Palestine 1948, 57; Rey 1883, 421; Riley-Smith 1971, 210, no. 21; Röhricht 1887, 249.

17. Khirbat KAFFA   1549.1888, alt. 150 m.
Cr. *Caphet, Cafetum*

Certain rents in *Cafetum* belonged in February 1200/1 to the fief granted to the *scribanus* Soquerius by Aymar, Lord of Caesarea (*Cod. Dipl.* (1), 288–289, no. 9; *RRH*, 205 no. 768). In February 1207/8 the lands of *Caphet* marched on the west with those of *Pharaon* (Far'un) and *Seingibis* (Kh. Nisf Jubail), the border separating them being marked apparently by the *Cauea Ficuum* (Wadi at-Tin) (*Cart. des Hosp.* (2), 65, no. 1251; *RRH*, 220, no. 819).

Khirbat Kaffa occupies a rounded hill-top, 3 km. south-east of Tulkarm, with views extending over the Wadi at-Tin and the coastal plain to the west. It is still inhabited, with a group of houses clustering about a wely. Sherds from the slopes east, south and west of the houses include Byzantine and early Islamic wares, nothing diagnostic of the 9th to 11th centuries, but a representative sample from the 12th to 14th as well as some modern china.

Visited 18.11.1983.

Bibliography:
Cart. des Hosp. (2), 65, no. 1251 (1207/8); *Cod. Dipl.* (1), 288–289, no. 9 (1200/1); *RRH*, 205, no. 768 (1200/1); 220, no. 819 (1207/8).

Beyer 1936, 38–39; 1940, 196; Clermont-Ganneau 1888(1), 334–337; Conder 1890, 35, no. 40; Conder and Kitchener 1881(2), 195; Gophna and Porat 1972, 220, no. 109; Palestine 1929, 52; 1948, 62; Rey 1883, 420; Röhricht 1887, 246.

18. KAFR JAMMAL (near)   1544.1821, alt. 190 m

Pottery collected by the 1967–68 Survey from a hill-top site 800 m. north of the village of Kafr Jammal includes types datable between the 9th and the 14th century.

Not visited.

Bibliography:
Gophna and Porat 1972, 226, no. 160.

19. KAFR SALLAM   Not located
Cr. *Caruasalim, Cafarsalem;* Med. Ar. *Kafr Sallām*

The site of Kafr Sallam has yet to be found. Documentary sources, however, allow its likely position to be established within the limits of a few square kilometres.

Al-Muqaddasi, in the late 10th century, writes that Kafr Sallam was,

"One of the villages of the district of Caesarea. It is very populous, and has a mosque. It lies on the high road (from Ar Ramlah northwards)" (transl. Le Strange, 60–61).

Elsewhere the same writer describes Kafr Sallam with Darayya, Bait Lihiya and Kafr Saba as a village in the province of Syria,

"larger and more sumptuous than are many of the chief towns in the Arabian Peninsula" (p. 12)

He also records that it lay within a day's journey of Ramla, Nablus and Caesarea (pp. 96–98).

By the middle of the 11th century, Kafr Sallam seems to have been abandoned by its population, possibly as a result of the unstable political conditions in Palestine at that time. Probably for this reason Nāsir-i Khusraw, travelling from Caesarea to Ramla in 1047, was led to equate the village with Kafr Saba (grid ref. 144.176: transl. Le Strange, 21), though we know from al-Muqaddasi that they were two separate places. Some physical remains of the village would still have been standing, however, for in March 1065 a group of German pilgrims led by Siegfried, Archbishop of Mainz, and the Bishops of Utrecht, Bamberg and Ratisbon were attacked by local Arabs as they proceeded towards Jerusalem and were forced to take refuge for two days in the deserted "castle" of Kafr Sallam (*in quoddam castellum uacuum Caruasalim nomine*). Finally they were rescued by the Fatimid governor of Ramla, under whose protection they were able to complete their pilgrimage (Marianus Scottus, 558–559; cf. Lambert of Hersfeld, 165–171).

Further topographical indications are provided by a charter of September 1131 by which Walter I Garnier, Lord of Caesarea, confirmed the gifts that his father Eustace and he had made to the Order of St. John. These included various properties in Qaqun, some lands given by H. Lumbardus,

"two carrucates of land in *Cafarsalem* for sowing and harvesting; and besides, adjoining that land, ... two carrucates of land extending from the beginning of the land belonging to Rambald that is worked in the Marsh (*in Maresco*) as far as the river" (*Cart. des Hosp.* (1), 84, no. 94; *RRH*, 35, no. 139).

It would thus appear that Kafr Sallam lay somewhere to the west of Qaqun, on the edge of the marshland which at that time surrounded the lower course of the Nahr Iskandaruna and its tributaries.

The memory of the town seems to have persisted through the 12th century, but unfortunately no source specifies whether it was inhabited. In his Description of the Holy Places, written around 1172, Theodoric lists the ancient and modern towns and villages that one would pass travelling from Lydda to Acre through the coastal plain: they include *Caphargamala* (Kafr Saba?),

Capharsemala (Kafr Sallam?), *Cacho* (Qaqun) and *Caesarea* in that order (XXXIX: ed. Bulst, 43; cf. 74 n. 2). In 1225, the Arab geographer Yāqūt also mentions Kafr Sallam as

> "a village of the Filastin province, lying between Nablus and Kaisariya, and four leagues from Kaisariya" (Le Strange 1890, 472).

His statement, however, is probably based on earlier sources.

Kafr Sallam was therefore on the road from Caesarea to Nablus, and on that from Caesarea to Ramla, and within a day's journey from all three towns. It follows that it should be sought in the coastal plain north of the point at which these two routes came together. It is therefore not possible to identify it with Kafr Saba (see above), Ras al-ʿAin (grid ref. 143.168: cf. C. Wilson, in Le Strange 1890, 472) or Kafr Sa (grid ref. 149.181: cf. Rey 1883, 419; Röhricht 1887, 246), all of which lie too far to the south. It remains uncertain, however, which course the road from Caesarea took in the 10th and 11th centuries. The course of the Roman road from *Antipatris* (Ras al-ʿAin) to Caesarea in this area is now well documented (Dar and Applebaum 1973) (see Figs. 1 and 3). It would have been joined by the road from *Neapolis* (Nablus) just west of the present Burgata village (grid ref. 1463.1924: Dar and Applebaum 1973, 97; fig. 2M), and from there have proceeded north to cross the Nahr Iskandaruna at or near the Jisr al-Maktaba, and thence on to Kh. Zalafa/Zilipheh (144.202) and Hadera (142.204). Almost any point on the stretch of road between Burgata and Zilipheh would correspond with the evidence in the charter of 1131. If the site lay on this road, it would probably have been located, like most Roman sites in this area, on the edge of the dry red soils overlooking the flood plain (Dar and Applebaum 1973, 97–99; fig. 4). Possible sites include Tall Shuqaifa (1463.1938) and Tel Nurit (1458.1984); at the latter medieval and Ottoman-period sherds have been found besides pre-Roman and Byzantine (see Site 38, below). Alternatively, the town might have been situated on the eastern route, which passed through Qaqun, thereby avoiding the crossing of the Nahr Iskandaruna. In this case, a position north-west of Qaqun and west of Kh. al-Jalama would be indicated.

Corroborative evidence for locating Kafr Sallam in this general area comes from an earlier source. The Jerusalem Talmud records the names of three Jewish villages whose wine was forbidden because of their proximity to three Samaritan villages. Among these, the wine of ʿEn Kushi was declared suspect because it lay near to the Samaritan village of Kefar Shalem (Neubauer 1868, 173). Kefar Shalem has been variously identified with Sallama, near Jaffa (132.162: Avi-Yonah 1940, 18), and with Dair Abu Sallama, east of

Lydda (146.150: Avi-Yonah 1976, 73). Neither suggestion seems very convincing. ʿEn Kushi, however, has recently been identified with Kh. Kusiya (1516.2029), 6·5 km. north of Qaqun; and it has also been suggested that Kefar Shalem may have been located at Kh. al-Jalama (Zertal 1977). The latter equation may be questioned on the grounds that the medieval sources, Frankish and Arabic, seem to differentiate clearly between Jalama and Kafr Sallam. The evidence from the Talmud, however, would support the location of Kafr Sallam somewhere near Kh. al-Jalama.

In summary, Kafr Sallam seems likely to have been in origin a Samaritan village on the road between *Neapolis* and *Caesarea*. Its prosperity in early Islamic times was probably due in part to the continued commercial importance of Caesarea as a port and market and to the establishment of Ramla as provincial capital in the 8th century. Its fortunes fell, however, and it became deserted in the period of insecurity resulting from the Seljuk incursions in the 11th century. After the Crusader conquest it may have been repopulated; but the fact that it is not listed among the villages that Baybars granted to his amirs in 1265 suggests that it was then finally abandoned and, in time, forgotten.

Bibliography:
Cart. des Hosp. (1), 84, no. 94 (1131); Lambert of Hersfeld, 165–171 (1065); Marianus Scottus, 558–559 (1065); al-Muqaddasi, 12, 60–61, 96–98 (c.985); Nāsir-i Khusraw, 21 (1047); *RRH*, 35, no. 139 (1131); Theodoric, XXXIX (ed. Bulst, 43) (1172); Yāqūt (in Le Strange, 1890, 472) (1225). Beyer 1936, 46, 50; Clermont-Ganneau 1896(2), 338; Le Strange 1890, 471–472; Rey 1883, 419; Röhricht 1887, 246.

20. KHIRBAT KAFR SIBB   1526.1946, alt. 90 m.
    Cr. *Cafresur*; Hebr. *Ḥ. Siv*

Cafresur is mentioned in a charter of December 1253 by which John Laleman, Lord of Caesarea, sold to the Order of St. John the village of *Damor* in the plain of Acre (Delaville le Roulx, *Archives*, 184, no. 80; *Cart. des Hosp.* (2), 749–750, no. 2661; *RRH*, 319, no. 1210). Unfortunately the document was in a bad state of repair when it was studied by Delaville le Roulx and he presents only a précis of its contents. From this it would appear that if the Hospitallers failed to pay the 12,000 bezants due for *Damor* then John Laleman was bound to pay them damages of 16,000 bezants. Clearly this condition make no logical sense, and it is likely that some intervening clauses have been lost; the clause relating to damages would more plausibly have referred to another transaction, such as perhaps a loan, whose terms have not been communicated to us. If it was indeed John Laleman, and not the Hospital, who was liable to pay damages, then *Cafresur* would have been in his possession in 1253, for it is cited as the security for the money. More than this, its boundaries are also defined. To the east lay *Socque* (Shuwaika), to the west *Caco* (Qaqun), to the south *Turrarme* (Tulkarm) and *Casal Neuf* (Burin) and to the north *Iheure* (Yamma). These topographical details allow it to be identified with Khirbat Kafr Sibb.

The *khirba* occupies a rounded hillock on the edge of the plain. Pottery evidence suggests occupation from the Roman period (Yeivin 1955, 84) through to the 14th century, while remains of walls, cisterns and other rock-cut features illustrate the former extent of settlement. Just south of the *khirba*, at Bahan, a Byzantine church was excavated in 1953–55; this seems to have continued in use for some time after the Muslim conquest (for references, see below).

Near the foot of the hill, to the west, stands the *maqam* of Jamāl al-Dīn (d. 1269: see pp. 80–81). The present building is a modern concrete replacement of an earlier structure, destroyed apparently since 1944. Photographs show that this was roughly square in plan, built in well-dressed ashlar with a wide pointed-arched opening on the east and probably, as now, on the north and west (see Pls. VI–VII). Its dome had a somewhat pointed profile with a cylindrical pinnacle, and it rested on an octagonal socle with squinches on the inside. The 13th-century tomb inscriptions recorded by the Dept. of Antiquities in 1944 are discussed below (pp. 80–81, nos. 5–6).

Visited 16.11.1983.

Bibliography:
Cart. des Hosp. (2), 749–750, no. 266 (1253); Delaville le Roulx, *Archives*, 184, no. 80 (1253); *RRH*, 319, no. 1210 (1253).

Beyer 1936, 40, 54, 57; Gophna and Porat 1972, 215, no. 66; Guérin 1874(2), 349; Israel 1964, 1411; Palestine 1933, 7; 1948, 58; Röhricht 1887, 251; Yeivin 1955, 84.

On Bahan: Avi-Yonah 1975, 306; Bagatti 1979, 185–186; Ovadiah 1970, 26–27, no. 14; Ovadiah and Gomez de Silva 1982, 125, no. 4; Yeivin 1955, 83–84.

21. Khirbat KAFR SUR   1563.1834, alt. 280 m.

The Survey of 1967–68 notes Byzantine, medieval and Ottoman-period material from the site.

Not visited.

Bibliography:
Conder and Kitchener 1881(2), 165; Gophna and Porat 1972, 224, no. 147.

22. Khirbat AL-KARNUS   1576.1907, alt. 210 m.

Pottery from the site collected by the Survey of 1967–68 includes a piece of yellow glazed *graffita* pottery, besides Byzantine glass, mosaic tesserae and coarse wares. Other

Pl. VI. Kh. Kafr Sibb (site 20): Maqam of Jamāl al-Dīn from E (photo. 1944, courtesy of the Israel Dept. of Antiquities and Museums).

Pl. VII. Kh. Kafr Sibb (site 20): Maqam of Jamāl al-Dīn, interior from N showing inscription no. 6 (photo. 1944, courtesy of the Israel Dept. of Antiquities and Museums).

sources mention ruined buildings, rock-cut wine-presses and tombs.

Not visited.

Bibliography:
Conder and Kitchener 1881(2), 195; Gophna and Porat 1972, 218, no. 93; Palestine 1929, 59; 1948, 58.

23. KEFAR VITKEN (KEREM) 1402.1977, alt.10 m.

This is the site of the discovery of a coin hoard of Mamluk date, including a die for minting Venetian gold ducats of the 15th century.

Bibliography:
Israel Museum Journal, 3 (1984), 90; Y. Porath, personal communication.

24. KILUDIYA   1468.1862, alt. 60 m.
Cr. *Calodia, Calosia:* Hebr. *Kefar Yaᶜaves*

In 1135, the village lands of *Arthabec* (al-Maghair) were defined on the east by those of *Kalensua* (Qalansuwa) and on the south by those of *Calodia* (*Cart. des Hosp.* (1), 97, no. 115; *RRH*, 39, no. 159). *Calosia* also appears in January 1153, along with *Calanthone* (Qalansuwa) and *Caco* (Qaqun), in a confirmation of properties belonging to the Hospitallers granted by Pope Eugenius III (*Cart. des Hosp.* (1), 167, no. 217; *RRH Ad*, 18, no. 280b). These references suggest that *Calodia* lay near to Qalansuwa and south or south-west of it. The site, however, has eluded detection until recent times, mainly because it did not appear on maps of the region until the 1940s. In 1940, it was scheduled as an archaeological site, under the name "Kh. Klodya" (*Palestine Gazette*, 1034 (1 Aug. 1940)); and two years later it appeared on a British Army map (1:25,000 series) as "Klûde".

Reports by J. Ory record Kiludiya as a Roman-Byzantine site of some significance, covering the top of a rounded hillock with remains of cisterns, mosaics and foundations of large well-dressed stones; also noted was a stepped basin built of concreted rubble (*PAM*, 12.3.1940; 16.7.1940; 7.4.1944). Today the site is partially covered by buildings.

Not visited.

Bibliography:
Cart. des Hosp. (1), 97, no. 115 (1135); 167, no. 217 (1153); *RRH*, 39, no. 159 (1135); *Ad*, 18, no. 280b (1153).

Beyer 1936, 45; 1951, 186; Clermont-Ganneau 1901(1), 336; Israel 1964, 1412; Palestine 1948, 62; Rey 1883, 420; Röhricht 1887, 247.

25. Khirbat MADD AD-DAIR 1412.1966, alt. 20 m.
Cr. *Casale Latinae, casale quod fuit Eustachii, Montdidier Mondisder, Mons Dederi*; Hebr. *Kibbutz Ma^cbarot, Hafita.*

The history of Kh. Madd ad-Dair in the 12th and 13th centuries is closely connected with that of al-Burj al-Ahmar (see below, Part Two). In April 1158, Pope Hadrian IV confirmed the possessions of the Benedictine monastery of St. Mary Latin in Jerusalem. They included

"in the territory of Caesarea, the Tower of Latina (Burj al-Ahmar), the village that belonged to Eustace (Kh. Madd ad-Dair) and land in Qaqun" (*RRH*, 85-86, no. 331; Sinopoli, nos. 3-4).

These same lands and villages were reconfirmed as belonging to the Abbey by Pope Alexander III in March 1173 (Holtzmann, 57, no. 2; Sinopoli, no. 5); and, despite their loss to the Mamluks in 1265, by Pope Benedict XI in March 1304 (Sinopoli, no. 10: *terrim de Latina et Montem Dederi*). It seems likely that the village had been given in alms to the Abbey by Eustace Garnier, the first lord of Caesarea (1105/10-1123), who was himself buried in the church of St. Mary Latin in Jerusalem in 1123 (*RRH*, 89, no. 342). Certainly it was in the Abbey's possession by December 1135, when it is referred to as *Casale Latinae* (the village of Latina), lying to the north of *Arthabec* (al-Maghair) (*Cart. des Hosp.* (1), 97, no. 115; *RRH*, 39, no. 159).

After the conquest of the area by Saladin in the late summer of 1187, the Abbey seems to have leased all its lands in the territory of Caesarea to the Order of St. John. In October 1189, Pope Clement III asked the Bishop of Banyas (Valania) to look into the terms of the lease of *Montdidier, Turriclee* and the other lands and assess whether it was placing too great a strain on the Hospital's resources (*Cart. des Hosp.* (1), 559, no. 879; *RRH Ad*, 46-47, no. 682a). When the area returned to Frankish hands in September 1191, however, it appears that it was the Templars rather than the Hospitallers who took possession of it, for in May 1236 they were paying rent for the two villages to the Abbey. At that time an agreement was reached between the Abbot of St. Mary Latin and the Master of the Hospital to hand them over to the Hospitallers as soon as the Templars had vacated them (*Cart. des Hosp.* (2), 501, no. 2141; *RRH Ad*, 66, no. 1072a). The Templars, however, seem to have taken their time about leaving and the hand-over of *Turris Rubea, Mondisder* and the lands in *Caco* did not take place until 7 August 1248 (*Cart. des Hosp.* (2), 673-675, no. 2482; *RRH*, 306, no. 1164). The new lease, which included in effect all the possessions of the Abbey in the territory of Caesarea, was renewed again in October 1267 (*Cart. des Hosp.* (3), 166, no. 3283; *RRH*,

354, no. 1356); but by this time the area had fallen to the Mamluks.

Unlike al-Burj al-Ahmar and Qaqun, Madd ad-Dair is not mentioned in the Arabic sources which record Baybars's division of the conquered lands among his amirs. It seems quite likely, therefore, that the settlement was dismantled along with other Frankish installations near the coast and the place abandoned.

The site occupied by Kh. Madd ad-Dair is a low rounded hill forming part of the inland *kurkar* ridge, 4 km. from the sea, just south of the point at which it is cut through by the Nahr Iskandaruna. The river, which is also known in Frankish sources as the *flum de Mondidier* (*Eracles*, XXXIII.7: p. 373), was fordable at this point by a bridge dating from Roman times (Dar and Applebaum 1973, fig. 2). Although the name *Rochetaillée* is more usually applied to the Nahr al-Faliq than to the Nahr Iskandaruna, it seems possible that the place marked *Roche taille, castrum, casale* between Caesarea and Arsuf on a map of the 13th century it to be identified with Kh. Madd ad-Dair (cf. Röhricht, *Karten*, no. 16; *Atlas of Israel*, sheet I/3, B).

Be that as it may, the archaeological evidence does suggest the existence of a small castle, in addition to the medieval village. In the 1870s, the Survey of Western Palestine noted,

"Part of a ruined vault, with a cistern to the south, cemented inside" (Conder and Kitchener 1881(2), 140).

More details are provided by an anonymous report in the Department of Antiquities in Jerusalem:

"The surface is strewn with small stones. There are remains of vaults on the hill; one is a barrel vault 6 paces by 10 paces with two manholes in the roof and an entrance on the south; the other is one metre above ground with the springing of the vault only remaining [see Pl. VIII]. Down the hill westward is a reservoir 6m.55 square with 1m.10 thickness of wall, built of square medium-sized stones in thick mortar. A fragment of a fluted shaft inserted in the west wall at the base was hollowed through to form an outlet for the water. The reservoir is coated with a reddish cement in the interior. Beside it is a built trough of [the same] character [as] the reservoir and a stone trough" (*PAM*, 21.8.1922).

In 1937, J. Ory recorded that the western (or northern?) wall of the surviving barrel-vault was about 12 m. long. Its internal measurements were 8·65 (E–W) × 5·30 m., and it was 3·00 m. high, though it seems unlikely that he was measuring to the original floor level (*PAM*, 9.5.1937). Remains of a ruined *birka* have also been recorded some 50-60 m. south-west of the cistern or reservoir already noted (D. C. Baramki, *PAM*, 13.7.1943).

None of these features has survived the expansion, since 1945, of Kibbutz Ma^cbarot, whose buildings now

Pl. VIII. Kh. Madd ad-Dair (site 25): remains of S vault of medieval tower looking E (photo. courtesy of the Israel Dept. of Antiquities and Museums).

cover the site. An RAF photograph, however, suggests that the two medieval vaults on top of the hill shared a common dividing wall. It seems likely in fact that they represented the basement for a tower somewhat similar to the Red Tower (al-Burj al-Ahmar). To judge from the figures given, this might have measured overall about 12·5 × 16 m., with walls some 1·70–2·00 m. thick (see Fig. 9). The door noted in the south wall of the intact chamber in 1922 would appear to have been the door in the spine wall between the two compartments, and not

KHIRBAT MADD AD-DAIR-
Tentative reconstruction

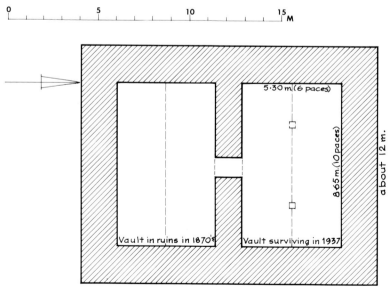

Fig. 9. Khirbat Madd ad-Dair (site 25): plan of the Crusader tower (tentative reconstruction based on Conder and Kitchener 1881; and J. Ory, PAM, 1937).

one set in the building's outer wall. Whether this tower was enclosed by an outer enceinte, as at the Red Tower, is uncertain though it seems plausible.

Visited Nov. 1983.

Bibliography:
Cart. des Hosp. (1), 97, no. 115 (1135); 559, no. 879 (1189); (2), 501, no. 2141 (1236); 673–675, no. 2482 (1248); (3) 166, no. 3283 (1267); Holtzmann, 56–59, no. 2 (1173); *RRH*, 39, no. 159 (1135); 85–86, no. 331 (1158); 306, no. 1164 (1248); 354, no. 1356 (1267); *Ad*, 46–47, no. 682a (1189); 66, no. 1072a (1236); Sinopoli, nos. 3–5 and 10 (1153, 1173, 1304).

Beyer 1936, 43–45; Conder and Kitchener 1881(2), 140; Israel 1964, 1410; Langé 1965, 94, 184; fig. 43; Palestine 1929, 127; 1948, 56; Paley and Porath 1979, 238–239; Rey 1883, 423; Röhricht 1887, 247, 253.

26. AL-MAGHAIR   1401.1916, alt. 40 m.
Kh. Bait Lid, Hannuna; Cr. *Arthabec* (?); Med. Ar. *Maghār*

In December 1135, the village of *Arthabec* was sold to the Order of St. John for 500 bezants by Isimbard, a knight of Caesarea. The village had evidently been held as a rear-fief, since 60 of these bezants went to Arnulf de Haynis, the chief fief-holder, and 150 to Walter I, Lord of Caesarea. The appurtenances included woods, pastures and waters. The village lands were bounded on the east by those of *Kalensua* (Qalansuwa), on the south by *Calodia* (Kiludiya), on the west by the Castle of Roger the Lombard ('Umm Khalid) and on the north by the village of the Latina monastery (Kh. Madd ad-Dair) (*Cart. des Hosp.* (1), 97, no. 115; *RRH*, 39, no. 159). The only known medieval site to correspond with these geographical indications is al-Maghair, a village also recorded as *Maghār* by Yāqūt in 1225 (Le Strange 1890, 498). (Note that Kh. 'Umm Sur, 1431.1900, has yielded no evidence of medieval occupation, but only coarse pottery of the 6th and 19th centuries.)

Today the site of al-Maghair is deserted, the buildings that stood there earlier this century having been demolished and their foundations ploughed out. The *khirba* occupied a slight rise, on the inland *kurkar* ridge; to the north and west the ground slopes down to the dry bed of a stream. Included amongst the modern building debris are numerous *kurkar* blocks, coarse pottery ranging from Byzantine to grey-fired 19th-century wares, one piece of medieval glazed slip-painted ware and debris suggesting glass-working. In 1936, the presence of column-drums suggested to J. Ory that this was the site of a Byzantine church (*PAM*, 24.3.1936); and in 1941, a mosaic was found during the construction of a road to a near-by army camp (*PAM*, 15.4.1941). Rock-cut *kokim* with *loculi* and *arcosolia* are also recorded (*PAM*, n.d.).

Visited 17.11.1983.

Bibliography:
Cart. des Hosp. (1), 97, no. 115; *RRH*, 39, no. 159.

Beyer 1936, 40, 44–45, 53; Conder and Kitchener 1881(2), 135; Israel 1964, 1411; Le Strange 1890, 498; Palestine 1929, 200; 1948, 57; Rey 1883, 418; Röhricht 1887, 247.

27. MAJAHID SHAIKHA   1387.1960, alt. 30 m.

Glazed medieval pottery has been found at this site by the 'Emeq Hefer Survey. The Antiquities Department lists also record scattered mosaic tesserae and a wely. It has been suggested that this building marks the burial place of 'Ayaz al-Tawil and others from Saladin's army, who lost their lives in the skirmish at the *Nahr al-Qasab* (Iskandaruna) in September 1191 (C. W. Wilson, in Bahā' al-Dīn, 285 n.).

Not visited.

Bibliography:
Bahā' al-Dīn, 285.

Israel 1964, 1410; Palestine 1929, 203; 1948, 56; Y. Porath, personal communication.

28. AL-MAJDAL   1511.1831, alt. 170 m.
Cr. *Casal Moyen*

In 1176, King Baldwin IV confirmed the Hospitallers' possession of a village called *Casal Moyen* situated near to *Kalenson* (Qalansuwa), which John of Arsuf had sold them for 3,000 bezants (*Cart. des Hosp.* (1), 342, no. 497; *RRH Ad*, 32, no 539b). Since it lay near to Qalansuwa, this village cannot be identified with *Casel Maen* (Bait Dajan) between Jaffa and Lydda (cf. *contra* Röhricht, *RRH Ad*, 32). Furthermore, it seems that it was in the seigneury of Arsuf. A site which fits these geographical indications as well as having abundant archaeological evidence for medieval occupation is al-Majdal, which overlooks the coastal plain from a position about 5 km. east of at-Tira.

The archaeological evidence suggests that a large settlement existed here in Roman and Byzantine times. The Survey of Western Palestine noted, in 1873,

> "walls, traces of a considerable town, a tank, caves, and cisterns ... and rock-cut tombs" (Conder and Kitchener 1881(2), 202).

A buried barrel-vaulted chamber (4·76 × 9·20 m.) built in ashlar may still be entered in the field north-west of the wely. Pottery finds indicate occupation of the site in the early Islamic period, continuing at least as late as the 14th century, while some fragments of grey-fired coarse ware also attest activity in the late 19th or early 20th century.

The site is now deserted. The only building standing is the wely of Shaykh "Musharaf" (i.e. "unknown") (Pl.

IX). This is some 5 m. square, with walls 1·80 m. thick, roofed with a roughly constructed pendentive dome. The walls are built of reused blocks, with a pair of reused column-drums (diam. 0·47 m.) serving as jambs for a rectangular door on the north.

Visited 17–18.11.1983.

Bibliography:
Cart. des Hosp. (1), 342, no. 497; *RRH Ad*, 32, no. 539b (1176).

Alt 1931, 33 n. 2; Beyer 1936, 45; 1940, 196; Conder and Kitchener 1881(2), 202; Israel 1964, 1412; Palestine 1929, 203; 1948, 63.

29. *Malue, Maluae*   Not located

Malu(a)e is mentioned twice in Crusader sources, but its precise location remains unknown. The first reference is in a continuation of the *Gesta Francorum* which lists the castles (*munitiones*) constructed by King Baldwin I (1100–18). The names recorded are *Mons Regalis* (Shaubak), *Turris Neapolitana* (Nablus), *Malue, Caun Mons* (Qaimun), *castrum in Achon* (Acre) and *Scandalion* (Iskandrun, between Acre and Tyre) (*RHC Occ* (3), 543). This list appears to be arranged in a rough geographical sequence from south-east to north-west, suggesting that *Malue* lay somewhere between Nablus (175.181) and Qaimun (160.230).

The second reference is contained in a charter of June 1156 by which Baldwin III confirmed the privileges that his predecessors, Baldwins I–II and Fulk of Anjou, had made to the Hospital of St. John in Nablus. These included the right to inherit the worldly goods left by pilgrims who died intestate between *castellum Beleismum* (Kh. Balʿama: 177.205), which lay between Janin and Nablus, and *Lubanum* (Lubban Sharqiya: 172.164), lying between Nablus and Jerusalem; and of those dying on the road

"from that platform (*ab perrone illo*), which represents the boundary dividing the land of Qaqun (*Cacho*) from that of *Maluae*, as far as the same *Lubanum*" (*Cart. des Hosp.* (1), 183–184, no. 244; *RRH*, 82, no. 321).

From this we may deduce that the land of *Maluae* adjoined that of Qaqun, and that the boundary between the two was marked by some kind of natural or artificial earthwork at the point where it was crossed by the road along which pilgrims normally travelled from Acre or Caesarea to Nablus, and thence on to Jerusalem. It does not necessarily follow, however, that either Qaqun or *Maluae* lay on this road.

Unfortunately we are still left in doubt as to which road was intended, the Roman road which crossed the Nahr Iskandaruna at the Jisr al-Maktaba and reached the mouth of the Wadi Nablus through Burin and

Pl. IX. al-Majdal (site 28): Maqam of an unknown shaikh, looking west with at-Tira (site 39) in distance (photo. author).

Tulkarm, or a more easterly one passing through Qaqun itself (see Fig. 3). Either seems possible, though it is uncertain how far west the land of Qaqun would have stretched. The second point of uncertainty is knowing which of the two places lay closer to Nablus. If *Maluae* lay north of Qaqun, then it would have been in the vicinity of Kafr Sallam (site 19), also unlocated. If it lay south, closer to Nablus, it may be possible to narrow down the possibilities. The lands of Qaqun were bounded on the east by those of *Cafresur* (Kh. Kafr Sibb), whose lands were in turn defined to the south by those of Tulkarm and *Casal Neuf* (Burin) (*Cart. des Hosp.* (2), 749–750, no. 2661). Thus, if a block of land belonging to *Maluae* lay south of Qaqun, it could only have been between the lands of Qaqun and Burin. *Maluae* itself would therefore have been south or south-west of Qaqun and west of *Cafresur*. A site on the Roman road such as Tall Shuqaifa is therefore not implausible; but no trace of any castle now remains.

Another consideration, however, might suggest the location of *Maluae* in or near the flood plain of the Nahr Iskandaruna north-west of Qaqun. The name of this river in Crusader sources is *Flum Salé*, the "Salt River". The Arabic word for salt is *milḥ*, and for saltings *mallāḥa*. The PEF map marks the area around the lower course of the river as *El Muâlha*, "the salt soil" (Palmer 1881, 175). This area might perhaps be the *terra Maluarum* in which Baldwin I constructed his castle.

A third possibility would be to identify *Maluae* with Kh. Kafr Sibb, Burin or Tulkarm. Excavations at the first two sites might perhaps shed some light on this question.

J. Prawer and M. Benvenisti locate the *munitio Malue* [*sic*] at Kh. an-Nairaba, 6·5 km. east of Tulkarm up the Wadi Nablus (1594.1914). This identification is untenable in the present state of evidence: first, because there are too many other villages between it and Qaqun for them to have shared a common boundary; secondly, because despite archaeological investigation of the site (Conder and Kitchener 1881(2), 198; Palestine 1929, 140; 1948, 58; Y. Porath, personal communication), it has so far revealed no evidence of medieval settlement.

Bibliography:
Cart. des Hosp. (2), 65, no. 1251 (1207/8); *Cod. Dipl.* (1), 288–289, no. 9 (1200/1); *RRH*, 205, no. 768 (1200/1); 220, no. 819 (1207/8).
Beyer 1936, 12–14; 1940, 182, 196; Johns 1937, 33 (F4); Rey 1883, 422.

30. Kh. NISF JUBAIL   1536.1872, alt. 140 m.
Cr. *Mezgebinum, Seingibis*

In February 1200/1, certain rents in *Mezgebinum* were listed as belonging to the fee of the *scribanus* Soquerius (*Cod. Dipl.* (1), 288–289, no. 9; *RRH*, 205, no. 768). The fact that the village is listed between *Pharaon* and *Cafetum* reinforces the suggestion made by Clermont-Ganneau (1888(1), 334–337) that this is the same as *Seingibis* which, in February 1207/8, was granted along with *Pharaon* (Farʿun) to the Hospitallers by Juliana, Lady of Caesarea (*Cart. des Hosp.* (2), 65, no. 1251; *RRH*, 220, no. 819). At this time the lands of the two villages, which the charter refers to as a single *casale*, marched on the east with the *Cauea Ficuum* (Wadi at-Tin) and *Caphet* (Kh. Kaffa), on the south with *Phardesi* (Fardisiya), on the west with *Calanchun* (Qalansuwa) and on the north with the Wadi at-Tin, here called *Cauea Artais*. The grant was made in free and perpetual alms and included all the villagers, cultivated and uncultivated lands, hills and plains.

The site occupies a promontory about 500 m. long and 150 m. wide, extending towards the north. Farʿun lies 1·5 km. to the north-west. Masses of tumbled blocks of stone, including counterweights for olive-presses, litter the site or are built into its field walls. Occupation is also attested by a number of bottle-shaped cisterns cut into the rock and by scatters of plain white mosaic tesserae. Despite a certain quantity of Roman and Byzantine pottery, however, the only evidence for later medieval occupation consists of a piece of rilled grey-fired amphora with white external painting and a fragment of early Islamic polychrome ware. It would appear, therefore, that by the 12th century the site was already abandoned and its lands taken over by near-by Farʿun.

A ruined watch-tower built of field stones and a lively growth of cactus suggest at least seasonal occupation in the 19th century or later, though no grey-fired pottery was found.

Visited 18.11.1983.

Bibliography:
Cart. des Hosp. (2), 65, no. 1251 (1207/8); *Cod. Dipl.* (1), 288–289, no. 9 (1200/1); *RRH*, 205, no. 768 (1200/1); 220, no. 819 (1207/8).
Beyer 1936, 36–39; 1940, 196; Clermont-Ganneau 1888(1), 334–337; Conder and Kitchener 1881(2), 210; Gophna and Porat 1972, 221, no. 116; Röhricht 1887, 246, 249.

31. QALANSUWA   1485.1878, alt. 30 m.
Cr. *Calanchun, Calanson, Calansue, Calanthone, Calanzon, Calenchum, Calenson, Calenzon, Calenzun, Calumzum, Kalenson, Kalensu, Kalensue*; Med. Ar. *Qalansuwa*.

History

Before the Crusades, Qalansuwa was a station on the principal coast road between Cairo and Damascus. It is recorded in the geographical guide of Ibn Khurradādhbih (c.820/5–c.911) as lying 20 miles from Lajjun and 24 from Ramla (cf. Hartmann 1910, 675–676; Quatremère 1837 (1, 2), 274); and this seems to have been the basis for al-Muqaddasi's statement (c.985) that it lay within a day's journey of both places (transl. Le Strange, 95; cf. 97).

On 8 April 1128, *Kalensu* was given to the Hospitallers by the knight, Geoffrey (or Godfrey) of Flujeac, in the presence of King Baldwin II and of his army on campaign against Ascalon. The donation charter itself is known only from an entry in an 18th-century inventory. This refers to Qalansuwa as a "castle" (*castel apellé Kalensu, situé dans le terroir de Césarée*); but as none of the later texts which confirm the same charter describe the place as anything more than a village, it seems likely that *castel* represents here a mistaken reading of *casale* (*Cart. des Hosp.* (1), 78, no. 83; *RRH Ad*, 9–10, no. 121a).

Goffridus de Flaui (or Flaiaco) is referred to earlier in the company of Eustace and Walter Garnier in January and June 1126 (*Cart. des Hosp.* (1), 71, no. 74; 73, no. 77; *RRH*, 27–28, nos. 112–113). He appears to have held Qalansuwa as a rear-fief of the lord of Baisan, who in turn held it from the lord of Caesarea. Thus, when in 1129 King Baldwin II confirmed the gift in the royal court in Jerusalem, John of Baisan and his brother Hugh appeared with Godfrey as the grantors (*Cart. des Hosp.* (1), 78–79, no. 84; *RRH*, 32, no. 130; cf. La Monte and Downs 1950, 59); and two years later, on 21 September 1131, Walter I Garnier, Lord of Caesarea, confirmed the gift of *Calumzum* to the Hospital in perpetuity (*Cart. des Hosp.* (1), 84, no. 94; *RRH*, 35, no. 139).

Qalansuwa seems to have remained in Hospitaller hands throughout the period of Frankish occupation of the area. It was confirmed as theirs by Pope Eugenius III in January 1153 (*Cart. des Hosp.* (1), 167, no. 217; (4), 313; *RRH Ad*, 18, no. 280b), and by King Baldwin III in July 1154 (*Cart. des Hosp.* (1), 172, no. 225; *RRH*, 75, no. 293). The Order had probably established a house there by September 1131, when Brother Gerard of *Calumzum* appears as witness to the charter of Walter Garnier. He may be the same Brother Gerald of *Kalensue*, who witnessed the sale of *Arthabec* (al-Maghair), an adjoining village, to the Hospital in December 1135 (*Cart. des Hosp.* (1), 97, no. 115; *RRH*, 39, no. 159).

In the 12th and early 13th centuries, the Hospitallers held other lands around Qalansuwa. In February 1151/2, they bought *Teira* (at-Tira), *juxta Calanson*, but then granted it to Robert of Sinjil for a reduction in the rent that they were paying him for the "land of *Emaus*" (*Cart. des Hosp.* (1), 156, no. 202; *RRH*, 69, no. 274). They possessed *Calosia* (Kiludiya) by January 1153 (*Cart. des Hosp.* (1), 167, no. 217). In 1176, they purchased *Casal Moyen* (al-Majdal), *près de Kalenson* from John of Arsuf (*Cart. des Hosp.* (1), 342, no. 497; *RRH Ad*, 32, no. 539b). And in February 1207/8, they received from

Juliana, Lady of Caesarea, the twin villages of *Pharaon* (Farʿun) and *Seingibis* (Kh. Nisf Jubail), described as lying east of *Calanchun* (*Cart. des Hosp.* (2), 65, no. 1251; *RRH*, 220, no. 819). This last charter was witnessed by a brother named Symon of *Calanchun*, who also appears as witness to two other grants of land made to the benefit of the Hospital in Acre in February 1207/8 and December 1207 (*Cart. des Hosp.* (2), 64, no. 1250; 79, no. 1276; *RRH*, 220, no. 818; 221, no. 824). Although direct evidence is lacking, it seems quite possible that by this date, and perhaps already in the 12th century, Qalansuwa had become the site of a Hospitaller commandery responsible for administering the Hospital's possessions in the southern part of the lordship of Caesarea (cf. Riley-Smith 1967, 429 n. 4).

Our understanding of the character of the settlement at Qalansuwa in Crusader times is unfortunately limited by the nature of the surviving evidence, most of which comes from the Hospitallers' Cartulary. It is certain, however, that it consisted of more than just the installations of the Order of St. John. An undated charter issued by the Master, Roger of Moulins (October 1177–1 May 1187), for instance, confirms the right granted to the "inhabitants" of *Kalenson* by his predecessor, Raymond of Le Puy (1125–58), to water their animals at the cistern of the place (*Cart. des Hosp.* (1), 350, no. 510: *RRH Ad*, 34, no. 554b). Unfortunately the full text does not survive. It may be compared, however, with another charter, perhaps of the same date, by which the same Master confirmed the *usages, facultés et coutumes* which Raymond of Le Puy had granted to the "inhabitants" of *Gibelin* (Bait Jibrin) (*Cart. des Hosp.* (1), 350, no. 509). In this case more details are known to us from an earlier confirmation made by the Master Gilbert of Assailly (*Cart. des Hosp.* (1), 272–273, no. 399). Bait Jibrin was, it seems, a *ville neuve* founded by the Hospitallers, and the inhabitants were in this case Frankish burgesses settled in the *faubourg* outside the castle (see Prawer 1980, 119–126; Riley-Smith 1967, 435–437). A similar kind of settlement may also have existed at Qalansuwa, but proof is lacking. The inhabitants of Qalansuwa, however, certainly included Franks and were not simply native Syrians. A burgess of Jerusalem named Peter Magnus (Le Grand) *de Calenzone* appears, for example, as witness to a charter of Baldwin of Mirabel in 1167 (*Cart. des Hosp.* (1), 255, no. 371; *RRH*, 113, no. 433).

In 1166, a charter of Hugh, Lord of Caesarea, refers to *Petrus de Fossato, vicecomes Calenzun*, and to *dominus Paganus de Calenzun* (*Cart. des Hosp.* (1), 243, no. 350; *RRH*, 111, no. 426). Now the terms of the donation of Qalansuwa to the Hospital by Walter I of Caesarea in 1131 suggest an outright gift in free and perpetual alms (see above). Any burgess settlement established by the Hospital there should therefore in theory have been subject to the Order's own judicial control (see Prawer 1980, 122–125). How is it possible then that thirty-five years later we find a knight and a viscount of Caesarea, and presumably therefore a burgess court, established in the same place? Unfortunately we do not possess enough information to provide any very satisfactory explanation. It is possible that as Qalansuwa developed in the 12th century and as new lands were brought under cultivation beyond the limits of those originally granted to the Hospital, these might have been claimed by the lord of Caesarea in whose territory they lay. Alternatively, lands, burgage plots or rents in Qalansuwa might have been leased back to the lord of Caesarea under the terms of charters which have not survived. However it came about, it seems likely that there had developed at Qalansuwa, by 1166, a settlement of Franks judicially independent of the Hospitallers, to whom the village had been granted in 1128 (on the relationship between burgesses and their seigneurs, see Prawer 1980, 327–339).

In 1187, Qalansuwa fell to Saladin (*Gesta Henrici II*, ed. Stubbs (2), 23). Doubtless it was returned to the Franks in 1191 after the battle of Arsuf; and in 1207/8 it was, as we have seen, once more in the hands of the Hospitallers. It was lost to the Mamluks in 1265, when its lands were divided by Baybars between two of his amirs, ʿIzz al-Dīn Aydamur al-Ḥalabī al-Ṣāliḥī and Shams al-Dīn Sunqar al-Rūmī al-Ṣāliḥī (Ibn al-Furāt (2), 80; al-Maqrīzī (1, 2), 13). In Mamluk times, at-Ṭīra seems to have taken over Qalansuwa's former role as a road station between Lajjun and Ramla. None the less, the main road would still have passed through it. In Rabīʿ I 737 H. (28 October–6 November 1336), the cup-bearer Qūsūn al-Nāṣiri ordered the construction of a cistern at Qalansuwa endowed with a piece of land (see below, Apendix 2, no. 8).

DESCRIPTION

The principal medieval buildings surviving in the centre of Qalansuwa today include a tower, a first-floor hall now used as a mosque, and various vaulted structures (see Fig. 10).

Of the tower (*A*), only the north and part of the west walls now survive, standing to a maximum height of 12·30 m. The north wall is 12·05 m. wide, narrowed by an off-set of 0·05 m. at a level of 8·25 m. above the ground (Pl. X). Its thickness is uncertain, but was probably between 2 and 3 m. The masonry consists of stone blocks laid somewhat roughly in courses between 0·54 and 0·60 m. high, with mortared rubble filling the core. Some of the quoins have drafted margins on either or both of their exposed faces, and a number of the other facing stones appear to represent attempts at patching. A house is now built against the south side of the wall, its plan apparently corresponding with that of the tower.

Its ground floor is vaulted with four high groin-vaults supported on a central square pier; but although this already existed by 1919 (K. A. C. Creswell, *PAM*, 1919), it is uncertain whether it corresponds with the medieval system of vaulting. The building of an upper storey to the house in 1935, "abutting the old masonry and entailing the removal of some of it", is recorded by R. W. Hamilton (*PAM*, 21.3.1935) (see Pl. XI).

The hall (*B*) lies some 40 m. east of the tower. It is about 16·50 m. wide and 28 (E) to 30 (W) m. long, the north wall being set at right-angles to the side walls while the south wall is slanted towards the east (see Fig. 11). The south and adjacent parts of the east and west walls are the best preserved, surviving up to 8·5 m. (Pls. XII–XV; Fig. 12). Up to around 4 m. from each of the two southern corners, the walls are faced with large ashlars, 0·57 m. high and finely dressed with rusticated faces and drafted borders. The remainder of the wall faces, however, are built with smaller smoothed ashlars whose alternating course heights of 0·31 and 0·26 m. allow them to follow through with the facing of the corners every two courses. It seems therefore that the wall belongs to a single phase of construction despite the different appearance of its two types of facing. Among the larger stones limestone and sandstone are used, while the smaller work is more usually sandstone. Some late Ottoman patching is also visible high up in the wall (cf. Pl. XV).

The principal entrance to the building was apparently the large first-floor doorway which survives (though blocked) in the south wall (Pl. XIII). This is 1·60 m. wide and 2·85 m. high, and is covered by a flat lintel. It is set back from the wall face within a pointed-arched recess, 2·33 m. wide and 0·40 m. deep. Although the arch springs from the same level as the top of the door, it is given a somewhat stilted appearance by the fact that its imposts are corbelled slightly inwards, with hollowed chamfers on their lower edges. The voussoirs and most (but not all) of the blocks forming the door jambs are smoothly dressed, in contrast to the rustication of the surrounding wall face. The lunette above the lintel is filled with three courses of ashlar with joggled interstices, producing a chevron-patterned effect; the intention of this arrangement was probably in part decorative, but it would also have had the effect of spreading the pressure bearing on the stone lintel below.

This doorway was probably once reached by means of a wooden ramp or staircase, the partially blocked beam-slots for which may still be seen just below it. Directly under them is another doorway, which leads into the undercroft. This door is 1·40 m. wide with jambs 0·33 m. thick, and it is covered by a pointed arch; the voussoirs are smoothly dressed, while some of the blocks forming the jambs have shallowly drafted edges. The former existence of a pair of wing doors, opening inwards, is

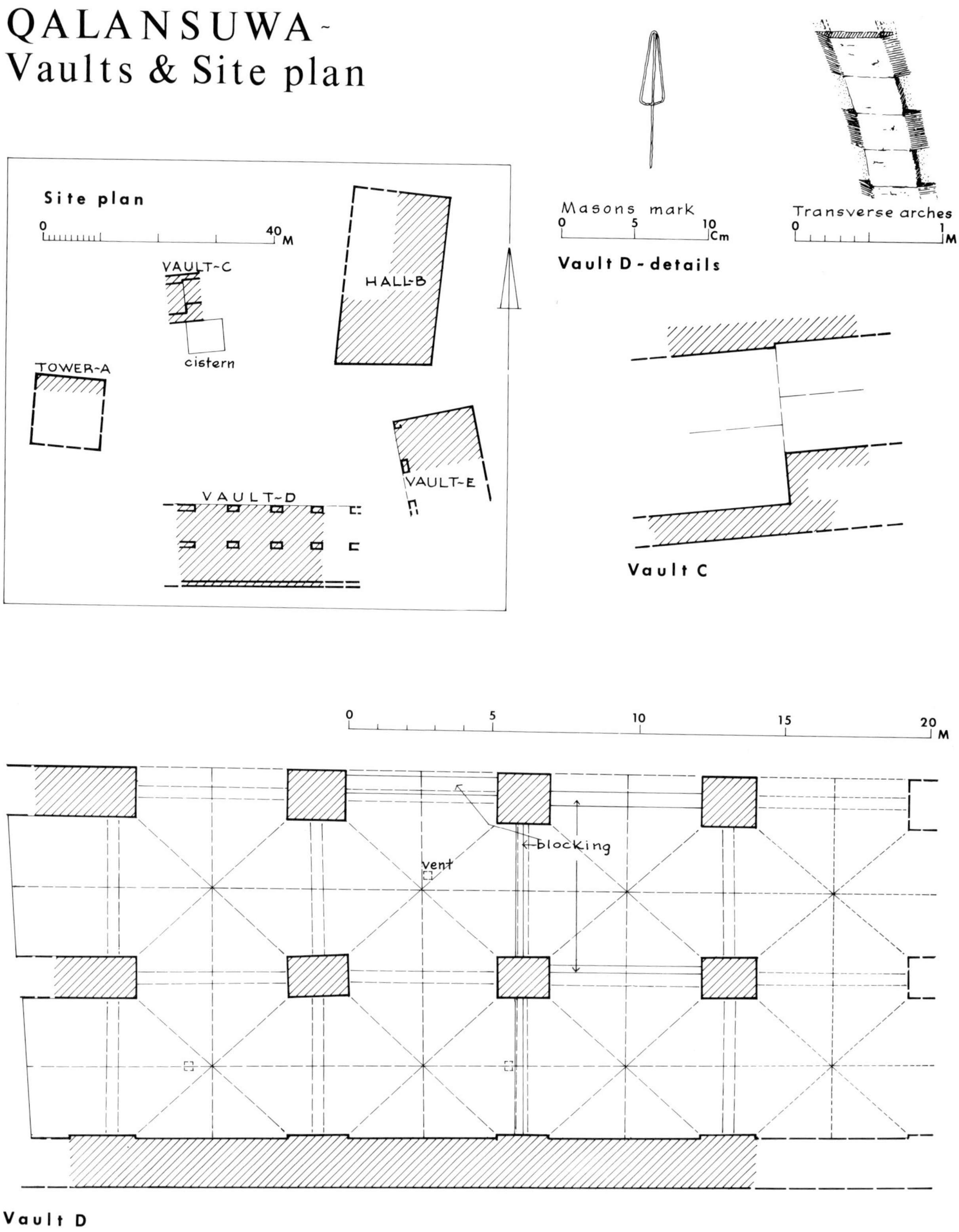

QALANSUWA -
Vaults & Site plan

Fig. 10. Qalansuwa (site 31): plans of medieval buildings in the village centre (BSAJ Survey 1983).

Pl. X. Qalansuwa (site 31): Tower A, N wall from NE (photo. author).

Pl. XI. Qalansuwa (site 31): Tower A, showing construction of modern house on the medieval foundations (photo. 1935, courtesy of the Israel Dept. of Antiquities and Museums).

indicated by the survival of two stone pivot-blocks and by the holes for a draw-bar. The doorway opened into a segmentally-arched passage, 1·58 m. wide and 2·08 m. long, the inner end of which is covered by another pointed arch but without rebated jambs.

The undercroft measures 12·75 × 24·6/25·3 m. internally and the north, east and west walls are some 1·90 m. thick. It is vaulted with eight bays of rising groin-vaults, arranged in two rows of four bays each, separated from one another by shallow transverse arches (0·09 × 0·37 m.). A hexagonal vent (diam. 0·48 m.) survives in the vaulting of the north-east bay. The vaulting springs from three piers some 1·65 m. square, arranged down the centre of the room and from rectangular pilasters, 1·65 m. wide, projecting 0·90 m. from the walls. Piers, wall faces and vaults are built of smooth ashlars. The area is now divided up by partition walls and not all the bays are accessible. In addition to the door already described on the south, another also existed on the east in the third bay from the north. It was

not possible to enter this bay, and only the top of the pointed arch of the door appears above ground level on the outside (Pl. XVI). It seems, however, to have been some 1·90 m. wide. Lancet windows also survive in the west wall of the south-western bay and in the east wall of the north-eastern one. They are 0·90 m. wide and 2·10 m. high on the inside, narrowing probably to around 0·10 m. in width on the outside, though in each case the window is now blocked and the external face is below ground level. It seems possible that there would have been some kind of opening in the external walls of each bay. A rock-cut cistern of uncertain dimensions exists below the north-eastern bay.

Nothing survives of the first-floor room of the building apart from its south wall and the adjacent parts of the east and west walls. The principal doorway in the south wall opened into a passageway about 2 m. long and 1·80 m. wide, covered by a high pointed barrel-vault. From the left-hand side of this a stair led off to the roof (see below). The doorway itself is now blocked on

QALANSUWA -
Hall plans

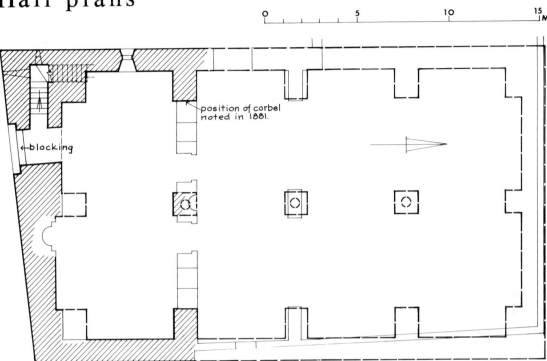

First Floor

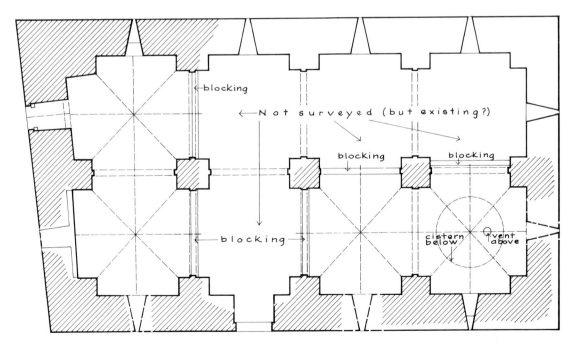

Ground Floor

Fig. 11. Qalansuwa (site 31): plan of medieval hall (BSAJ Survey 1983).

Pl. XII. Qalansuwa (site 31): Medieval hall from SW photo. author).

the outside and the passage forms a small room, used by
the muezzin for broadcasting the call to prayer and
providing access, via the medieval stair, to the minnaret.

The mosque dates from around 1911 (K. A. C.
Creswell, *PAM*, 1919). It consists of a prayer hall of two
groin-vaulted bays taking up the southern end of the
first floor and enclosed on three sides by the standing
medieval walls (Pl. XV). The vaults, however, appear
to be modern. On the north it is preceded by a *liwan*,
which has recently been extended to the far end of the
platform created by the medieval basement to make an
enlarged outer prayer hall. Since the interior of the
mosque proper is covered with plaster and paint, it is
hard to tell how much of the fabric is medieval and how
much late Ottoman.

Victor Guérin, who saw the building in the 1870s
before it was converted into a mosque, mistakenly
identified it as the remains of an aisled church, facing
east. The three eastern apses which he claims to have
seen can have existed only in his own imagination. Some
of the other details that he records, however, may be
based on more reliable observations:

"The aisles were separated one from another by
monolithic columns of which only the positions are
recognizable, and which were probably surmounted by
corinthian capitals; for, in a particular house, I found a
beautiful one of white marble, which had been hollowed
out in the form of a mortar by the inhabitants of the
village; these people told me that they had found it on the
site of the church. The other capitals and the column-

Pl. XIII. Qalansuwa (site 31): Medieval hall, south doorways (photo. 1919, Creswell Archive, courtesy of the Ashmolean Museum, Oxford).

shafts that supported them have disappeared; they presumably came from an earlier building" (1874(2), 351).

Like Guérin, the officers of the Survey of Western Palestine recognized only three of the four pairs of bays of the building; they did not, however, identify them as belonging to a church. To them it appeared that the vaulting of the first floor sprang from piers, measuring 4 × 5 ft. (1·22 × 1·52 m.), built directly over those of the undercroft. Their plan also shows two corner pilasters and at least three others 4 ft. (1·22 m.) wide projecting 5 ft. 10 in. (1·78 m.) from the side walls. Two of these pilasters probably survive incorporated into the northern wall of the early 20th-century mosque (see Fig. 11;

Pl. XIV. Qalansuwa (site 31): Medieval hall, S wall from SE (photo. author).

and Pl. XV). On the east face of the western one, the SWP records a large corbel and impost moulding, from which there seems to have sprung a transverse arch composed of voussoirs some 0·40 m. square in section (Fig. 13). The responding half of this arch would doubtless have been supported by the pier in the centre of the room. On this evidence the vaulting would therefore have consisted of eight bays of groin-vaults separated by thick transverse arches.

There remains an inconsistency, however, in the descriptions of the piers in the centre of the room. Guérin states that they were monolithic columns, though he admits that he saw none in position. The officers of the SWP record only rectangular piers; but

Pl. XVI. Qalansuwa (site 31): Medieval hall, ground-floor door in E wall (photo. author).

their plan does not indicate any of these as extant. In place of the northern pier, however, they record a column, 1 ft. 8 in. (0·51 m.) in diameter, to which, they assert, belonged a corinthianesque marble capital which they saw lying in the street outside. Because they thought that this column stood on the line of the building's north wall, they interpreted it as the *trumeau* of a large double window (Conder and Kitchener 1881 (2), 199–200). It is therefore uncertain whether the vaulting in the centre of the room was supported by rectangular piers or columns, or whether perhaps the columns (which would in any case have been reused antique spolia) served simply as reinforcements inside masonry piers.

The only surviving window is in the west wall of the south-west bay (Pl. XVII). This is set high in the wall in the centre of the bay and was evidently intended only for admitting light. It has a double splay, narrowing to 0·48 m. from 1·05 m. on the inside and widening to 0·69 m. on the outside, with a rebate for a shutter or glass 0·35 m. from the outside wall face. The opening is 1·71 m. high, corresponding to three courses of the larger size of masonry facing, with a blind arch cut from the lintel and a sloping sill beneath.

Pl. XV. Qalansuwa (site 31): Medieval hall from W, showing the mosque newly constructed. Note the fine ashlar pilaster on the inside of the W wall (photo. 1919, Creswell Archive, courtesy of the Ashmolean Museum, Oxford).

QALANSUWA -
Hall elevations

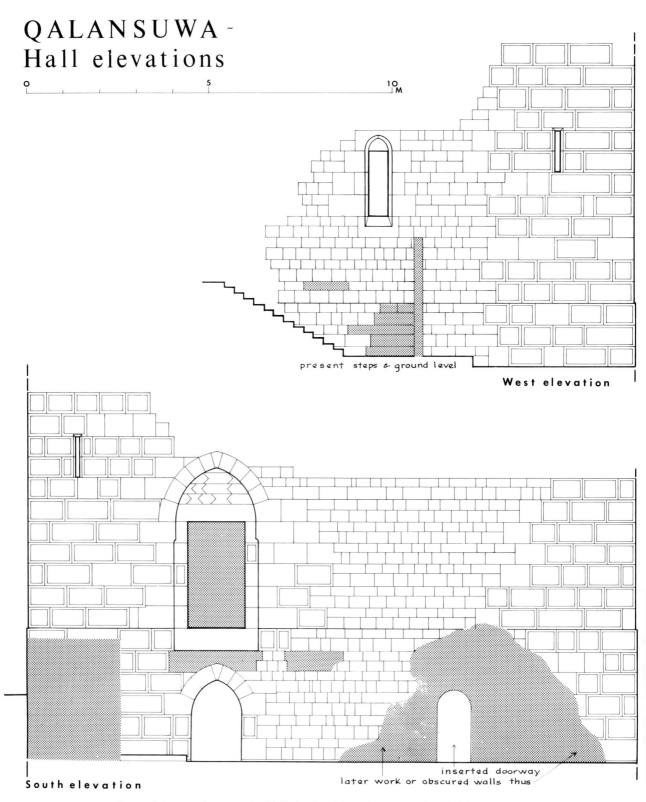

present steps & ground level

West elevation

South elevation

inserted doorway
later work or obscured walls thus

Fig. 12. *Qalansuwa (site 31): medieval hall, elevation of the south and west walls (BSAJ Survey 1983).*

QALANSUWA ~
Hall ~ sections & details

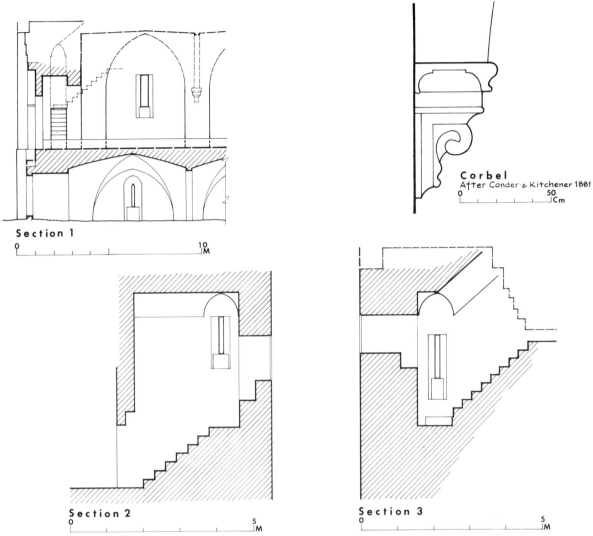

Section 1

0 ⊢⊣⊣⊣⊣⊣⊣⊣⊣⊣⊣ 10
M

Corbel
After Conder & Kitchener 1881
0   50
⊢⊣⊣⊣⊣⊣⊣⊣⊣⊣⊣ Cm

Section 2

0 ⊢⊣⊣⊣⊣⊣ 5
M

Section 3

0 ⊢⊣⊣⊣⊣⊣ 5
M

Fig. 13. Qalansuwa (site 31): medieval hall, sections and details (BSAJ Survey 1983).

The south-western angle of the building contains the staircase to the roof, built within the thickness of the walls. As remarked above, this leads off from the west side of the main entrance passage. It is built in well-cut ashlar masonry, laid in 0·57 m. courses. The lower stair passage is 0·90 m. wide and is covered by a horizontal pointed barrel-vault. The upper part is only 0·83 m. wide, and covered instead by a rising barrel-vault, which intersects the first to form a small groin-vault over the landing, where the stair turns to the right (Pl. XVIII). This landing is lit by identical slit-windows in

the south and west walls, the latter being set one course (0·57 m.) higher than the other. They are each three courses (1·71 m.) high on the inside and only two (1·14 m.) on the outside, the sides narrowing from 0·47 m. wide inside to 0·17 m. outside, with a chamfered outer edge (Pl. XIX).

Four different types of masonry mark were recorded on the inside facing of the stair; and one mark of a different type was found on the corresponding outer face of the same wall (see Fig. 14).

Various other medieval vaulted structures survive at

Pl. XVII. Qalansuwa (site 31): Medieval hall, first-floor window in W wall (photo. author).

measure about 5·30 (E–W) × 4·40 (N–S). The vaults are rubble-built except for a transverse arch of ashlar between each of the piers and pilasters (Pl. XXI).

The northern end of another similar range of vaulting (*E*) survives just south of the hall and runs south from it.

Some large rock-cut cisterns are known by the villagers to exist just south of the hall and between it and the tower. They are now blocked, but were apparently in use when Guérin visited the village (1874(2), 351).

The arrangement of these medieval buildings does not appear to form any very coherent plan, though it seems likely that the area enclosed by them was originally an open space or courtyard. The character of their masonry and construction is entirely consistent with a date in the 12th century. It seems very probable therefore that they represent part of a complex of buildings erected by the Hospitallers. Unfortunately, since no two of the buildings directly adjoin one another it is impossible to establish any structural relationship between them; and their architecture cannot be dated to

Pl. XVIII. Qalansuwa (site 31): Medieval hall, staircase (photo. author).

Qalansuwa in different stages of delapidation. Some 25 m. west of the hall, lie the remains of two barrel-vaults (*C*), 3·65 m. and 5·20 m. wide respectively, set end on to one another and aligned roughly east–west (see Fig. 10). The second vault now runs at most only 4·80 m. west of its junction with the first. The upper part of the outer facing of the common south wall of these vaults is coated with a pinkish-orange mortar bearing a herringbone pattern of trowel marks; this appears to represent the north side of a cistern or tank, the rest of which is now destroyed.

About 30 m. south of this there survives a range of three double bays of groin-vaults (*D*) supported by rectangular piers (1·40/1·70 m. × 1·80/2·00 m.) and a solid wall on the south. It extends for some 25 m. from east to west, but evidently once continued further in both directions. The northern side presents a row of pointed-arched openings, well built with smooth well-dressed ashlar masonry (see Pl. XX). One masonry mark was recorded (Fig. 10). The bays themselves

QALANSUWA ~
Hall

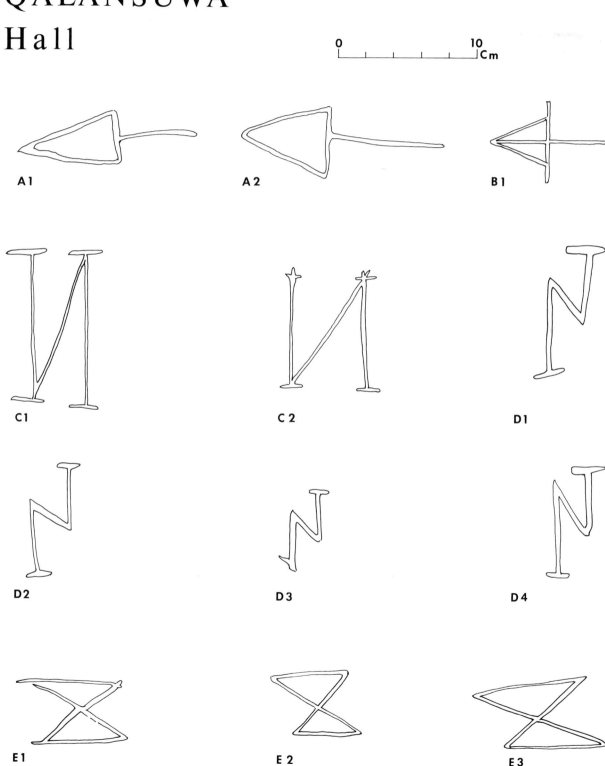

Fig. 14. Qalansuwa (site 31): medieval hall, masonry marks (note that all are from the staircase except B1, which comes from the outer face of the west wall).

Pl. XIX. Qalansuwa (site 31): Medieval hall, stair window in W wall (photo. author).

within precise enough limits to form any chronological sequence of building. If the same practice was followed here as in many other villages taken over by the Franks in the 12th century, however, it is possible that the tower represented the earliest construction, built perhaps soon after the Hospitallers took control or even before by Geoffrey of Flujeac. The hall may have been built later in the 12th century. It would perhaps have been used both as a residence for the brethren living in Qalansuwa, and as their *curia* or administrative building. The ranges of groin-vaulted buildings were presumably used for the storage of agricultural produce. Apart from the tower, none of the buildings in Qalansuwa appears to have had any specifically defensive purpose; even the hall, though solidly built, had lancet windows and at least two doors at ground level. Possibly the buildings recorded here were enclosed by outer defences that have not survived. By the middle of the 12th century, however, the area was fairly well insulated from serious Muslim raiding, and it is equally possible therefore that Qalansuwa

developed at that time as an open-planned settlement. Nothing is known of the overall plan of the medieval village, however, nor of the whereabouts of the *curia* of the lord of Caesarea's viscount. Air photographs provide little useful information; indeed, on the contrary, they show how entirely different the early 20th-century plan is to what we now know of the lay-out of the 12th-century buildings. Evidently to find out more about medieval Qalansuwa there is a need for more archaeological and topographical work, including excavation and a watching brief to be kept on all public works and rebuilding carried out there.

In 1919, K. A. C. Creswell recorded and photographed the remains of a medieval *maqam* surviving in a ruined state west of the village, near to the well (Pl. XXII). Neither the building nor apparently the memory of it have survived.

> "A little to the west of the village, and quite near to the well, are remains of a little mausoleum of superior quality. On the east side are the remains of a tunnel-vaulted chamber running north and south, with two doorways in its west side. The northern one leads into the corner—all that now exists—of a little mausoleum. A squinch is set across this angle on a splay-face cornice. This squinch must have converted the square lower part of the mausoleum into an octagon measuring about 7 feet (2·13 m.) a side. The arch of the semi-dome forming the squinch has a thin key-stone and well-cut voussoirs with irregular extrados. In the left-hand corner of the spandrel is a little cockle-shell niche. The masonry has a rubble core and the cement is of good quality.
>
> "The north-east corner of this interesting fragment, which may be as early as the XIIth century, is in danger of collapsing, but the D.M.G. has promised to have it consolidated.
>
> "Alongside the above is a little cenotaph, composed of odd pieces of stone. One of these is an Arabic inscription of seven lines, dated 737 H. (1336)" (*PAM*, 1919).

The text of this inscription, recording the construction of a cistern by Qūsūn al-Nāṣiri, is given below (Appendix 2, no. 8; Pl. XXXVIII). The mausoleum itself seems likely to be Mamluk of the late 13th century. It may be compared with the mausoleum of the amir Aydughdī Kubakī (*c.* 1289) in Jerusalem (Walls 1974, 49–50; fig. 14; pl. XVII) and that of Abū Hurayra (1274) at Yibna (Mayer (LA) and Pinkerfeld 1950, 21–24; figs. 1–11). Like them it probably incorporated reused Crusader fragments, thereby giving the impression of being earlier than it actually was.

Visited 23.2.82, 18.11.82, 20.5.83, 14–17.11.83, 22.11.83, 3.7.84.

Bibliography:

Cart. des Hosp. (1), 78, no. 83 (1128); 78–79, no. 84 (1129); 84, no. 94 (1131); 97, no. 115 (1135); 156, no. 202 (1151/2); 167, no. 217 (1153); 173, no. 225 (1154); 243, no. 350 (1166); 255,

Pl. XX. Qalansuwa (site 31): Vaulted range D, central opening on N (photo. author).

Pl. XXI. Qalansuwa (site 31): Valted range D, interior looking W (photo. author).

Pl. XXII. Qalansuwa (site 31): Maqam W of the village, remains viewed from NW (photo. 1919, Creswell Archive, courtesy of the Ashmolean Museum, Oxford).

no. 371 (1167); 342, no. 497 (1176); 350, no. 510 (1177/87); (2), 64–65, nos. 1250–51 (1207/8); 79, no. 1276 (1207); (4), 313 (1153); *Gesta Henrici II*, ed. Stubbs (2), 23; Ibn al-Furāt (2), 80; al-Maqrizī (1, 2), 13; al-Muqaddasī, transl. Le Strange, 95, 97 (c. 985); *RRH*, 32, no. 130 (1129); 35, no. 139 (1131); 39, no. 159 (1135); 69, no. 274 (1151/2); 75, no. 293 (1154); 111, no. 426 (1166); 113, no. 433 (1167); 220, nos. 818–819 (1207/8); 221, no. 824 (1207); *Ad*, 9–10, no. 121a (1128); 18, no. 280b (1153); 32, no. 539b (1176); 34, no. 554b (1177/87).

Abel 1940, 41, no. 6; Bagatti 1979, 133; Benvenisti 1970, 15, 19, 173–174, 198, 267, 311, 345; Beyer 1936, 41–42, 45, 50–51; 1940, 185; 1951, 186; Conder 1874, 15; 1875, 92–93; in Palestine Exploration Fund 1881, 277–278; Conder and Kitchener 1881(2), 165, 199–201; figs.; Deschamps 1939, 23; Enlart 1925(2), 266; Guérin 1874(2), 350–352; Hartmann 1910, 675–676; Israel 1964, 1412; Johns 1937, 25 (F4); Karmon 1961, 58; Langé 1965, 94, 180; fig. 43; Le Strange 1890, 476; Meistermann 1936, 469; Ory 1975, 199; Palestine 1929, 214; 1948, 62; Prutz 1881, 174–175; Quatremère 1837(1, 2), 258, 274; Rey 1883, 420; Riley-Smith 1967, 69n., 135, 429, 437n.; 1971, 210, no. 25.

32. QAQUN   1497.1962, alt. 50 m.
    Cr. *Caccho, Cacho, Caco, Cacto, Chaccahu, Chaco, Caqo, Caque, Chao, Chaquo, Cocto, Quaquo*; Med. Ar. *Qāqūn*; Hebr. *Yikon*.

HISTORY

Archaeological evidence suggests that an Arab village already existed at Qaqun before the Crusades. During the 12th century, its population included Frankish settlers dependent on the castle (see below), native Syrian Christians (*Cart. des Hosp.* (1), 171, no. 223; *RRH Ad*, 19, no. 298a) and possibly some Muslims; but according to Benjamin of Tudela there were no Jews there in 1163 (transl. Adler, 20).

The character of the Frankish settlement in Qaqun in the 12th century appears to have been essentially seigneurial. By 1110, the village was held by Eustace Garnier as part of his lordship of Caesarea (*Cart. des Hosp.* (1), 21–22, no. 20; *RRH*, 12, no. 57). The lord of Caesarea was represented in Qaqun by a viscount, who would also probably have acted as castellan and have presided over the burgess court. His counterpart for dealing with judicial affairs concerning the native Syrians was an Arabic-speaking interpreter known as a dragoman (cf. Riley-Smith 1972, 15–19). Both officials are recorded as holding land in the village in the 12th century. The Viscount Walter, for instance, alienated a *curtile* (enclosed piece of land) in September 1131 (*Cart. des Hosp.* (1), 83–84, no. 94; *RRH*, 35, no. 139), and witnessed another charter in the Archbishop's court in Caesarea in December 1135 (*Cart. des Hosp.* (1), 97, no.

115; *RRH*, 39, no. 159). A later viscount, James (or Jacob), witnessed a charter in 1175 (*Cart. des Hosp.* (1), 322–323, no. 470). A dragoman of Qaqun named Peter appears with Viscount Walter as witness to the same charter of December 1135; and in 1146 he sold some land to Walter I, Lord of Caesarea, for 200 bezants (*Cart. des Hosp.* (1), 133, no. 168; *RRH*, 61, no. 243). To judge by his name, Peter could have been either Frankish or Syrian Christian in origin.

As early as 1110, Eustace Garnier had granted to certain of his knights the possession of *uillani* in Qaqun (*Cart. des Hosp.* (1), 21–22, no. 20; *RRH*, 12, no. 57). By *uillani* we should probably understand Arab villagers, who together with their families and heirs became in effect serfs, their lands and other material possessions also being made the property of the knights (cf. Prawer 1980, 203). Other Franks who held lands or rents in Qaqun are known to us by name. H. Lumbardus, for instance, held and then alienated two carrucates in Qaqun during the lifetime of Eustace Garnier (d. 1123); and in 1131, Walter I Garnier exchanged another piece of land with a man named Alo(n) (*Cart. des Hosp.* (1), 83–84, no. 94; *RRH*, 35, no. 139).

The composition of a knight's fee in Qaqun granted to a certain James by Hugh, Lord of Caesarea, is described in a charter of 1161. The principal part of this fee consisted of the rent from a cistern amounting to 25 bezants a year; in addition Hugh undertook to provide for the maintenance of two mounts for James and his squire, and for the restoration of losses resulting from military service inside or outside the kingdom (*domi forisque*); if James took a wife, he was to be paid a further 25 bezants and five for maintenance as well as 20 *modii* of wheat (*RRH*, 98, no. 373).

Beside these Frankish settlers of Qaqun, we know of a Bernard of Qaqun who appears as a lay witness at the court of the Bishop of Ramla-Lydda in 1138/9 (*RRH*, 46, no. 190; Delaborde, 49–50, no. 20); and Hugh of Qaqun, who witnessed a charter of Walter I of Caesarea 1146 (*Cart. des Hosp.* (1), 133, no. 168; *RRH*, 61, no. 243).

The Hospitallers had been given lands *juxta Caccho* by Eustace Garnier and certain *uillani* by some of his knights before September 1110 (*Cart. des Hosp.* (1), 21–22, no. 22: *RRH*, 12, no. 57). In September 1131 their holdings there included some houses with their appurtenances and curtileges, and four carrucates of arable land, all of which had been given them by Eustace Garnier; two carrucates given them by H. Lumbardus, with Eustace's consent; a curtilege which the Viscount, Walter, had given them with the consent of Walter I Garnier; and another which Walter I Garnier had previously exchanged with Alo(n). It seems likely that the Hospitallers were maintaining a house in Qaqun by this date, since one of their brothers who witnessed this

charter in Caesarea is named Aldebrandus Chaco (*Cart. des Hosp.* (1), 83–84, no. 94; *RRH*, 35, no. 139). In 1146, Walter I of Caesarea ran into financial difficulties in Acre and in order to extricate himself bought back a piece of land from Peter, the Dragoman of Qaqun, for 200 bezants and sold it for 800 bezants to the Hospital together with a house and a threshing floor lying next to the communal cistern (*Cart. des Hosp.* (1), 133, no. 168; *RRH*, 61, no. 243; cf. La Monte 1947, 148). The Hospitallers' possessions in Qaqun were confirmed by Pope Eugenius III in January 1153 (*Cart. des Hosp.* (1), 167, no. 217; *RRH Ad*, 18, no. 280b), and by King Baldwin III in July 1154 (*Cart. des Hosp.* (1), 173, no. 225; *RRH*, 74, no. 293). In the same year, Hugh, Lord of Caesarea, also granted them a piece of land which the Syrian Christians were using as a threshing floor, next to a garden already owned by the Hospital (*Cart. des Hosp.* (1), 171, no. 223; *RRH Ad*, 19, no. 298a).

In 1175, Baldwin, Lord of Ramla, gave to the Hospital a certain Syrian Christian named John, together with his family and heirs. This John had formerly been a cistern-keeper at *Cafferrus*(?) (probably *Caphaer* = Kafr ad-Dik, which Baldwin sold to the Hospital in the same year: *Cart. des Hosp.* (1), 336, nos. 487–489; *RRH Ad*, 31–32, no. 530a–c), but had been incapacitated by a spot on the eye. By giving him away, Baldwin was therefore probably showing more charity towards the man and his family than piety towards the Hospital. The only witness to the act, apart from the man's two brothers, was James, the Viscount of Qaqun. It seems likely, therefore, that whatever livelihood the Hospitallers were able to find the man would have been in Qaqun (*Cart. des Hosp.* (1), 332–323, no. 470).

The Benedictine Abbey of St. Mary Latin in Jerusalem possessed lands in Qaqun by April 1158, when its right to them was confirmed by Pope Hadrian IV (Holtzmann, 55; Sinopoli, 140, nos. 3–4; *RRH*, 85, no. 331). It was reconfirmed by Pope Alexander III in March 1173 (Holtzmann, 57, no. 2; Sinopoli, 140, no. 5). In or by October 1189, however, the Abbey had leased its lands in Qaqun and the two villages that it held in the territory of Caesarea, *Montdidier* (Madd ad-Dair) and the Red Tower (Burj al-Ahmar), to the Hospital (*Cart. des Hosp.* (1), 559, no. 879; *RRH Ad*, 46–47, no. 682a). These two villages were apparently occupied by the Templars after the Frankish reconquest in 1191, but in the agreement of May 1236 by which the Abbot of St. Mary Latin undertook to restore them to the Hospitallers no mention is made of the lands of Qaqun (*Cart. des Hosp.* (2), 501, no. 2141; *RRH Ad*, 66, no. 1072a). It seems possible, therefore, that the Hospital had managed to hold on to these lands. In August 1248, both villages and the lands and possessions of the Abbey in the territory of Qaqun were formally leased to the Hospital for 800 bezants a year (*Cart. des Hosp.* (2), 673–675, no.

2482; *RRH*, 306, no. 1164: see p. 86). This, however, is the only direct evidence that we have for the Hospital holding lands in Qaqun in 13th century.

The question of the Templars' interests in Qaqun is difficult to assess. It has already been remarked that there is no certain evidence that they leased land there from St. Mary Latin in 1236. On 30 April 1187, however, there is mention of a Templar "convent" in the village of *Caco*, from which the Master of the Temple, Gerard of Ridefort, summoned a force of perhaps 20–30 knights to rendezvous with him at the castle of *La Fève* (al-Fula) in the Jezreel plain in order to intercept a Muslim force that was about to enter Galilee (see Kedar and Pringle 1985, 168). The French sources relating this event, which ended in the destruction next day of the entire Templar force near Nazareth, present a number of problems. All of them say that when the Master heard of the Muslims' approach, he sent word to the Templar "convent" (or commandery) at *Caco* and that the force of knights from there arrived back at *La Fève* the same day before nightfall. Two versions say that the village of *Caco* lay four miles (say 6·5 km.) from *La Fève* (*Eracles, RHC Occ* (2), 39; *Continuation de Guillaume de Tyr*, ch. 25 (ed. Morgan, 38)); one, the Chronicle of Ernoul, gives the distance as four leagues, which could be interpreted as a four-hour journey, but even this reads "miles" in one version (ch. XII: ed. de Mas Latrie, 145–146). Now Qaqun lies some 45 km. from al-Fula and although this distance might perphaps be covered in a four-hour ride it could not be mistaken for four miles. Secondly, the village and castle of Qaqun belonged to the Lord of Caesarea in 1175 and did so still in 1253 (*Cart. des Hosp.* (2), 749–750, no. 266; *RRH*, 319, no. 1210). It is therefore difficult to see why a force of 20–30 Templar knights should have been stationed there in 1187, unless perhaps they had been granted the castellanry after 1175, the date of the last mention of a viscount; none of the sources refers to a castle, however, only to a convent. These considerations lend weight to the possibility that the village which all three sources call *Caco* might not have been Qaqun at all, but another place with a similar name. One that might fit this description is Kh. Qara, four miles (6·5–7 km.) east of al-Fula; this is referred to as *Cara* among the villages (including al-Fula) belonging to the Abbey of Mount Tabor in 1103 (*Cart. des Hosp.* (2), 827, no. 2832; *RRH*, 6, no. 39) and 1146 (*Cart. des Hosp.* (2), 824, no. 2829) and *Kara* in 1107 (*Id.*, 826, no. 2831). The identification of a Templar commandery or indeed any Templar possessions at Qaqun in the 12th or 13th centuries is therefore open to serious doubt, though in mitigation it may also be recalled that our knowledge of their 12th-century possessions is in any case very slight, owing to the loss of their archives in Jerusalem in 1187.

The castle of Qaqun is first mentioned in May 1123, when the Constable and Regent of the Kingdom,

Eustace Garnier, and the Patriarch of Jerusalem, Warmund, mustered troops there (*ante castellum quoddam quod Cacho incolae regionis nominant*) from Tiberias, Acre, Caesarea and Jerusalem to oppose the Egyptians who were attacking Jaffa by land and sea. This campaign ended with the victory of the Franks at *Ibelin* (Yibna) and was soon followed by the death of the Constable (Fulcher of Chartres, III, 18, 1 (ed. Hagenmeyer, 664–665; transl. Ryan, 241–242); William of Tyre, XII, 21 (*RHC Occ*, 1, 543–544); Prawer 1975(1), 305; Runciman 1954(2), 165–166). In view of its strategic significance, as illustrated in this and later campaigns, and of the importance attached to it in administering part of the lordship of Caesarea, it seems likely that the castle was an early foundation, built perhaps before or soon after the fall of Caesarea to the Franks in May 1101. It may be recalled that King Baldwin I is credited with building a castle at *Malue*, somewhere near Qaqun, before 1118 (see no. 29 above). The strategic significance of Qaqun was enhanced not only by its castle but also no doubt by its water supply, which as we have seen was partly a seigneurial monopoly (*RRH*, 98, no. 373) and partly communally owned (*Cart. des Hosp.* (1), 133, no. 168; *RRH*, 61, no. 243), and by its agricultural land. In 1172, the pilgrim Theodoric refers to it as *castellum a modernis Cacho nominatum, in fertilissima terra situm* (XXXIX: ed. Bulst, 43; ed. Tobler, 89). The castle is also shown on a map of the first half of the 13th century (Röhricht, *Karten*, no. 16).

Qaqun would have fallen to Sultan Baybars in 1265 when he took Caesarea and Arsuf. The following year he restored the castle and reconstructed the church as a mosque (Ibn al-Furāt (2), 101; al-Maqrīzī (1, 2), 40). If the same pattern was followed here as at Ramla (1268) and elsewhere, this would most probably have been the Latin parish church rather than one belonging to the Syrian Christians (cf. Riley-Smith 1971, 216, 218). Baybars evidently intended making Qaqun not only his principal military base in the Sharon plain, but also the centre of a new administrative district replacing those of Caesarea and Arsuf, which had now ceased to exist (Riley-Smith 1971, 208–209). During the Mamluk period, the district of Qaqun stretched from the Nahr al-ʿAuja (Nahal Yarkon) in the south to the Nahr az-Zarqa beyond Caesarea in the north. Beyond this lay an area dependent on Pilgrims' Castle (ʿAtlit), which remained in Christian hands until 1291.

In late November 1271, an attempt was made by King Hugh of Cyprus and Jerusalem and Prince Edward of England, with a company of Templars, Hospitallers, Teutonic Knights and knights and sergeants of the kingdom, to recapture the castle of Qaqun. According to the Frankish accounts, as it approached Qaqun the army raided some encampments of Turcomans, killing a large number of Muslims and capturing an even greater quantity of livestock. The *Estoire de*

Pl. XXIII. Qaqun (site 32): Site of the castle from SE. Note medieval tower-keep and, to the right, a rounded tower of late Ottoman date (photo. author).

Pl. XIIIA. Qaqun (site 32): Village mosque (right) and medieval tower-keep (left), from N (photo. author).

Pl. XXIV. Qaqun (site 32): Medieval tower-keep from NW (photo. 1919, Creswell Archive, courtesy of the Ashmolean Museum Oxford).

Eracles says that they then returned to Acre with their booty, leaving the *tor de Quaquo* untaken (*RHC Occ* (2), 461: cf. Sanudo, ed. Bongars, 224); but the Templar of Tyre relates that before retiring,

> "they besieged some Saracens in a tower that stands at *Caco*, very strongly surrounded by ditches full of water, and would have taken it; but our people were too fearful of remaining there because of the cry that had gone out through the land; and the Saracens had already assembled from all parts; and so our men departed and came to Acre with all speed, safe and sound" (*Gestes des Chiprois*, ed. Raynaud, 200–201).

Just how near the Franks may have come to taking the castle is suggested by the Muslim sources. These record that in the Crusader attack on Qaqun the paymaster of the Mamluks (*ustādh-dār*), Ḥusām al-Dīn, was killed and another amir wounded, and that the governor of the place was forced to leave. The news was serious enough for Baybars, when he heard of it in Aleppo on December 4, to return immediately to Damascus and set in train a relief operation. This was led by the amir Jamāl al-Dīn Aqush al-Shamsī with troops from ʿAin Jalut. On their approach the Franks withdrew from Qaqun, but were overtaken and harried by the Mamluks, leaving a number of men killed and horses and mules hamstrung. According to the Muslim commander of Qaqun, Bajkā al-ʿAlāʾi, the latter numbered 500 head (Ibn al-Furāt (2), 155; al-Maqrīzi (1, 2), 101; cf. al-ʿAyni, 246, 248; Riley-Smith 1971, 243).

For as long as the Franks were to remain in the Holy Land, the Mamluk base at Qaqun was to represent for them a threat both to ʿAtlit (Pilgrims' Castle) and to their very survival in the country (cf. Burchard of Mount Sion, ed. Laurent, 83 (1283); Ricoldus de Monte Crucis, ed. Laurent, 107 (1290s); Quatremère 1837(2, 1), 225). For reasons which remain obscure, it was identified in this period with Michmethath, a place mentioned in the Book of Joshua (XVI.6; XVII.7; cf. Burchard, ed. Laurent, 83; Röhricht, *Karten*, nos. 1 (Florence, *c.*1300) and 18 (Sanudo, *c.*1320)).

Qaqun was soon integrated into the coastal road system from Cairo to Damascus reinstituted by Baybars (cf. Hartmann 1910, 686–693). In the 15th century, it is listed by Khalil al-Ẓāhirī (d. 1468) as one of the stations on the road passing through Lydda, al-ʿAuja, and at-Tira and continuing on to Damascus through Fahma, Jinin, Zirʿin, ʿAin Jalut and Baisan; it also served as a relay station for snow taken from Syria to Egypt (Quatremère 1837(1, 2), 255; (2, 2), 91, n. 34).

In 1293/4, the town suffered an earthquake that was also felt in Gaza, Ramla and Karak (Quatremère 1837(1, 2), 254; Kallner-Amiran 1951, 228). The subsequent rebuilding included a large caravanserai, constructed by ʿAlam al-Dīn Sanjar al-Jawlī (amir 1299; died 1345), sometime governor of Gaza (Quatremère 1837(1, 2), 255; Mayer (LA) 1933, 198).

Among those buried at Qaqun in the Mamluk period was Yalbughā al-Yaḥyāwī, a former governor of Hama and Aleppo, who was executed there in Jumada I 748 (9 August–7 September 1347) (Mayer (LA) 1933, 250). Some other burials are recorded on the epitaphs published below (Appendix 2, nos. 1–3).

DESCRIPTION OF THE CASTLE

Before 1947, Qaqun was a sizeable Arab village occupying a low rounded hill on the eastern edge of the coastal plain. After its evacuation in the war of 1948, the village buildings were systematically levelled so that today only the medieval tower-keep, built on the highest part of the hill, and some derelict structures immediately surrounding it are still left standing (Pl. XXIII).

The tower survives today to a maximum height above ground level of 8·5 m. (Pl. XXIV–XXVII; Fig. 15). Its base measures 14·53 (N) × 17·65 m. (E) externally, with walls some 2·80 m. thick. The walls narrow at a level of 0·30 m. below the springing of the ground-floor vault, and on the north face there is another off-set 1·90 m. below this one. The south-west corner of the tower, including about half of the south wall and three-quarters of the west wall, has completely collapsed. Most of the remainder, however, survives to just above the level of the first floor.

The tower was constructed of large well-dressed blocks of ashlar, for the most part apparently antique spolia recut or refaced for their new purpose. They included a column-drum (or perhaps a milestone) with a cylindrical shaft (diam. 0·58 m.) and a square base, inserted into the west wall; and two fragments of architrave, one with a sculpted frieze that had been planed down and all but obliterated by the medieval masons. The larger ashlars (up to 0·50 m. high) tend to be concentrated at the base of the walls or at the corners,

Pl. XXV. Qaqun (site 32): Medieval tower-keep from NE. Note offset and splay-base arrow-slit in N wall and reused antique cornice fragment in E wall (photo. author).

Pl. XXVI. Qaqun (site 32): Medieval tower-keep from SE (photo. author).

where some of them also have drafted edges. There is no consistency in the course heights, however, and many of the courses do not follow through from one corner to the next. This seems more often the result of reuse of earlier material than to denote any difference in building periods. The course heights inside the tower and on the upper parts are usually around 0·30 m. In places, particularly on the south, some galletting of small stone chips is also visible; and on the south and east, the wall face is scarred by traces of buildings that were later constructed against it.

The ground floor of the tower is now choked with fallen rubble and a virulent growth of cactus. Its interior would have measured some 8·90 × 12·00 m. A report of 1922 suggests that it was originally roofed with four bays of groin-vaults, supported by a rounded pier in the centre of the room (*PAM*, 18.8.1922). This pier is now invisible, but a photograph taken by K. A. C. Creswell in 1919 suggests that it may have been square rather than rounded, at least at the level of the springing of the vaults (Pl. XXIV). The surviving inside face of the east wall also puts in doubt the theory of groin-vaults. This wall still displays the springing of one side of a continuous barrel-vault, and what remains of the west wall suggests the same. In the centre of the north wall, however, is a shallow rectangular pilaster from which there springs another line of vaulting which intersects the inside halves of both barrel-vaults (Pl. XXVIII). The responding half of this vault evidently sprang from the central pier, as did a second identical vault whose

Pl. XXVII. Qaqun (site 32): Medieval tower-keep from S, showing arrow-slit in S wall (photo. author).

QAQUN
Survey 1983

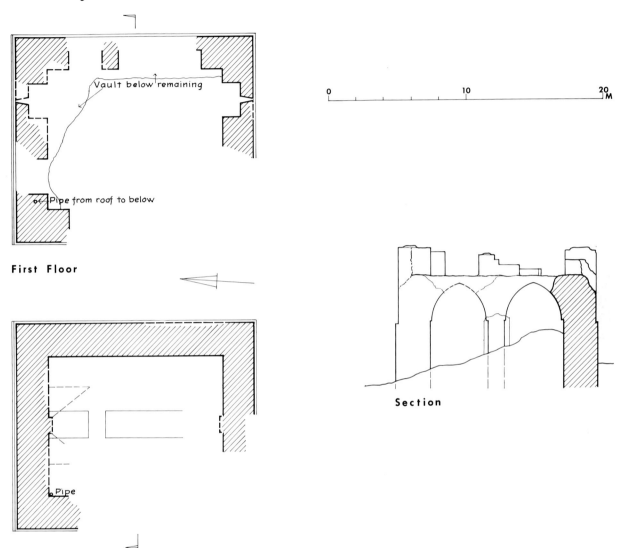

First Floor

Basement

Section

Fig. 15. Qaqun (site 32): medieval tower-keep, plans and section of existing remains (BASJ Survey 1983).

remains may still be seen in Creswell's photograph (Pl. XXIV). Thus the ground-floor vaulting would appear to have consisted of a pair of barrel-vaults, side by side, separated by a central pier from which sprang two intersecting vaults (see Fig. 16). All the vaults seem to have had pointed profiles; they were built of rubble masonry, contrasting with the ashlar of the vertical wall facing (course heights 0·28 m.). In a secondary phase, a rough wall of rubble and earth-mortar was constructed down the centre of the room from north to south,

enclosing the central pier. In the northern half was a rounded doorway, whose arch is now barely visible above ground. This wall seems to have been a village construction built after the tower was already ruined. A wely of al-Khidr (the Green) existed in the north-west corner of it until 1947.

The remains of the first floor are even more fragmentary than those of the ground floor (see Fig. 15). The walls at this level were about 2·65 m. thick. They were pierced, however, by casemated arrow-slits, two in

QAQUN
Reconstruction

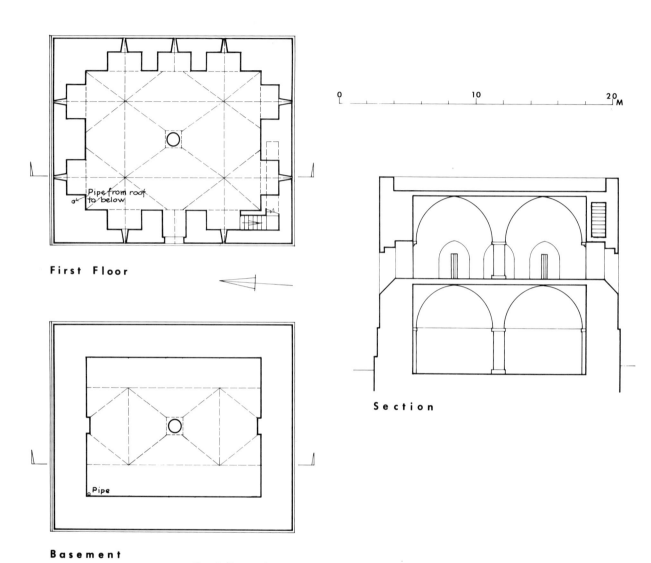

First Floor

Basement

Section

Fig. 16. Qaqun (site 32): medieval tower-keep, suggested reconstruction.

the north wall, three in the east, two in the south and possibly another three in the west, though one of these may have alternatively have been the main entrance to the tower. The best-preserved casemate is in the south wall (Pl. XXIX). It is 2·62 m. wide and 1·64 m. deep; the arrow-slit was 0·80 m. wide, narrowing on the outside to 0·05 m. with a chamfered outer face (Pl. XXVII). Neither the top of the arrow-slit nor the vaulting of the casemate survives, and indeed even the floor has been robbed out. The sides of the casemate, however, have preserved on them a plaster facing

covering a layer of coarse potsherds set in mortar. The casemate that faces this one in the north wall was apparently similar in design and proportions, though without a chamfered outer face. Although only half of its arrow-slit survives, the part that does includes the base, which has a sloping sill terminating in a serif-like splay at the bottom (Pl. XXX; Fig. 17).

In the north-west corner of the tower, an earthenware pipe is built into the rubble core of the wall (Fig. 18). This is made up of cylindrical sections, 24 cm. long and 15·8 cm. in overall diameter, which slot one inside the

Pl. XXVIII. Qaqun (site 32): Medieval tower-keep, spring of basement vaulting from inside face of N wall, seen from SE. Note later blocking to right. Course heights to left, 0·28 m. (photo. author).

next. The fabric is red, with a grey fracture, and is hard and coarse, containing fine white grits; it resembles some of the 13th-century coarse wares from the Red Tower. The pipe debouches through the vault into the north-west corner of the ground-floor room. It seems unlikely, however, that it originally terminated here. More likely, it would have run down the corner of the room to take water from the roof into a cistern below the tower's ground floor. The fact that the pipe is built inside the upper part of the tower but outside the lower part suggests that it was installed while the upper part was still being built. Similar water pipes may be seen in the 12th-century convent buildings in Bethany inserted into cavities hollowed out of existing wall faces and simply covered by a coating of mortar and plaster; and others have been excavated at St. Mary in the Valley of Jehoshaphat in Jerusalem (Johns 1939, 126; fig. 4).

It is uncertain how the first floor was vaulted. This vaulting, however, need not necessarily have been related in any way to the arrangement of the casemates, which would have been enclosed by their own individual barrel-vaults. The space to be enclosed was about 9·20 × 12·30 m. Quite possibly, therefore, it was covered by four bays of groin-vaults, supported by a central pier constructed directly over that of the ground floor.

There remains the question of the position of the main entrance and the method of communicating between the floors. No trace of any ground-floor door has been detected, though one may possibly have existed in part of the tower that has collapsed. The principal entrance

Pl. XXIX. Qaqun (site 32): Medieval tower-keep, casemated arrow-slit in S wall, from N (photo. author).

ARROWSLITS

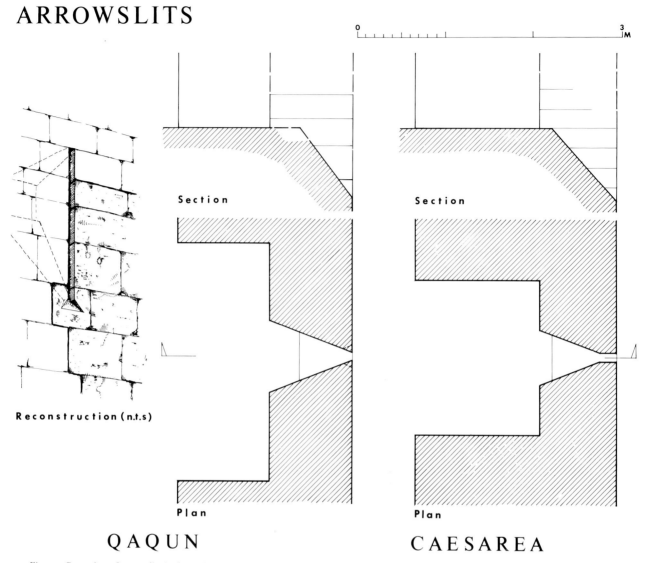

Fig. 17. Comparison of arrow-slits in the north wall of the tower at Qaqum (site 32) and the north town wall of Caesarea (BSAJ Survey 1983 and 1979).

to towers of this kind, however, was sometimes at first-floor level, even if another door existed below. The only point at which there could have been a first-floor door at Qaqun would have been in the parts of the west and south walls that no longer exist, since no door is to be seen in the other surviving parts of the structure. It is possible that this angle may also have contained the stair leading to the roof; this could perhaps have led off from one side of either of the two window casemates near the south-west corner; such an arrangement also existed in the 12th-century tower at Khirbat al-Kurmil (*Carmel*), south-east of Hebron (Rey 1871, 103–104; fig. 30; cf. Conder and Kitchener 1881(3), 372–374; fig.). A stair linking the ground- and first-floor is mentioned by the

Survey of Western Palestine (Conder and Kitchener 1881(2), 195), but it is uncertain if this was original; the medieval stair, if one existed, might also therefore have been in the south-west corner. One advantage of inserting a staircase inside the corner of a building was that it would be less likely to obstruct any doors or windows that the builders might wish to insert into the walls. The disadvantage, however, was that it could weaken the stability of the structure. This could perhaps explain why it was this corner of the tower that collapsed first.

The masonry style used in constructing this building and its fragmentary state of preservation make it extremely difficult to tell whether or not what remains

Pl. XXX. Qaqun (site 32): Medieval tower-keep, splay-base arrow-slit in N wall (photo. author).

either at *Crac* or elsewhere in Syria (1934, 258–259; fig. 21 and 53b; pl. LXXIVb). Plunging arrow-slits with splayed bases are also found in the second 12th-century phase at Beaufort Castle (pre-1190) (Deschamps 1939, 204; fig. 18). And an arrow-slit in the Hospitaller mill at Khirbat Kurdana (*Recordane*), near Acre, is splayed both at the bottom and at the top (see Pl. XXXI); this building probably dates to the late 12th or early 13th century (cf. Benvenisti 1970, 248–252, 288). The bases of these arrow-slits, however, are broadened in the shape of a stirrup (*base à étrier*), whereas the one at Qaqun seems more modestly proportioned and more triangular in shape. It finds closer parallels with examples nearer at hand in the town walls of Caesarea. A detailed survey of these walls has yet to be made. Most of its arrow-slits, however, appear to be casemated and to have plunging sills designed to give the defenders a raking field of fire across the inclined face of the glacis (see Fig. 17). Not all the arrow-slits have splayed bases, but those that do seem to be situated in the later parts of the walls (e.g. the north gate-tower: Rey 1871, fig. 56). It seems likely therefore that they belong to one of the 13th-century building phases: 1219–20, 1228 or 1251–52 (cf. Hazard 1975, 85–88).

It would appear therefore that the first floor of the tower at Qaqun with its casemated arrow-slits is likely to

QAQUN

0 _____ 10
Cm

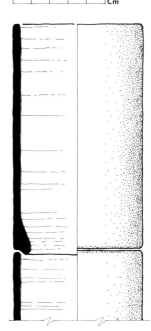

Fig. 18. Qaqun (site 32): section of ceramic pipe built into north-west corner of medieval tower (BSAJ Survey 1983).

belongs to one or more periods of construction. Certain horizontal divisions are visible in the rubble core; but such features are commonplace in medieval buildings of this kind and do not necessarily denote different periods of construction (cf. Fig. 34).

The design of the tower and the style of its masonry may be compared with other Frankish work of the 12th and early 13th century. Its plan with vaulting carried on a central pier is similar to that of the *donjons* of Qal'at Yahmur (12th-c.) and Sahyun (1108/32) in Syria and the tower at the south-eastern corner of the *faubourg* of 'Atlit (1218–)(see above, pp. 16–18).

The only significant architectural features of the tower are its casemated arrow-slits. Arrow-slits set in casemates and with plunging sills and splayed bases may be seen in the towers and curtains on the outer west wall at *Crac des Chevaliers*, dated *c.*1170–1220; the embrasures of the first period of work at *Crac* (pre-1170) are quite different, and Deschamps also notes that arrow-slits of this kind are unknown in medieval Muslim fortification,

Pl. XXXI. Khirbat Kurdana: Arrow-slit in Crusader mill-house (photo. author).

date to the second half of the 12th century or the first half of the 13th. It is unlikely to date to after the Mamluk conquest, and whatever additions Baybars made to the castle have therefore either disappeared or should be sought elsewhere; perhaps they were confined to the outer defences. The first documentary reference to a castle at Qaqun, however, comes from 1123, and reasons have been advanced above for thinking that it had been built by Eustace Garnier within the first two decades of the 12th century. How can this apparent contradiction between archaeological and written evidence be reconciled? First, it is possible that arrow-slits with the modeslty splayed bases seen at Qaqun were already being built by the Crusaders before 1150; there is in any case not enough evidence to be certain. Secondly, it could be that Eustace Garnier's castle did not originally include a central tower. Towers are common features of most of the early castles built by the Franks on the Holy Land, however, and it would seem surprising if the one at Qaqun were not an original feature, especially as it

occupies the highest point of the site. The keep probably was therefore an original feature, though it may have undergone later remodelling sometime in the late 12th or 13th century, before the Mamluk conquest. Clearance work and excavation may one day perhaps provide a more definitive answer.

Other Features

Some 12 m. south of the tower lie the remains of an underground cistern with a semi-circular barrel-vault constructed of ashlars. It measures about 5·37/5·56 (E–W) × 5·71/5·86 m. (N–S), with rounded corners and is coated inside with pink plaster containing crushed pottery and sherds of rilled amphorae. The original opening is a circular manhole, 0·80 m. wide, in the crown of the vault. In a later period another inlet was inserted in the north-west corner, fed by a ceramic pipe similar to the one found built into the tower. It seems therefore that this was a 5th- to 7th-century cistern which continued in use into the 12th or 13th century.

Remains of another fortification encircle the hill top, with rounded towers surviving south-east and north-west of the tower. These, however, are very roughly built with irregular stones and earth mortar. They seem unlikely to date to before the 19th century.

The ruins of the mosque, another casualty of the post-1948 destruction, lie north-west of the tower. In 1947, S. A. S. Husseini wrote of this building:

> "Only the domed part is ancient, the rest of the building is new. North of al-Jamiʿ [the mosque] is an enclosed yard containing graves and a cistern" (*PAM*, 22.7.1947).

The inscriptions from the mosque are discussed below (Appendix 2, nos. 2–4). Other features noted in 1947 include,

> "in the village, Bir el-Hilu, a large built well with three openings; near it are some traces of building foundations.
> "To the west is a medieval graveyard known as Maqbarat es-Satiriya.
> "Further west is Bir el-Khan, south of [the] school, which is said to have been built on the remains of el-Khan. South of Bir el-Khan is a marble column buried in the ground and said to belong to the grave of el 'Jawili'" (*PAM*, 22.7.1947).

This well and the wely of al-Jawlī lying on the west side of the village may very well represent the site of the khan built by ʿAlam al-Dīn Sanjar al-Jawlī in the early 14th century. An undated inscription seen in the mosque in 1922 also refers to a reservoir (*hawd*), which could also possibly have been connected with the road-station (*PAM*, 18.8.1922).

Pottery collected from Qaqun shows, as would be expected, a continuous sequence of types from Byzantine and early Islamic up to modern times.

Visited 22.7.82, 30.5.83, 22.7.83, 15–16.11.83, 3.7.84.

Bibliography
Amadi (ed. de Mas Latrie, 212) (1271); al-ʿAynī Badr al-Dīn, 246; 248 (1271); Benjamin of Tudela (transl. Adler, 20) (1163); Burchard of Mount Sion (ed. Laurent, 83) (1283); *Cart. des Hosp.* (1), 21–22, no. 20 (1110); 83–84, no. 94 (1131); 97, no. 115 (1135); 133, no. 168 (1146); 167, no. 217 (1153); 171, no. 223 (1154); 172, no. 225 (1154); 183–184, no. 224 (1156); 322–323, no. 470 (1175); (2), 673–675, no. 2482 (1248); 749–750, no. 2661 (1253); (3), 166, no. 3283 (1267); *Continuation de Guillaume de Tyr*, XXV (ed. Morgan, 38) (1187); Delaborde, 49–50, no. 20 (1138/9); Delaville le Roulx, *Archives*, 72–73, no. 4 (1135); 80–81, no. 8 (1146); 24 and 181, no. 78 (1248); 184, no. 80 (1253); 40 and 230, Addnl. no. 2 (1267); *Eracles, RHC Occ* (2), 39 (1187); 461 (1271); Ernoul, XII (ed. De Mas Latrie, 145–146) (1187); Fulcher of Chartres, III, 18, 1 (ed. Hagenmeyer, 664–665; transl. Ryan, 241–242) (1123); *Gestes des Chiprois*, 200 (1271); Holtzmann, 55 (1158); 57, no. 2 (1173); Ibn al-Furāt (2), 101 (1266); 155; 159 (1271); al-Maqrīzi (1, 2), 40 (1266); 101 (1271); Ricoldus de Monte Crucis (ed. Laurent, 107) (1290s); Röhricht, *Karten*, no. 1 (c.1300), 16 (1200/50), 18 (c.1320); *RRH*, 12, no. 57 (1110); 35, no. 139 (1131); 39, no. 159 (1135); 46, no. 190 (1138/9); 61, no. 243 (1146); 74, no. 293 (1154); 82, no. 321 (1156); 85, no. 331 (1158); 98, no. 373 (1161); 306, no. 1164 (1248); 319, no. 1210 (1253); 354, no. 1356 (1267); *Ad*, 18, no. 280b (1153); 19, no. 298a (1154); Sanudo (ed. Bongars, 224) (1271); Sinopoli, 140, nos. 3–4 (1158) and 5 (1173); Theodoric, XXXIX (ed. Bulst, 43; ed. Tobler, 89) (1172); William of Tyre, XII, 21, *RHC Occ* (1), 543–544 (1123).

Abel 1940; Bagatti 1979, 185; Benvenisti 1970, 15, 19, 173–174, 198–199, 276, 311, 313; Beyer 1936, 12, 17–18, 40–41, 44–45, 50–51, 56–57, 84; 1940, 185; 1951, 155, 172, 180, 278; Conder and Kitchener 1881(2), 152–153, 195; Deschamps 1939, 23 n. 5; Guérin 1874(2), 346–348; Hartmann 1910, 692; Israel 1964, 1410; Jaussen and Abel 1923, 85, 94; Johns 1937, 25 (F4); Karmon 1961, 58–60; Langé 1965, 94, 180; fig. 43; Le Strange 1890, 475; Mayer (LA) 1933, 198, 250; Meistermann 1936, 470; Palestine 1929, 216; 1948, 56; Prawer 1975(1), 305; Prutz 1881, 167, 174; Quatremère 1837(1, 2), 254–256; (2, 1), 225; (2, 2), 91–92 n. 34; Rey 1883, 419; Riley-Smith 1967, 125, 485; 1971, 208, 218, 242–243.

33. AR-RAS
1560.1842, alt. 280 m.

Ar-Ras is today a small hilltop hamlet in the area southeast of Tulkarm. The 1967–68 Survey reports Byzantine, medieval and Ottoman pottery.

Not visited.

Bibliography:
Conder and Kitchener 1881(2), 166; Gophna and Porat 1972, 223, no. 138; Palestine 1929, 222; 1948, 63.

34a. SHAIKH MUHAMMAD
1418.1989, alt. 30 m.
b. KHIRBAT ASH-SHAIKH
1417.1984, alt. 19 m.
MUHAMMAD
Hebr. *Elyashiv*

These two sites, less than 500 m. apart, lie on the inland *kurkar* ridge, north of the Nahr Iskandaruna and of its crossing point at Kh. Madd ad-Dair. The ʿEmeq Hefer Survey records glazed pottery.

Not visited.

Bibliography:
Palestine 1929, 164; 1948, 56; Y. Porath, personal communication.

35. SHUFA
1579.1869, alt. 320 m.

The 1967–68 Survey recovered from this site a piece of green and yellow glazed slip-ware with a coarse red fabric, similar to that found at the Red Tower (al-Burj al-Ahmar) in Phases B and C and datable to the 12th or early 13th century.

Not visited.

36. SHUWAIKA
1535.1936, alt. 110 m.
Cr. *Soeta, Socque*; Med. Ar., *al-Shuwayka*

In February 1200/1, various rents in *Soeta* formed part of the fief of the *scribanus* Soquerius (al-Shuwayki?) granted him by Aymar, Lord of Caesarea (*Cod. Dip.* (1), 288–289, no. 9; *RRH*, 205, no. 768). The village of *Socque* is also mentioned in December 1253 as belonging to John Laleman, Lord of Caesarea, and as defining the eastern border of the lands of *Cafresur* (Kafr Sibb) (Delaville le Roulx, *Archives*, 184, no. 80; *Cart. des Hosp.* (2), 749, no. 2661; *RRH*, 319, no. 1210). Baybars divided the lands of *al-Shuwayka* between two of his amirs in 1265 (Ibn al-Furāt (2), 81; al-Maqrīzi (1, 2), 14).

In the 1870s, V. Guérin noted a white marble corinthian capital and a masonry-lined well in the village. The latest pottery in the Palestine Museum collection is 6th-century.

Not visited.

Bibliography:
Cart. des Hosp. (2), 749, no. 2661 (1253); *Cod. Dip.* (1), 288–289, no. 9 (1200/1); Delaville le Roulx, *Archives*, 184, no. 80 (1253); Ibn al-Furāt (2), 81; al-Maqrīzi (1, 2), 14; *RRH*, 205, no. 768 (1200/1); 319, no. 1210 (1253).

Abel 1940, 41, no. 17; Beyer 1936, 38, 40, 67; Conder 1890, 31, no. 22; Conder and Kitchener 1881(2), 153; (3), 404; Guérin 1874(2), 353; Palestine 1933, 21; 1948, 58; Rey 1883, 424; Riley-Smith 1971, 210, no. 30.

37. AT-TAIYIBA
Med. Ar. *Ṭayyibat al-Ism*

1513.1858, alt. 80 m.

In 1265, Baybars divided the lands of *Ṭayyibat al-Ism* between two of his amirs (Ibn al-Furāt (2), 80; al-Maqrizi (1, 2), 13). In the later Mamluk and Ottoman periods, part of the village lands were held as *waqf* by the mosque of Hebron (Jaussen and Abel 1923, 85).

Byzantine, medieval and Ottoman pottery is noted by the 1967–68 Survey from the northern part of the village.

Not visited.

Bibliography:
Ibn al-Furāt (2), 80; al-Maqrizi (1, 2), 13.

Abel 1940, 41, no. 7; Beyer 1936, 14; Conder and Kitchener 1881(2), 166; Gophna and Porat 1972, 221, no. 123; Guérin 1874 (2), 352; Israel 1964, 1412; Jaussen and Abel 1923, 85, 93–94; Palestine 1948, 63; Riley-Smith 1971, 210, no. 32.

38. TEL NURIT

1458.1984, alt. 10 m.

The destroyed site of Tel Nurit was identified by the ʿEmeq Hefer Survey in the flood plain of the Nahr Iskandaruna in 1982. Surface remains included sherds of the medieval and Ottoman periods. This represents a possible location for Kafr Sallam (site 19) or for *Maluae* (site 29).

Not visited.

Bibliography:
Paley, Porath and Stieglitz 1982, 261.

39. AT-TIRA
Cr. *Teira*; Med. Hebr. *Bytr*; Med. Ar. *al-Ṭira*

1455.1821, alt. 70 m.

At-Tira seems likely to mark the location of the *mutatio Betthar* that is mentioned on the road between *Antipatris* (Ras al-ʿAin) and *Caesarea* by the Pilgrim of Bordeaux (A.D. 333) and other late Roman sources (see Neef 1981; Avi-Yonah 1976, 41).

In February 1151/2, the village of *Teira*, near to *Calanson* (Qalansuwa), was being held in fee by Pisellus of Sinjil (*casale S. Egidii*) from Walter Malduiz. On 5 February of that year, the Order of St. John bought the village from Pisellus, with the consent of Walter, for 1,000 bezants and granted it to Robert of Sinjil and his heirs. In return Robert granted the Hospital a reduction of 100 bezants a year on the rent that they were paying him for land at *Emaus* (cf. *Cart. des Hosp.* (1), 149–150, no. 192 (1150)) and paid 400 bezants as compensation to Walter Malduiz. The agreement between Robert and the Hospital was reversible if he or his heirs at any time claimed the full rent of 500 bezants a year for the land at *Emaus* (*Cart. des Hosp.* (1), 155–157, no. 202).

After the Mamluk conquest of the area in 1265 the village may well have been temporarily abandoned. It is not included in Baybars's grants of estates of that year; and in 1333, the Jewish traveller Isaac Ḥelo records *Bytr*, a town between Sabastiya and Arsuf, as a mass of ruins amongst which was to be found the tomb of Rabbi Eliazar Modain (transl. Carmoly, 252–253). At about this time, however, the Arab writer Khalil al-Ẓāhiri noted *al-Ṭira* as a road station on the coastal route from Cairo to Damascus, lying between *al-ʿAuja* (Ras al-ʿAin) and *Qaqūn* (transl. Quatremère 1837(2, 2), 91 n. 34; cf. Hartmann 1910, 692; Avi-Yonah 1970; Sauvaget 1941, 66 n. 265).

Not visited.

Bibliography:
Cart. des Hosp. (1), 155–157, no. 202 (1151/2); Delaville le Roulx, *Archives*, 86–88, no. 12 (1151/2); *RRH*, 69, no. 274 (1151/2); Isaac Ḥelo (transl. Carmoly, 252–253) (1333); Khalil al-Ẓāhiri (transl. Quatremère 1837(2, 2), 91, n. 34).

Avi-Yonah 1970; Beyer 1936, 14; 1940, 165; 1951, 178; Conder 1890, 31, no. 28; Conder and Kitchener 1881(2), 166; Guérin 1874(2), 355; Hartmann 1910, 692; Neef 1981; Palestine 1948, 62; Sauvaget 1941, 66, n. 265.

40. TULKARM
Cr. *Turcarme, Turrarme*; Med. Ar. *Ṭurkarm*

1527.1909, alt. 110 m.

In November 1212, *Turcarme* was given to the Order of St. John along with some houses in Acre and Tyre by Aymar, Lord of Caesarea, as pledge for a loan of 2,000 bezants, 110 *modii* of barley and 60 of wheat (*Cart. des Hosp.* (2), 150, no. 1400; *RRH Ad*, 57, no. 859b). In December 1253, the village (*Turrarme*) was still the property of the Lord of Caesarea, John Laleman, when it was mentioned as defining the southern border of the lands of *Cafresur* (*Cart. des Hosp.* (2), 749–750, no. 2661). Baybars divided the lands of Tulkarm between two of his amirs in 1265 (Ibn al-Furāt (2), 80; al-Maqrizi (1, 2), 13).

The development of Tulkarm as a small town, beginning in early Ottoman times and encouraged by the construction of the railway at the end of the 19th century, has unfortunately obscured the earlier features of the village.

Bibliography:
Cart. des Hosp. (2), 150, no. 1400 (1212); 749–750, no. 2661 (1253); Delaville le Roulx, *Archives*, 184, no. 80 (1253); Ibn al-Furāt (2), 80; al-Maqrizi (1, 2), 13; *RRH*, 319, no. 1210 (1253); *Ad*, 57, no. 859b (1212).

Abel 1940, 40, no. 3; Beyer 1936, 39–40, 63; 1951, 281; Conder 1890, 31, no. 23; Conder and Kitchener 1881(2), 161–162; Guérin 1874(2), 353; Palestine 1948, 58; Riley-Smith 1971, 210, no. 33.

41. 'UMM KHALID 1375.1929, alt. 30 m.
Mukhalid; Cr. *Castellare Rogerii Longobardi*; Hebr. *Nathanya*

In December 1135, the lands of the castle (*castellare* or *castellaris*) of Roger the Lombard were cited as defining the western boundary of those of *Arthabec* (al-Maghair) (*Cart. des Hosp.* (1), 97, no. 115; *RRH*, 39, no. 159). It is uncertain whether or not this Roger is the same Rogerius Lombart who witnessed the sale of a vineyard by Peter of St. Gaultier to the Holy Sepulchre in Jerusalem in 1129 (*RRH*, 32, no. 129; cf. Beyer 1936, 44). Possibly he or one of his progenitors was among the Lombards who sailed with the Genoese fleet that helped capture Caesarea in May 1101, though he might equally have been an immigrant from the time of the First Crusade.

The site of Roger's castle has now been all but obliterated by the expansion of the modern town of Nathanya, founded in 1929. Some remains of it were seen, however, by J. S. Buckingham in 1816, by the officers of the Survey of Western Palestine in 1873 and by an anonymous writer in 1922 (*PAM*, 21.8.1922); and they survived in very much the same condition until as late as September 1946, when they were surveyed by J. C. B. Richmond for the Palestine Department of Antiquities (see Pls. XXXII–XXXIII; Fig. 19).

The most detailed description is that of the Survey of Western Palestine, which, despite certain inaccuracies that will become apparent later, is worth citing in full:

"Remains of a ruined vaulted building exist here. It appears to have formed one side of a small fortress, and may perhaps be of Crusading origin. A stone ring was found in the north wall for tying a horse or mule to, which suggests that this was in the interior, and that the vault ran round a central area. The vault is 82 feet [25·01 m.] long by 22 feet [6·71 m.] wide inside, the walls 5 feet [1·52 m.] thick. A loophole 18 inches [0·46 m.] wide, and a door closed [i.e. blocked] and 3½ feet [1·07 m.] wide, exist in the south or outer wall. In the north wall is a similar loophole, stopped up, and a door 7 feet [2·13 m.] wide.

"In the south-[east] corner are remains of a small tower 21 feet [6·40 m.] square inside originally; the north wall of this is broken down. The tower projects 5 feet [1·52 m.] beyond the south wall, and has on that side an entrance [or alcove] 7 feet [2·13 m.] wide, with two loopholes above.

"The door in the north wall of the vault has an arch, with a very flat point, 8 feet [2·44 m.] diameter, 3 feet [0·92 m.] high. The roof of the vault is also pointed, and covered with hard brownish cement, like that used at Caesarea. This extends down to the springing of the vault arch. The pointed arches of the windows and doors are also comparatively flat.

"The masonry is of stones 8 inches [0·20 m.] and 9

Pl. XXXII. '*Umm Khalid* (*site 41*): Medieval building from S (*photo. pre-1947, courtesy of the Israel Dept. of Antiquities and Museums*).

Pl. XXXIII. 'Umm Khalid (site 41): Medieval building from SE (photo. pre-1947, courtesy of the Israel Dept. of Antiquities and Museums).

'UMM KHALID
After J.C.B. Richmond, Sept 1946

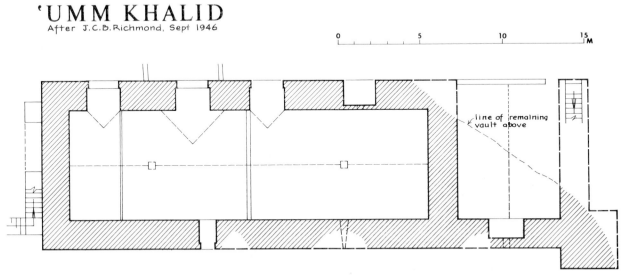

Fig. 19. 'Umm Khalid (site 41): plan of medieval building identified as part of the Castle of Roger the Lombard (after survey by J. C. B. Richmond, 1946, redrawn by courtesy of the Israel Dept. of Antiquities and Museums).

inches [0·23 m.] square [or high?], roughly dressed and carefully coursed, like the masonry at Caesarea.

"In the roof are square manholes. In the north-west [?] corner a staircase 8 feet [2·44 m.] wide leads up parallel to the north [?] wall; seven steps remain.

"The total height of the vault is over 20 feet [6·10 m.]; the doorways are some 12 feet [3·66 m.] high. There are remains of an upper storey. The stone used is the soft friable sandstone of the neighbourhood" (Conder and Kitchener 1881(2), 142–143).

The remains described here appear to have represented the south range and south-east corner of a rectangular complex, perhaps some 33 m. square, planned about a central courtyard. The later descriptions and plan of it, however, compel us to modify the Survey of Western Palestine's observations in certain respects. First, the main vaulted chamber seems to have been only 22·25 m. long, with walls 1·64 m. thick. In 1922 it was subdivided to accommodate two families; by this date an upper storey had also been added, reached by an external stair on the west. Richmond's plan (1946) also records two other blocked doors in the north wall, similar to the one already noted by the SWP, and a low vaulted alcove of uncertain purpose opening in the outer face of this wall (cf. Reich 1983, fig. 21).

Secondly, the feature that the SWP took to be a tower, 6·40 m. square internally, seems more likely to have been the truncated surviving southern end of the east vaulted range of the complex. Richmond's plan shows the north wall of this to have been a later blocking. In place of a door in its south wall, his plan shows an alcove; and although he does not indicate the two arrow-slits referred to by the SWP, they are clearly represented on photographs of the 1930s and 1940s (see Pls. XXXII–XXXIII). The south-east corner of the complex, however, was reinforced by a small turret, 3·44 m. square which projected 1·22 m. from the south wall; this appears to have been completely solid, at least in the lower part of it that survived.

Thirdly, there is the question of the staircase. The SWP indicates a stair 2·44 m. wide in the north-west corner of the building, parallel to the north wall; but no such feature could be found in 1922 and in view of the alignment of the vault the description sounds implausible. Richmond, on the other hand, indicates a staircase barely 1 m. wide set within the thickness of the east wall; but it is not clear whether he considered this to be an original feature or a later insertion. The external staircase on the west was, as we have seen, a 19th-century addition to provide access to the house built on top of the vault. It is thus uncertain whether there was originally an upper floor and whether any of the stairs recorded were original features.

The water supply for the castle seems to have been from wells (Biyarat Kawirk) on the east side of the hill. One of these was built, according to the SWP, of masonry similar to that of the castle, and in 1922 it was still covered by a pointed-arched vault with a square hole in it. Adjacent to it was a cemented trough or cistern, 4·57 m. square (another source indicates 3 × 4 m.: *PAM*). Between the castle and this well were six circular rock-cut features interpreted by the SWP as granaries, 1·52 m. in diameter and 1·83–3·05 m. deep, as well as a circular cistern, 3·66 m. in diameter constructed of masonry similar to that of the castle (Conder and Kitchener 1881(2), 143; *PAM*, 21.8.1922).

Bibliography:
Cart. des Hosp. (1), 97, no. 115 (1135); Delaville le Roulx, *Archives*, 72, no. 4 (1135); *RRH*, 39, no. 159 (1135).

Bagatti 1979, 184–185; Benvenisti 1970, 276; Beyer 1936, 44–45; Buckingham 1822(1), 218; Conder and Kitchener 1881(2), 142–143; Israel 1964, 1410; Langé 1965, 94, 180; fig. 43; Palestine 1929, 208; 1948, 56; Reich 1983, 110–111; figs. 20–23; Wilson 1880(3), 113.

42. YAMMA
1532.1973, alt. 90 m.
Cr. *Iheure*; Med. Ar. *Yammā*; Hebr. Ḥ. *Yaḥam*.

In December 1253, the village of *Iheure* belonged to a knight called Isambart and its lands defined the northern boundary of those of *Cafresur* (Kh. Kafr Sibb) (*Cart. des Hosp.* (2), 749–750, no. 266; *RRH*, 319, no. 1210). This Isambart may be the same Isembardus, knight of Caesarea, who witnessed a charter in 1200/1 (*RRH*, 205, no. 768). In 1265, Baybars divided the lands of Yamma between two of his amirs (Ibn al-Furāt (2), 81; al-Maqrīzī (1, 2), 14 n. 15).

The site is today still occupied by an Arab village and a new domed mosque of reinforced concrete is under construction. The lists of the Antiquities Department mention ruined walls and cisterns beneath the village, traces of a rock scarp and enclosing wall on the north-west and west, and various antique spolia (*PAM*, 16.8.1932; 21.9.1932; cf. Palestine 1948, 57).

Visited 16.11.1983.

Bibliography:
Cart. des Hosp. (2), 749–750, no. 2661 (1253); Delaville le Roulx, *Archives*, 184, no. 80 (1253); Ibn al-Furāt (2), 81; al-Maqrīzī (1, 2), 14 n. 15; *RRH*, 319, no. 1210 (1253).

Abel 1940, 41, no. 14; Beyer 1936, 40, 44; Israel 1964, 1411; Palestine 1929, 262; 1948, 57; Riley-Smith 1971, 210, no. 35.

43. KHIRBAT AZ-ZAHRAN
1579.1911, alt. 230 m.

Khirbat az-Zahran is a hill-top site overlooking the Wadi Nablus from the south, some 4·5 km. east of Tulkarm. Though deserted, ruined dry-stone walls and rock-cut cisterns attest previous occupation. In 1941, S. A. S. Husseini noted in the middle of the site,

> "a large cross-vaulted chamber known as ʿAqdat Sabbuba. The vault is supported on piers built at the four corners; some of the piers have a moulded frieze. It appears that the vault was built [with] reused stones from the Kherba, and probably is not earlier than the 18th century A.D.
>
> "Some of the stones lying about in the chamber bear a rough diagonal dressing. Near-by are remains of walls and heaps of building stones. Along the north and north-west sides, where the hill has a straight edge, remains of a retaining wall [are] seen" (*PAM*, 27.8.1941).

Pottery from the site in the Palestine Museum includes three sherds of early Islamic unglazed white ware (8th-11th century), ten of hand-made village ware (12th century on) and two of green-glazed slip-ware; to these the 1967-68 Survey has added two pieces of late 13th- to 14th-century glazed slip-painted ware. Evidently the site was occupied at various times during the Middle Ages, possibly continuously, while the existence of diagonally-tooled masonry suggests that some kind of building, perhaps a tower, might have stood here during the period of Frankish occupation.

Not visited.

Bibliography:

Gophna and Porat 1972, 218, no. 88; Palestine 1929, 193; 1948, 58.

44. ZAITA   1550.1990, alt. 100 m.
Med. Ar. *Zayta*

In 1265, Baybars divided the lands of Zaita between three of his amirs (Ibn al-Furāt (2), 80; al-Maqrīzi (1, 2), 13).

The present village occupies the north-western part of a hill top, rising between 40 and 50 m. above the valleys of streams on the north and south. The mosque is built of reinforced concrete. In 1932, however, N. Makhouly noted that the arches inside the mosque were supported on two Byzantine columns, one of which was spirally fluted; in the courtyard he also saw a "sculptured stone of Arabic type". Another two marble columns were built into the *maqam* of Shaykh Sulayman west of the village (*PAM*, 21.9.1932).

Visited 18.11.1983

Bibliography:

Ibn al-Furāt (2), 80; al-Maqrīzi (1, 2), 13.

Abel 1940, 40, no. 2; Beyer 1936, 38; 1942, 184-186; 1951, 257; Conder and Kitchener 1881(2), 153; Guérin 1874(2), 346; Palestine 1929, 263; 1948, 57; Prutz 1881, 172-173; Riley-Smith 1971, 210, no. 36.

APPENDIX 1

POTTERY FROM SITES IN THE CENTRAL SHARON PLAIN

Groups of medieval pottery derived from surface sherding and, in one case (the Red Tower), from excavation were inspected and identified from 22 sites in the central Sharon region. This material came in part from sites surveyed by the British School in 1983, in part from the survey made by the Archaeological Survey of Israel in 1967-68 (inspected by kind permission of Z. Yeivin and Y. Porath) and in part from the sherd collection of the Department of Antiquities in Jerusalem, amassed for the most part at the time of the British Mandate (1918-48).

The geographical distribution of 31 identifiable categories of pottery is indicated in Table 4. More detailed descriptions of most of these types will be found below in the report on the pottery from the Red Tower (al-Burj al-Ahmar: site 4).

Most of the pottery found on sites in this area in the Crusader period, although similar to types found elsewhere in the Crusader states, seems likely to have been produced locally. Such types include handmade pottery, with or without painted decoration, and the painted amphorae whose fabrics, it may be noted, correspond with that of the drain-pipe built into the wall of the tower-keep at Qaqun (site 32). Glazed common wares (including cooking pots), green and yellow slip-wares and monochrome graffita wares similar to those found in this area have also been excavated at Caesarea (see Pringle 1985b). Of the wide range of pottery imported from overseas that is found at Caesarea, however, very little seems to have filtered through to the inland parts of its territory. We may note, however, a piece of 12th-century Byzantine graffita ware from the Red Tower and possible examples at Kh. Bait Sama (site 2) and Fardisiya (site 10); late 12th- to early 13th-century Cypriot graffita pottery from the Red Tower, Kh. Bait Sama and possibly al-Majdal (site 28); and St Symeon ware imported from the region of Antioch occurring at Qaqun.

Glazed pottery imported overland from central Syria, however, is much more plentiful than any of the seaborne imports. Raqqa-type wares, with either an opaque turquoise glaze or black painting under a clear turquoise glaze, are found at Kh. Burin (site 3), the Red Tower, Kh. Dairaban (site 5), Fardisiya (site 10), Kh. Hanuta (site 12), Kh. Kaffa (site 17), Kh. Kafr Sibb (site 20), al-Majdal (site 28), and Qaqun (site 32). Later 13th- to 15th-century under-glaze painted wares similar to types found in Syria and Egypt occur at Kh. Bait Sama (site 2), Kh. Burin (site 3), the Red Tower (site 4), Kh. Kafr Sibb (site 20), al-Majdal (site 28) and Qaqun (site 32). In the same period, however, locally produced lead-glazed wares, particularly monochrome glazed green or yellow slip-wares and slip-painted wares, achieve an even higher representation.

Table 4. Medieval pottery from sites in the central Sharon

Site nos.:	2	3	4	5	9	10	12	15	16	17	18	20	22	25	26	28	30	32	35	37	43	44
Early Islamic:																						
Painted amphora	●	●	●				●		●	●		●					●					●
White unglazed	●	●	●					●										●		●		
Polychrome gl.	●	●	●			○					●	●				●	●					
Graffita	●	●														●						
Lamp												●										
12th c.–1260s:																						
Handmade	●	●	●			●	●			●		●		●		●	●	●		●	●	
+ painting	●	●	●			●				●		●				●		●				
Painted amphora	●	●	●								●											
Gl. common	●	●	●						●		●	●				●		●				
Gl. green and yellow slipware		●	●			●				●		●							●			
Monochr. Gr.	●	●	●			●				●		●	●			●		●				
Byz. Gr.	○	●				○																
Cypriot Gr.	●	●														○						
St. Symeon																		●				
Alkaline gl.:																						
White			●			●																
Turquoise		●	●	●		●										●		●				
+ black UGP		●				●	●			●		●				●		●				
Other																		●				
1260s onwards:																						
Gl. common			●						●							●						
Gl. monochr. slip	●	●	●			●	●		●	●	●	●				●	●	●		●		
Gl. slip-painted	●	●	●		●	●	●		●	●	●	●			●	●	●	●		●		
Yell. and green gouged										●						●	●	●				
UGP:																						
Black u. turq.			●									●										
Black u. clear	●		●																			
1300 onwards:																						
UGP:																						
Black and blue		●	●									●				●		●				
Black and turq.		●	●															●				
Blue and white		●	●															●				
Moulded gl.																●		●				
Pipes			●				●			●												
Turkish polychr.			●			●																
China/porcelain		●	●						●	●					●			●				

Abbreviations: Gl. = Glazed; Gr. = Graffita; Monochr. = Monochrome; Turq. = Turquoise; U. = Under; UGP = Under-glaze painted.

APPENDIX 2

ARABIC INSCRIPTIONS

by D. S. Richards

(St. Cross College and the Oriental Institute, Oxford)

In the late 1940s there were deposited in the Department of Antiquities at Jerusalem several field notes taken by Mr. S. A. S. Husseini, which contain details of six funerary inscriptions. They were accompanied by photographs. The original stones to my knowledge no longer survive. Therefore, to publish this brief account of some lost Muslim epigraphy, I must rely entirely on the surviving notes and the available photographs. All the passages in quotation marks are Husseini's. It must be recognized that the photographs by themselves are not satisfactory for establishing the texts which follow, but they do allow one some slight chance of controlling Husseini's readings.

The epitaphs are themselves unexceptional. If one compares them with the sample of eighty-five from Damascus, edited by K. Moaz and S. Ory, their contents correspond closely with the elements identified in that work (1977, 162). The *basmala* begins nos. 1, 2, 3 and 5. Most likely it was also at the head of no. 4, which perhaps then exhibited a Koranic verse, as do nos. 1, 3 and 5 (in the first two cases Kor. 55, vv. 26–27, and in the other Kor. 9, v. 21). The confession of faith is found only in no. 6. The tomb is designated in three cases (nos. 1, 3 and 5) by the phrase "This is the grave of ... (*hādhā qabr* ...)." Possibly it also formed part of no. 4. No. 2 has the phrase "This was made for ... (*mimmā ʿumila bi-rasm* ...)."

The name of the deceased then follows, introduced in nos. 1, 3, 4 and 5 by a pious formula. The child in no. 2 (his age at death is specified) is referred to as "*al-walad al-ṣāliḥ*, the righteous child". The deceased in no. 1 is described as "the shaikh", and the two amirs of nos. 4 and 5, neither of whom can be identified, have basic military "titles". In no. 6, I prefer to interpret the *al-faqīr* as a "function" ("the ascetic"), rather than as a pious epithet, "the needful" [*sc.* of God etc.]. Then, in all but no. 6 and the incompletely read no. 1, the date of death is given, followed in nos. 3, 4 and 5 by the "pious invocation", which in these examples is of the commonly found variety.

Qaqun (Site 32).

Husseini's notes on Qaqun are dated 22.7.1947.

1. Epitaph for Shaykh Muḥammad ibn al-Ḥājj ...
Photograph PAM 038,600. Plate XXXIV.

"Qabr [tomb of] esh-Sheikh Abu Sha'r with an inscribed tomb stone." Above line (i) at the top of the ogival stone is a winged motif with a pendant loop at the centre. The lines of the text are separated by horizontal bands. The inscription in relief is executed in a fair *naskhi* probably of the 7th/13th century. Compare Moaz and Ory 1977, nos. 66 and 67 and the typical Ayyubid motifs there found.

(i)   بسم الله الرحمن الرحيم

(ii)   كل من عليها فان ويبقى وجه ربك

(iii)   هذا قبر الفقير إلى الله تعا[لى]

(iv)   [ا]لشيخ محمد بن الحاج عب[د]

(v)   [‐ ‐ ‐ ‐ ‐ ‐ ‐ ‐ ‐ ‐]

Pl. XXXIV. *Qaqun, Inscription no. 1 : Epitaph for Shaykh Muḥammad ibn al-Ḥājj (photo. courtesy of the Israel Dept. of Antiquities and Museums).*

In the name of God the Merciful, the Compassionate.
(ii) "All that is upon it [the earth] is transient, but the
face of your Lord endures" [Kor. 55, vv. 26–27]. (iii) This
is the grave of the one needful of God Almighty (iv) the
Shaykh Muḥammad ibn al-Ḥājj ʿAb[d] (v) ...

Husseini read *al-ʿabd al-faqīr*, "the servant needful
etc.", but the photograph gives no justification for this.
The "ibn" in the name of the deceased, omitted by
Husseini, seems clear above the "d" of Muhammad.

2. Epitaph of Aḥmad ibn Mūsā (688 H./A.D. 1289)

There is a reference in the notes to a photograph
(PAM 038,589) but I have not had access to it.

"An inscribed marble column fragment was found
deposited among a heap of stones near the house of
Mohd. Ahmad Nasr Allah; it is said to have been
removed from the SW side of Maqbarat el Kabbara
which appears to be also partly a medieval cemetery.
Mohd. Nasr Alla[h] was instructed to remove and keep
this stone in the mosque yard."

(i)	بسم الله الرحمن الرحيم
(ii)	مما عمل برسم الولد الصالح
(iii)	احمد بن موسى توفى ليلة
(iv)	عاشورا إلى رحمة الله سنة
(v)	ثمان وثمانين وستماية
(vi)	وكان عمره سبع سنين

In the name of God the Merciful, the Compassionate.
(ii) This was made for the righteous child (iii) Ahmad
ibn Mūsā. He died on the eve of (iv) ʿĀshūrā [and passed]
to the mercy of God in the year (v) six hundred and
eighty-eight [3 February 1289]. (vi) He was seven years
old.

3. Epitaph for Muḥammad ibn ʿĪsā (792 H./A.D. 1390)

Photographs PAM 12632 and 038,591 (the latter is of
a squeeze). Plate XXXV.

North of the mosque (*al-jāmiʿ*) there was an enclosed
yard containing graves and a cistern. "One of the graves
is said to belong to esh Sheikh ʿAmmar (of Zeita village
and of the Fiddiyat family). On the west end of the
grave is an inscribed tomb stone which is said to have
been removed from the mosque wall and re-built in its
present position."

There is a report by N. Makhouly, dated 22 January
1936, which refers to a "marble slab 792 A.H. built to
wall at the back of the mosque". This is more than likely
a reference to the present inscription, and photograph
PAM 12632 (Pl. XXXV) appears to show the slab still
in position on the wall of the mosque.

*Pl. XXXV. Qaqun, Inscription no. 3: Epitaph for Muḥammad ibn ʿĪsā (792
H./A.D. 1390) (Photograph PAM 12632: Courtesy of the Israel Dept. of
Antiquities and Museums).*

Husseini in his transcription has by mistake treated
lines (iv) and (v) as one, and numbered the remainder
accordingly. The rectangular slab (of marble, as it
seems) exhibits a *naskhī* script, in which some of the
diacritical points are represented by carefully formed
rings. The lines of text are separated from one another
by bands and there are signs that a plain border enclosed
the whole.

(i)	بسم الله الرحمن الرحيم
(ii)	كل من عليها فان ويبقى وجه
(iii)	ربك ذو الجلال والاكرام عز لله
(iv)	هذا قبر العبد الفقير إلى الله
(v)	تعالى محمد بن عيسى [توفى] إلى
	رحمة الله
(vi)	تعالى في جمادى الاول سنة اثنين
	وتسعين وسبعماية
(vii)	رحمة الله عليه وعلى من ترحم عليه

The suggested completion of the line (v) seems to me to be at least partially legible from the photograph, but line (vii) is impossible to verify.

> In the name of God the Merciful, the Compassionate. (ii) "All that is upon it [the earth] is transient, but there endures the face (iii) of your Lord, possessed of glory and graciousness" [Kor. 55, vv. 26–27]. Power be unto God. (iv) This is the grave of the servant needful of God (v) Almighty, Muḥammad ibn ʿIsā. [He died and passed] to the mercy of God (vi) Almighty in Jumādā I in the year seven hundred and ninety-two [17 April–16 May 1390]. (vii) The mercy of God be upon him and upon those who pray for mercy to be shown him.

4. Unidentified inscription

An anonymous report in the PAM Qaqun file, dated 18.8.1922, refers to an inscription for which there is no photograph and no transcription.

"In the wall of the mosque is inserted an inscribed slab with no dating referring to the 'Haud' or reservoir."

Kh. Kafr Sibb (Site 20)

There follow two inscriptions from the deserted village of Kafr Sibb. Husseini made his notes concerning them and his transcriptions on the 12th August 1944. I also have had access to transcriptions of nos. 5 and 6 in a different and unidentified hand with rough sketches of the tomb on which the inscriptions were found and an indication of their positions upon it.

5. Epitaph for al-ʿAlāʾī (666 H./A.D. 1267)

Photograph PAM 31779 (and of a squeeze PAM 30911). Plate XXXVI.

"On the south side of the gable top of this grave is another inscribed marble slab; the inscription is incomplete and might have belonged to the neighbouring southern grave known as that of Sheikh Surur. Dimensions: length 42 cm., width 20 cm."

[– – – – – – – – – – –]

(i)   العلائي المجاهد المرابط

(ii)   في سبيل الله توفا [sic] ليلة

(iii)   السبت سابع وعشرين

(iv)   من ربيع الاول سنة ستة [sic]

(v)   وستين وستماية رحمه الله

(vi)   ورحم من ترحم عليه امين

Pl. XXXVI. Kh. Kafr Sibb, Inscription no. 5: Epitaph for al-ʿAlāʾī (666 H./A.D. 1267) (Photograph PAM 30911: courtesy of the Israel Dept. of Antiquities and Museums).

al-ʿAlāʾī, the warrior, the campaigner (ii) in the Path of God. He died on the eve of (iii) Saturday, the twenty-seventh (iv) of Rabiʿ I in the year six (v) and sixty and six hundred [Saturday = 17 December 1267]. May God have mercy upon him (vi) and have mercy upon those who pray for mercy to be shown him. Amen.

6. Epitaph for Jamāl al-Dīn Aqūsh al-Bakrī (?) (686 H./A.D. 1269)

Photograph PAM 31780. Plates VII and XXXVII.

"Remains of a settlement on a low hill. On W. side is a domed tomb chamber with an open courtyard enclosed by a wall ... Under the dome is a double built graves [sic]. The southern grave is that of the Sheikh Jamal ed Din, it has a gabled top. On the N. side is an inscribed marble slab, it bears 8 lines in a very shallow relief. (Dimensions: length 67 cm., width 28 cm.)"

The various lines of the inscription are separated one from another by relief bands. Between lines 4 and 5 is a

In line (ii) Husseini omitted the *minhu*. The reading of the nisba in line (v) is very doubtful. Husseini has "[al-Ykri]," while the anonymous notes have "[al-?di]," where the question mark represents a consonantal outline as in Arabic "b" but without diacritical points.

> **In the name of God the Merciful, the Compassionate. (ii) "Their Lord gives them good tidings of mercy from Himself (iii) and acceptance" [Kor. 9, v. 21 (incomplete)]. This is the grave of the one needful (iv) of God's mercy, the Amir, the warrior for the Faith, (v) Jamāl al-Dīn Aqūsh al-Bakri [?]. (vi) He died on the first day of Jumādā (vii) I in the year sixty-eight (viii) and six hundred [27 December 1269]. God have mercy on him.**

IRTAH (SITE 15)

The last of the funerary inscriptions, a short and undated one, was recorded by Husseini on a trip to Irtah. The notes are dated 29.6.1941.

7. *Epitaph for the ascetic Bāyazīd*

Husseini describes in his notes a small structure of two square chambers, both domed, which he calls the *Maqam en-Nabi Yaᶜqub* (the shrine of the Prophet Jacob) (see Pls. IV–V).

"Near the E. side of the entrance [of the western chamber] stands a marble column, its top diam. is 25 cm. On the upper end of the column the following inscription is incised in provincial naskhi script."

(i)   الفقير بايزيد

(ii)   لا اله الا الله

(iii)   محمد رسول الله

> **The ascetic Bāyazīd. (ii) There is no god but God. (iii) Muḥammad is the Prophet of God.**

QALANSUWA (SITE 31)

8. *Inscription recording the construction of a cistern (737 H./A.D. 1336)*

Plates XXII and XXXVIII.

There is one more inscription which is different in character. The slab of stone, upon which it was engraved, was found by K. A. C. Creswell in 1919 being used as a tombstone next to a ruined mausoleum west of the village (see above p. 56). The text records the foundation of a cistern by the amir Qūsūn (or Qawsūn), who came to Egypt in 720 H./A.D. 1320–1, and played a major role in the third reign of the Sultan al-Nāṣir Muḥammad. He acted as regent during the very short reigns of two of al-Nāṣir's sons, al-Manṣūr Abū Bakr and al-Ashraf Küçük, but was overthrown and imprisoned

Pl. XXXVII. Kh. Kafr Sibb, Inscription no. 6: Epitaph for Jamāl al-Dīn Aqūsh al-Bakri (?) (686 H./A.D. 1269) (photo. courtesy of the Israel Dept. of Antiquities and Museums).

field devoid of text, divided into two by a broader vertical band, on each side of which is a bold six-petalled rosette (also in relief). These two motifs interrupt the bands above and below them.

(i)   بسم الله الرحمن الرحيم

(ii)   يبشرهم ربهم برحمة منه

(iii)   ورضوان هذا قبر الفقير

(iv)   إلى رحمة الله الامير الغازي

(v)   جمال الدين اقوش [البكرى]

(vi)   توفى في مستهل جمادى

(vii)   الا(١)ول سنة ثمان وستين

(viii)   وستماية رحمه الله

Pl. XXXVIII. Qalansuwa, Inscription no. 8, recording the construction of a cistern (737 H./A.D. 1336) (photo. Creswell Archive, courtesy of the Ashmolean Museum, Oxford).

in Alexandria, where he was killed in Shawwāl 742 H./April A.D. 1342 (see Ibn Ḥajar (3), 342–4).

The text has been published and is well known. A study of Creswell's photograph has not enabled me to suggest a reading for the damaged word at the beginning of line (vii), nor to arbitrate between the readings given for the end of that same line.

In the name of God the Merciful, the Compassionate. "We shall surely reward them according to the best of their actions" [Kor. 16, v. 99]. (ii) There ordered the construction of this blessed and auspicious cistern (*ḥawḍ*), in the days of our Lord the Sultan (iii) al-Malik al-Nāṣir, the servant needful of God Almighty, his most Noble Excellency Sayf al-Dīn, the Support (iv) of the Community, the Refuge of the Religion, the Illumination of the State, Qūsūn al-Nāṣirī (v) the Cupbearer (may God Almighty glorify his victories and at the last crown his deeds with pious works) in his desire for the face of God Almighty (vi) as a pious foundation for all God's people. The endowment for it is the plot of land to the west of the cistern (vii) . . . in the last ten days of Rabīʿ I in the year 737 [28 October–6 November 1336], and [praise be] to God.

See Mayer (LA) 1933, 187–8; *RCEA* (15), no. 5708; cf. Mayer (LA) 1931, 146; Van Berchem 1922, 288–9, note 4.

PART TWO

Excavations at the Red Tower
(al-Burj al-Ahmar)
1983

I. HISTORICAL INTRODUCTION

The Red Tower (*La Tour Rouge* or *Turris Rubea* to the Crusaders, *al-Burj al-Ahmar* to the Mamluks) was the name given in the 13th century to a small castle, comprising a tower-keep and a surrounding wall, which formed the centre of a village and territory of the same name lying in the southern part of the lordship of Caesarea. As with other "red" place-names in Palestine, such as Khan al-Ahmar near Baisan (cf. Mayer (LA) 1932), the colour seems more likely to refer to the red-orange sandy soil (*hamra*) surrounding the site than to the colour of the building itself. The remains of the Red Tower are situated in the Sharon plain, about 9 km. due east of the modern coastal resort of Nathanya, roughly midway between the sea and the mountains of Samaria. The motor road, built in 1926 to link the site of Nathanya with Tulkarm at the mouth of the Wadi ash-Sha'ir (or Wadi Nablus), passes 150 m. south of the ruin.

Despite archaeological evidence for Byzantine occupation of the site, no certain mention of it occurs in documentary sources before the 12th century. Attempts to equate it with the Jewish village of *Burgātā* or *Burqātā*, whose wine was forbidden by the Jerusalem Talmud because of its proximity to the Samaritan village of *Birath Soreka* (= Tulkarm?) (cf. Neubauer 1868, 173) are not conclusive; and their apparent endorsement by modern maps which mark the site "Horvat Burgata" is perhaps unfortunate. The modern Arabic name for the site, Khirbat al-Burj al-'Atut (the ruin of the fallen tower), whose phonetic similarity to *Burgātā* seems to have been a principal cause of this confusion, is first recorded only in the 19th century, when it would accurately have described the state of the *medieval* tower, by then in an advanced stage of delapidation (Guérin 1874(2), 349; Conder and Kitchener 1881(2), 178).

In the 12th century, the site was known by entirely different names. In a confirmation of the rights and possessions of the Benedictine Abbey of St. Mary Latin (or Latina) in Jerusalem, granted by Pope Hadrian IV on 21 April 1158, it is listed as "the Tower of Latina (*turris Latinae*) in the territory of Caesarea", along with "the village that had belonged to Eustace" (Kh. Madd ad-Dair) and land in Qaqun (*RRH*, 85–86, no. 331; cf. Holtzmann, 55; Sinopoli, 140, nos. 3–4; Mayer (HE) 1977, 216–220; Beyer 1936, 43–44). The Abbey's possession of these lands was reconfirmed by Pope Alexander III on 8 March 1173 (*RRH*, 86, no. 331; Holtzmann, 57, no. 2; Sinopoli, 140, no. 5) and by

Benedict XI on 15 March 1304 (Sinopoli, 141, no. 10). How the monks came to possess them is uncertain, though it seems likely that Madd ad-Dair (*Montdidier*) had been granted them by Eustace Garnier, the first Lord of Caesarea (1105/10–1123) (see above, pp. 37–39). Eustace and his successor Walter I Garnier (1123–49/54) were both buried in the abbey church of St. Mary Latin (*RRH*, 89, no. 342). If the Red Tower was not included in Eustace's original gift, therefore, it seems plausible to assume that it would have been added to the Abbey's endowments by Walter when he made provision for the eventual repose of his own body and soul before his death, which occurred between 1149 and 1154 (cf. Hazard 1975, 93, 95–96; La Monte 1947, 147–148).

Between July and August 1187, following Saladin's destruction of the Latin army at Hattin, this area was lost to the Franks (*Gesta Henrici II*, ed. Stubbs (2), 23) and it seems likely that the castle was abandoned. It was probably reoccupied in or soon after September 1191, when King Richard I of England retook the coastal plain around Caesarea and defeated Saladin at the battle of Arsuf (Prawer 1975(2), 80–83; Runciman 1954(2), 55–57). It may have been at this moment that the castle was taken over by the Templars, who by 1236, were paying rent for it to the Abbey (*Cart. des Hosp* (2), 501, no. 2141; *RRH Ad*, 66, no. 1072a). There is no evidence however, that they had ever held it before 1187; nor is there any reason to seek a connection between this castle and the Master of the Templars, Arnald de Turre Rubea (1180–84), whose name is derived from Torroja in Aragon (Bulst-Thiele 1974, 99–105; cf. Mayer 1936, 44).

While the date of the Templars' occupation of the Red Tower is therefore open to speculation, their eventual loss of it is better documented. It seems that in the period of turmoil between the fall of Jerusalem to Saladin in 1187 and the retaking of Acre by the Third Crusade in 1191, the Benedictine community of St. Mary Latin, without a home and short of funds, had leased all their possessions in the territory of Caesarea to the Hospital, even though these lands, which included *Montdidier* (Kh. Madd ad-Dair) and *Turriclee* (al-Burj al-Ahmar) were as yet still in Muslim hands. On 11 October 1198, Pope Clement III instructed the Bishop of Banyas (Valania) to examine the terms of this lease and decide if it was not placing too great a strain on the

Hospital's finances (*Cart. des Hosp.* (1), 559, no. 879; *RRH Ad*, 46–47, no. 682a). It was evidently allowed to stand, however, for its general terms were later put into effect. In May 1236, an agreement was reached between Robert, Abbot of St. Mary Latin (now transferred to Acre), and Guérin, Master of the Hospital, by which the Abbot undertook to respect the obligations imposed on him by the lease of *Montdidier* and *Tourre-Rouge* to the Hospital and to hand them over as soon as the Templars had left (*Cart. des Hosp.* (2), 501, no. 2141; *RRH Ad.*, 66, no. 1072a). Copies of this agreement were entrusted to the Archbishop of Nazareth and the Abbot of the Templum Domini (*RRH*, 280, no. 1072). It was not until 7 August 1248, however, that the formal handing over of the two *casalia* and of the Abbey's possessions near *Caco* (Qaqun) was made by Abbot Peregrinus to John de Ronay, Grand Preceptor and Vice-Master of the Hospital. On this occasion the lands concerned were described as follows:

> "Our village (*casale*) of *Mondisder* with all its rights and appurtenances, and our other village which is called the Red Tower (*Turris Rubea*), similarly with its rights and appurtenances, and all the lands and possessions which we and our monastery have or are seen to have in the territory of the village called *Caco*, that is to say including the men, women, woods, wastes, plains and mountains, pastures, cultivated and uncultivated lands, waters and water channels (*aquarum discursibus*), and all other written and unwritten (rights) appertaining to the aforesaid villages and lands" (*Cart. des Hosp.* (2), 673–675, no. 2482).

The rent agreed for these lands was 800 bezants a year (*ad pondus Acconensi*), to be paid in two instalments on the Feast of the Nativity of the Blessed Virgin Mary (September 8) and on Ascension Day respectively. It was to be paid whatever the state of the country and whether or not the Hospitallers were still able to collect their rents from the villages, so long as Acre or Tyre remained in Christian hands. If both cities fell, then the payment of rent was to be suspended until one or the other of them were retaken. In this way, the Abbey was to be guaranteed a steady income from its possessions, at the expense if need be of the Hospital, for as long as it was likely to continue in existence itself. The lease was to be renewed every 25 years (*Cart. des Hosp.* (2), 673–675, no. 2482; *RRH*, 306, no. 1164).

The lease was indeed renewed, apparently on the same terms as before, on 29 October 1267, through the mediation of the Patriarch of Jerusalem, William II of Agen (*Cart. des. Hosp.* (3), 166, no. 3283; *RRH*, 354, no. 1356). Since the renewal was not due until 1273, the need for mediation may perhaps reflect a reluctance on the part of the Hospital to comply with its terms. If so, a likely cause is not hard to find; for in March and April 1265, Caesarea and Arsuf had fallen to Sultan Baybars. *Al-Burj al-Aḥmar* is included in the list of captured lands

lying in the territories of these two cities with which he enfeoffed his amirs later in the same year (Ibn al-Furāt (2), 81; al-Maqrīzī (1, 2), 14; cf. Riley-Smith 1971, 209, no. 11; Abel 1940, 41, no. 13; *pace* Beyer 1936, 43).

The fate of the castle after its capture by the Mamluks is not recorded. It seems unlikely that either of the two amirs, Nāṣir al-Dīn al-Qaymarī and Sayf al-Dīn Balabān al-Zaynī al-Ṣāliḥī, between whom the village and its lands were divided, would actually have resided there (cf. Ziadeh 1953, 40–44; Irwin 1977, 65–67). The administrative importance of the site would therefore probably have quickly lapsed. As for its defensive role, in 1265 Baybars systematically destroyed the city walls of Caesarea and Arsuf and began the policy followed by later Mamluk rulers of dismantling all the Frankish castles of the coastal plain and expelling its settled population, so as to reduce it to an inhospitable waste, peopled only by nomads, dangerous and uninviting to any future Christian attempt at colonization (Ayalon 1965, 7–12). The principal Mamluk stronghold in the area from 1266 onwards was Qaqun, situated on the eastern edge of the plain and on the main Damascus to Cairo coast road (Ibn al-Furāt (2), 101; see above pp. 22–25). There would have been no place for the Red Tower in this new defensive scheme, and the probability is that it was dismantled in or soon after 1265, along with many other castles in the coastal plain of Palestine. The evidence for the destruction and for its date, however, will be discussed below in the light of the archaeological evidence (p. 128).

Unlike Qaqun, which receives various mentions in later 13th- and 14th-century sources, both Frankish and Arabic, the Red Tower disappears from the written record from 1265 until the 19th century. In June or July 1870, Victor Guérin refers to it under the name of al-Burj al-ʿAtut:

> "Au sud-ouest de cet oued [nahr Iskandaruna], s'élève sur un monticule, à la distance de 2 kilomètres, un fortin d'origine musulmane; il est aujourd'hui abandonné" (1874(2), 349).

The site was visited again in May 1873 by the officers of the Survey of Western Palestine. At this time the tower's state of preservation seems to have been little different to what it is today, save that the eastern ground-floor vault was still partly intact, running 7·6 m. (25 ft.) north from the surviving south wall of the tower. The remains are described as follows:

> "Remains of a tower, apparently part of a Crusading castle. The wall remaining measures 30 feet [9·15 m.] east and west, and on the inside, towards the north, is a vault 25 feet [7·63 m.] long (north and south) and 12 feet [3·66 m.] broad. This is about 20 feet [6·10 m.] high. The wall on the south reaches up to a height of 40 to 45 feet [12·20–13·73 m.], and has inside it a buttress dividing the building into two aisles, north and south. The walls of the vault are 5 feet [1·53 m.] thick; in the west wall is a small

archway about 3 feet [0·92 m.] high, the arch pointed with two rings of voussoirs, five in the inner, seven in the outer [see Fig. 27b], the keystones cut away to form the point of the arch. In the south wall, high up, is a loophole window some 4 feet [1·22 m.] high and three feet [0·92 m.] wide inside, and about 6 inches [0·15 m.] wide outside. The direction of the south wall is 104°; it is 8 feet [2·44 m.] thick, built of very hard limestone, rudely dressed with soft white mortar and a packing of small stones 3 inches to 4 inches[0·07–0·10 m.] wide. The ashlar measures 1 foot by 1½ feet [0·30 × 0·46 m.], to 2 feet by 1½ feet [0·61 × 0·46 m.]; the arches seen were all pointed, the arch of the vault a tunnel-vaulting of smaller stones than those in the walls. The masonry is laid in courses with the vertical joints carefully broken. The place is inhabited by a peasant family" (1881(2), 178).

Reports made to the Department of Antiquities of the British Mandatory Government, including one by K. A. C. Creswell (1919), then a captain in the Royal Engineers, add little of substance to this description by the Survey. Photographs from the early 1920s, however, show that at that time the area north of the surviving south wall of the tower was occupied by a number of rough stone-built houses (see Pl. XXXIX; Fig. 20a). A

report of 1922 also noted traces of an ancient reservoir near the well north-east of the tower, and a heap of squared stones and a column shaft lying a short distance north of the ruin, near a depression in the ground which seemed to the writer of the report to indicate the location of a cistern (*PAM*, 25.8.22). At this time the *khirba* was registered as state land, administered by the Department of Antiquities (cf. Palestine 1929, 26; 1948, 57).

In June 1945, the Department carried out some consolidation work on the east side of the surviving wall of the tower (*PAM*: 20.6.45). After the Arab–Israeli war of 1948, the remaining buildings of the hamlet north of the tower were destroyed by bulldozer. Already before this the eastern vault of the tower, visible in early photographs (Pls. XL–XLI), had also fallen or been destroyed. More consolidation work has since been done on the remaining part of the south wall, however, by the Israel Department of Antiquities. Today the site is surrounded on three sides by citrus plantations and on the south by a pair of large septic tanks. The wells just north-east of the tower have been replaced by a small pumping station. Apart from these intrusions of modern civilization, however, the site is now abandoned.

Pl. XXXIX. The Red Tower (al-Burj al-Ahmar), from the S-E (photo. pre-1947, courtesy of the Israel Dept. of Antiquities and Museums).

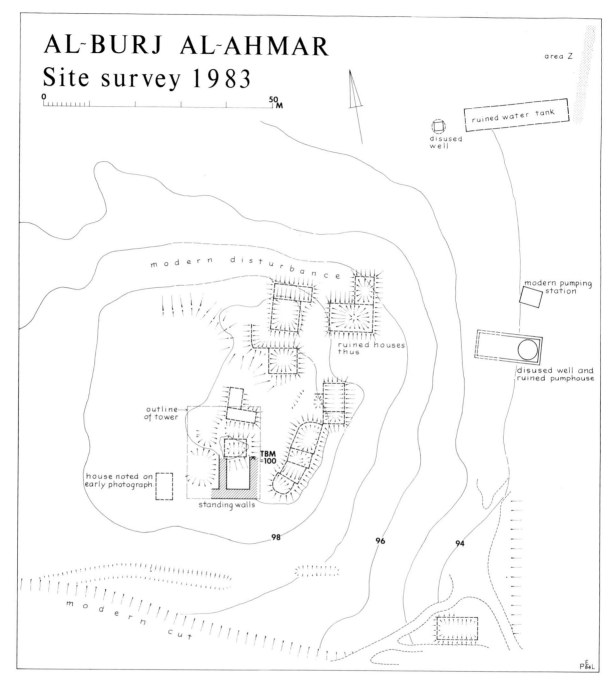

Fig. 20a. The Red Tower: site survey 1983.

Pl. XL. The Red Tower(al-Burj al-Ahmar): S wall from NW, showing intact E barrel-vault (photo. pre-1947, courtesy of the Israel Dept. of Antiquities and Museums).

Pl. XLI. The Red Tower (al-Burj al-Ahmar): S wall from SE (photo. pre-1947, courtesy of the Israel Dept. of Antiquities and Museums).

II. EXCAVATION STRATEGY

Before the excavation began, the visible remains at the site consisted of the south wall and part of the ground floor of the medieval tower-keep and some ruined mud and stone buildings of more recent date lying north and east of it. These buildings were grouped around the summit of a low knoll of roughly rectangular shape (Fig. 20a). The immediate aims of the excavation were, first, to establish the ground plan of the tower and, as far as resources permitted, its relationship to other contemporary structures built around it; and secondly, to recover objects of daily use, particularly coins and pottery, in order to establish a chronology for this and other sites in the region and to provide a fuller picture of the life of its inhabitants. Excavation was therefore concentrated on the tower itself, with other smaller soundings being made north and west of it (see Fig. 20b).

The initial choice of areas for excavation was influenced in part by the prior existence of two deep scoops, made apparently by a bulldozer at some time since 1948; these had removed much of the upper overburden of soil and rubble in two areas close to the visible remaining parts of the tower. In one of these, just north of the tower (Area B), a sounding, 2·5 × 5 m., was therefore excavated down to bedrock, in order to obtain a preview of the cultural sequence of the site. In the second area (Area C), a trench 2 m. wide was dug across the line of the destroyed western ground-floor chamber of the tower, exposing its collapsed west wall and its flagstone floor. Excavation here was later extended west to examine the foundation trench of the west wall (Area C1) and south to investigate what lay behind a medieval blocking wall, the line of which coincided quite by chance with the southern section line of our trench (C4).

In the area of the eastern ground-floor chamber of the tower, a long trench 1·50 m. wide was laid out north and south to follow the line of the central spine wall of the tower and to establish the position of the north wall (Area A). At the northern end of this trench, post-medieval buildings were encountered and the area of the trench was therefore enlarged (Area A2) in order to investigate them. A second trench (A1) was also dug at right angles to the first, across the line of the eastern

tower chamber, to provide, together with the trench in Area C, a complete cross-section through the tower; but when this became unsafe to work, owing to its depth and the looseness of its sides, it was extended up to the north wall of the tower (Area A3).

Two other soundings of 2 × 3 m. were also made as westward extensions to the trench of Area C–C1, in order to sample the stratification of the area of fairly level ground extending west of the tower (C2–C3). The outer of these (C3) picked up the outer wall of the castle; and the south return of the same wall, already partially visible in the side of a machine excavation made when the sewage ponds were dug, was investigated by means of another 3 × 4 m. sounding (C5).

On the final day of excavation, an attempt was made to locate the doorway which should have linked the two ground-floor chambers of the tower. This was quickly found by clearing out an early 20th-century pit in Area A. The west side of the door was also uncovered (Area C6). But time did not permit us to complete excavation of these areas, and they were promptly backfilled. A small area of topsoil was also excavated on the east side of the tower (Area D) to locate the outer face of the wall.

The depth of the overburden of collapsed medieval masonry as well as the difficulty of shifting large numbers of heavy blocks of stone from deep trenches placed severe restraints on what a small group of volunteers could achieve in the time available. A further limiting factor was the joint decision made by the excavator with the Department of Antiquities to backfill the trenches before the winter rains, so as to ensure the future preservation of the monument; this was in fact done by machine within days of the completion of archaeological work on the site. In spite of these difficulties, the main objectives of the excavation were achieved, thanks largely to the hard work of the volunteers. More could doubtless be learnt if a larger area were to be uncovered. But this can now be left to a future date, when it may perhaps be possible to combine such as excavation with careful consolidation of the exposed masonry, so as to allow the castle to be seen again as a standing medieval building.

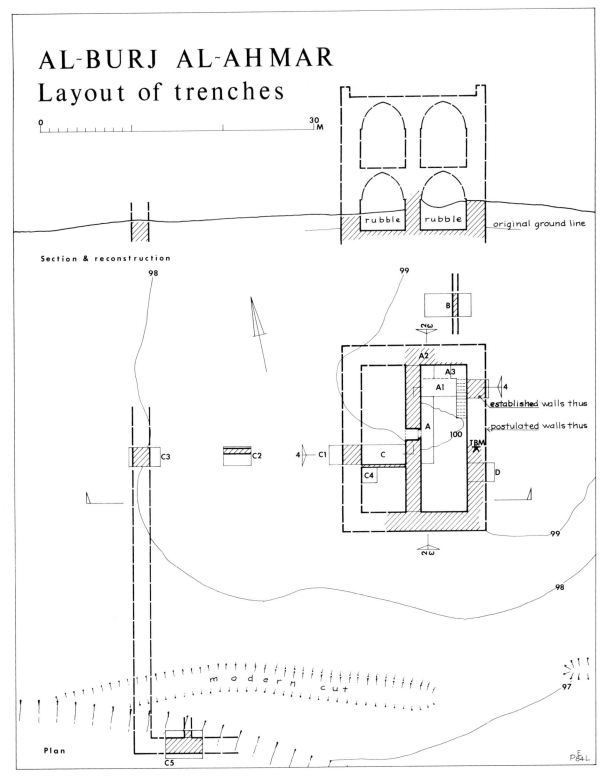

AL-BURJ AL-AHMAR
Layout of trenches

0 —————————— 30 M

rubble   rubble   original ground line

Section & reconstruction

established walls thus

postulated walls thus

TBM

modern cut

Plan

Fig. 20b. The Red Tower: layout of trenches 1983.
(Note: temporary bench mark [TBM] = 100 m. above site datum [ASD] = c. 42 m. above sea level)

III. THE STRUCTURAL DEVELOPMENT OF THE SITE

1. THE MEDIEVAL TOWER
(Areas A–A3, C, C1, C4, C6, D)

PHASE A—BYZANTINE AND EARLY ISLAMIC

Layers predating the construction of the tower were excavated in two areas, at the north-western corner of the east tower chamber (Area A) and on either side of the tower's west wall (Areas C and C1).

In Area A (Fig. 21b), bedrock consisting of red sand (*hamra*) was encountered at 95·60 m. ASD. This was overlain by a layer of brown sandy soil (**156**) containing charcoal flecks; this layer was about 0·90–1·00 m. thick, the surface rising slightly towards the east. The only finds from it were two sherds of combed Byzantine coarse ware.

In Area C (Fig. 21a), the same sandy bedrock (at 96·15 m. ASD) was overlain by a harder grey clayey layer (**103**), 0·36 m. thick, containing small pieces of white mortar, charcoal and pottery. The pottery included Byzantine rilled amphora and cooking-pot sherds as well as some later Byzantine or early Islamic grey-surfaced rilled amphorae with white painting. The upper part of the same layer (**94**) was similar, but with less charcoal; the pottery included some unglazed early Islamic types with a fine white fabric and, on the surface, some 12th-century intrusions. These layers sealed the mouth of a pit of uncertain dimensions (**111**), cut into bedrock, from which two Byzantine coarse-ware sherds were recovered.

West of the tower (Area C1) the excavation was not continued to bedrock because of the dangerousness of the trench. The layer corresponding to layer **94** east of the tower wall, however, was excavated from 97·05 m. ASD. to a depth of some 0·70 m. before excavation was abandoned. It was light brown, loose and sandy, containing charcoal and small pieces of mortar (**83 + 113**). The same range of Byzantine and early Islamic pottery was recovered from it, as well as some glass.

These brown sandy or clayey layers overlying bedrock may perhaps be interpreted as field soil, which accumulated gradually from the 6th to the 8th century. Evidently there was occupation at this period near-by. Either this area was not built on, however, or what structures there were would have been destroyed and levelled prior to the construction of the tower.

PHASE B—CONSTRUCTION OF THE MEDIEVAL TOWER

The tower was rectangular in plan, measuring some 19·7 m. (N-S) × 15·5 m (E-W) overall, with walls about 2·2 m. thick (see Fig. 24). Its ground floor consisted of two barrel-vaulted chambers, built side by side and aligned north–south, separated from each other by a spine wall running down the centre of the building.

Foundations and Floors

In the area west of the tower (Area C1), the beginning of construction work was represented by a spread of charcoal (**82**) at 97·05 m. ASD, no more than 0·02 m. thick; this may perhaps represent the burning-off of vegetation before the laying-out of the medieval buildings began. This layer was in turn cut by the foundation trench (**84**) of the west wall of the tower (**12**). This trench extended 0·34 m. from the outer face of the wall and was probably about 1·80 m. deep, judging by its depth on the other side. Finds from its fill included Byzantine and early Islamic wares (including a piece of 9th- to 11th-century glazed polychrome ware), as well as some glazed cooking-pot fragments and other medieval coarse wares. The wall itself (**12**) was 2·17 m. thick and coated on the outside with a white mortar render.

The foundation trench, once filled, was overlain by a dark brown layer (**81**), 0·15 m. thick, containing charcoal and small white stones and becoming looser and greyer in the northern part of the trench. This was in turn covered by a deposit of crushed limestone, 0·20 m. thick but thinning out to the north where it was overlain by lenses of dark red and orange sand, containing white stones. These deposits (**79**) seem likely to represent building debris associated with the work of construction on the upper part of the tower. They were themselves cut through by a pit (**80**), 0·28 m. deep and 0·26–0·38 m. wide though splaying out at the top, which contained a loose fill of small pieces of mortary rubble. This had the appearance of a post-hole, perhaps intended to support part of the scaffolding associated with the construction of the wall (see Fig. 23).

On the inside of the tower, the ground level was lowered by some 0·50 m. The surface thus exposed was pierced by three stake holes (**97**): the first two about 0·15 m. deep and 0·10 m. wide, spaced 0·35 m. apart, and the third about 0·07 m. deep and 0·16 m. deep placed 0·14 m. east of the first two (see Fig. 23). It is not certain whether these belonged to the period of construction of the tower or to an earlier phase.

The foundation trench (**93**) of the west wall (**12**) was 0·40 m. wide on the inside, narrowing to 0·16 m. at the bottom, and was 1·20 m. deep (see Fig. 21a). It was evidently filled in as the wall was constructed, as was shown by the mortary spreads which interspersed its fill level with each course of the wall. The fill was otherwise brown-orange, containing mortar, charcoal and lumps of the layers through which it had been cut. Finds were similar to those in **84** and included another piece of 9th- to 11th-century glazed polychrome ware.

The area inside the tower was then levelled up with red sand (**92**) to form a flat surface at 96·55 m. ASD; in this sand was found a piece of turquoise alkaline-glazed pottery. Over this layer was laid a flag-stone floor at 96·75 m. ASD (Pl. XLII). The stones forming this floor (**33**) were up to 0·34 × 0·50 m. in size and 0·21 m. thick. They were bedded in strong white mortar containing smallish stones, which also sealed the gaps between them. The arrangement of the flags was singular. A

Pl. XLII. The Red Tower (al-Burj al-Ahmar): Spine-wall of tower from W, showing paved floor of W chamber and section through collapsed rubble (compare Fig. 21a) (photo. author).

single line of stones was arranged longitudinally down both sides of the chamber and three rows of stones were set the same way down the centre; the other blocks were arranged at right angles to these. However, the rows forming the spine down the middle of the room were not placed centrally, but were displaced by the width of one block to the west (see Fig. 23). The flag-stone floor ran up against the west (**12**) and east (**18**) walls of the chamber.

At the northern end of the eastern chamber (Area A), excavation was able to show conclusively what had already been suspected from examination of the standing remains of the tower, namely that its spine wall (**18**) had been built only after the foundations and lower parts of the outer walls of the tower (**12**, **44**, **100**, and here **101**) had been constructed. In this area the north wall (**101**) was set in a foundation trench (**155**) 0·90 m. deep with a flat bottom (95·64 m. ASD); this was 1·10 m. wide on the inside, narrowing to 0·55 m. (see Fig. 27a). The fill was of medium brown earth containing pieces of mortar and lumps of backfill from the layers through which it had been cut; it contained Byzantine and early Islamic pottery, together with some medieval coarse ware. The wall was built from the base up in ashlar and had a chamfered plinth just below the level of the prepared ground surface inside the tower.

The tower's spine wall (**18**) abutted the inner face of the north wall (**101**). Its foundation trench (**154**) was 0·36–0·52 m. wide at the top, narrowing almost to nothing at the bottom, and was 1·00 m. deep, or about 0·10 m. lower than the north wall (see Fig. 21b). This trench cut through the fill of the foundation trench of the north wall (**155**). Its own fill consisted of a backfilling of the layers through which it had been dug, including red sand (bedrock) and lumps of darker soil, with increasing amounts of rubble and mortar towards the bottom. The finds were almost exclusively Byzantine. The tops of both these backfilled trenches were then levelled up with red sand. No evidence was found for any "made" floor in this phase, though it could be that there was one that was later removed.

The excavated evidence for dating the foundations of the tower is far from conclusive. There were no coins from this phase. The pottery from the foundation trench in Area A consisted entirely of unglazed sherds, mostly residual Byzantine or early Islamic coarse wares, though including six sherds of medieval amphorae with white painting on the outside. In Area C–C1, the assemblage was similar, though here some glazed pottery was also found, including two sherds of 9th to 11th-century polychrome ware found in the foundation trench one either side of the wall, eight sherds from cooking pots and two from green-painted slip-wares, possibly of the early 12th-century. From beneath the stone floor (**33**) of the western chamber came a tiny piece of turquoise alkaline-glazed pottery (context **92**); but although this

AL-BURJ AL-AHMAR
Trenches A & C - sections

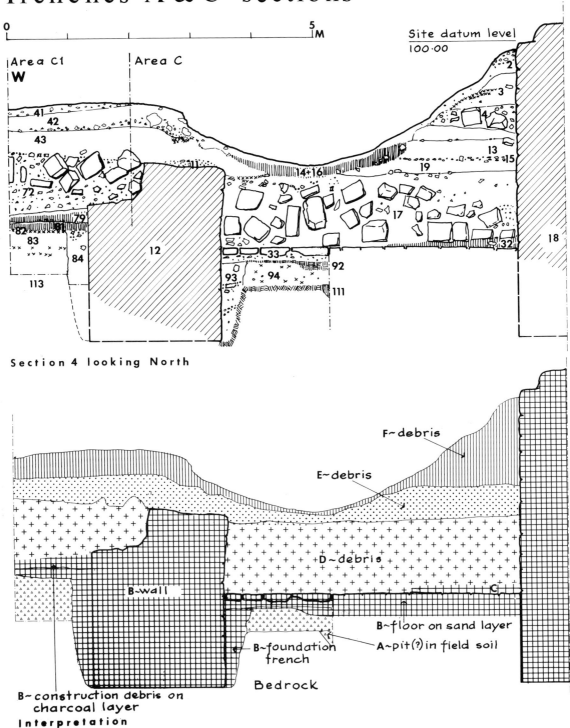

Site datum level
100.00

Area C1   Area C

W

0   5 M

Section 4 looking North

F~debris

E~debris

D~debris

B~wall

B~floor on sand layer

A~pit(?) in field soil

B~foundation trench

Bedrock

B~construction debris on charcoal layer

Interpretation

Fig. 21a. The Red Tower: Trench C–C1, Section 4 looking north.
(For structural sequence see Fig. 37)

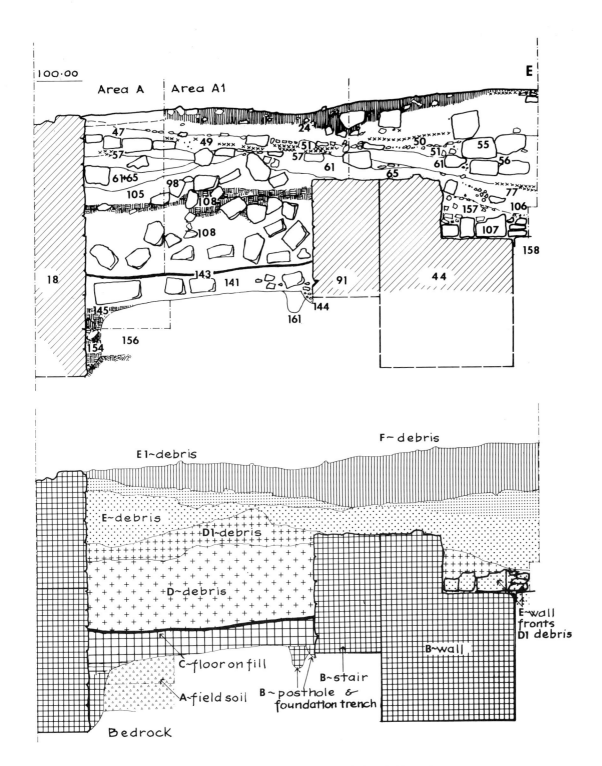

Fig. 21b. The Red Tower: Trench A, Section 4 looking north.
(For structural sequence see Fig. 35)

AL-BURJ AL-AHMAR
Trench A-section

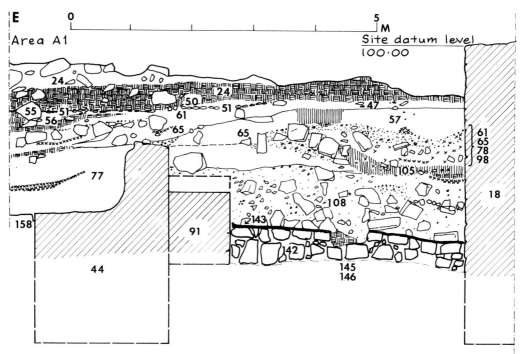

Section 4 looking South

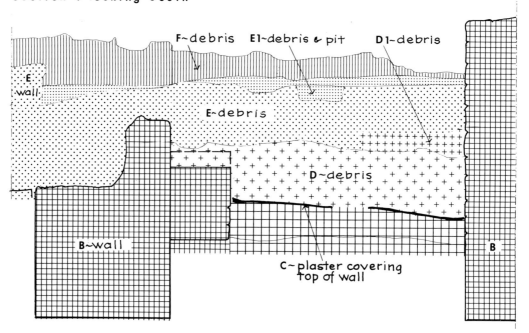

Interpretation

Fig. 22a. The Red Tower: Trench A, Section 4 looking south.
(For structural sequence see Fig. 35)

Trench C, C1-section

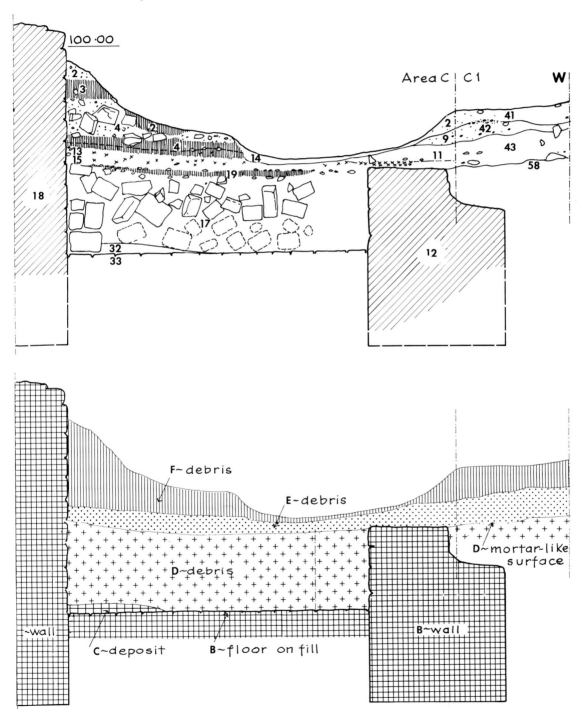

Fig. 22b. *The Red Tower: Trench C–C1, Section 4 looking south.*
(*For structural sequence see Fig. 37*)

AL-BURJ AL-AHMAR
Trenches C,C1,C4

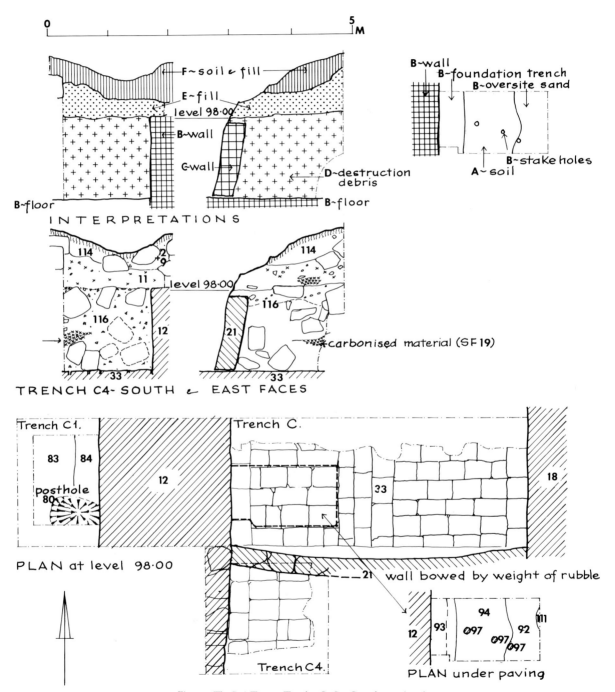

Fig. 23. The Red Tower: Trenches C, C1, C4: plans and sections.
(For structural sequence see Fig. 37)

AL-BURJ AL-AHMAR
Tower-plan

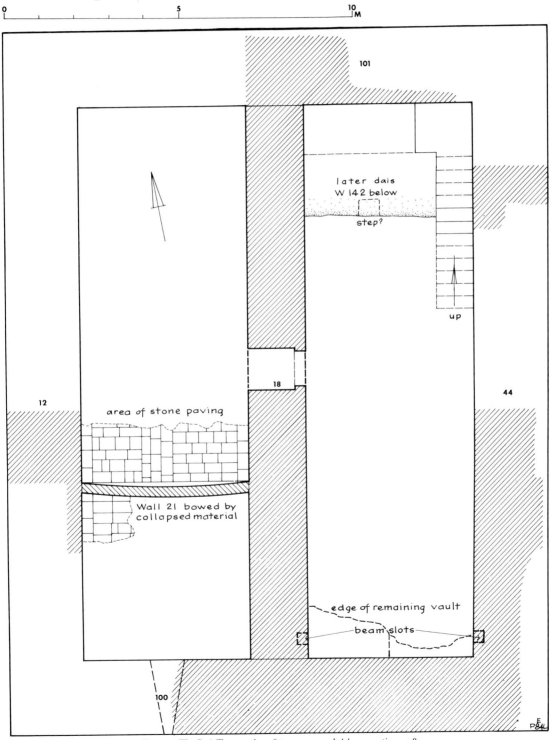

0   5   10 M

101

later dais
W 142 below

step?

up

12

area of stone paving

18

44

Wall 21 bowed by
collapsed material

edge of remaining vault

beam slots

100

Fig. 24. The Red Tower: plan of tower as revealed by excavation, 1983.

might suggest a 12th-century date for the floor, it does not necessarily affect the dating of the tower wall which structurally precedes it. More significant for dating this group perhaps is the absence of certain types of glazed and unglazed pottery diagnostic of the later 12th or 13th centuries. On archaeological grounds a date in the first half of the 12th century therefore seems likely for the construction of the tower.

Masonry of the Tower

The masonry of the tower is best studied at the south wall, which still survives to a height of some 14 m. above

the floor level inside the tower (or 12 m. above ground level outside) (Pls. XLIII–XLIV; Figs. 25a–b). This wall is 2·13 m. thick at its base. It is faced inside and out with ashlars between 0·33 and 0·46 m. in height. Where the core is exposed, it is seen to have been laid course by course with the facing. The fill consists of largish blocks, some roughly squared and evidently reused, set in a reddish sandy mortar containing a small amount of chalk and other rubble.

On the south face, thirty-six courses of the facing survive above ground level. The building work was carried out in at least three stages, defined by a 0·05 m.

Pl. XLIII. The Red Tower (al-Burj al-Ahmar): S wall from S (photo. author).

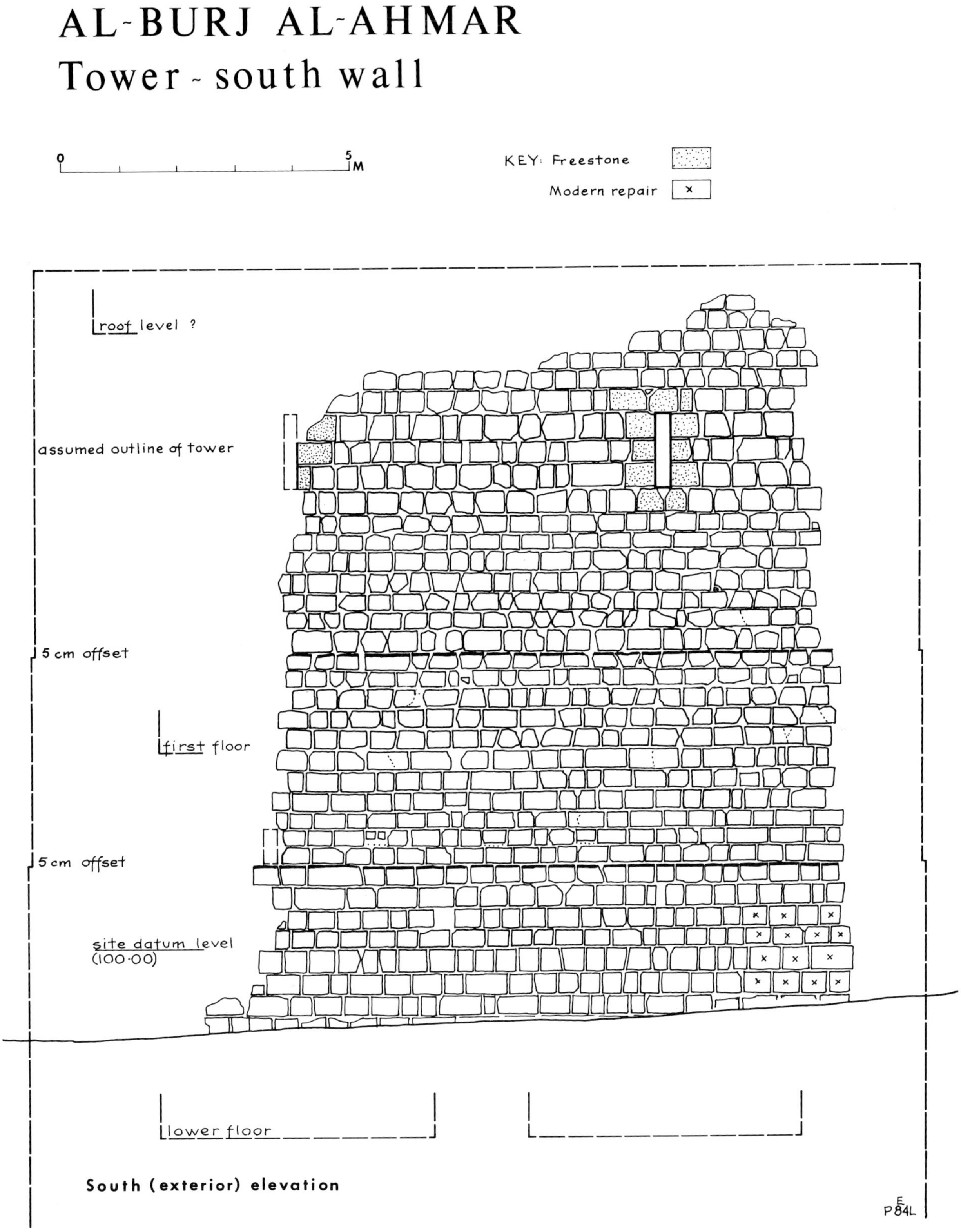

AL-BURJ AL-AHMAR
Tower - south wall

0 |_____|___|___|___|___| 5
                            M

KEY: Freestone [▓▓▓]

Modern repair [x]

roof level ?

assumed outline of tower

5 cm offset

first floor

5 cm offset

site datum level
(100·00)

South (exterior) elevation

lower floor

E
P 84L

Fig. 25a. The Red Tower: South tower wall elevation from south.

offset between each stage: the lowest stage of eight courses (2·50 m.) took the building up to the level of the springing of the first-floor vault; the second, eleven courses high (3·10 m.), took the wall up to just above the level of the first floor; and the third completed the full surviving height of the wall (see Fig. 34). Some later repairs are visible on the east side of the surviving wall and one or two of the blocks low down in the facing have also been replaced in recent times (see Fig. 25). It is clear, however, that not all of the original facing stones are bedded correctly. One in particular, in the fourth course above ground level, is not only bedded the wrong way but is also severely burnt on one face; evidently it had come from an earlier building that had been destroyed by fire. Most of the facing blocks indeed seem to be reused; many have rounded edges and it is probably partly for this reason that there is galletting between them, using largish stones up to 0·12 m. across. The pointing, where it survives, is thickly applied and extends over the face of the blocks to form a flat surface; the mortar used for it is white, containing some orange sand, and has horizontal or herring-bone trowel

Pl. XLIV. The Red Tower (al-Burj al-Aḥmar): S wall from N (photo. author).

AL-BURJ AL-AHMAR
Tower-south wall

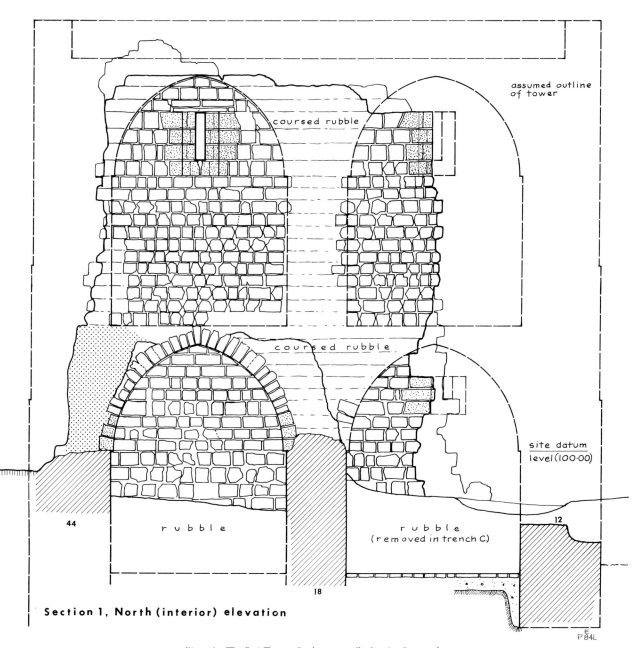

0   5 M

KEY: Freestone
Modern repair

assumed outline of tower

coursed rubble

coursed rubble

site datum level (100.00)

44   rubble

rubble (removed in trench C)

18

12

Section 1, North (interior) elevation

E P 84L

Fig. 25b. The Red Tower: South tower wall, elevation from north.

impressions made in it, presumably in order to receive some kind of plastering or render. Similar pointing may be seen in the Benedictine convent building at Bethany and in the Templar castle of *Maldoim* (Qalᶜat ad-Damm) between Jerusalem and Jericho.

The Ground Floor of the Tower

The ground-floor or basement vaulting of the tower consisted of two barrel-vaults with pointed profiles arranged north-south (see Fig. 24). They were each 4·80–4·85 m. wide, 15·54 m. long and 6·00 m. high. They were constructed of irregular pieces of split stone set in mortar, springing from three courses of finely dressed voussoirs along either side. The ceiling was covered with a fine white plaster. Two slots for wooden centring (0·35 m. wide, 0·55 m. high and 0·31 m. deep) survive in the east vault, 0·40 m. from the south wall. One of the key-stones found in the collapse at the northern end of this vault had set in it an iron ring (see Fig. 56, no. 18).

The two vaults were divided by a spine wall (**18**), 1·65 m. thick, roughly in the centre of which was a door opening from the eastern into the western chamber. This was evidently the door seen by Conder and Kitchener in 1873, but since completely covered by debris. It was 0·92 m. wide with jambs 0·35 m. thick,

widening to 1·13 m. on the west. The arch was pointed and had a double row of voussoirs on both faces. The door would probably have been about 2·0 m. high, but time did not permit it to be excavated down to the threshold (Fig. 27b).

No evidence for any doorway was found in the outer wall of the tower. It seems unlikely that there would have been one in the western half of the tower, for if so the door in the spine wall would have opened the wrong way. This chamber did, however, have a small rectangular window in its south wall, 4·20 m. above floor level. It was about 1·00 m. high and 0·60 m. wide, narrowing to the outside; but only the east reveal survives (see Fig. 25). In the east chamber, the only possible position in which there could have been a door would have been in the east wall directly opposite the door in the spine wall; this is the only place where the wall is not either standing or revealed by excavation. It is quite possible, however, that there was no door at all at this level.

The Staircase

The eastern chamber communicated with the first floor by means of a massive stone staircase (**91**), built against the north and east sides of the room (Pls. XLV–XLVI; Figs. 24 and 26). This staircase was structurally

Pl. XLV. The Red Tower (al-Burj al-Ahmar): Excavated N end of E tower chamber, showing staircase arch from S (compare Fig. 26) (photo. author).

Pl. XLVI. The Red Tower (al-Burj al-Ahmar): Excavated N end of E tower chamber from W, showing remains of staircase and Wall 142 (photo. author).

later than the walls of the tower against which it was built. Whether it was an original feature or a later insertion is therefore not absolutely certain, though it seems reasonable to assume that it was part of the original design. The lower part of the stair, built against the east wall, was 1·08 m. wide. The steps were made from large single blocks of stone (1·08 × 0·49 × 0·22 m.), forming treads 0·22 m. high and 0·32–0·34 m. wide. They were supported on a solid rising plinth of rubble masonry faced with roughly squared reused blocks. At the north-east corner of the room, the staircase would have turned to the left and have continued up through the barrel-vault to the floor above. This part of it was 1·37 m. wide and was carried on a semi-vault of which only the base and springers survived, constructed of finely cut ashlars.

The foundation of the staircase was slighter than those of the tower walls and was set in a narrow foundation trench (**144**) filled with yellow clay and stones (see Fig. 21b). In the angle where it changed direction there was a post-hole (**161**), some 0·32 m. deep and 0·25–0·30 m. wide (Fig. 26). Its purpose is uncertain; it might perhaps have been either for a scaffolding post or for a post supporting a wooden balustrade for the stair.

The First Floor

The vaulting arrangement of the first floor may be reconstructed using the evidence of the surviving south wall and the ground plan as revealed by excavation (see Figs. 25b and 34). It seems likely that it was vaulted with six bays of groin-vaults, arranged in two rows of three bays each, corresponding to the line of the barrel-vaults beneath. These vaults would have sprung from rectangular pilasters, one of which (1·65 m. wide and projecting some 0·25–0·30 m.) still survives on the south wall, and presumably from two rectangular piers in the centre of the room built directly over the spine wall of the ground floor.

The south wall narrowed to about 1·75 m. at first-floor level. In it were two rectangular windows, about 1·70 m. high and 1·0 m. wide, narrowing to 0·30 m. on the outside. Their function seems to have been to provide light rather than positions for firing arrows from, since they would have been 4 m. above floor level. If this reconstruction of the vaulting system is correct, there could also have been three more openings in each of the two longer walls and a further two in the north wall. Alternatively it is possible that one of these bays contained the principal first-floor entrance to the tower; but further excavation, particularly in the area east of the tower, would be necessary to determine exactly where and at what level this entrance was.

The first floor had a tesselated pavement consisting of plain white limestone tesserae, 3–4 cm. across, interspersed with larger chunks of broken marble veneer. A large amount of this material, including several

AL-BURJ AL-AHMAR
Tower staircase

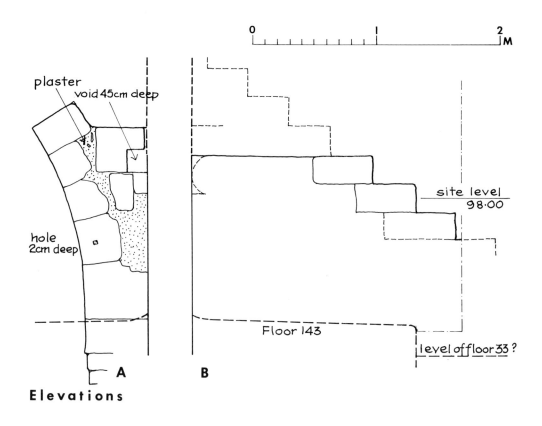

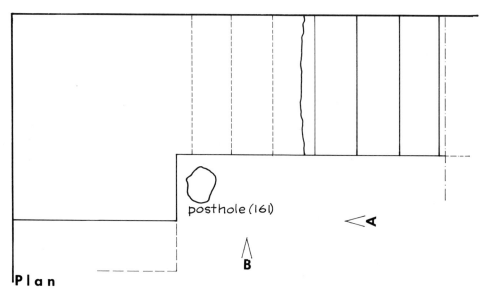

Fig. 26. *The Red Tower: plan and elevations of staircase.*

fragments still held together in a mortar bedding, were found in the collapse of the first-floor vault into the northern part of the east ground-floor chamber (Area A). Also found in this collapse were two pieces of white wall-plaster, decorated with grey painted lines.

Phase C—Later Alterations to the Medieval Tower

In a later phase a rough dry-stone wall (**142**) was constructed across the northern end of the east ground-floor chamber of the tower, 2·64 m. from the north wall (Area A). This wall was 0·46–0·61 m. wide and 0·40–0·60 m. high, with what may have been a step 0·60 m. wide in the centre; it was constructed with two courses of reused blocks and no mortar (Pl. XLVI; Figs. 22a and 27a). The wall was evidently intended to do no more than serve as revetment for levelling up the area between it and the north wall. The fill for this levelling (**121 + 141 + 146**) consisted of blocks of stone packed with red-brown earth containing quantities of 13th-century pottery, a dispersed hoard of 24 base silver coins, fragments of metalwork, glass, bones and other rubbish. The coins suggest a date for the fill after the time of the Third Crusade (1189/91) (see pp. 128; 175, nos. 5–28).

The fill and the wall were then covered with a coating of beaten clay and plaster (**143**), which ran up against the tower and stair walls. It would thus have formed a kind of dais, 3·20 m. wide and 0·60 m. high, extending beneath the stair vault to the end of the chamber (Fig. 24). It was unfortunately not possible to locate the floor level of the rest of the chamber, because of the dangerous state of the south section of the trench.

Another wall (**21**) was also built across the western chamber of the tower, 4·80 m. from its south wall (Pl. XLVII; Figs. 23–24). This was constructed with a single thickness of stone blocks, 0·27–0·29 m. wide, and was covered on both sides with pink plaster. It was built directly on top of floor **33** and ran against walls **12** and **18**. It survived, like the west wall (**12**), only 1·20 m. above the floor level; and the collapse of the vault above had caused it to bow out by some 0·20 m. towards the south. Its function is unexplained. If it had an opening in it, this must have been more than 1·20 m. above the floor; and the enclosed space south of it (Area C4) was apparently empty when the vaulting collapsed.

The existence of a stone floor in the western chamber would have made it easier to keep clean, and this may explain why little rubbish had accumulated on it when it was buried. A deposit of brown soil (**32**) running up against the east and cross walls (**18** and **21**), however,

Pl. XLVII. The Red Tower (al-Burj al-Ahmar): W tower chamber, Wall 21 from NE (photo. author).

contained material similar to that found beneath the raised dais in the east vault. This even included fragments from the same painted handmade jar (Fig. 42, no. 7). It would appear therefore that the floor was not swept between the period of the laying of the plaster floor in the eastern vault and the collapse of the tower, and this in turn would suggest that no great lapse of time occurred between the two events.

Phase D—The Destruction of the Medieval Tower

The tower was subsequently destroyed in a methodical fashion. The facing and up to half of the rubble core of the east and west walls (**44** and **12**) were robbed out, causing the walls to fall outwards under pressure from the vaulting (see Figs. 21–22). The collapse of the west wall extended at least 13 m. from the base of the wall (see below, Area C2). In both ground-floor chambers the barrel-vaults seem to have fallen straight downwards; rows of voussoirs were found in these areas piled next to each other directly where they had fallen.

It seems likely that fire was used in undermining the outer walls. On the west, the heat had reactivated some of the lime mortar, so that the top of the collapsed rubble (**58**) appeared, on excavation, like a hard mortared surface almost indistinguishable from the surviving mortared core of the wall. Beneath this hard crust, however, the rubble became looser (**72**) (Figs. 21a, 22b).

In the same area (C–C1) the collapsed rubble of the western wall had been levelled off at around 98 m. ASD, or 1·20 m. above the medieval floor level. The collapse of the vault inside the chamber (**17**) had caused the cross-wall (**21**) to bow out by some 0·20 m. to the south (Fig. 23), suggesting that the central part of the vault had fallen before the southern part (**116**). A lens of carbonized material found in the collapse south of the cross-wall appears to have been derived from the first floor; it is analysed below (pp. 187–191).

In the eastern chamber, the collapsed rubble (**108**, **133**) and the north wall (**101**) were levelled off at about the same level (98 m. ASD), though the east wall (**44**) and staircase (**91**) survived some 0·40 m. higher than that (Figs. 21b, 22a). The south wall, however, was allowed to remain standing; and indeed most of it survives to this day almost to its full height. The southern part of the east ground-floor vault also survived for some 7·6 m. in length until sometime after the First World War (see Pls. XL–XLI). Evidently the intention of the destroyers was to leave the castle indefensible, and when they had achieved that aim they saw no point in expending further time or energy in demolishing it.

The date of the destruction should obviously be placed after 1189, the *terminus post quem* for the group of finds sealed by the plaster floor in Phase C. The finds from the collapse, however, suggest that the upper layers of the rubble continued to be disturbed and picked over (perhaps by people in search of building materials) for a century or more before finally being levelled off and sealed by other deposits. The pottery from it includes wares of the late 13th and 14th centuries, among them a large amount of handmade village pottery as well as glazed cooking pots, slip and slip-painted wares and under-glaze painted pottery. A 16th-century Ottoman coin (no. 33: context **116**) found south of the cross wall in the western vault (Area C4) seems certain to be intrusive; but two Mamluk coins, dated 1363/77 (no. 32: context **114**) and 1380/1 (no. 30: context **114**) respectively, found lying on the levelled surface of the collapse, provide a more plausible terminal date for this phase in 1380 or after.

Phase D1—The Upper Layers of Collapse in Areas A–A3

Because of the looseness of the rubble deposits in areas A–A3, the upper layers of the medieval collapse were treated as a separate sub-phase to reduce the possibility of the group of finds from Phase D being contaminated by intrusions from Phase E. The range of pottery from these layers, however, turns out to be little different to that from Phase D. The only coin from this sub-phase is a Mamluk issue dated 1343/4 (no. 29: context **98**).

Phase E—Later Medieval and Post-Medieval Occupation

Following the destruction of the tower and the levelling out of the resultant pile of rubble, the areas examined by excavation were covered by further tipping of building debris, which in places (Area A1) reached a depth of over a metre. These deposits, however, cannot represent simply the upper layers of destruction of the medieval castle, for they also contained quantities of ash, fragments of dometic ovens, animal bones and pottery of the 18th century and later. They were evidently therefore the result of continued occupation of the site; but in the areas excavated there was at first little evidence for structures associated with this occupation.

In Area C, no trace of any buildings was found at all, even though a photograph from the 1920s shows a house standing near this position (Figs. 21a, 22b). Bulldozing in this area after 1948, however, had removed the upper layers in places to within 0·25 m. of the top of the medieval destruction. Immediately over this destruction was a layer of brown soil containing charcoal flecks (**19**), 0·16–0·20 m. thick, overlain in turn by a 0·08 m. thick spread of small stones and pottery representing an exposed surface (**15**). This was then covered by a grey ash layer (**13**), 0·20–0·30 m. thick, disturbed, however, by roots and rodent holes where it ran against the tower wall (**18**). The pottery from these layers differed in a number of respects from that of the destruction layers. Glazed cooking pots, for example, which accounted for over 17% of the pottery assemblage of Phase D in this area, were completely absent, indicating that few or none of the finds from this group were likely to have been derived from the earlier phase. The group does include yellow glazed slip-painted and green glazed slip-ware, however, as well as some under-glaze painted and an increasing proportion of handmade village pottery; but grey-fired coarse wares, which are a feature of the late Ottoman groups, are almost completely absent. The two Mamluk coins already referred to (see Phase D) provide a *terminus post quem* of 1380/1. These layers therefore seem likely to represent domestic rubbish from occupation of the site from the late 14th century onwards.

In Area A, the layers of tipping were more confused and it was not possible to define a distinct 14th- or 15th-century phase of occupation (Figs. 21b, 22a, 27a). As in Area C, however, it seems that there were at first no buildings. Just east of the eastern wall of the tower (**44**), however, there were found traces of what may have been the room of a house (Fig. 21b). Just over half of the outer part of the tower wall had been robbed out in Phase D in this area (A1) down to a level of 97·7 m. ASD. Part of the rubble (**157**) associated with this robbing was now cleared away and the remainder faced with a crude walling of reused stones (**107**) running east–west. The surviving mortar core of the tower wall (**44**) served as a floor, which was also extended to the east with a layer of paving stones (**158**). The extent of this room, however, if such it was, is not known. The fill (**77**) which subsequently covered its destruction contained two sherds of 18th-century Kütahya pottery (see Fig. 51, nos. 88–89).

West of this, in the area covering the collapsed eastern vault of the tower, there accumulated a pile of red and grey ash and silts, interspersed with blocks of stone from destroyed buildings and fragments of domestic ovens. Some of these ovens were found more or less *in situ*. They had evidently been set originally into the ground surface in the open air. They consisted of domed circular structures, some 0·50 m. in diameter with walls 0·02–0·04 m. thick, made of fired clay. Their bases were normally made up of layers of broken coarse pottery, most of it Byzantine and presumably collected for this purpose from elsewhere on the site.

Eventually, after serving for an indeterminate length of time as an area of waste ground between houses, the area was itself partially built over. The walls of the first building to be constructed did not survive. A white plaster floor (**40**) was uncovered in Area A2, however,

extending some 2·4 m. and 1·8 m. respectively from the north and east sides of the trench (Figs. 27a–28). It seems likely that this floor extended at least 4 m. further north where it appeared in Area B (**164**) (Fig. 29b). The plaster was laid on a bedding of red sand. To the south of it was uncovered an area of stone paving (**48**), covering a rectangular area measuring some 1·5 (E-W) × 2 m. (N-S). The paving stones were all reused blocks, up to 0·25/0·30 × 0·50/0·60 m. in size and 0·20 m. thick. A difference of only 0·03 m. was recorded between the levels of the two floors (*c.* 99 m. ASD). Although the walls of the building did not survive, it seems likely that the plaster floor represented the interior of the house and the paved floor part of the yard in front of the main door. One may envisage this courtyard lying south of the house and enclosed on the west by the surviving top of the tower's spine wall (**18**), on the south by the north wall of the village house occupying the surviving tower vault and on the east by what appears to have been a rough dry-stone wall made of reused blocks of stone (**55**). It would thus have measured some 6·2 (E-W) × 8 m. (N-S), the ground sloping down slightly towards the east.

PHASE E1—CONTINUED POST-MEDIEVAL OCCUPATION

The building erected at the end of Phase E was subsequently destroyed. Its plaster floor (**40**) was overlain by a layer of red sandy clay, up to 0·15 m. thick, probably representing the collapse of its walls which would have been either of mud or of mud and stone, of which the latter had been robbed for reuse. The demolition debris extended into the courtyard area, where mixed layers of grey and red-brown soil containing lumps of charcoal and plaster were found (**49** and **56**), overlying the external paving (**48**) and running up against the east wall (**55**).

The first phase of rebuilding consisted of a wall (**39**), 0·65 m. wide, surviving only one course (0·32 m.) high, which ran north–south and probably abutted the northern surviving end of the spine wall of the tower (**18**) (see Fig. 28). No floor level was found associated with this wall.

This wall was subsequently incorporated into another, more substantial wall (**23**, **38**), 0·75 m. wide and surviving to a height of 0·80 m. This followed the same course as the first, but turned at right angles to the east some 0·60 m. from the north end of the trench (Fig. 28). It was constructed with irregularly-shaped stones bonded with red sandy clay. The excavated part of it seems to represent the west and part of the north sides of a rectangular building, some 3 × 6·5 m., aligned east–west, which could be traced on the ground surface even before excavation began (see Fig. 20). In the area excavated just south of it (Area A1) was found a spread

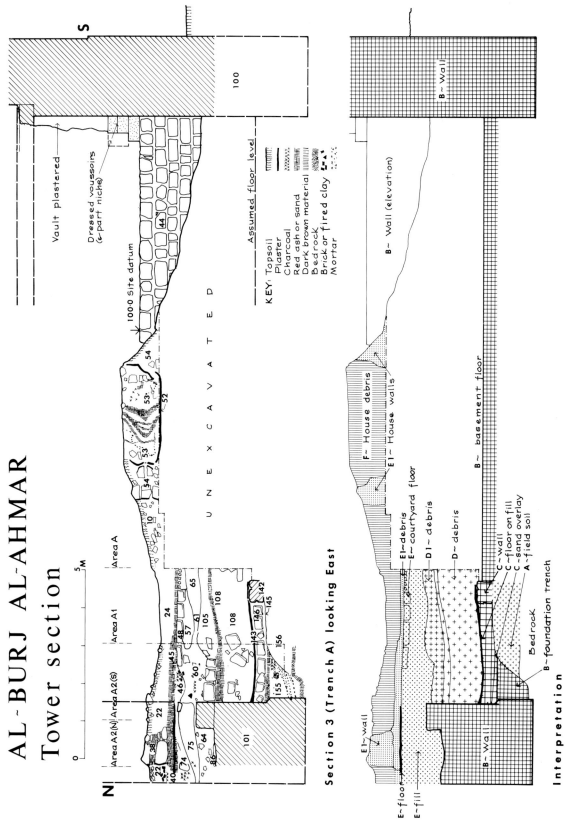

AL~BURJ AL~AHMAR
Tower section

KEY: Topsoil
Plaster
Charcoal
Red ash or sand
Dark brown material
Bedrock
Brick or fired clay
Mortar

Section 3 (Trench A) looking East

Interpretation

Fig. 27a. The Red Tower: Trench A, section 3 looking east.
(For structural sequence see Fig. 35)

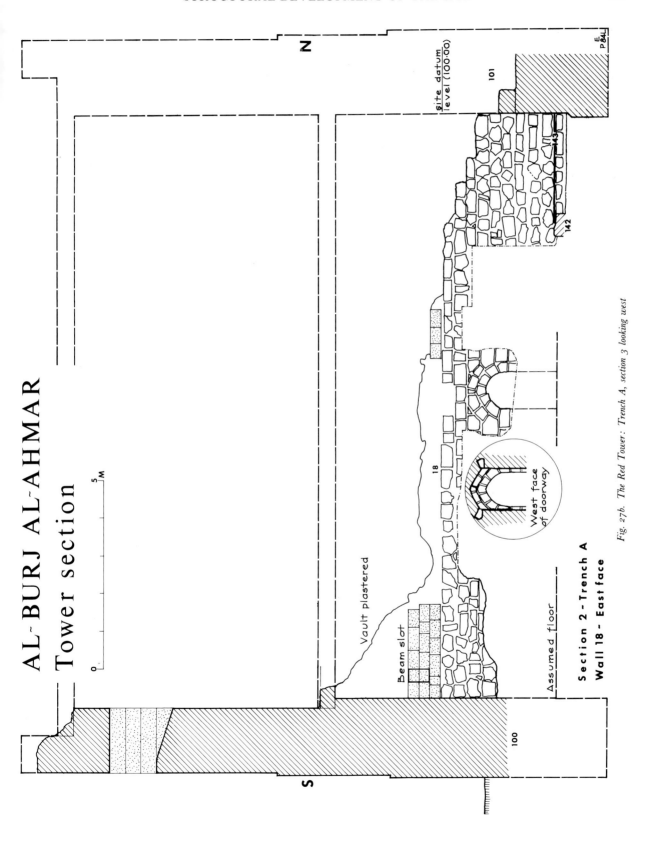

Fig. 27b. The Red Tower: Trench A, section 3 looking west

AL-BURJ AL-AHMAR

Trenches A1, A2

Plans and sections

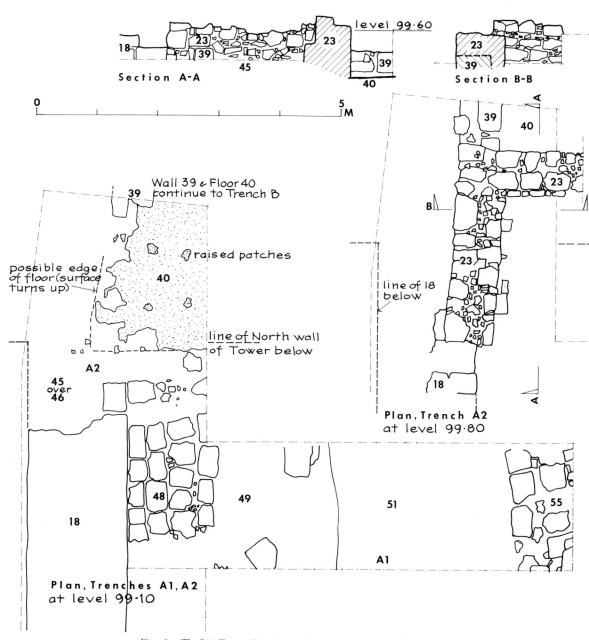

Fig. 28a. The Red Tower: Trenches A1–A2: plans and sections of later features.
(For structural sequence see Fig. 35)

Interpretation

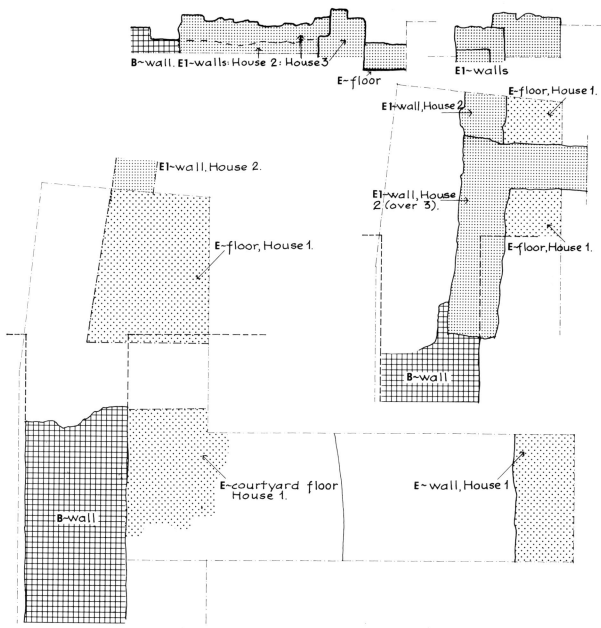

Fig. 28b. The Red Tower: Trenches A1–A2: plans and sections of later features.
(For structural sequence see Fig. 35)

of smallish stones (**51**), probably representing simply a weathered surface rather than deliberate cobbling, which ran up against the row of large stone blocks (**55**) that delimited the east side of the yard (Figs. 21b, 22a, 28a).

Further south (Area A), remains of another building were excavated (Figs. 20, 27a). This seems to have been a house, measuring some 5 × 6 m. overall, with walls of mud and stone (**54**) and its floor and interior wall faces covered with white plaster (**52**). The roof, which had collapsed into the building, was evidently of wood covered with layers of mud (**53**). At the western end of the building, a pit (**160**), 2 m. wide and 1·2 m. deep, had been dug to give access to the vaulted space inside the doorway which had formerly connected the two ground-floor chambers of the tower (Fig. 27b). The sides of the pit and of the exposed medieval masonry were covered with lime wash. Presumably this space had been used as a place for storage. The relationship between this building and the others north of it is not very clear, because the intervening area was not completely excavated. Evidently the building could only have been constructed after the destruction of the house occupying the surviving part of the eastern tower vault, since it is in part built over it; this vault was still standing in the 1920s.

Traces of other houses were also visible north and east of the standing remains of the tower before excavation began (Fig. 20). Some of these were also standing in the 1920s.

PHASE F—FINAL ABANDONMENT AND DESTRUCTION

Finds from the collapse of the southernmost building (Area A) included fragments of 78 r.p.m. gramophone records and British Army ammunition, archaeological evidence of the military use of the site during the 1947–48 war. The date of abandonment of the other buildings is less certain. It seems likely that those to the north (Area A2) were already derelict by this time.

2. THE AREA NORTH OF THE MEDIEVAL TOWER
(Areas B–B1)

PHASE A—BYZANTINE

In the area north of the medieval tower bedrock was estimated (although it was not quite reached) at around 95·5 m. ASD (see Fig. 29). It was overlain by a sandy clay deposit (**76**) containing four sherds of Byzantine pottery. Above this the soil became browner (**71**) and contained more pottery, including rilled amphorae and cooking pots with horizontal loop handles, besides a copper coin probably of the fifth century A.D. (no. 4). The top of this layer was represented by a horizontal surface at around 96 m. ASD, covered with a spread of coarse pottery and tile fragments. Above this the soil, though similar, became still darker (**68**, **88**) and contained small pieces of charcoal besides more Byzantine pottery. Through this layer, which in the eastern part of the trench was up to 0·45 m. thick, was cut a feature running east–west for at least 3 m. and turning to the south at the eastern end of the trench (**67**, **87**). The full extent of this feature could not be ascertained because of the smallness of the area excavated (see Fig. 29a). It seems possible, however, that it represented the robbed foundations of a wall. Its depth was as much as 0·45 m. in the eastern part of the trench and its width at least 0·60 m. It had a yellow sandy fill, containing large stones, some lumps of dark brown earth (derived presumably from the layers through which it was cut) and very little pottery.

PHASE B—MEDIEVAL CONSTRUCTIONS

The area was subsequently levelled down to 96·3 m. ASD on the west and to 96·55 m. ASD on the east, the division between these two surfaces being defined by a stone wall (**28**) running north–south across the excavated area. This wall had no visible foundation trench on the west side, where its base was no more than 0·15 m. below the ground surface; on the east, however, a narrow foundation trench was discerned, filled with mortar and small stones. The wall was 0·62 m. wide and survived to 0·90 m. or three courses in height, including the foundations (Pl. XLVIII). It was built of reused ashlars, some well cut but others rougher and with broken edges, bonded with hard reddish mortar. The northern part of the foundation appeared to incorporate some masonry foundations surviving at the bottom of the robber trench (**67**) of Phase A.

East of the wall there was a flat surface of trampled earth and mortar (**30**), containing a great deal of charcoal (Fig. 29a). The pottery from this was mostly Byzantine, but also included at least five sherds of medieval amphorae. Cut into this layer, 0·55 m. from the wall, was a stake-hole (**31**), 0·14 × 0·22 m. across and 0·20 m. deep; the charcoal remains of the lower part of the extracted stake were found next to it. Overlying the mortary layer (**30**) and the stake hole (**31**) was a spread of charcoal (**35**), up to 0·05 m. thick, containing shapeless fragments of iron and copper, as well as a silver ring (see Fig. 54, no. 2). This layer ran up against the wall (**28**). The pottery consisted of undistinguished coarse ware, probably mostly Byzantine except for one piece of medieval handmade pottery.

To the west of the wall, the levelled surface of the Byzantine layers (**68**, **67**) was covered by a spread (**66**) of trampled stones (up to 0·05 × 0·10 m.) and pottery sherds. These were overlain by a thin (c. 0·10 m.) layer (**59**) of reddish sand containing small stones which also ran up to the wall (**28**). In it, against the wall, was found an iron knife (see Fig. 58, no. 29). The layer also included a high proportion of coarse pottery, mostly Byzantine, but also some medieval sherds: these included coarse wares, a green *graffita* sherd and a piece of yellow slip-ware. Despite the preponderance of Byzantine pottery in these layers, they would seem to represent a medieval phase associated with the construction of the castle buildings north of the tower. The "negative" stratification, caused by the levelling down of the area prior to the commencement of building work, and the thinness of the deposits themselves do not allow for much precision in dating the phase, though the glazed pottery is at least consistent with a date in the 12th or 13th century.

Pl. XLVIII. The Red Tower (al-Burj al-Ahmar): Trench B, looking E and showing Wall 28 (compare Fig. 29B) (photo. author).

AL-BURJ AL-AHMAR
Trench B plans

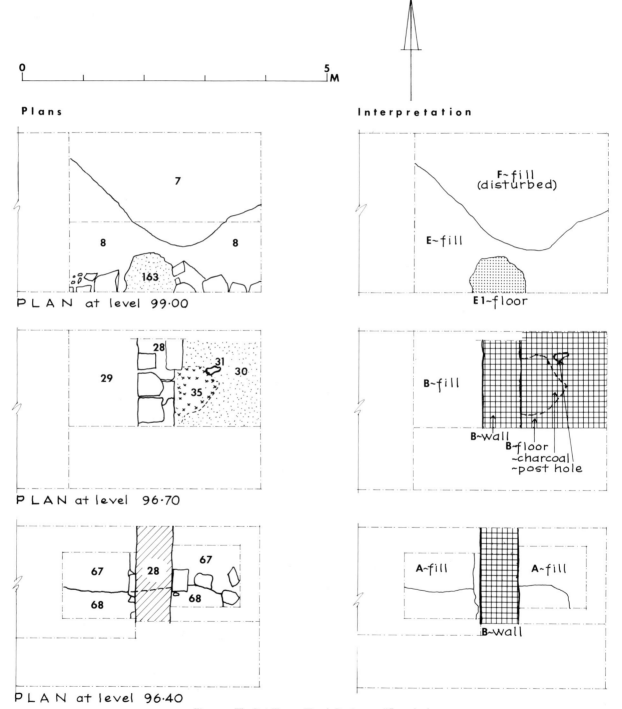

0   5
M

Plans

Interpretation

7

8   163   8

PLAN at level 99·00

F-fill
(disturbed)

E-fill

E1-floor

28
29   31   30
35

PLAN at level 96·70

B-fill

B-wall
B-floor
-charcoal
-post hole

67   28   67
68   68

PLAN at level 96·40

A-fill   A-fill

B-wall

Fig. 29a. The Red Tower: Trench B, plans at different levels.
(For structural sequence see Fig. 36)

Sections

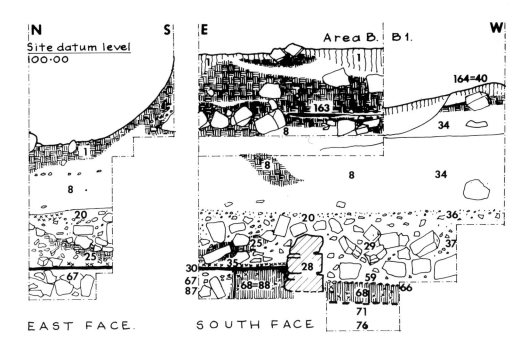

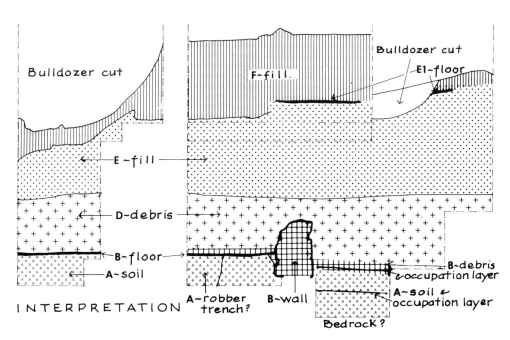

Fig. 29b. The Red Tower: Trench B, sections looking east and south.
(For structural sequence see Fig. 36)

PHASE D—DESTRUCTION OF THE CASTLE BUILDINGS

In a subsequent phase, the upper part of the medieval wall (**28**) was thrown down and the area covered by more than a metre of stones and rubble. Some of this material evidently came from the collapsed tower itself; it included, for example, fragments of mortar bearing the characteristic herring-bone pattern of trowel impressions that can still be seen on the pointing of the surviving part of the tower wall. The stones also included a segment of a rough antique limestone column drum, 0·40 m. high and 0·41 m. in diameter. The destruction debris (**25, 29, 37**) was levelled out at around 97·4–97·5 m. ASD (**20, 36**). The finds from it were not very numerous. They included some handmade village pottery (about 4%) and one sherd each of green-on-cream slip-ware and monochrome green *graffita* ware.

PHASE E—LATER MEDIEVAL AND POST-MEDIEVAL OCCUPATION

The top of the medieval destruction was overlain by a deposit 1·20–1·50 m. thick of grey and red ash and silt. The finds were similar to those from the layers overlying the destruction in Area C, and included sherds of green glazed slip-ware and yellow glazed slip-painted ware, one piece of Syrian under-glaze painted ware, just six sherds of grey coarse ware but an increasing proportion (12·4%) of handmade village pottery. This evidence and the discovery of a coin dated 1388/9 (see p. 176, no. 31) lying on the surface of the medieval destruction (in context **8**) suggest that these ash layers accumulated as a result of continued occupation of the site from the late 14th century onwards.

PHASE E1—STRUCTURES ASSOCIATED WITH POST-MEDIEVAL OCCUPATION

Over the ash and silt deposits, from around 98·7 m. ASD upwards, there accumulated layers which indicated several phases of building activity. Their remains, however, had been badly mauled by the bulldozer and by animal burrows, and they were therefore examined only in section. They seem to have consisted of houses with mud and stone walls and with plaster floors. One of these floors (**164**) represented the northern continuation of a floor (**40**) excavated in Area A2. The building remains were in turn overlain by more deposits of ash and silt. The finds from them were all treated as being unstratified, because of the disturbance.

3. AREA C2 WEST OF THE MEDIEVAL TOWER

PHASE A—BYZANTINE AND EARLY ISLAMIC

Bedrock (*hamra*) was encountered in this area at 96·46–96·66 m. ASD, sloping down towards the east (see Fig. 30). It was covered by a layer of light brown soil (**138**), darker in places, containing charcoal. This layer was 0·30–0·40 m. thick. It contained only coarse unglazed pottery, including two rilled amphora sherds with grey surfaces and white painting, indicating a date for the group in the 6th to 8th centuries.

Set into the surface of this layer were the bottom courses of two roughly built walls (Fig. 30). The first (**135**), running east–west, was 0·60 m. wide and survived 0·25 m. high. The second (**136**) abutted the first at the western end of the excavated area; its thickness was not determined. Neither wall appeared to have a foundation trench and no trace of mortar was found in their construction.

PHASE B—MEDIEVAL

The wall foundations of Phase A were surrounded and covered by a layer of light brown soil (**132, 137**), 0·20–0·25 m. thick, which also contained pieces of crushed limestone and mortar. It seems quite possible that this corresponds with the layers immediately predating the construction of the medieval tower in Area C1 (**83, 113**). Although most of the pottery from it was Byzantine or early Islamic, similar to the finds from the underlying layer (**138**), this layer also contained some coarse wares of medieval type as well as four fragments of glazed cooking pots.

The surface of this layer was defined by a spread of small stones at 97·05–97·20 m. ASD. This surface seems to relate to the period of use of the medieval castle.

PHASE D—DESTRUCTION OF THE MEDIEVAL CASTLE

The weathered surface of Phase B was directly overlain by layers of building destruction, 0·80–1·00 m. thick (**117, 127**). These comprised tips of red sand, mortar and rubble sloping downward from east to west. Some of this debris seems likely to have come from the collapse of the west wall of the tower itself. Finds from these layers were sparse. They included, however, three sherds of glazed thin-walled cooking pots from the bottom 0·10 m. of the destruction (**127**) and a single sherd of handmade pottery from higher up (**117**).

PHASE E—LATER MEDIEVAL OCCUPATION

The top of the medieval destruction was overlain by a grey ashy layer (**104**) containing layers of pinkish-orange or yellow ash and charcoal. This layer, which was up to 0·50 m. thick, contained a similar range of glazed and unglazed pottery to that from the same phase in Area C.

AL-BURJ AL-AHMAR
Trench C2

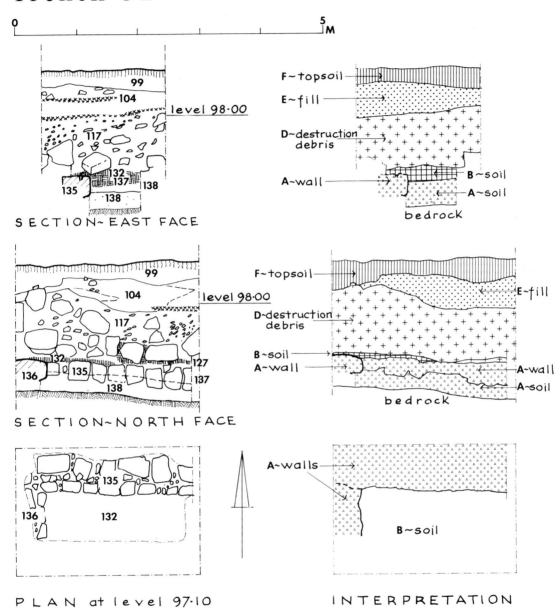

Fig. 30. The Red Tower: Trench C2, plan and sections.
(For structural sequence see Fig. 38)

PHASE F—TOPSOIL

The topsoil (**99**) in this area contained the same range of later medieval pottery as that found stratified in the layers beneath it. The almost complete absence of grey-fired coarse ware or other post-medieval types suggests either that this area was no longer inhabited after the 15th century or that the upper layers which might have contained such material had been removed by 20th-century bulldozing (but see Area C3 below). Photographs of the 1920s show this area ploughed and cultivated.

4. AREA C3 WEST OF THE MEDIEVAL TOWER

PHASE A—BYZANTINE AND EARLY ISLAMIC

Bedrock, at 96·20 m. ASD, was overlain in this area by a layer (**128**) some 0·15 m. thick of reddish sandy soil, containing charcoal flecks (see Fig. 31). The pottery consisted entirely of Byzantine coarse ware. Above this the soil became lighter in colour (**165**). The finds (amalgamated with those of layer **124** above) included quantities of Byzantine pottery, some glass, white mosaic tesserae and a triangular grey marble floor tile.

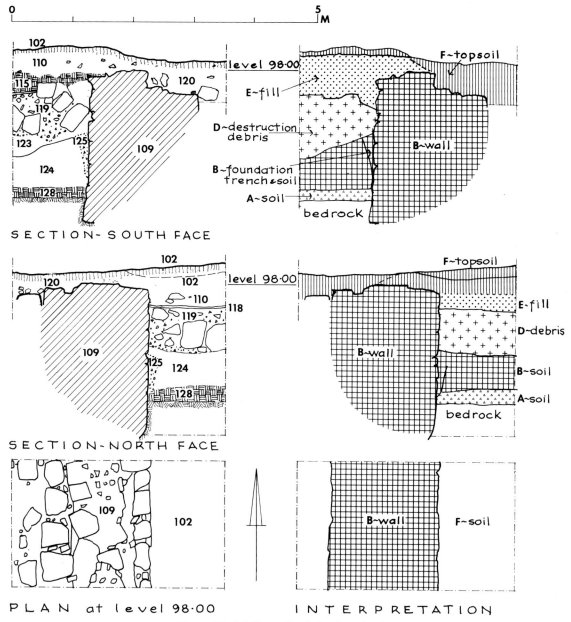

Fig. 31. The Red Tower: Trench C3, plan and sections.
(For structural sequence see Fig. 38)

PHASE B—CONSTRUCTION OF THE OUTER CASTLE WALL

The castle phase is represented in this area by a wall, some 1·70–1·80 m. thick, built north–south across the excavated area 21·20 m. in front of the west tower wall. Its foundations were some 1·3 m. deep and its surviving height about 1·1 m. Its construction was similar to that of the tower itself, with two facings of rough ashlar blocks and a core which included reused ashlars and other stones bonded with a light yellow-brown mortar containing red sand.

The foundation trench (125) of the wall was about 0·15 m. wide, narrowing down to nothing, and was filled with small stones in a hard clayey matrix. Although it was recorded from around 96·8 m. ASD, it is uncertain from what precise level the trench had been cut, since the upper part of the layer through which it was dug (165) had subsequently been disturbed (124). There was therefore no floor or surface found associated with the wall. The combined finds from the layers associated with the contruction of the wall (124, 125, 165) were predominantly Byzantine, but also included some rilled amphorae of medieval type, some of them with white external painting.

PHASE D—DESTRUCTION OF THE MEDIEVAL CASTLE

The medieval wall was destroyed down to around 98 m. ASD. The layers of destruction on its eastern side were some 0·65–1·10 m. thick and consisted of large blocks and other stones from the ruined structures lying in tips of orange or reddish mortary rubble, with occasional patches of burning (119, 123). The surface of the destruction was relatively flat (97·65 m. ASD) and was covered by a 0·03 m. spread of reddish sand and mortar (118), dipping towards the south where it also contained large stones. The few finds from these layers were mostly Byzantine, but also included some medieval coarse ware, three sherds of thin-walled glazed cooking pot and a piece of green-glazed slip-painted ware.

PHASE E—LATER MEDIEVAL OCCUPATION

Some 0·20–0·40 m. of further deposits separated the top of the medieval destruction from topsoil. These comprised red and grey ashy layers (110, 115), containing some large stones. The finds included handmade pottery, green and yellow glazed slip-painted and green-glazed slip-ware, but no 19th-century grey coarse ware; a date from the late 13th or 14th century onwards therefore seems to be indicated.

PHASE F—TOPSOIL

The finds from the topsoil (102, 120) were similar to those from Phase E, but also included a certain proportion (12%) of 19th-century grey-fired coarse ware.

5. AREA C5 SOUTH-WEST OF THE MEDIEVAL TOWER

PHASE B—CONSTRUCTION OF THE OUTER CASTLE WALL

The first archaeological phase represented in this area was the construction of a wall (139), 1·80 m. thick running east–west (see Fig. 32). It was built with a coursed rubble core consisting of stones set in yellow sandy mortar and was faced with rough ashlars. Only two courses, or 0·70 m., of the facing survived on the north side, and only one on the south. The foundations, 0·55 m. deep, were set directly into the bedrock (hamra). On the north, the foundation trench (149) was overlain by a mortar floor (148), some 0·12 m. thick, which was also laid directly on to the bedrock and ran up against the face of the wall. The mortar of this floor was similar to that of the wall itself. If any earlier layers or topsoil had existed on this side of the wall before its construction, they were evidently removed by the builders. On the south side of the wall, however, it is possible that the foundation trench (147) had been dug from a higher level; but the archaeological strata of this area had unfortunately been removed by a mechanical excavator after 1948. The foundation trenches on both sides of the wall contained a fill of light brown earth with mortar and limestone fragments; no finds were recorded from either of them.

The thickness and method of construction of the wall are closely comparable with those of the medieval wall (109) excavated in Area C3. It seems very likely, therefore, that it represents a continuation of the same wall to enclose the southern side of the castle. It appears in effect, to run parallel with the south wall of the tower and 21·7 m. in advance of it.

PHASE E—LATER MEDIEVAL OR POST-MEDIEVAL OCCUPATION

Over the mortar floor (148) on the north side of the wall (139), there accumulated a layer of grey ash (153), some 0·14 m. thick, containing fragments of domestic clay ovens. Into this was set the foundation of a second wall (151) which abutted the north face of the first wall and ran northward from it. It was 1·09 m. thick and survived two courses or about 0·60 m. high. It was built with reused blocks of stone and was probably once bonded with earth mortar; but this had long since weathered away. On both sides of this wall were laid areas of rough cobbling (150, 152), consisting of small stones set in whitish grey ashy mortar. They ran up against the wall and against the earlier wall (139). The

AL-BURJ AL-AHMAR
Trench C 5, & Well

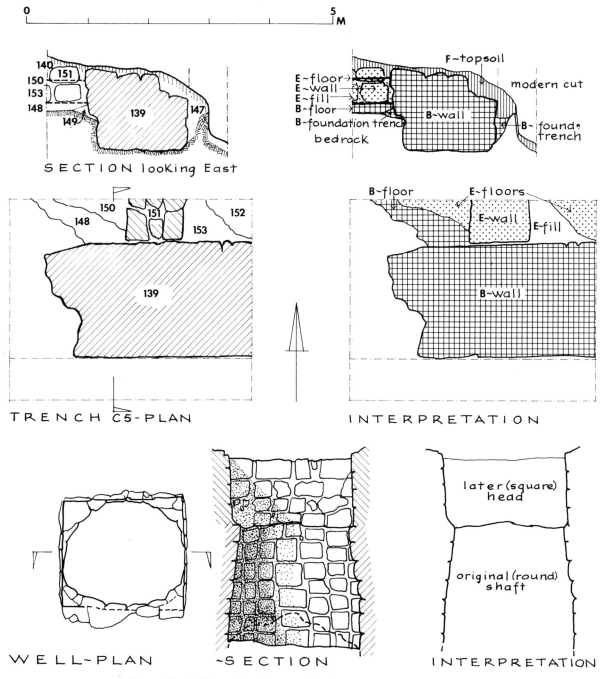

Fig. 32. *The Red Tower: Trench C5 and well north-east of the Khirba, plans and sections.*
(For structural sequence see Fig. 38)

floor west of the wall (**150**) had been relaid at least once. Both these floors were in turn overlain by a further deposit of grey ash, from which three unglazed sherds, including one handmade, were recovered. These represent the sum total of stratified finds from this area. It seems reasonable, however, to assign these layers and their associated building remains to one of the phases of later or post-medieval occupation that have been observed elsewhere on the site. Whether or not the medieval wall (**139**) was still standing to any appreciable height when wall **151** was built against it is uncertain; it is possible, however, that it was used simply as a foundation for the later structure of which wall **151** formed part.

Phase F—Topsoil and Disturbance

The archaeological features in the western and southern part of this area were completely destroyed by mechanical excavator when the modern sewage tanks were built. This work has also removed all trace of the south-west corner of the castle.

6. OTHER FEATURES NORTH-EAST OF THE KHIRBA

The Wells

Remains of two wells survive on the north-eastern side of the *khirba*. They are now both disused, having been replaced by a modern bore-hole and pumping station. The northern and probably the earliest well lies some 70 m. north-west of the medieval tower (see Figs. 20a and 32). It has a circular shaft, faced with rough (probably reused) ashlars; it is 1·7 m. in diameter but widens slightly as it descends. The well is now blocked 3 m. below ground level. The upper 1·1 m. has been rebuilt in a secondary phase to a rectangular plan, and measures some 1·7 × 2·0 m. It seems likely that this was the well used by the post-Crusader occupants of the site (Phase E), but whether it owes its origins to the 12th century or earlier is uncertain. On the east side of it lie the remains of a concrete tank, some 5 × 23 m., orientated east–west. This probably represents a modern rebuilding of the tank seen in 1922 (see above, p. 27; Fig. 20a).

The second well lies some 50 m. south of the first (see Fig. 20a). Its shaft is also cylindrical, over 4 m. in diameter and faced with small finely cut ashlars. The well is blocked 17 m. below the surface. Over its mouth there was constructed in Mandate times a small pumping station, remains of which and of its pumping machinery still survive. The well itself may be compared with two others in the same area, one at Jaljuliya (1454.1733) and the other south-east of Qaqun (1509.1953); all three seem likely to date from the late 19th or early 20th century.

The modern pumping station lies just north of this well.

Spread of Byzantine Pottery (Area Z)

Just north-east of the tank associated with the first well (see Fig. 20a), ploughing around the edge of the orchard adjoining the site had turned up a dense spread (**70**) of Byzantine coarse pottery, extending for some 20 m. from north to south. This pottery consisted almost exclusively of rilled amphora sherds with vertical loop handles.

IV. SUMMARY AND DISCUSSION

PRE-CRUSADER OCCUPATION (PHASE A)

Apart from a stone knife blade (Fig. 62, no. 1), which may indicate human activity on the site in the Chalcolithic period (fourth millennium B.C.), the earliest finds at the Red Tower date from the 5th century A.D. Structures of this period, however, proved elusive, probably because in the areas excavated the medieval builders had removed most of the earlier strata when levelling the site for the construction of the castle. In most areas, brown soil containing pottery of the 5th to 7th A.D. centuries directly overlay the natural red sandy bedrock (*hamra*). Slight traces of walls were found in Areas B and C2, but in both cases the excavated areas were too restricted to allow any building plan to emerge.

A dense concentration of amphora sherds thrown up by ploughing north-east of the castle (Area Z) and other sherds scattered among the citrus groves round about suggest that occupation in the Byzantine period was not restricted to the castle mound. The pottery from this period, however, consists almost entirely of coarse wares (e.g. amphorae and cooking pots), and apart from some pieces of glassware and numerous white mosaic tesserae there is no evidence to suggest that in social or economic terms the settlement ranked as anything more than a small agricultural village.

The pottery and glass finds also indicate that occupation persisted after the Muslim Arab conquest of 636, though whether it continued without a break up to the appearance of the Crusaders in Palestine in 1099 is more difficult to tell. The relatively small quantity of material from these intervening centuries and the total absence of structural evidence in the areas excavated is again probably due largely to the levelling of the site in the 12th century.

THE CRUSADER CASTLE (PHASE B)

The medieval castle consisted of the tower-keep or *donjon*, from which the site takes its name, surrounded by an encircling wall almost square in plan and measuring about 60 m. on each side (see Fig. 33). The central tower measured 19·7 m. (N–S) × 15·5 m. (E–W) and had walls 2·20 m. thick (see Fig. 34). It had two stories. The lower one was 0·50 m. below the medieval ground level and was covered by a pair of barrel-vaults set side by side; the upper one was probably more spacious, with six bays of groin-vaults supported by two masonry piers in the centre of the room. The roof, which doubtless at one time had a crenellated parapet, would have been 13 m. above ground level.

The principal entrance to the tower has yet to be located. The excavations, however, have narrowed down the range of possible locations for it to the centre of the east wall at ground-floor level, or somewhere in the north, east or west walls at first-floor level. The existence of a massive stone staircase linking the ground floor and first floor would imply that only one entrance would have been necessary; but at which level remains uncertain. An entrance at first-floor level would no doubt have been more secure and more in keeping with normal western practice (Finó 1970, 175; Brown 1976, 65f.); but among other 12th-century Crusader towers and *donjons* ground-floor entrances seem to be rather more common than first-floor ones (cf. Pringle 1983a, 170).

In view of the paucity of natural lighting allowed into the basement, it seems improbable that it would have been intended for anything more than storage. To judge by the way that the door in the spine wall opens, the western chamber could only have been entered from the eastern one. It had a well-laid flag-stone floor and it is not impossible that it served as some kind of strong room, at times perhaps even as a prison. The purpose of the small room, 4·80 m. square, that was later partitioned off at its south end remains a mystery. Access to the eastern chamber could have been via the staircase or perhaps through a door in the outer east wall. Its floor seems to have consisted of no more than beaten earth and plaster. The stone staircase constructed against its east and north walls led up through the vaulted ceiling to the first floor.

Such evidence as we have from the first floor suggests that it represented the residential area, or *piano nobile*, of the tower, with painted plaster walls and a pavement composed of a mixture of plain white mosaic tesserae and fragments of antique marble. Floors of a similar kind have been recorded in other 12th-century Crusader buildings in Palestine, including the first-floor cloister of St. Mary Latin itself in Jerusalem, the conventual buildings of the abbey of St. Mary in the Valley of Jehoshaphat (Johns 1939, 125–126, 130–131; pl. LVIII.1) and the church of the Agony of the Saviour in the Garden of Gethsemane (Orfali 1924, pl. XV, XIX–XX, XXII). No trace remains of the staircase that would have led up to the roof; possibly, as at Safita

Castle, it was also built in a corner of the room against the inside face of the walls.

The outer wall of the castle was investigated at only two points, west and south-west of the tower respectively. It was 1·70–1·80 m. thick and constructed in a similar fashion to the wall of the tower itself. Presumably it would have had a defended gateway and perhaps towers at two or more of the angles. The south-west corner, however, has unfortunately been completely destroyed by the construction of the modern sewage works.

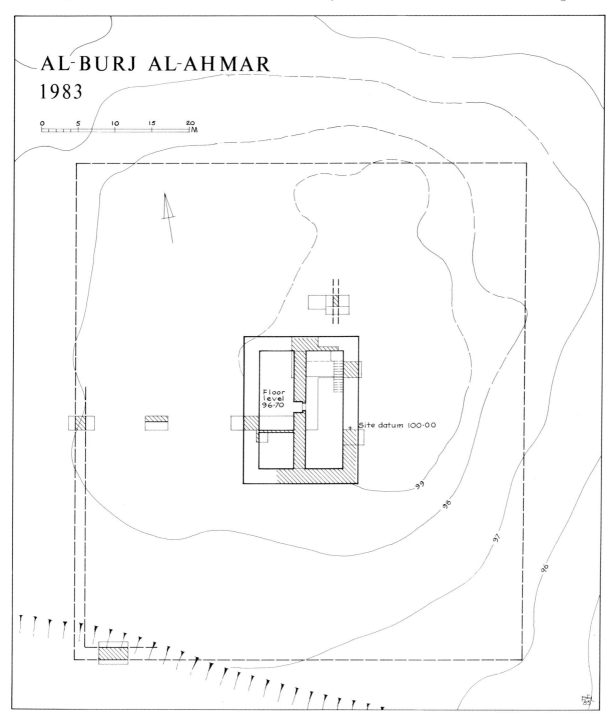

AL-BURJ AL-AHMAR
1983

0   5   10   15   20
M

Floor
level
96·70

Site datum 100·00

99

98

97

96

Fig. 33. The Red Tower: plan of the Crusader castle as revealed by excavation 1983.

Further excavation would be needed to obtain more information about this wall and to tell whether it was surrounded by any form of defensive ditch. Traces of an outbuilding of some kind were found in the bailey north of the tower (Area B), but in too restricted an area to tell its plan.

Examination of the remains of the tower suggests that although it was evidently built in stages (five of which are summarized in Section 2 of Fig. 34), these would all have belonged to a single programme of construction. The vertical stages defined by offset courses in the masonry correspond more or less with the optimum seasonal building heights for church towers and tower-keeps recorded in the West; documentary and architectural evidence suggests these to have been between 3·0 and 3·7 m. (cf. Renn 1968, 25–26). It may therefore have taken

AL-BURJ AL-AHMAR
Reconstruction of tower

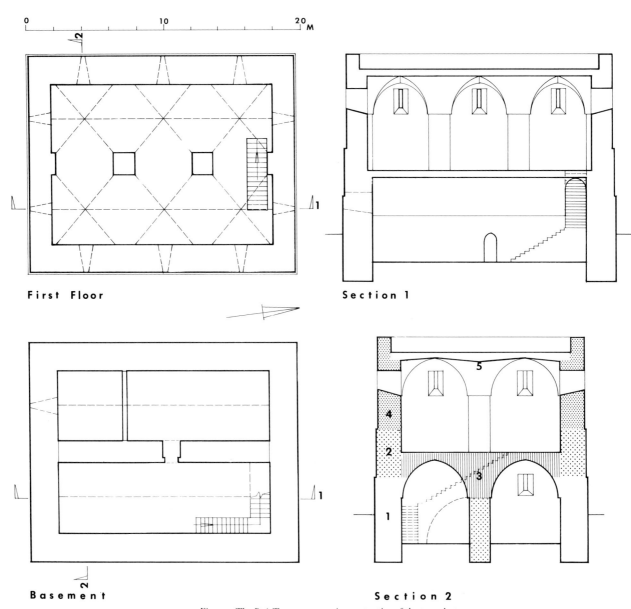

Fig. 34. The Red Tower: suggested reconstruction of the tower-keep.

three to four seasons to complete the basic structure of the tower (assuming that stages 2 and 3 were combined in one season). The similarity between the tower's masonry and that of the outer wall also indicates that this too belonged to the same programme of construction.

So much then for the form of the building. But when was it built, by whom, and for what purpose? As we have remarked already, the pottery and other finds recovered from the layers associated with its construction suggest that the tower's foundations were laid sometime in the first half of the 12th century. It may therefore safely be identified with the "Tower of Latina" that was standing by 1158. It may also be compared with a number of other similar Crusader structures also dating to the 12th century. As mentioned above (p. 15), the plan of the tower is broadly comparable with the tower at al-Bira, which existed by 1124, and with that of Madd ad-Dair, with which it is likely to be roughly contemporary. The tower at al-Bira also stood at the centre of a rectangular enceinte, in this case 60 × 45 m.; and a type-site for this kind of 12th-century Crusader castle is to be found in Qal‘at Yahmur in Syria, dating perhaps before 1137 and certainly before 1177 (see Fig. 4). Other 12th-century Crusader castles of this have been discussed above (pp. 15–18).

None of this archaeological and comparative evidence, however, allows us to tell precisely the year or even decade of the 12th century when the Red Tower was built. In order to approach an answer to this question, we must consider the likely historical context of its construction. As noted, it seems highly probable that the village and its lands were granted to the Bendictines of St. Mary Latin by one or other of the first two lords of Caesarea, Eustace (1105/10–23), who also granted them Madd ad-Dair (*Montdidier*), or Walter I (1123–49/54). It remains uncertain, however, whether the castle would have been built before or after this transfer took place.

The construction of a small castle of this type would indeed fit logically into the historical context of the extension of the lord of Caesarea's control over his territorial domains during the first half of the 12th century. This was still a period of insecurity in the coastal plain, when the granting of fiefs would have gone hand-in-hand with the construction of strongholds to enforce Frankish dominion in the countryside. As the century proceeded and as the Franks were better able to contain and finally to extinguish the threat of Egyptian raids from Ascalon, the need to fortify or to maintain in a state of defence a site such as the Red Tower would gradually have decreased. Thus it could be that by the time when it was given to the Benedictines, the castle (assuming that it existed by then) would have lost much of its military significance.

If the site had been given to the monks early in the century, however, say before 1130, then the possibility arises that the monks themselves might have been responsible for building the castle. As has been observed, its plan is similar to that of the castle at al-Bira built by the canons of the Holy Sepulchre, which in 1124 served as refuge for the local Frankish population during an Egyptian raid. Later in the century we find this building complex being used by the canons as an administrative centre for running their estates in the area, under the control of their steward (see Pringle 1985a, 157). But the later administrative centre built by the same canons at al-Qubaiba had no *donjon* nor even a tower; apparently by the 1130s or 1140s this was considered unnecessary.

Whether the Red Tower was built by the Benedictines, however, or as seems more likely by the lord of Caesarea or one of his vassals, by the time when the monks were firmly in possession of it (1158) its function is more likely to have been administrative than military. The principal interest of the monks in their estates in the area would, after all, have been in their revenues; and although John of Ibelin informs us that the monastery of St. Mary Latin owed the service of fifty sergeants to the royal army (ch. CCLXXII, p. 426; cf. Sanudo, 194), it seems improbable that this obligation would have necessitated for them the construction of works of defence or the maintenance of permanent garrisons (cf. Smail 1956, 90–92). But it may also be questioned whether the Benedictines would have needed to maintain such an installation at all (or, for that matter, the one at Madd ad-Dair) simply in order to collect revenue, in cash or kind, from their lands thereabouts. Quite possibly, by the latter half of the 12th century the castle was surplus to their needs. Unfortunately our excavations have provided no evidence that might have a bearing on the possible use to which the castle was put in the 12th century. And although we know that a Templar garrison was installed in it by 1236, there is no evidence, archaeological or written, for Templar occupation of the site before the Third Crusade.

THE CASTLE AFTER THE THIRD CRUSADE (PHASE C)

The relative peace and stability of conditions in the Sharon Plain were rudely shattered in July 1187 by Saladin's destruction of the royal army at Hattin and his swift conquest of the entire Latin Kingdom of Jerusalem except for Tyre. After the treaty of Jaffa in September 1192, by which the Sultan formally ceded back to the Franks the lands that they had managed to regain since 1189, the coastal plain as far south as Ascalon (which remained unfortified) returned to Frankish hands, but the inner hill country of Samaria, including the town of Nablus, remained in the possession of the Muslims (cf. Prawer 1975(2), 99; map VII). In these changed political circumstances the security of the coastal region could less easily be taken for granted. Thus we find Arsuf being refortified by Richard I in 1191, by John of Ibelin in 1240, and by the Hospitallers in 1261 (Benvenisti 1970, 132–133). Caesarea was refortified by John of Brienne, Leopold of Austria and the Hospitallers in 1218, destroyed by a Mamluk raid in 1220 and refortified again in 1228 and by King Louis IX of France in 1251 (Hazard 1975, 86–89). And further north, the Templar fortress of Pilgrims' Castle (ʿAtlit) was built from 1218 onwards (Johns 1947; 1975). In the central Sharon, Qaqun may also have been refurbished in the later 12th or 13th century.

The Red Tower also seems to have been cleaned up in the 13th century, though the archaeological evidence does not allow us to say whether it was also refortified. The work documented by the excavation entailed the construction of a raised dais at the north end of the west ground-floor chamber. This was formed of a rough wall built across the chamber, with an in-fill of masonry blocks and loose earth thrown in behind it, the whole platform thus created being then sealed by a beaten clay and plaster covering. From the fill came a large quantity of rubbish, including broken pottery, glass, metalwork, animal bones (including pig) and, to judge by traces adhering to some of the bronzework, pieces of leather, cloth and other organic materials which have not survived. The dating comes from a hoard of 24 coins comprising only two types, *deniers* of Amaury (1163–c. 1219) and of the bishopric of Le Puy (c.1189–); together these provide a *terminus post quem* of c.1189. The hoard, however, was spread over an area of some 4 m.² and appeared to have been thrown into the fill along with the other rubbish. Thus it does not seem likely that the types were current when they were deposited, and the date of their final disposal in this position could therefore be some time later than the date of the coins themselves. The group of finds from this area is closely comparable to the group of finds from a similar deposit of earth lying on the floor of the western chamber, directly beneath the collapse of the vault; and the ceramic finds from these two areas even include pieces from the same handmade painted jug (Fig. 42, no. 7). From this two conclusions may be drawn: first, that the material used to form the platform at the north end of the east chamber included rubbish that had been lying around in the basement of the tower; secondly, that between the time of this partial cleaning operation and the destruction of the tower, no attempt was made to complete the clearance of rubbish from the stone floor of the west chamber. This suggests that no great period of time elapsed between these two events.

The purpose of the raised platform is uncertain; neither is it known whether its construction was an isolated operation, or was connected with a more extensive *mise-en-valeur* of the castle. In view of the dating evidence and the other considerations made above, however, it seems possible that it occurred after the Hospitallers took possession of the castle in 1248. It may perhaps represent part of their cleaning-up operation after the Templars had at last handed the site over to them. The finds from this phase could in this case have represented mostly rubbish left behind by the departing Templar garrison.

THE DESTRUCTION OF THE CASTLE (PHASES D AND D1)

The castle was destroyed in a methodical fashion. The east and west walls of the tower were undermined, causing them to fall outwards and the vaults straight downwards. Rubble from the collapse extended as far north as Area B and as far west as Area C2. Only the south wall of the tower and part of its east ground-floor vault was left standing. The outer castle wall in Area C3 was also destroyed down to the same level as the west wall of the tower. A mass of carbonized material found in the collapsed rubble in Area C4 (Fig. 23) would appear to represent debris from a hearth established on the first floor of the tower, immediately above, in its final phase of occupation (see pp. 187–191).

The destruction must obviously have taken place after the *terminus post quem* of c.1189 provided by the coin hoard, and later too than the refurbishment carried out in Phase C, whose date seems likely to be 1248 or after. The finds from the upper layers of the destruction debris, however, include pottery of the late 13th and 14th centuries; and a *terminus ante quem* of c.1390 is indicated by a Mamluk coin of 1343 (no. 29) found in the upper destruction debris and by three others of 1363/77 (no. 32), 1380/1 (no. 30) and 1388/9 (no. 31) respectively found lying on its surface. The destruction could thus have occurred at any time between c.1248 and c.1390. The balance of probability, however, is that it happened in or soon after 1265, when Baybars took possession of the whole Sharon Plain south of the Nahr az-Zarqa and destroyed the fortifications of Caesarea, Arsuf and other Frankish castles of the area (see above p. 24). The later finds from the upper destruction layers probably represent rubbish which found its way into the pile of rubble as it was picked over by local villagers, or perhaps by the Mamluks from Qaqun, searching for building materials.

LATER AND POST-MEDIEVAL OCCUPATION (PHASES E AND E1)

In around 1390, what remained of the pile of rubble created by the collapse of the major part of the tower was finally levelled out over most of the site. It was from the weathered surface of this levelling that the three Mamluk coins came which enable us to date it (nos. 30–32).

Over the top of this were found deposits of ash, further building remains, pottery and faunal material indicat-

ing domestic use of the site between the end of the 14th century and modern times. These strata were too confused, however, to allow any more precise definition of the exact phases of occupation to be attempted; and it is uncertain even whether occupation would have been

AL-BURJ AL-AHMAR
Area A1-A3 structural sequence

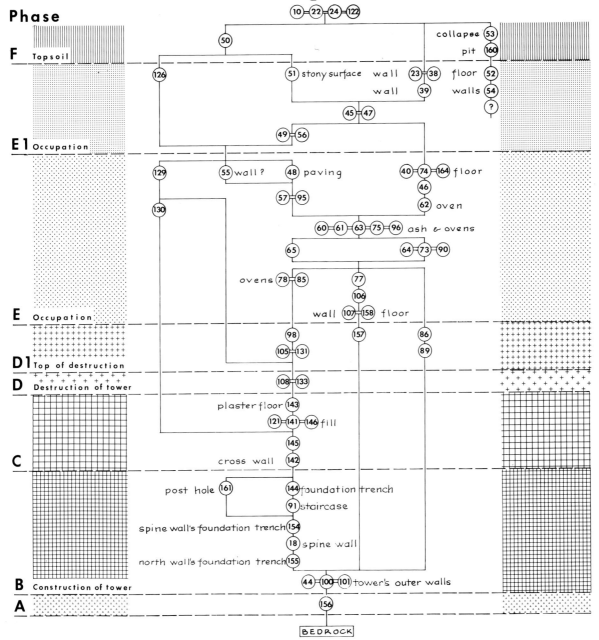

Fig. 35.

continuous, intermittent or seasonal. The Red Tower is not mentioned among the taxable inhabited villages in the Ottoman survey of 1596/7. In 1870, Victor Guérin remarked that it was abandoned; though the officers of the Survey of Western Palestine recorded one family living in the surviving east vault of the tower in 1873. A small group of peasant houses can be seen on the photographs taken just after the First World War, and their remains are identified on our site plan (Fig. 20a).

The occupation debris from these five centuries could therefore be the result of seasonal occupation by nomads, whose presence in the Sharon Plain is known to us from the same survey of 1596/7; or it may perhaps be the result of occupation of a seasonal or intermittent kind by villagers from the hill country who are recorded in the later 19th century descending into the plain in autumn and early spring to sow and reap harvests from the arable farmland there, or in the summer to graze their animals (Amiran 1953, 199–201; fig. 5).

FINAL ABANDOMNENT (PHASE F)

The small settlement that had developed around the ruins of the tower during the relatively stable period of the British Mandate was abandoned during the period of inter-communal strife in 1947 and used subsequently as a military post by Israeli troops holding the plain against the Arab forces in Tulkarm. Thus until the armistice in 1949 the castle again assumed a military role.

AL-BURJ AL-AHMAR
Area B structural sequence

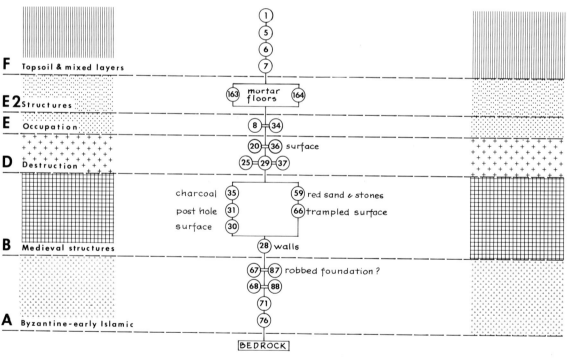

Fig. 36.

AL-BURJ AL-AHMAR
Area C, C1,4,&6 structural sequence

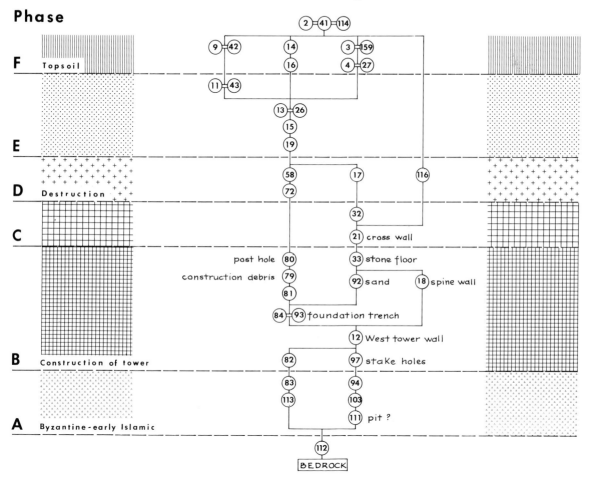

Fig. 37.

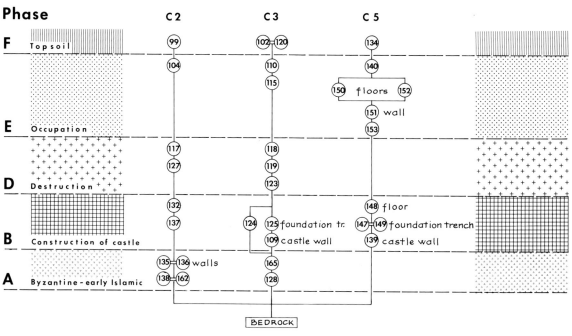

Fig. 38.

PART THREE

The Finds from the Red Tower 1983

I. POTTERY

Over 17,000 sherds of pottery were recovered from the excavations at the Red Tower. Because the material was so fragmentary, however, very few complete forms were reconstructable and the typology that follows contains individual descriptions of only 90 pieces. A high degree of selectivity is of course quite usual in publications of the pottery from excavations. In order to present a more comprehensive picture of the ceramic assemblage from the Red Tower, however, a sherd-count was also carried out on each group of finds from each individual context, no material being excluded. The results of this analysis are shown in Tables 5–10 and summarized in Fig. 39.

The pottery from Phase A (5th to 12th centuries) consists almost entirely of unglazed coarse wares, most of it probably of the 5th to 8th centuries. Byzantine and early Islamic coarse wares also occur as residual material in all subsequent phases, but because of the abraided condition of most of the sherds it is not always possible to tell precisely the proportions of residual to contemporary material. A rough indication is provided, however, by considering the proportions of rilled and comb-decorated sherds, which can usually be assigned to the 5th to 8th centuries. In Phase A these represent almost half of the total assemblage. In Phase B they fall to 35%, and thereafter they remain at a level of between 3·5% and 10%. It is possible to estimate therefore that between 7% and 20% of the coarse pottery from subsequent phases is residual Byzantine or early Islamic material. (The fact that rilled, comb-decorated and plain sherds may come from the same pot does not affect this argument.)

Phase B represents layers and features associated with the construction of the 12th-century castle (c.1100–50). As already indicated, however, a high proportion, perhaps around 70%, of the pottery from these layers is likely to be residual. Small quantities of material from the 9th to 11th centuries are also identifiable, however, their relative paucity being due in some part to the removal of the more recent layers by the builders of the castle. Amongst the more recent coarse wares from Phase B may be noted grey rilled amphorae with white external painting (2·21%) and other red- or brown-bodied amphora sherds with similar painting (4·13%). Unglazed fine white wares, typical of early Islamic contexts elsewhere, account for 3·46% of the assemblage. The glazed pottery includes two sherds of 9th- to 11th-century polychrome ware from the foundation trenches of the tower (see no. 78), one alkaline-glazed sherd, one graffita sherd (no. 71), three sherds of glazed slip ware, besides twelve of common or kitchen wares. In all, the glazed pottery accounts for less than 2% of the whole assemblage in this phase.

The pottery from Phase C, derived from a period of occupation of the castle after the Third Crusade (c. 1191–c.1265), shows a marked change from that of the earlier periods. First of all, there appears to be very little residual pottery in these layers; the proportion of rilled and comb-decorated sherds suggests no more than about 7%. On the other hand, a sizeable proportion of the coarse-ware sherds have white slip-painting on the outside (14·24%). A second feature of this group is that glazed sherds now account for over 18% of the total, though only one in twenty-four of them (or 0·76% of the total) come from glazed table wares; most of the glazed sherds are from cooking pots. Medieval handmade painted pottery makes its first appearance in this phase. Most of the 32 sherds of this type, however, came from the same pot (no. 7), so that while it is certain that such pottery existed on the site in the mid-13th century it seems unlikely to have been in general use by the occupants of the castle.

The finds from Phase D, the layers of destruction of the castle, suggest a rather mixed group of material derived in part from the final phase of Frankish occupation of the castle and in part from the Arab villagers who continued to occupy the site. This village material seems from stratigraphical evidence to span the period from c.1265 until c.1390. Much of the common glazed pottery, which accounts for 13·10% of this assemblage, seems to have come from the final Frankish occupation. White painting on amphora sherds, however, virtually disappears, and the relatively high incidence (9·77%) of rilling and comb-decoration also suggests a greater proportion of residual Byzantine pottery creeping back into the assemblage; some of this Byzantine pottery was contained in the collapsed rubble from the tower itself, while evidence from a later phase (E) indicates that sherds were often collected by the villagers to form the bases for their clay ovens. More persuasive ceramic evidence for the occupation of the site by *fallahin* in this phase is to be found in the increase in the proportion of handmade pottery (11·23%). The finer glazed wares include slip-wares, mostly mono-chrome green in colour (1·32%), slip-painted wares (0·48%) and under-glaze painted wares (0·55%). Most of these seem likely to date from the late 13th or 14th century, though it remains possible that some of them were derived from the Frankish occupation of the castle before 1265.

Phase D1 represents the uppermost layers of destruc-tion in Area A1, datable from its finds to c. 1350–90. The pottery from it continues the same general trends identified in Phase D. Thus, the proportion of hand-made wares continues to rise (38·54%); that of glazed cooking pots continues to decline (2·67%), while other glazed wares actually increase their share slightly (5·48%). The presence of two sherds of imported graffita ware, however, one 12th-century (no. 72) and the other 13th-century (no. 73), betrays an element of residual material even in this group.

Phases E (c. 1390–c. 1920) and E1 (c. 1920–1948) represent occupation of the site from the end of the 14th century until the end of the British Mandate. This occupation was not necessarily continuous, and was in any case quite possibly of a seasonal kind. It is unfortunate that the deposits were too mixed to allow the chronological development of the ceramic assemb-lage over these 450 years to be precisely documented. The general trends, however, are clearly seen in the tabulated figures. In Phase E, the proportion of handmade pottery returns to about the level that it had occupied in Phase D (12·19%); and in Phase E1 it drops again to 4·70%. It is unlikely that all of the handmade pottery in Phase E1 is residual, however, since such pottery was being produced in villages of the West Bank to within the past decade. One reason for its decline at the Red Tower, however, seems to be that towards the end of the 19th century it was being replaced by technically superior wheel-made pottery with a charac-teristic dark grey fabric. This ware represents only 5·87% of the assemblage in Phase E, but increases to 34·47% in Phase E1. Similar pottery is still made today in the Gaza Strip, but it seems likely that the material at al-Burj al-Ahmar was derived from an as yet unidenti-fied source nearer at hand. Glazed cooking pots virtually disappear from the site after the end of the 14th century. Their place was apparently taken first by the handmade wares and later by the grey-fired pottery. Fine glazed pottery also continues to be rare in these layers, though three pieces of 18th-century Turkish pottery (nos. 88–90) show that occasional items of fine ware did continue to reach the site and that not all of the glazed pottery from these later phases can therefore be regarded as residual.

One striking feature of the ceramic assemblages of all the phases at the Red Tower is the predominance of coarse wares. Even allowing for an element of residual

Byzantine material in all phases, the sherd-count indicates that coarse wares represent over 70% of the pottery of each phase (see Fig. 39). This preponderance could perhaps be explained in part by the sampling procedure, since large amphorae could be expected to produce more sherds on breaking than say glazed plates or bowls. But this inherent bias does not prevent glazed pottery predominating over unglazed on other medieval sites, where the same system of sherd-counting has been used (e.g. Genoa, see below). A more plausible explanation therefore seems to lie in the nature of the site itself. From the 5th century, the site of the Red Tower seems to have been occupied by nothing more than an agricultural village settlement, to which for a period of about 150 years during the 12th and 13th centuries were added the Frankish residents of the castle. Thus, in Byzantine and early Islamic times, almost all the pottery consists of cooking pots and amphorae. Only two sherds of fine Byzantine table-ware were found, and even these were unstratified; while fine early Islamic glazed wares account for only seven sherds before the construction of the castle.

The functional significance of the relative propor-tions of different wares in the 12th century and later could perhaps be assessed more easily if comparative data existed from other contemporary sites in Palestine. In the absence of such data, however, a comparison can still be made with a contemporary site of a very different kind in Italy in order to illustrate the potential value of such analyses. This site is the archbishop's palace of San Silvestro in the *centro storico* of Genoa, excavated between 1971 and 1976 (see Andrews and Pringle 1977; Pringle 1977).

In Fig. 40, the proportion of glazed pottery in the assemblages from roughly contemporary phases at the Red Tower and Genoa are compared. As can be seen, in the 12th century, glazed wares were already six times more common in Genoa than at the Red Tower though glazed kitchen wares were still relatively uncommon in Italy. Glazed cooking pots came into general use in Palestine at least a century earlier than in Italy, and in the mid-13th-century Frankish phase at the Red Tower they account for some 18% of the total assemblage, as compared with only 3·5% in Genoa in the same period. But thereafter, while at the Red Tower their proportion declined to almost nothing by the end of the 14th century, at Genoa it continued to increase up to 33% by the same date. The figures for glazed fine wares tell a somewhat different story, while displaying no less significant a contrast. At Genoa the proportion of fine glazed pottery continued to rise throughout the period from the 12th century to the 15th century, achieving about 49% in the period 1404–72; at the Red Tower, on the other hand, it represents a feeble proportion in all phases, never going above 5·5%. Taking all the glazed

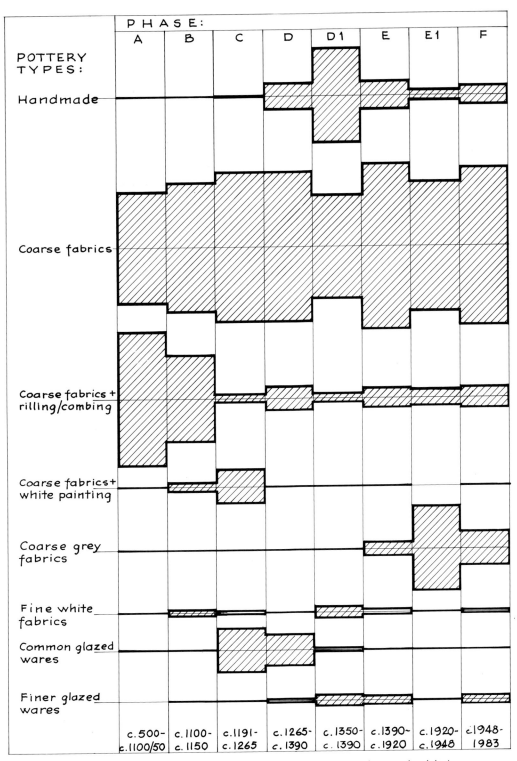

Fig. 39. The Red Tower: Relative percentage distribution of pottery types by phase over the whole site.

pottery together, it can be seen that at the Red Tower the 13th-century Frankish phase represented a peak in the use of glazed pottery on the site, a feature no doubt to be explained by the changed cultural and functional status of the site in this period rather than by chronology, since glazed pottery had been in common use in Palestine for several hundred years before the castle was built. In Genoa, on the other hand, the proportion of glazed pottery continued a steady rise from the 12th to the 15th century, reaching over 77% by the end of that period.

An archbishop's palace in Italy and a village and castle in Palestine are of course two so completely different settlement types that it seems hardly necessary to analyse in detail why their pottery assemblages should differ so greatly. It is to be hoped, however, that future excavators of medieval sites in Palestine and Syria will pay more attention to the pottery than has been done in the past and enable some more fruitful

comparisons to be made between different classes of site in the same geographical area.

Note on the Pottery Illustrations:

The colours of glazes or paints represented in Figs. 41–51 are identified in the text by the following letters:

(a) indicates solid black in the figure;
(b) indicates diagonal shading in the figure;
(c) indicates vertical shading in the figure;
(d) indicates horizontal shading in the figure;
(e) indicates cross-hatching in the figure;
(f) indicates stippling in the figure; and
(g) indicates the absence of any shading in the figure.

The extent of glaze on the outside of vessels is shown by a dotted line, and of slip by a broken line. The following abbreviations may also be noted: d. = diameter; h = height; r. = radius.

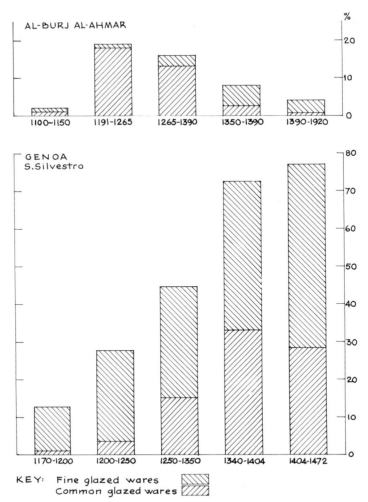

Fig. 40. Comparison of the percentage representation of glazed pottery in roughly contemporaneous assemblages at Genoa (San Silvestro) and al-Burj al-Ahmar (The Red Tower).

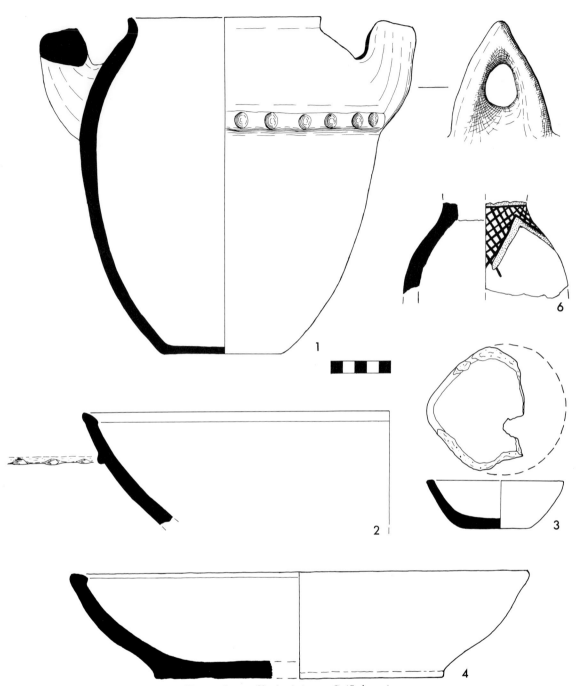

Fig. 41. Pottery: Handmade (nos. 1–6) (Scale 1 : 3).

1. UNGLAZED HANDMADE WARES

Leaving aside two stray sherds from Phases A and B, handmade pottery first appears at the Red Tower in the 13th century in Phase C. Most of the fragments from this phase, however, came from a single, though exceptionally fine, painted jar (no. 7), pieces of which were found scattered between Areas A and C. Handmade wares only achieve a significant proportion of the total ceramic assemblage in Phases D (11·23%), D1 (38·54%) and later, that is to say after the destruction of the castle. It seems likely that most of this material came from the village settlement that was subsequently established on the site in the late 13th and 14th centuries. From the 15th century onwards (Phases E–E1),

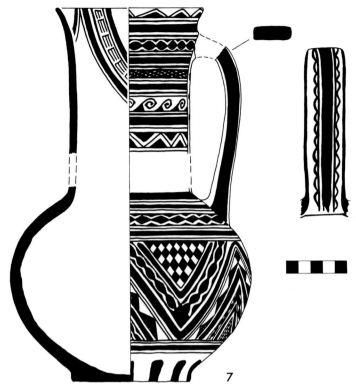

Fig. 42. Pottery: Handmade painted jug (no. 7) (Scale 1 : 3).

handmade pottery accounts for 12·19% and then 4·70% of the total assemblage, its decline probably being due to the development of the technically superior grey-fired wheel-made pottery towards the end of the 19th century.

In all phases except C non-painted handmade wares are significantly more common than painted.

(A) NON-PAINTED HANDMADE WARES.

From as early as Phase D (*c*.1265–*c*.1390) the non-painted handmade pottery includes both smoothed or burnished types and globular calcite-gritted cooking pots with basket handles, often with incised decoration on the handles (cf. St. Mary of Carmel, 13th century: Pringle 1984a, 95, nos. 1–4).

> 1. Fig. 41. (P49) Two-handled jar with thumb-impressed ridge on shoulder, almost complete (h. 27·5; max. d. 15·5 cm.). Fabric black with white gritty inclusions, brown on surface, very coarse, fairly hard, burnished both sides. Context 110 (*c*.30 fragments), Area C3, Phase E.
>
> 2. Fig. 41. (P51) Large hemi-spherical basin (d. *c*.50 cm.), rim fragment. Fabric grey-buff, with cream-pink exterior, burnished inside and over rim with some trace of red colouring on rim, very coarse, fairly hard. Thumb-impressed ridge around shoulder. Context 108, Area A1, Phase D.

> 3. Fig. 41. (P63) Spouted saucer (h. 4·0; d. 10·2 cm.). Fabric grey with red-brown burnished surface, very coarse, fairly hard. Context 133, Area A3, Phase D.
>
> 4. Fig. 41. (P64) Large flat-bottomed basin with curving sides (h. 8·5; d. 38 cm.). Fabric grey with red-brown surface, very coarse containing white grits, fairly hard, burnished inside. Context 133 (2 fragments), Area A3, Phase D.
>
> 5. Not illustrated. (P37) As no. 4. Context 85, Area A2, Phase E.

(B) PAINTED HANDMADE WARES

In no phase other than C are more than one in ten of the handmade sherds painted. It is also noticeable that the painted pieces in the earlier phases, including no. 7 (Phase C) and no. 10 (Phase D), are of a higher technical quality than those of the later periods (cf. Franken and Kalsbeek 1975, 172).

> 6. Fig. 41. (P61) Closed form, fragment of shoulder and base of neck. Fabric grey, burnished orange-brown on outside, very coarse, fairly hard. Painting in red (a) and white (f). Context 133, Area A3, Phase D.
>
> 7. Fig. 42. (P77 + 79 + 92) Jar with globular body, high vertical neck, slightly everted rim and vertical strap-handle (h. 29·8; d. 19·9 cm.). Fabric buff-cream, very coarse, fairly hard. Burnished cream exterior, with red painted design (a). Contexts 32 (17 fragments), 141 (7 fragments) and 146 (6 fragments), Areas A and C, Phase C.

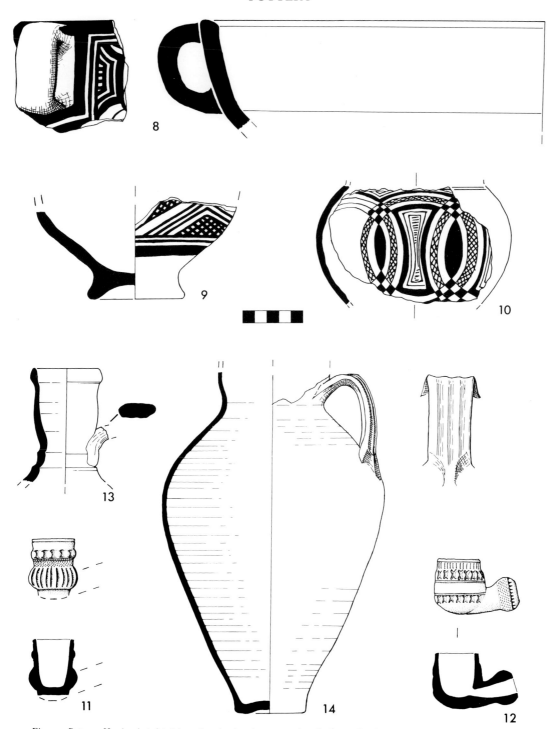

Fig. 43. Pottery: Handmade painted (nos. 8–10), pipes (nos. 11–12) and other unglazed wares (nos. 13–14) (Scale 1 : 3).

8. Fig. 43. (P39) Large cylindrical vessel with flattened inwardly sloping rim and thick vertical strap handle (d. *c.* 56 cm.). Fabric orange-brown, very coarse, medium hard. Burnished reddish brown on inside with black painting on rim. White slip and black (a) geometrical pattern painted on outside. Context 95, Area A2, Phase E.

9. Fig. 43. (P42) Closed form, fragment of pedestal base. Fabric brick red, very coarse, fairly hard. Trace of cream slip and burnishing on exterior, with black (a) geometrical painted design. The quality of this piece is far inferior to that of no. 7. Context 98 (6 fragments), Area A1, Phase D1.

10. Fig. 43. (P62) Closed form, fragment of globular body (d. 16 cm.). Fabric light yellow-green to buff, coarse with red, black and white grits, fairly hard. Textile impressions on the inside surface. Exterior smoothed and painted with black (a) design. Context 133 (7 fragments), Area A3, Phase D.

(c) SMOKERS' PIPES

Handmade pipe bowls of terracotta appear at the Red Tower after *c.*1390 (Phase E). They are often elaborately decorated with stamped or rouletted impressions. At Tall Qaimun, such pipes are dated "Mamluk" (Ben-Tor and Rosenthal 1978, 70; fig. 6.1–2), and at Hama despite the questionable nature of the stratigraphy they seem to have been present on the Citadel before its destruction in 1401 (Poulsen 1957, 280, nos. 1069–1081). Taken together, the evidence from these three sites would therefore support a date for the appearance of such pipes in Syria and Palestine towards the end of the 14th century or early in the 15th. Pipe-smoking became very common throughout the Turkish empire from the early 17th century onwards, however, with the introduction of the tobacco plant from the New World. Indeed, the similarity of our nos. 11 and 12 to 18th- and 19th-century pieces from Ottoman Greece suggests that they may be considerably later than Mamluk in date (see Robinson 1985). Three examples have also recently been published from excavations in Beirut (Turquety-Pariset 1982, 37–38, nos. 25–27; figs. 4–5).

> 11. Fig. 43. (P23) Fragment of pipe bowl. Fabric grey with red-brown polished surface, fine, hard. Context 75, Area A2, Phase E.
>
> 12. Fig. 43. (P24) Pipe bowl with stem attachment, almost complete. Fabric as no. 11. Context 75, Area A2, Phase E.

2. UNGLAZED WHEEL-MADE WARES

Unglazed wheel-made wares represent the largest class of pottery present at the Red Tower in all phases. They were sorted into three main categories: those fired in an oxidizing atmosphere (here described as "Coarse fabrics"), those fired in a reducing atmosphere ("Grey fabrics") and finer types with a white, cream or sometimes slightly pink fabric ("White fabrics").

(A) COARSE FABRICS

Residual Byzantine and early Islamic coarse pottery was common in most contexts. A fairly high proportion of this material (over 50% in Phase A) consists of sherds decorated with fine combing or coarser rilling, both produced by running a serrated edge across the surface of the vessel. These sherds seem to have come mostly from round-bottomed amphorae with rounded shoulders, vertical necks and round-sectioned vertical loop handles on the shoulders (cf. Bethany: Saller 1957, 206, no. 7051; 209, nos. 7312–13); or from hemi-spherical cooking pots with inward-sloping cut-away rims, round-sectioned horizontal loop handles and closely fitting lids (cf. Bethany (Saller 1957, 246, no. 3338); Pella, late 6th to mid-8th century (McNicoll *et al.* 1982(2), pls. 138.1, 140.7 and 143.2); Khirbat al-Mafjar, mid-8th century (Baramki 1944, 71, 74 (ware 18a); fig. 13)).

Such pottery is poorly represented in Phase C. Instead, the unglazed coarse pottery of this phase consists almost entirely of contemporaneous material of the 13th century. The commonest types of vessel represented are amphorae, sometimes with white painting on the outside. Unfortunately no complete profiles survive. They seem, however, to have had a roughly cylindrical form, with gently rilled sides (the rilling produced in this case by the potter's fingers, not by a serrated edge as on the earlier types), a hollow base to allow the vessel to stand on a flat surface, a pair of opposing vertical strap handles and a narrow vertical rim (see nos. 15–18). The fabrics are orange-buff to grey, containing grog and white grits. Surfaces are washed buff or grey and are often painted with wavy lines of white slip. These medieval amphorae are well fired, with a metallic ring to them, quite unlike the earlier Byzantine or early Islamic types. White-painted sherds are already present by the early 12th century in Phase B, in which they represent 4·13% of the total assemblage. In Phase C (mid-13th century) they achieve 14·24%, and thereafter virtually vanish from the record. These figures, however, underestimate the total proportions of sherds coming from white-painted vessels, since not all the fragments from them would have been painted.

From Phase D onwards, unglazed coarse wares continue to represent the largest class of pottery in all phases. Most of this material seems likely to be contemporaneous rather than residual, though as indicated above Byzantine coarse wares probably still accounted for 10–20% of all subsequent assemblages. The fragmentary condition of the material, however, and the mixed stratigraphy of Phase E (*c.*1390–*c.*1920) prevents any typological development being identified.

> 13. Fig. 43. (P68) Pitcher, fragment of rim, neck and handle attachment. Fabric pink-buff with creamy wash on surfaces, coarse, fairly hard. Context 131, Area A3, Phase D1.
>
> 14. Fig. 43. (P99) Jug with strap handle, almost complete except for rim (h. *c.*28; max. d. 18·2 cm.). Fabric grey, red-brown at edges with smooth buff exterior surface, fairly fine with white gritty inclusions, hard and finely potted; heavy rilling inside. Context 126 (22 fragments, + another 54 probably from the same vessel), Area A3, Phase E1.

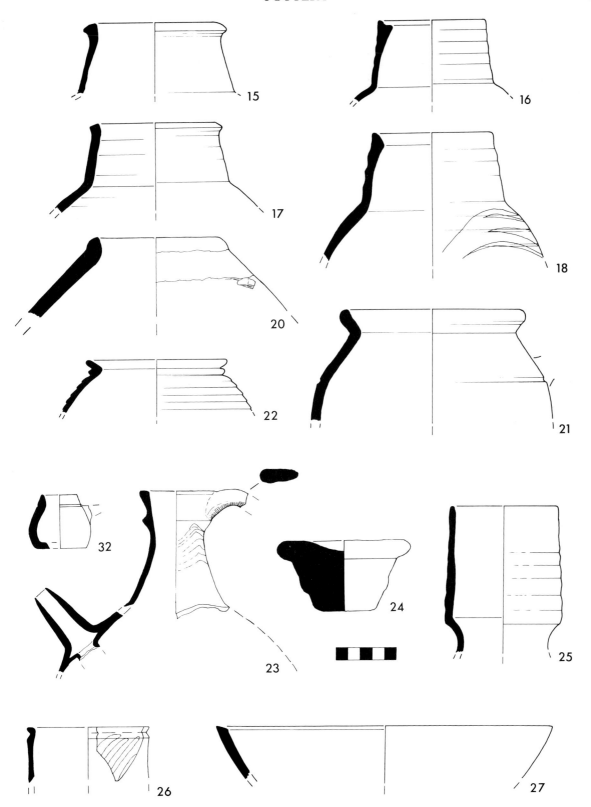

Fig. 44. Pottery: Unglazed coarse wares (nos. 15–17, 32) (Scale 1:3).

15. Fig. 44. (P55) Amphora, rim fragment (d. 11·6 cm.). Fabric pink-brown, grey on surfaces, coarse, fairly hard. Context 116, Area C4, Phase D.

16. Fig. 44. (P31) Amphora, rim fragment (d. 9·0 cm.). Fabric pink-orange, quite fine with some small white inclusions, hard, with surface wash. Context 84, Area C1, Phase B.

17. Fig. 44. (P87) Amphora, rim fragment (d. 10·8 cm.). Fabric red-brown to grey, with white inclusions, coarse with grey surface wash, hard and metallic sounding. Context 146, Area A1/3, Phase C.

18. Fig. 44. (P85) Amphora, rim fragment (d. 10·0 cm.). Fabric as no. 16, orange to grey, with white slip-painting on outside. Context 146, Area A1/3, Phase C.

19. Not illustrated. (P98) Canteen, fragment of body and strap handle. Fabric as no. 16. Context 141, Area A1/3, Phase C.

20. Fig. 44. (P54) Hole-mouthed jar, rim fragment. Fabric grey with red-brown surface, coarse, very hard, crudely made. Context 116, Area C4, Phase D.

21. Fig. 44. (P29) Jar, fragment of out-turned rim (d. 15·4 cm.) and handle attachment. Fabric pink-brown, coarse, hard. Context 78, Area A1, Phase E.

22. Fig. 44. (P41) Olla, fragment of everted rim (d. 11·5 cm.) and rilled body. Fabric orange with grey external surface, coarse with white inclusions, hard. Cf. Pella, 6th to 7th century (McNicoll *et al.* 1982(2), pl. 138, nos. 6–10). Context 94, Area C, Phase A.

23. Fig. 44. (P88) Pitcher, fragments from rim and neck with attachment for flat oval-sectioned handle, and from body and spout. Fabric red with greyish exterior, coarse containing white grits, fairly soft and crumbly. Traces of white slip-painting on exterior. Cf. Pella, mid-8th century (Smith *et al.* 1980, pl. XXX; McNicoll *et al.* 1982, pl. 142·1); Caesarea, Crusader period (Pringle 1985b, no. 1). Context 146 (9 fragments), Area A1/3, Phase C.

24. Fig. 44. (P52) Amphora stopper (11·0 × 5·7 cm.). Fabric pinkish orange to grey with pink wash, very coarse, fairly hard. Probably residual from 6th or 7th century. Context 108, Area A1, Phase D.

25. Fig. 44. (P86) Pipe (?), fragment of plain rim (d. 9·0 cm.). Fabric orange-pink with buff external wash, coarse with white inclusions, hard and metallic sounding. Context 146, Area A1/3, Phase C.

26. Fig. 44. (P32) Albarello, rim fragment (d. 10 cm.). Fabric orange-buff, quite fine with white inclusions, hard. White slip-painting on outside. Context 84, Area C1, Phase B.

27. Fig. 44. (P30) Hemi-spherical cooking pot with cut-away inward-sloping rim to take a lid (d. 28 cm.). Fabric grey, grey-brown on inside face, coarse, hard. Cf. Khirbat al-Mafjar, 8th to 13th century (Baramki 1944, 71, 74 (wares 18ab); fig. 13); Abu Ghosh, 10th to 11th century (de Vaux and Steve 1950, 127; pl. B.18); Capernaum, early Islamic (Loffreda 1983, 361–362; figs. 8.1–3 and 12.5–6); Jerusalem Citadel, early Islamic (Geva 1983, 69; pl. 7a). Context 84, Area C1, Phase B.

28. Fig. 45. (P60) Large basin or mortarium, with beaded rim, comb-decorated exterior and handle attachment (d. 48 cm.). Fabric light brown-orange, very coarse with grey gritty inclusions, fairly hard. Cf. Tall Qaimum, Byzantine or early Islamic (Ben-Tor and Rosenthal 1978, 73; fig. 7.10); Pella, mid-8th century (McNicoll *et al.* 1982(1), 146; (2), pl. 145.6). Context 124 (31 fragments), Area C3, Phase B.

(B) GREY FABRICS

In Phases A and B (and residually in some later phases) there are found a few fragments of rilled amphorae with a dark reddish brown fabric and grey exterior surface, decorated with white slip-painting. These belong to a class of amphora common in the late 7th and 8th centuries in Palestine and Transjordan. They have been excavated, for example, at the Amman Citadal (Harding 1951, 12, nos. 41 and 66), Pella (McNicoll *et al.* 1982(1), 146; (2), pls. 62b and 146·3), Khirbat al-Mafjar (Baramki 1944, fig. 3.1–3), Bethany (Saller 1957, 209, no. 7042; fig. 39) and Kursi (Tzaferis 1983a, 58–59; fig. 7.1).

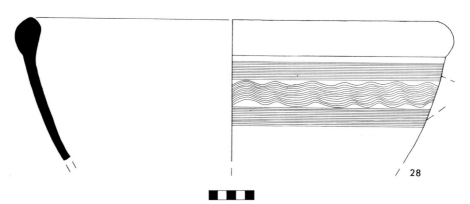

Fig. 45. Pottery: Unglazed basin or mortarium (no. 28) (Scale 1 : 4).

Fragments of another type of coarse unglazed pottery with a distinctive grey or black fabric appear in significant quantities from Phase E onwards, achieving 5.87% of the total assemblage in that phase and 34.47% in Phase E1. Only small quantities of this ware were found in Area C, probably because here the uppermost layers had been bulldozed away. Grey-fired pottery of this type was produced from around the middle of the 19th century (Stern 1978, 5; fig. 1.4) and it is still made today in the region of Gaza (cf. Gatt 1885). It seems likely, however, that the finds at the Red Tower would have come from a source nearer at hand, though where has yet to be precisely determined. Forms consist mostly of rilled amphorae, somewhat similar to the 13th-century examples but smaller and with rounded bases; and pitchers (*ibrīq*, pl. *abārīq*) with narrow vertical collars and globular bodies. Some of the sherds are also comb-decorated.

(c) White Fabrics

Wares with a white (or buff to pink) fabric are normally somewhat finer and softer than the other unglazed wares. Forms comprise mostly bowls and water jars or jugs. Fine white fabrics are common in the early Islamic period (e.g. Abu Ghosh, 9th to 11th century: de Vaux and Steve 1950, 127–130; pl. C–D); and in Phase B (early 12th century, including residual material) they represent 4.71% of the pottery in Area A and 9.00% in Area C. The finds of white wares from later phases tend to have somewhat coarser fabrics and a few pieces from Phase D onwards (e.g. nos. 29–31) have incised decoration.

> 29. Fig. 48. (P76) Closed form, fragment from shoulder and base of neck. Fabric grey-buff, pinkish in section with white external slip, coarse, fairly soft. Incised decoration on outside. Context 17, Area C, Phase D.
>
> 30. Fig. 48. (P36) Closed form, body fragment. Fabric buff-grey, quite fine, fairly hard. Incised decoration on outside. Context 85, Area A2, Phase E.
>
> 31. Fig. 48. (P74) Closed form, body fragment. Fabric white-buff, quite fine, fairly hard. Incised decoration on outside. Context 46, Area A2, Phase E.

3. LAMPS

> 32. Fig. 44. (P56) Beehive lamp, fragment. Fabric buff, rather coarse, hard. Context 116, Area C4, Phase D.
>
> 33. Fig. 46. (P50) Lamp, made in a two-piece mould, oval-shaped (8.5 × 10 × 3.8 cm.), with low oval base-ring, a round hole in the top, pulled-up handle, little decoration. Spout burnt. Fabric pink, coarse containing grog, soft. Context 110, Area C3, Phase E.
>
> 34. Fig. 47. (P67) Lamp, made in two-piece mould, oval-shaped (8.3 × 12 × 4 cm.), with rounded base, handle pulled up and over, spout burnt. Fabric white, fine, hard.

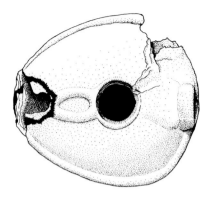

33

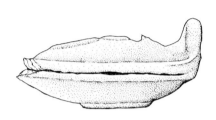

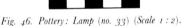

Fig. 46. Pottery: Lamp (no. 33) (Scale 1 : 2).

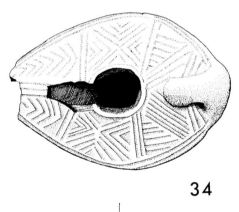

34

Fig. 47. Pottery: Lamp (no. 34) (Scale 1 : 2).

Geometrical pattern on upper surface. Cf. St. Mary of Carmel, 13th century (Pringle 1984a, 97, no. 9); al-Fula (*La Fève*), 12th or 13th century (Kedar and Pringle 1985). Context 133 (6 fragments), Area A3, Phase D.

35. Not illustrated. (P19) Saucer lamp with pinched spout, missing most of sides. Fabric pink-buff, grey in fracture, rather coarse with white inclusions. Probably residual. Context 75, Area A2, Phase E.

4. LEAD-GLAZED WARES

(A) LEAD-GLAZED COMMON OR KITCHEN WARES

Lead-glazed cooking pots are almost entirely absent from the Red Tower before the construction of the castle, even though they are attested elsewhere in Palestine from perhaps as early as the 8th century and certainly from the 10th (for discussion, see Pringle 1985b, 176). In Phase B they represent only 1·15% of the total assemblage, and in Phase C 18·39%. In Phase D the proportion drops to 13·01%. Most of the sherds of glazed cooking pots from this phase, however, come from the collapse of the tower vault in Area C, and it therefore seems likely that they were derived from the final phase of Frankish occupation. They include the sherds of a glazed cooking pot (similar to nos. 36–43 below) found together with carbonized food remains, which appear to have fallen with the first floor of the tower (see below, pp. 187–191). After Phase D glazed common wares virtually disappear from the site, though pieces of identifiable 14th-century types from Phase D1 onwards indicate that not all of the finds from later strata are residual.

The normal types of cooking pot of the 13th century at the Red Tower consist of globular vessels with vertical or out-turned rims and horizontal strap or oval-sectioned handles. A thick dark brown glaze covers the inside of the base and is sometimes splashed on the shoulder of the pot. The fabrics are thin, hard and brittle and tend to shatter into tiny fragments. For this reason no complete pots survive, though enough remains of some of them to indicate their general similarity to the more complete examples excavated near-by in Caesarea (Pringle 1985b, 176–177, nos. 3–8). Since the glaze on these pots does not cover the whole interior, it seems unlikely that its main purpose was to make them less porous. More likely the glaze was intended to make the vessel easier to clean in the area where food was most likely to burn or stick to the pan.

Note that in the drawings, the extent of glazing is indicated by stippling.

36. Fig. 48. (P82) Globular cooking pot, fragment of thickened rim. Fabric brick red to orange, coarse, finely potted, medium hard and metallic-sounding. Specks of brown glaze. Cf. Tall ʿArqa, 13th century (Thalmann 1978, 23, 25; fig. 32.3). Context 32, Area C, Phase C.

37. Fig. 48. (P58) Cooking pot, as no. 36, fragment of vertical thickened rim. Cf. Caesarea, Crusader period (Pringle 1985b, no. 5). Context 116, Area C4, Phase D.

38. Fig. 48. (P84) Cooking pot, as no. 36. Context 32, Area C, Phase C.

39. Fig. 48. (P57) Cooking pot, fragment of everted rim. Cf. Tall ʿArqa, 13th century (Thalmann 1978, 23, 25; fig. 32.2). Context 116, Area C4, Phase D.

40. Fig. 48. (P81) Cooking pot, as no. 39. Context 32, Area C, Phase C.

41. Fig. 48. (P83) Cooking pot, as no. 39. Context 32, Area C, Phase C.

42. Fig. 48. (P96) Cooking pot, as no. 39. Splash of dark brown glaze across shoulder, probably derived from another glazed vessel stacked on top of it in the kiln. Context 145, Area A1/3, Phase C.

43. Fig. 48. (P71) Cooking pot, fragment of beaded rim. Context 105, Area A1, Phase D1.

44. Fig. 48. (P97) Cooking pot, fragment of horizontal loop handle with oval cross-section. Cf. Caesarea, Crusader period (Pringle 1985b, nos. 5–6). Context 145, Area A1/3, Phase C.

Glazed common wares from the period immediately following the destruction of the castle (Phase D1 onwards) have a somewhat finer, lighter-coloured fabric and a thin even coating of light brown glaze. The fabric and glaze may be compared with those of the contemporary glazed slip-painted wares with which they are often associated (see nos. 64–69 below). The dating of these types seems likely to be late 13th- to mid-14th-century. Similar types are found at Tall Qaimun (Ben-Tor, Portugali and Avissàr 1979, 76; fig. 5.5) and St. Mary of Carmel (Pringle 1984a, 99, nos. 27–28).

45. Fig. 48. (P45) Flat-bottomed frying pan (*tegame*) with flaring sides, lid-seating and opposing lug handles (d. 27·8; h. 4·5 cm.). Fabric light orange-brown, medium fine with small white inclusions, hard. Fine light brown glaze on inside and rim. Context 98 (11 fragments), Area A1, Phase D1.

46. Fig. 48. (P44) Flat-bottomed frying pan, as no. 45 (d. 26·4; h. 4·0 cm.). Fabric pinkish orange, fire-blackened on base, somewhat coarse and porous, hard. Light brown glaze on inside and rim. Context 98 (4 fragments), Area A1, Phase D1.

47. Not illustrated. (P5) Frying pan, as no. 45, rim fragment. Burnt, so that glaze has acquired a dark green colour. Context 16, Area C, Phase F.

48. Fig. 48. (P93) Small cup, fragment of plain vertical rim (d. 14 cm.). Fabric orange-buff with exterior wash, fairly fine, quite hard. Light brown glaze on inside only. Context 130, Area A3, Phase E.

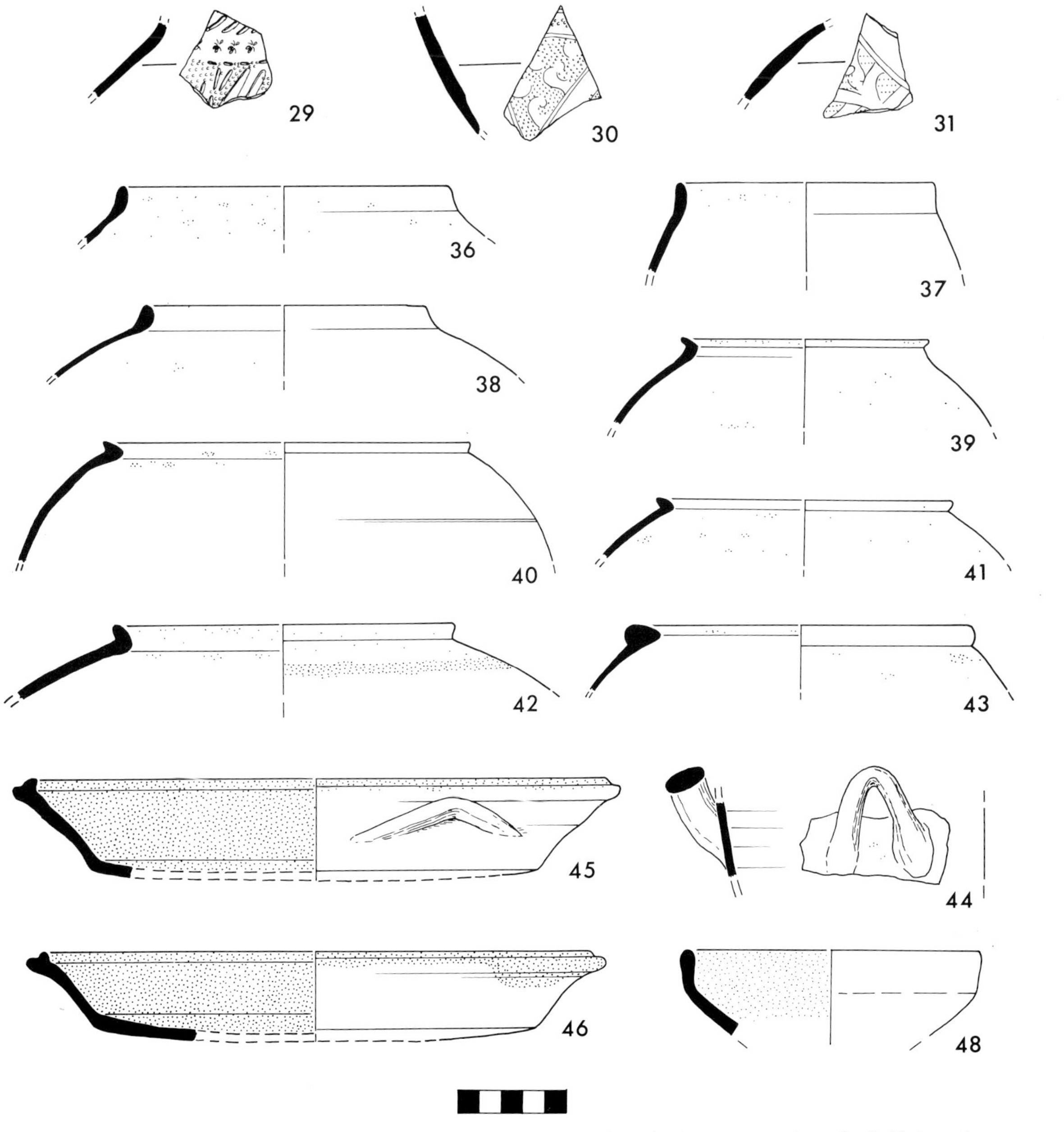

Fig. 48. Pottery: Unglazed white fabrics with incised decoration (nos. 29–31); lead-glazed common wares (nos. 36–48) (Scale 1:3).

(b) MANGANESE-PAINTED LEAD-GLAZED POTTERY

Only a single piece of manganese-painted lead-glazed pottery was found in the whole excavation.

49. Fig. 49. (P18) Hemi-spherical bowl, fragment of foot-ring base. Fabric orange-brown, coarse with white inclusions, fairly soft. Decoration consisting of seven radiating strokes painted in manganese brown (a) under a glazed which appears brown and pock-marked as though partially devitrified. Contexts 64 and 85, Area A2, Phase E.

5. GLAZED SLIP-WARES

(a) MONOCHROME GLAZED SLIP-WARES

Monochrome glazed slip-wares are already present during the Frankish occupation of the Red Tower (Phases B and C), but become more common after the destruction of the castle. This would tend to support the dating of most of the pottery of this type to the late 13th century onwards, as has already been proposed, for example, at Tripoli (Salamé-Sarkis 1980, 186–191

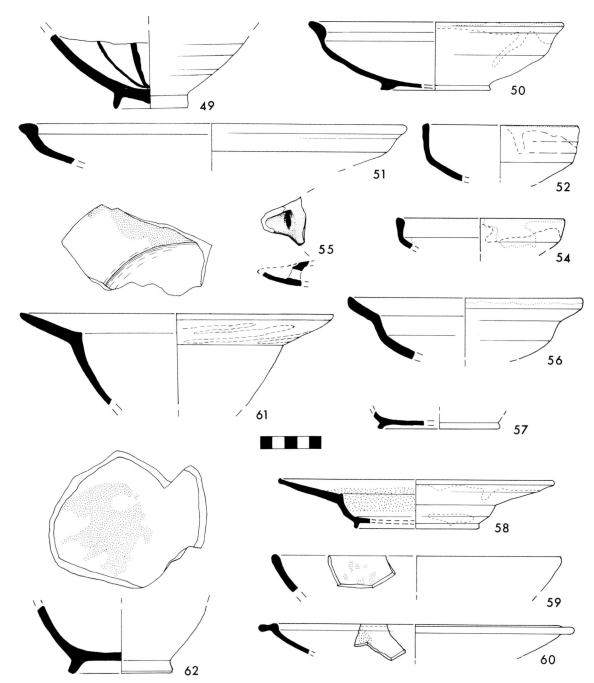

Fig. 49. Pottery: Manganese-painted lead-glazed (no. 49): monochrome glazed slip-wares (nos. 50–57); glazed slip-wares with green decoration (nos. 58–62) (Scale 1 : 3).

(Type A.III); figs. 29–31; pl. LXXII.8–9) and Tall Qaimun (Ben-Tor, Portugali and Avissàr 1979, 76; fig. 5.1).

50. Fig. 49. (P1) Bowl with thickened out-turned rim and low foot-ring base (d. 21; h. 5·5 cm.). Fabric pink-orange,

with red-brown external wash, somewhat coarse, hard; a hole is burnt in the base. Thin white slip on inside, spilling over rim, covered by bright green glaze. The slip and glaze of another similar vessel have stuck to the outside during firing, suggesting that the bowls were stacked upside down in the kiln, with no intervening stilts. Context 13 (13 fragments), Area C, Phase E.

51. Fig. 49. (P4) Basin, fragment of rim similar to no. 50 (d. *c.*32 cm.). Fabric pink, rather coarse, containing grog and white inclusions, fairly soft. Cream slip under bright green glaze. Cf. St. Mary of Carmel, (late) 13th century (Pringle 1984a, 103, no. 41). Context 14, Area C, Phase F.

52. Fig. 49. (P46) Cup, fragment of plain vertical rim (d. 13 cm.). Fabric pink, quite fine, hard. Cream slip beneath bright green glaze. Context 98 (3 fragments), Area A1, Phase D1.

53. Not illustrated. (P27) Cup, as no. 52. Fabric red-brown. Context 78, Area A1, Phase E.

54. Fig. 49. (P14) Cup, fragment of vertical thickened rim (d. 14 cm.). Fabric light red-brown, darker on outside surface, quite fine, fairly hard. Cream slip beneath green glaze. Context 57, Area A1, Phase E.

55. Fig. 49. (P90) Lamp, fragment of beak. Fabric brick red, coarse, fairly hard. White slip beneath pale green glaze. Context 146 (2 fragments), Area A1/3, Phase C.

56. Fig. 49. (P16) Bowl, fragment of flanged rim (d. 19 cm.). Fabric orange-brown, quite fine, fairly hard. Coated inside with thin light brown slip not covering whole surface, under dark brown glaze. Context 60, Area A2, Phase E.

57. Fig. 49. (P89) Bowl (perhaps as no. 58), fragment of low foot-ring base. Fabric brick red, rather coarse with small black inclusions, hard. Thin white slip under pale green glaze. Context 141 (2 fragments), Area A1/3, Phase C.

(B) GLAZED SLIP-WARES WITH GREEN SPLASHED DECORATION

The following pieces are distinguished from the monochrome slip-wares by having a clear or pale yellow glaze enlivened by splashes of green.

58. Fig. 49. (P95) Shallow bowl, with wide flanged rim and low foot-ring base (d. 22·5; h. 4·0 cm.). Fabric perhaps originally buff coloured but burnt, rather coarse. White slip beneath a clear glaze, coloured pale green (f) in places. For the form, cf. Caesarea, Crusader period (Pringle 1985b, 177, no. 12). Context 141, Area A1/3, Phase C.

59. Fig. 49. (P72) Hemi-spherical bowl, fragment of plain rim (d. 24 cm.). Fabric light orange-brown, quite fine with white inclusions, fairly hard. White slip on both sides. Yellow glaze splashed with green (f) on inside only. Context 105, Area A1, Phase D1.

60. Fig. 49. (P47) Bowl, fragment of flanged rim (d. *c.*26 cm.). Fabric pink, rather coarse, hard. Thin white slip inside, not extending to rim. Yellow glaze on inside and rim, splashed with green (f). Context 104 (2 fragments), Area C2, Phase E.

61. Fig. 49. (P101) Hemi-spherical bowl, fragment of broad flanged rim (d. 26 cm.). Fabric buff, fairly fine but containing some grog, white grits and mica, surfaces smoothed, medium hard. Pinkish cream slip on inside under clear somewhat opaque glaze with thick green (f)

decoration. Cf. Caesarea, Crusader period (Pringle 1985b, 179, nos. 20–21), probably from the same source. Contexts 141 and 146, Area A1/3, Phase C.

62. Fig. 49. (P91) Hemi-spherical bowl, fragment of foot-ring base. Form, fabric and decoration as no. 61. Context 146, Area A1/3, Phase C.

63. Not illustrated. (P11) Hemi-spherical bowl, fragment of foot-ring base, as no. 62. Context 32 (2 fragments), Area C, Phase C.

(C) GLAZED RESERVED SLIP-WARE

Only two fragments of glazed reserved slip-ware were recovered, both of them from topsoil in Area C. They have a clear glaze with green splashed decoration, somewhat like examples published from Caesarea (Pringle 1985b, 179, nos. 22–25).

6. GLAZED SLIP-PAINTED WARES

With the exception of one small and possibly intrusive sherd from Phase C (Context 141), glazed slip-painted wares appear only from Phase D onwards, suggesting a date for these types from the late 13th century onwards. All the types found at the Red Tower seem to be local Palestinian products, probably from the same potteries that were producing the bright green glazed slip-wares (nos. 50–54) and the flat-bottomed brown glazed frying pans (nos. 45–47) described above (cf. Tall Qaimun, 13th to 14th centuries: Ben-Tor and Rosenthal 1978, 67; fig. 5.1; Ben-Tor, Portugali and Avissàr 1979, 76; fig. 5.2). No identifiable 12th- or early 13th-century types were found (possibly excepting no. 67), even in residual contexts (cf. Caesarea: Pringle 1985b, 183, nos. 26–35).

64. Fig. 50. (P2) Basin, fragment of thickened flattened inward-sloping rim (d. 23·5 cm.). Fabric pink-orange, somewhat coarse containing grog, hard. Fine cream-coloured slip-painting inside and on rim, under almost colourless glaze. Context 8 (3 fragments), Area B, Phase E.

65. Fig. 50. (P69) Basin, fragment of foot-ring base. Fabric pink-orange, quite fine but containing grog and white grits, fairly hard. Yellow glaze over white slip-painting. Context 131, Area A3, Phase D1.

66. Fig. 50. (P10) Basin, fragment of hollowed disc base. Fabric pink-orange, somewhat coarse containing grog, medium hard. Yellow glaze. Context 26, Area C, Phase E.

67. Fig. 50. (P33) Bowl, fragment of flanged rim. Fabric brick red, coarse, quite hard. Cream slip-painting under yellow glaze on upper surface of flange only. Context 86, Area A2, Phase D1.

68. Fig. 50. (P75) Basin, fragment of vertical thickened rim with carinated side (d. 24 cm.). Fabric orange-brown, coarse with white inclusions, fairly soft. Fine yellow glaze. Context 105 (2 fragments), Area A1, Phase D1.

69. Fig. 50. (P65) Basin, fragment of foot-ring base. Fabric brown-orange, rather coarse with white and red inclusions, medium hard. Yellow glaze. Context 133, Area A3, Phase D.

7. GRAFFITA WARES

Graffita pottery was extremely rare or non-existent in all phases at the Red Tower. In all, graffita sherds numbered no more than eleven of local types, one of imported Byzantine and one of imported Cypriot type throughout the whole excavation. This is in marked contrast to Caesarea, where a wide range of graffita types is represented (Pringle 1985b, 183–193, nos. 37–69).

(A) COARSE LOCAL GRAFFITA WARES

70. Fig. 50. (P40) Basin, body sherd. Fabric grey-brown (burnt), coarse with white inclusions, hard. Cream slip. Green glaze. Incised decoration thick and uneven. Cf. Tall Hasban, Ayyubid-Mamluk periods (Lawlor 1980, fig. 1, no. 1070). Context 99, Area C2, Phase F.

71. Fig. 50. (P15) Bowl, fragment of flanged rim. Fabric brick red, coarse, medium hard. Thin cream slip on inside and splashed over rim, presenting mottled appearance where coarseness of fabric shows through, under green glaze on inside only. Probably early 12th-century. Context 59, Area B1, Phase B.

(B) GRAFFITA WARES OF BYZANTINE AND CYPRIOT TYPES

The only two pieces of imported graffita pottery were residual fragments in Phase D1.

72. Not illustrated. (P80) Bowl, body fragment. Fabric dark red, fine, hard. White slip. Yellow glaze. Probably 12th-century Byzantine. Context 89, Area A2, Phase D1.

73. Fig. 50. (P70) Bowl, fragment of high foot-ring base with out-turned lip. Fabric light grey, quite fine, very hard. Graffita design in roundel in base. Fine white slip, faintly greenish clear glaze with splash of brown (b). Tripod marks in base. Cypriot type IIIa (Dikigoropoulos and Megaw 1948, 82–83, 88–89; nos. 13–14; pl. VIII). The tendency to overfiring, with consequent blackening of the fabric, is a characteristic of the pottery of this type produced at Lemba in western Cyprus in the 13th century (Megaw and Jones 1983, 241). Context 105, Area A1, Phase D1.

8. ISLAMIC GLAZED WARES

(A) ISLAMIC ALKALINE-GLAZED WARES

Included in this category are all alkaline-glazed wares except those with under-glaze painting, which are treated separately below.

74. Fig. 50. (P59) Hemi-spherical bowl, fragment of flaring rim (d. 22 cm.). Fabric creamy, sandy, soft. Thin opaque pale blue (probably discoloured white) glaze on both sides. Context 121, Area A1, Phase C.

75. Fig. 50. (P12) Hemi-spherical bowl, fragment of flaring rim. Fabric creamy, sandy, soft. Opaque pale blue glaze on both sides, with streak of turquoise-green (f) on inside. Context 32, Area C, Phase C.

76. Fig. 50. (P9) Closed form, body fragment from near base. Fabric buff, pink in fracture, rather coarse, fairly soft. Thick opaque green glaze covering upper part of sherd. Context 24, Area A1, Phase F.

77. Fig. 51. (P43) Hemi-spherical bowl, fragment of flanged crinkled rim and gently scalloped body. Fabric white, sugary, soft. Thick (1 mm.) duck-egg blue-green transparent glaze on both sides. Probably an attempt at imitating celadon. Contexts 78 (1 fragment) and 98 (12 fragments), Area A1, Phase D1 (& E).

(B) EARLY ISLAMIC GLAZED POLYCHROME WARE

The pieces of glazed polychrome pottery described below (nos. 78–79) belong to a type with cream or buff fabric, covered by a thin white slip or wash and decorated in green, brown, yellow or purple under a thin clear glaze. It is dated at Abu Ghosh from the 10th to the 11th century (de Vaux and Steve 1950, 120–122; pls. A and XV.2), though production had probably already begun in the 9th. That pottery of this kind was produced in Palestine itself is proved by the discovery of a potter's workshop at Hammat-Tabariya, Tiberias (Oren 1971; Frierman 1975, 51–52). The material at Tiberias differs slightly from that at Abu Ghosh, however, suggesting that more than one centre of production existed. Other finds of this ware have been made in Caesarea, the Jerusalem Citadel (Geva 1983, 69–71; pl. 7a), Khirbat al-Mafjar (Baramki 1944, pl. XVI.4–5), Tall Qaimun (Ben-Tor and Rosenthal 1978, 67; pl. 18c (top right)) and Dhiban in Transjordan (Winnett and Reed 1964, 25; pl. 13.18).

78. Fig. 50. (P38) Bowl, fragment of foot-ring base. Fabric cream-coloured, rather coarse and sandy with occasional white inclusions, fairly hard. Thin creamy slip or wash on both sides, under clear glaze with turquoise green (f) decoration on inside only. Context 93, Area C, Phase B.

79. Fig. 50. (P8) Bowl, fragment of disc base. Fabric pink-buff, quite fine, hard. Decoration inside in pale green (f) and manganese brown (a), and under base in brown (a) only. Context 24, Area A1, Phase F.

9. UNDER-GLAZE PAINTED WARES

Under-glaze painted wares first appear at the Red Tower in Phase D (c. 1265–c. 1390). Although on stratigraphical grounds it is possible that some of this

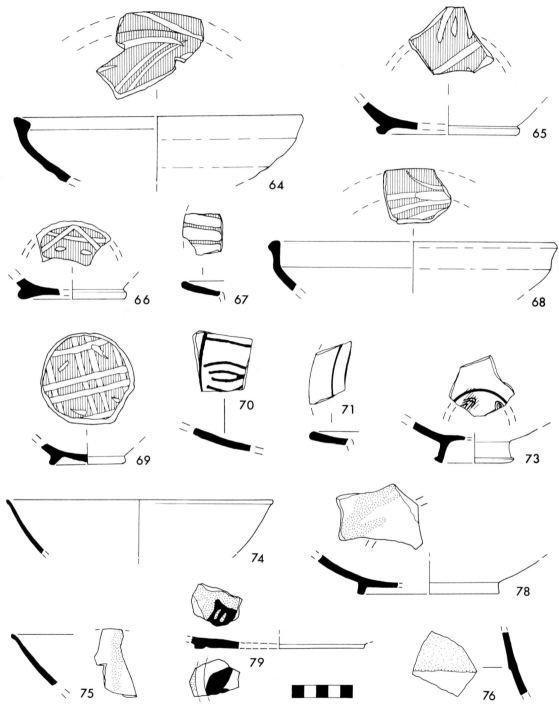

Fig. 50. Pottery: glazed slip-painted (nos. 64–69); graffita (nos. 70–73); alkaline-glazed (nos. 74–76); early Islamic polychrome (nos. 78–79) (Scale 1 : 3).

material might have come from the final phase of Frankish occupation of the site (*c.* 1248–65), typological comparison of the pieces illustrated here with material from Egypt and Syria suggests that most of it dates from the early or mid-14th century onwards. (I am grateful to Dr. Helen Philon for this observation.) As a group the under-glaze painted pottery from the Red Tower has more in common with the group from St. Mary of Carmel (Pringle 1984a, 107–109) than with that from Caesarea (Pringle 1985b, 196). Indeed, it now seems

Table 5   Distribution of pottery types by phase over the whole site

Phases:	A	B	C	D	D1	E	E1	F
Unglazed:								
Handmade	1	1	1	149	262	521	33	312
	0.06	*0.10*	*0.04*	*10.33*	*36.85*	*11.89*	*4.70*	*7.45*
+ painting			32	13	12	13		10
			1.21	*0.90*	*1.69*	*0.30*		*0.24*
Coarse fabrics	773	550	1587	865	301	2914	363	2653
	44.81	*52.83*	*59.80*	*59.99*	*42.33*	*66.53*	*51.71*	*63.36*
+ combing	356	152	9	55	7	184	10	149
	20.64	*14.60*	*0.34*	*3.81*	*0.98*	*4.20*	*1.42*	*3.56*
+ rilling	569	211	83	86	22	178	38	235
	32.99	*20.27*	*3.13*	*5.96*	*3.09*	*4.06*	*5.41*	*5.61*
+ white painting	12	43	378	13	4	1		2
	0.70	*4.13*	*14.24*	*0.90*	*0.56*	*0.02*		*0.05*
Grey fabrics	1	3	4	5	7	246	232	536
	0.06	*0.29*	*0.15*	*0.35*	*0.98*	*5.62*	*33.05*	*12.80*
+ combing						5	4	14
						0.11	*0.57*	*0.33*
+ rilling				1		6	6	26
				0.07		*0.14*	*0.85*	*0.62*
+ rilling + white painting	5	23		5		2		
	0.29	*2.21*		*0.35*		*0.05*		
White fabrics	7	36	50	14	36	122	2	70
	0.41	*3.46*	*1.88*	*0.97*	*5.06*	*2.78*	*0.28*	*1.67*
—moulded			1					
			0.04					
—incised				1	1	3		5
				0.07	*0.14*	*0.07*		*0.12*
—impressed						1		
						0.02		
Lamps		3	1	8	1	2		1
		0.29	*0.04*	*0.55*	*0.14*	*0.05*		*0.02*
Pipes						2	3	2
						0.05	*0.43*	*0.05*
Terra sigillata								2
								0.05
Glazed:								
Kitchen wares	1	12	488	189	19	24	4	21
	0.06	*1.15*	*18.39*	*13.10*	*2.67*	*0.55*	*0.57*	*0.50*
Slip-wares		1	6	19	13	85	3	81
		0.10	*0.23*	*1.32*	*1.83*	*1.94*	*0.43*	*1.93*
—green painted		2	9	3	2	6		4
		0.19	*0.34*	*0.21*	*0.28*	*0.14*		*0.09*
Reserved slip-wares								2
								0.05
Mn. painted						2		
						0.05		
Graffita—monochrome		1		1		6		3
		0.10		*0.07*		*0.14*		*0.07*
—Byz/Cypriot					2			
					0.28			
Slip-painted			1	7	7	37	4	33
			0.04	*0.48*	*0.98*	*0.84*	*0.57*	*0.79*
Islamic alkaline		1	4		12	3		3
		0.10	*0.15*		*1.69*	*0.07*		*0.07*
Islamic polychrome		2						3
		0.19						*0.07*

Table 5   (cont.)

Phases:	A	B	C	D	D1	E	E1	F
UGP				8	3	12		9
				0·55	0·42	0·27		0·21
—blue and white						2		
						0·05		
Turkish						3		
						0·07		
Tin-glazed								1
								0·02
Porcelain						10		
						0·02		
Totals	1725	1041	2654	1442	711	4380	702	4187
%	100·02	100·01	100·02	99·98	99·97	100·01	99·99	99·97

unlikely that the occupation of the site of the Carmelite monastery came to an end with the departure of the friars in 1291, since a number of the under-glaze painted types (and some of the others) should be re-dated to the 14th century. As at the Red Tower, these under-glaze painted types find parallels in both Syria and Egypt, and it is uncertain from which source they were derived (on the problems of origin, see Jenkins 1984). In contrast, the under-glaze painted types excavated at Caesarea would all seem to be 13th-century and to have been imported from Muslim Syria during the period of Crusader occupation (pre-1265).

The relative quantity of under-glaze painted pottery from the Red Tower is very small; in no phase does it represent even as much as one-percent of the ceramic assemblage.

(A) Wares with Black Painting under a Colourless or Turquoise Glaze

These wares correspond with Hama, type VII, the so-called "Raqqa Ware" (Poulsen 1957, 157–178).

80. Fig. 51. (P3) Jar, fragment of vertical neck with thickened flattened rim (d. 10·5 cm.). Fabric creamy white, sandy, soft and friable. Black decoration under a blue-turquoise glaze. Probably mid-14th century. Cf. Acre, 13th century (Pringle, no. 32); Metropolitan Museum, New York (Jenkins 1983, 20, no. 20). Context 11 (4 fragments.), Area C, Phase E.

81. Fig. 51. (P48) Bowl, fragment of foot-ring base. Fabric white, sugary, soft. Black decoration under a clear blue-tinged glaze on the inside only. Cf. Hama, 13th century (Poulsen 1957, 160, 166, 172; figs. 498, 519, 549). Context 104, Area C2, Phase E.

(B) Wares with Black and Blue or Turquoise Painting under a Colourless Glaze

These wares correspond with Hama, type XI, dated by Poulsen to the late 13th and 14th centuries (1957, 202–224), but probably mostly mid-14th-century in date.

82. Fig. 51 (P94) Bowl, fragment of flanged rim (d. 25·6 cm.). Fabric cream, sugary, very soft. Decoration in black (a) and turquoise-blue (f) under a clear glass. Mid-14th century. Context 130, Area A3, Phase E.

83. Fig. 51. (P35) Bowl, body sherd. Fabric as no. 82. Decoration in black (a) and cobalt blue (f) under a colourless glaze covering both sides. Early to mid-14th century. Cf. St. Mary of Carmel (Pringle 1984a, 107, no. 74); Hama (Poulsen 1957, 212; fig. 716); Ashmolean Museum, Oxford (Porter 1981, 41–42; fig. 8; pl. XXIX). Context 90, Area A2, Phase E.

84. Fig. 51. (P7) Bowl, fragment of flanged rim (d. 24·5 cm.). Fabric as no. 82. Black (a) and turquoise-blue (f) decoration under a colourless glaze. Context 17, Area C, Phase D.

85. Fig. 51 (drawn upside down). (P6) Jar, fragment from narrowing neck. Fabric as no. 82. Black (a) and turquoise-blue (f) calligraphic decoration under clear glaze on outside; glaze but no decoration on inside. Cf. Metropolitan Museum, New York (Jenkins 1983, 24, no. 26). Context 16, Area C, Phase F.

86. Fig. 51. (P66) Hemi-spherical bowl, fragment of plain rim (d. 30 cm.). Fabric as no. 82. Black (a) decoration on both sides with watery cobalt blue (f) added on inside, under colourless glaze. Cf. Hama, type XIc, 14th century (Poulsen 1957, 210–212). Context 133, Area A3, Phase D.

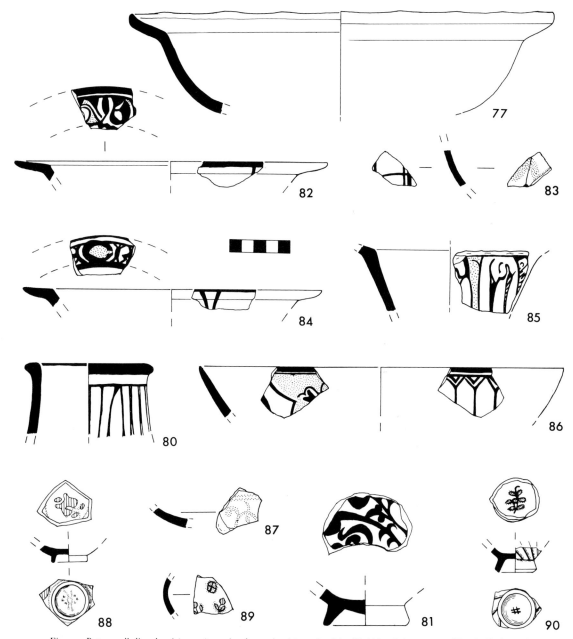

Fig. 51. Pottery: alkaline-glazed (no. 77); under-glaze painted (nos. 80–87); Turkish polychrome (nos. 88–90) (Scale 1:3).

(c) WARES WITH BLUE PAINTING UNDER A COLOURLESS GLAZE

These wares correspond with Hama, type XII, otherwise known as Syrain "blue-and-white" (Poulsen 1957, 224–230; cf. Lane 1971, 29–30; Carswell 1972b). Only two sherds were recovered from the Red Tower, both from Phase E. Their appearance therefore corresponds with the usual dating of this ware to the 14th century onwards. The two pieces from St. Mary of Carmel should also be reassigned to this date (cf. Pringle 1984a, 107–109, nos. 78–79).

87. Fig. 51. (P34) Bowl, body fragment from just above the base. Sugary white fabric, very soft. Blue decoration (f) under clear bluish glaze on inside only. Context 90, Area A2, Phase E.

POTTERY

Table 6 Distribution of pottery types by phase (Area A)

Phases:	A	B	C	D	D1	E	E1	F
Unglazed:								
Handmade			1 *0·05*	81 *24·77*	262 *36·85*	256 *10·57*	33 *4·70*	38 *3·36*
+ painting			15 *0·76*	8 *2·45*	12 *1·69*	4 *0·16*		
Coarse fabrics		48 *56·47*	1216 *61·63*	151 *46·18*	301 *42·33*	1593 *65·74*	363 *51·71*	567 *50·09*
+ combing	2 *100·00*	4 *4·71*	7 *0·35*	17 *5·20*	7 *0·98*	88 *3·63*	10 *1·42*	44 *3·89*
+ rilling		21 *24·71*	75 *3·80*	27 *8·26*	22 *3·09*	115 *4·75*	38 *5·41*	121 *10·69*
+ white painting		6 *7·06*	323 *16·37*	2 *0·61*	4 *0·56*	1 *0·04*		
Grey fabrics				1 *0·31*	7 *0·98*	235 *9·70*	232 *33·05*	291 *25·71*
+ combing						2 *0·08*	4 *0·57*	12 *1·06*
+ rilling						4 *0·16*	6 *0·85*	20 *1·77*
+ rilling + white painting		2 *2·35*		5 *1·53*		1 *0·04*		
White fabrics		4 *4·71*	50 *2·53*	6 *1·83*	36 *5·06*	54 *2·23*	2 *0·28*	16 *1·41*
—incised					1 *0·14*	2 *0·08*		
Lamps			1 *0·05*	7 *2·14*	1 *0·14*	2 *0·08*		1 *0·09*
Pipes						2 *0·08*	3 *0·43*	2 *0·18*
Glazed:								
Kitchen wares			270 *13·68*	8 *2·45*	19 *2·67*	18 *0·74*	4 *0·57*	3 *0·27*
Slip-wares			5 *0·25*	4 *1·22*	13 *1·83*	22 *0·91*	3 *0·43*	4 *0·35*
—green painted			8 *0·41*	1 *0·31*	2 *0·28*			
Mn. painted						2 *0·08*		
Graffita—monochrome						3 *0·12*		
—Byz/Cypriot					2 *0·28*			
Slip-painted			1 *0·05*	6 *1·83*	7 *0·98*	11 *0·45*	4 *0·57*	4 *0·35*
Islamic alkaline			1 *0·05*		12 *1·69*	1 *0·04*		1 *0·09*
Islamic polychrome								1 *0·09*
UGP				3 *0·92*	3 *0·42*	2 *0·08*		
—blue and white						2 *0·08*		
Turkish						3 *0·12*		
Tin-glazed								1 *0·09*
Porcelain								6 *0·53*
Totals %	2 *100·00*	85 *100·01*	1973 *99·98*	327 *100·01*	711 *99·97*	2423 *99·96*	702 *99·99*	1132 *100·02*

Table 7 Distribution of pottery types by phase (Areas C, C1, C4, C6)

Phases:	A	B	C	D	E	F
Unglazed:						
Handmade	1			64	154	214
	0·08			*6·46*	*10·53*	*10·95*
+ painting			17	5	6	5
			2·50	*0·50*	*0·41*	*0·26*
Coarse fabrics	546	186	371	648	1043	1349
	42·03	*57·76*	*54·48*	*65·39*	*71·34*	*69·00*
+ combing	329	27	2	22	86	87
	25·33	*8·39*	*0·29*	*2·22*	*5·88*	*4·45*
+ rilling	401	38	8	35	51	83
	30·87	*11·80*	*1·17*	*3·53*	*3·49*	*4·25*
+ white painting	12	21	55	11		1
	0·92	*6·52*	*8·08*	*1·11*		*0·05*
Grey fabrics	1	2	4		5	54
	0·08	*0·62*	*0·59*		*0·34*	*2·76*
+ combing					3	2
					0·21	*0·10*
+ rilling					2	1
					0·14	*0·05*
+ white painting	1	3				
	0·08	*0·93*				
White fabrics	7	29		8	42	31
	0·54	*9·00*		*0·81*	*2·87*	*1·58*
—moulded			1		1	
			0·15			
—incised				1		4
				0·10		*0·20*
Lamps		3		1		
		0·93		*0·10*		
Terra sigillata etc.						2
						0·10
Glazed:						
Kitchen wares	1	8	218	175		17
	0·08	*2·48*	*32·01*	*17·66*		*0·87*
Slip-wares			1	15	41	68
			0·15	*1·51*	*2·80*	*3·48*
—green painted		2	1	1	4	3
		0·62	*0·15*	*0·10*	*0·27*	*0·15*
Reserved slip-ware						2
						0·10
Graffita					2	
					0·14	
Slip-painted					13	20
					0·89	*1·02*
Islamic alkaline		1	3		2	2
		0·32	*0·44*		*0·14*	*0·10*
Islamic polychrome		2				2
		0·62				*0·10*
UGP				5	8	8
				0·50	*0·55*	*0·41*
Totals	1299	322	681	991	1462	1955
%	*100·01*	*99·98*	*100·01*	*99·99*	*100·00*	*99·98*

Table 8 Distribution of pottery types by phase (Area B)

Phases:	A	B	D	E	F
Unglazed:					
Handmade		1 / 0·42	3 / 3·95	45 / 12·43	30 / 4·14
+ painting				3 / 0·83	3 / 0·41
Coarse fabrics	171 / 50·74	164 / 69·20	43 / 56·58	240 / 66·30	484 / 66·85
+ combing	13 / 3·86	8 / 3·37	9 / 11·84	10 / 2·76	13 / 1·80
+ rilling	153 / 45·40	61 / 25·74	14 / 18·42	6 / 1·66	13 / 1·80
+ white painting					1 / 0·14
Grey fabrics		1 / 0·42	4 / 5·26	6 / 1·66	156 / 21·55
+ rilling			1 / 1·32		3 / 0·41
White fabrics				21 / 5·80	7 / 0·97
—incised				1 / 0·28	1 / 0·14
—impressed				1 / 0·28	
Glazed:					
Kitchen wares					1 / 0·14
Slip-wares		1 / 0·42		18 / 4·97	4 / 0·55
—green painted			1 / 1·32		
Graffita		1 / 0·42	1 / 1·32		
Slip-painted				10 / 2·76	3 / 0·41
UGP				1 / 0·28	1 / 0·14
Porcelain					4 / 0·55
Totals	337	237	76	362	724
%	100·00	99·99	100·01	100·01	100·00

10. TURKISH POLYCHROME GLAZED POTTERY

Three fragments of polychrome Turkish pottery were found in Phase E. All seem to be 18th-century products of the Armenian pottery industry established at Kütahya in west central Asia Minor (see Carswell 1972a; Lane 1971, 63–65).

88. Fig. 51. (P25) Coffee cup, base fragment. Fabric white, fine and chalky, fairly soft. Decorated in blue (f) and dark manganese purple (c) on both sides under a colourless glaze. The blue potter's mark under the base may perhaps be an illiterate attempt at copying the *Sivaz* mark. This and the use of purple would suggest a date between *c.*1740 and the end of the century or perhaps after (Carswell 1972a (2), 36–39). Context 77, Area A1, Phase E.

Table 9 Distribution of pottery types by phase (Area C2)

Phases:	A	B	D	E	F
Unglazed:					
Handmade			1 *12.50*	11 *21.57*	6 *6.82*
+ painting					1 *1.14*
Coarse fabrics	48 *65.75*	44 *59.46*	4 *50.00*	20 *39.22*	63 *71.59*
+ combing	12 *16.44*	6 *8.11*			
+ rilling	9 *12.33*	16 *21.62*		2 *3.92*	2 *2.27*
+ white painting		1 *1.35*			
Grey fabrics					1 *1.14*
+ white painting	4 *5.48*	3 *4.05*			
White fabrics				4 *7.84*	6 *6.82*
Glazed:					
Kitchen wares		4 *5.41*	3 *37.50*	6 *11.76*	
Slip-wares				3 *5.88*	3 *3.41*
—green painted				2 *3.92*	1 *1.14*
Graffita				1 *1.96*	3 *3.41*
Slip-painted				1 *1.96*	2 *2.27*
UGP				1 *1.96*	
Totals	73	74	8	51	88
%	*100.00*	*100.00*	*100.00*	*99.99*	*100.01*

89. Fig. 51 (P26) Cup, fragment of globular body. Fabric white, fine, medium hard. Decoration in black (a), turquoise (f) and managanese purple (c), under a colourless glaze. Context 77, Area A1, Phase E.

90. Fig. 51. (P22) Coffee cup, fragment of foot-ring base with spiral-fluted exterior. Fabric white, fine and chalky, fairly soft. Decoration in cobalt blue (f) and black (a) under a colourless glaze on both sides. The potter's mark, painted in black under the base, is an imitation of the crossed-swords mark of the Meissen factory, and is common on Kütahya coffee cups of the mid- to late 18th century, if not later (Carswell 1972a(2), 36–38, 95; fig. 21c; Lane 1971, 65, 114, no. 21). Context 75, Area A2, Phase E.

11. TIN-GLAZED POTTERY

Medieval Italian tin-glazed pottery, which is common on Frankish coastal and some inland sites in the 13th century, is completely absent from the Red Tower. The only tin-glazed sherd from the whole excavation was a modern piece decorated in blue-on-white, found in Phase F (Context 22).

12. PORCELAIN

The excavation produced ten sherds of porcelain. All of it, however, was modern and from Phase F.

Table 10   Distribution of pottery types by phase (Area C3)

Phases:	A	B	D	E	F
Unglazed:					
Handmade				55 *67·07*	24 *8·33*
+ painting					1 *0·35*
Coarse fabrics	8 *57·14*	108 *33·44*	19 *47·50*	18 *21·95*	190 *65·97*
+ combing		107 *33·13*	7 *17·50*		5 *1·74*
+ rilling	6 *42·86*	75 *23·22*	10 *25·00*	4 *4·88*	16 *5·56*
+ white painting		15 *4·64*			
Grey fabrics					34 *11·81*
+ rilling					2 *0·69*
+ white painting		15 *4·64*		1 *1·22*	
White fabrics		3 *0·93*		1 *1·22*	10 *3·47*
Glazed:					
Kitchen wares			3 *7·50*		
Slip-wares				1 *1·22*	2 *0·69*
Slip-painted			1 *2·50*	2 *2·44*	4 *1·39*
Totals	14	323	40	82	288
%	*100·00*	*100·00*	*100·00*	*100·00*	*100·00*

II. GLASS

Altogether 156 pieces of glass were recovered from contexts attributed to Phases A to E. The distribution of differently coloured fragments by phase is shown in the following Table.

In Phase A, predating the construction of the castle, most of the glass (over 95%) was blue-green in colour and probably Byzantine or early Islamic in date. Amongst the pieces in this group which can be dated

Table 11   Table showing the distribution of differently coloured glass fragments by phase

	Blue-green	Green	Yellow	Purple	Clear	Totals
Phase A	65	2	1	—	—	68
Phase B	10	1	—	—	1	12
Phase C	3	2	—	—	46	51
Phase D	4	1	—	—	5	10
Phase D1	—	1	—	—	5	6
Phase E	4	—	—	1	4	9

with reasonable certainty after the Muslim conquest may be noted the base of a small *unguentarium*, probably of the 7th to 8th century (no. 12), and the rim of a mould-blown cup of a type unlikely to date to before the 11th century (no. 23). The latter is therefore one of the latest datable finds from Phase A.

Although only a dozen fragments were recovered from Phase B, contemporary with the construction of the castle, they show the same preponderance of blue-green over other colours. It seems likely, however, that most of these and of the similar fragments appearing in later contexts are simply residual, like the large quantities of Byzantine coarse pottery that were found in all phases. The one certain medieval piece from this phase is the rim of a bowl of fine clear glass (no. 8).

In Phase C, dating from the period of occupation of the castle from the late 12th century up to its eventual destruction in around 1265, residual Byzantine glass is momentarily eclipsed by contemporaneous medieval glass. This glass is virtually colourless and soft. Unfortunately it had not survived as well as the earlier glass. On excavation it was usually found to have a thick purple-brown patination which easily flaked off. Poss-

ibly in part for this reason none of the pieces was found to be decorated. Recognizable forms included fragments of bottles (nos. 9, 17, ?13) and lamps (nos. 14–15). These finds may be compared as a group with those from Montfort Castle, which probably date from much the same period (Dean 1927, 40; fig. 56).

The only piece of decorated glass found in the excavation came from Phase E, dating from *c.* 1390 onwards. This was a piece of purple glass, decorated with a band of white enamel (no. 24).

GLASS OF THE BYZANTINE PERIOD

1. Fig. 52. (G14: SF3) Bracelet of green-blue glass with yellow and red trailing. Context 2, Area C, Phase F.

2. Fig. 52. (G8) Bowl, fragment of folded rim (d. 12 cm.). Blue-green. Context 124, Area C3, Phase B.

3. Fig. 52. (G2) Fragment of folded rim (d. 12 cm.). Blue-green. Context 83, Area C1, Phase A.

4. Fig. 52. (G22) Bowl, fragment of folded rim (d. 13·5 cm.). Blue-green. Context 141, Area A1/3, Phase C.

5. Fig. 52. (G21) Jug, fragment of high base ring. Green-blue. Cf. Isings 1957, forms 120d and 122 (4th- to 5th-c.). Context 108, Area A1, Phase D.

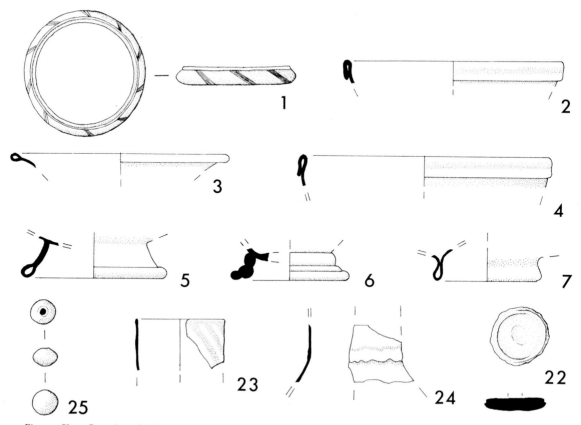

Fig. 52. Glass: Byzantine period (nos. 1–7); medieval mould-blown (nos. 22–23); enamelled (no. 24); faience bead (no. 25) (Scale 1 : 2, except no. 25 which is full-size).

6. Fig. 52. (G7) Fragment of coiled base. Blue-green. 5th- to 6th-century (inf. D. Barag). Context 124, Area C3, Phase B.

7. Fig. 52. (G19) Jug, fragment of small base ring. Blue-green. Cf. Isings 1957, forms 120a, 123, 124. Context 103, Area C, Phase A.

MEDIEVAL BLOWN GLASS

8. Fig. 53. (G17) Bowl, fragment of vertical rim (d. *c.*22 cm.). Clear. Context 35, Area B, Phase B.

9. Fig. 53. (G4) Bottle, fragment of narrow vertical rim (d. 3 cm.). Clear. Context 32, Area C, Phase C.

10. Fig. 53. (G20) Bowl, fragment of folded rim (d. 16). Clear. Cf. Hama (Riis 1957, 32; fig. 23). Context 73, Area A2, Phase E.

11. Fig. 53. (G12) Flask or bottle, fragment of slightly flaring neck with external trailing. Clear. Cf. Montfort Castle (Dean 1927, 40; fig. 56g). Context 146, Area A1/3, Phase C.

12. Fig. 53. (G1) Unguentarium, fragment of hollow base (d. 2·5 cm.). Apparently yellow, though heavy

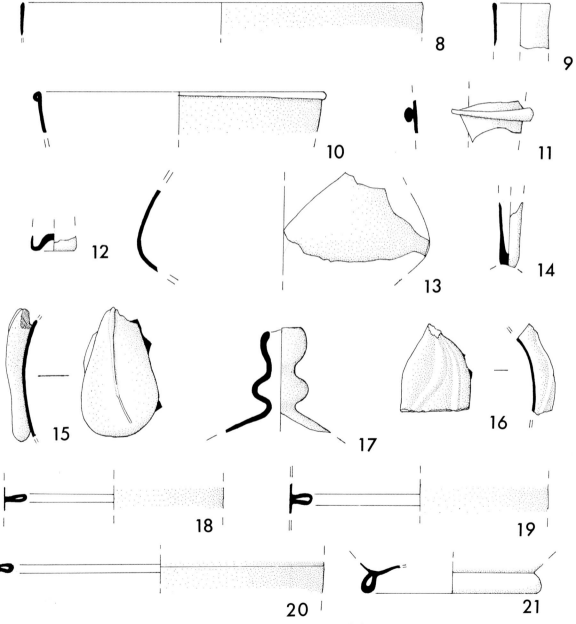

Fig. 53. Glass: medieval blown (nos. 8–21) (Scale 1 : 2).

pitting of surface makes colour hard to tell. 7th to 8th century (inf. D. Barag). Context 83, Area C1, Phase A.

13. Fig. 53. (G11) Closed form (bottle or lamp?), fragment of squashed ovoid body (max. d. 16 cm.). Clear. Context 146, Area A1/3, Phase C.

14. Fig. 53. (G3) Narrow vertical tube from inside the base of a lamp. Green-yellow. Cf. al-Mina (Lane 1937, 66; fig. 10v), Hama (Riis 1957, 38–39; figs. 60–61 or 62). Context 146, Area A1/3, Phase C.

15. Fig. 53. (G24) Hanging lamp, attachment for suspension ring. Clear. Cf. Montfort Castle (Dean 1927, 40; fig. 56b). Context 141, Area A1/3, Phase C.

16. Fig. 53. (G9) As no. 15. Context 116, Area C4, Phase D.

17. Fig. 53. (G23) Bottle, fragment of bulging neck and rim. Clear. Cf. Corinth, 11th to 12th century (Weinberg 1975, 135–136; fig. 15); Montfort Castle (Dean 1927, 40; fig. 56a). Context 141, Area A1/3, Phase C.

18. Fig. 53. (G6) Body fragment with vertical sides and folded interior ledge (d. 12 cm.). Clear. Context 32, Area C, Phase C.

19. Fig. 53. (G25) As no. 18 (d. 14 cm.). Context 141, Area A1/3, Phase C.

20. Fig. 53. (G16) As no. 18 (d. 18 cm.). Context 14, Area C, Phase F.

21. Fig. 53. (G5) Bowl or bottle, fragment of folded ring base (d. 10 cm.). Clear. Cf. Montfort Castle, bottle (Dean 1927, 40; fig. 56g); Hama, bowl (Riis 1957, 32; fig. 21). Context 32, Area C, Phase C.

MEDIEVAL MOULD-BLOWN GLASS

22. Fig. 52. (G15) Disc (d. 3·0–3·3; thickness 0·3–0·4 cm.), with central stem broken off. Clear. This piece seems rather too uneven to have been the base of a goblet (cf. Weinberg 1975, 138–139; figs. 23–24), though it is uncertain what else it could have been. Context 46, Area A2, Phase E.

23. Fig. 52. (G18) Cup, fragment of vertical rim with oblique ridge patterning (d. > 5 cm.). Very pale blue-green. Cf. Corinth, 11th to 12th century (Weinberg 1975, 139–140; figs. 26–27). Context 113, Area C1, Phase A.

MEDIEVAL GLASS WITH ENAMEL DECORATION

24. Fig. 52. (G13) Jug or flask, lower part of neck and shoulder. Dark purple, with white enamel band around the base of the neck. Cf. Hama (Riis 1957, 63–67, type F.I.5). Context 65, Area A1, Phase E.

FAIENCE

25. Fig. 52. (G10: SF1) Turquoise faience bead or pinhead (d. 0·6 cm.). Context 13, Area C, Phase E.

III. METALWORK

Metal objects of all kinds were found in the excavations, the largest group of medieval finds coming from Phase C, associated with the period of use of the castle in the 13th century. Much of the iron and bronze was heavily corroded. The following catalogue therefore represents a selection of the better preserved pieces. Most of the 19th- and 20th-century finds from Phase F, including quantities of British Army ·22 and ·303 ammunition (some of it live), have been excluded.

FINGER RINGS

1. Fig. 54. (SF 46) Plain silver finger ring of uniform thickness, convex outside (d. 2·2 cm.). Context 141, Area A, Phase C.

2. Fig. 54. (SF 7) Silver finger ring, made from flattish band of metal widening towards the bezel and joined underneath; no trace of decoration (d. 1·7–1·9 cm.). Context 35, Area B, Phase B.

COSMETIC RODS

The following two pieces belong to a class of object, also attested in antiquity, which is usually identified as intended for the application of cosmetic preparations to the eyes and face. It seems likely, however, that they could also be used for other purposes. At the Red Tower both examples came from layers associated with the construction of the castle. They may therefore either have been derived from earlier Muslim occupation of the site or from the initial Frankish occupation. In both instances, the presence of women which such objects might imply, would seem less surprising than it might in the period after the castle passed into the hands of the Military Orders.

3. Fig. 54. (SF 24) Bronze cosmetic rod, widening at one end with five pairs of circular grooves around the centre (length 13·5 cm.). Cf. Hama (Ploug et al. 1969, 62–66; figs. 24–25). Context 124, Area C3, Phase B.

4. Fig. 54. (SF 25) Part of bronze cosmetic rod, similar to no. 3 (length 4·5 cm.). Context 124, Area C3, Phase B.

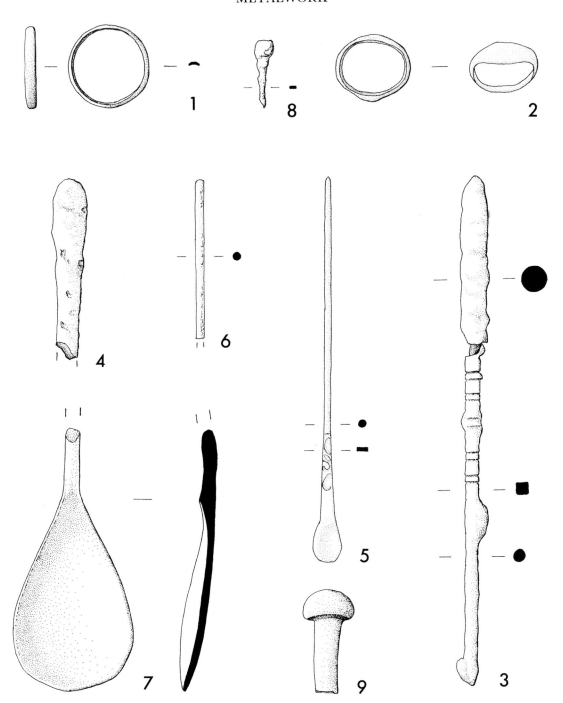

Fig. 54. Metalwork: Silver rings (nos. 1–2); objects of bronze (nos. 3–9) (Scale 1:1).

SPATULAS AND SPOONS

5. Fig. 54. (SF 12) Bronze spoon-shaped spatula, with traces of decoration towards the bowl (length 11·7 cm.). Cf. Hama (Ploug *et al.* 1969, 67; fig. 25, nos. 6–8). Context 105, Area A1, Phase D1.

6. Fig. 54. (SF 21) Fragment of bronze rod, perhaps the handle of a spoon or spatula (length 4·2 cm.). Context 85, Area A2, Phase E.

7. Fig. 54. (SF 22) Bronze spoon with oval bowl, handle missing. Cf. Hama (Ploug *et al.* 1969, 67–70; figs. 26–27). Context 130, Area A3, Phase E.

BRONZE PINS AND STUDS

8. Fig. 54. (SF 51) Bronze pin with rounded head and flattish stem (length 1·7 cm.). Context 146, Area A1/3, Phase C.

9. Fig. 54. (SF 43) Bronze rivet or stud, mushroom-shaped with rounded head and rounded stem (length 2·6 cm.). Cf. Hama (Ploug *et al.* 1969, 61–62; fig. 23, no. 8). Context 141, Area A1/3, Phase C.

SCABBARD OR SHEATH

10. Fig. 55. (SF 58a) Fragments of the bronze armature of a scabbard or sheath for a knife, with traces of what appears to be leather still adhering to them. The top of the sheath was strengthened with a band of thin metal while at intervals below this bands of copper wire were wound around it. Length unknown. The blade for which it was intended would have been about 3 cm. wide. Context 146, Area A1/3, Phase C.

BUCKLES AND BELT FITTINGS

11. Fig. 55. (SF 66) Bronze oval buckle with plate by which it was attached to the end of the belt. The plate was folded over the buckle and rivetted. Belt thickness *c.*2·5 cm. For this type of belt attachment, compare examples from Corinth, 9th century and later (Davidson 1952, 274,

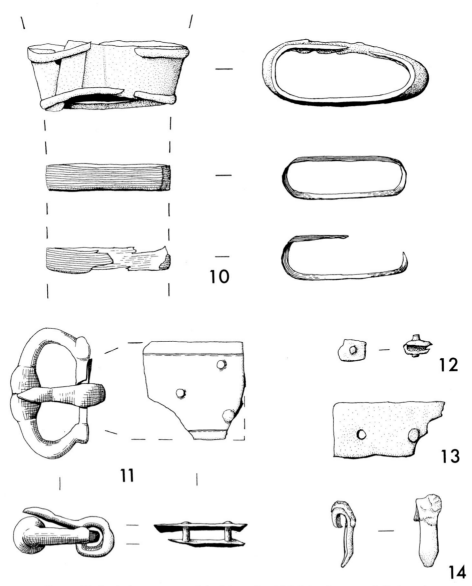

Fig. 55. Metalwork: bronze armature of sheath (no. 10) and belt fittings (nos. 11–14) (Scale 1 : 1).

nos. 2237–2239; pl. 115) and ʿAtlit Castle, 13th century (Johns 1934, pl. LX). For general comparisons for the shape of the buckle, compare Hama (Ploug *et al.* 1969, 85; fig. 35, no. 6), Montfort Castle (Dean 1927, 38; fig. 53f–j) and ʿAtlit Castle stables (Johns 1936, fig. 16.1–2). Context 146, Area A1/3, Phase C.

12. Fig. 55. (SF 65) Fragment of bronze strap-end, consisting of plate folded over leather and rivetted. Possibly part of no. 11. Context 146, Area A1/3, Phase C.

13. Fig. 55. (SF 58b) Fragment of bronze strap-end, found together with no. 10. Context 146, Area A1/3, Phase C.

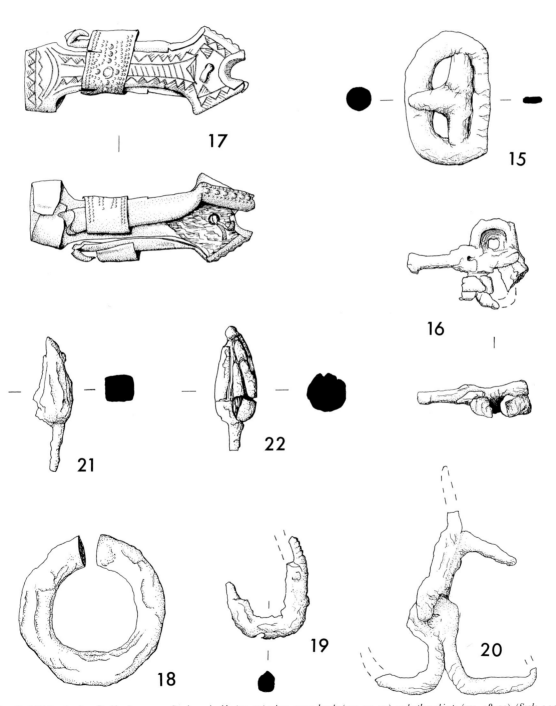

Fig. 56. Metalwork: Iron Buckles (nos. 15–16); brass buckle (no. 17); iron arrow-heads (nos. 21–22) and other objects (nos. 18–20) (Scale 1 : 2).

14. Fig. 55. (SF 44) Bronze tongue from buckle similar to no. 11 (length 1·6 cm.). Context 141, Area A1/3, Phase C.

15. Fig. 56. (SF 68) Iron oval-shaped buckle, for belt 5 cm. wide (dims. 7 × 4·5 cm.). This type has no attachment plate; the belt was attached by passing it round a bar behind the tongue of the buckle. For the general type, but in bronze, compare Corinth, 10th to 12th centuries (Davidson 1952, 272, nos. 2202–2204; pl. 114). Context 146, Area A1/3, Phase C.

16. Fig. 56. (SF 76) Iron oval- or kidney-shaped buckle, for belt about 3·5 cm. wide. Context 141, Area A1/3, Phase C.

17. Fig. 56. (SF 61) Brass buckle-cum-strap-end, with pieces of leather still adhering; made from thin sheet-metal wrapped around belt-end, with incised geometrical decoration on the face and repoussé decoration on the retaining ring (dims. 12 × 4·5 cm.). Probably 19th- or early 20th-century. Context 159, Area C6, Phase F.

17a. Not illustrated (SF 17) Fragment of buckle or strap-end (dims. 1·8 × 2·1 cm.). Context 121, Area A1, Phase C.

IRON RINGS AND HOOKS

18. Fig. 56. (SF 16) Iron ring (d. 8 cm.; 1·5 cm. thick), found attached to fallen voussoir from the east vault of the tower. Context 108, Area A1, Phase D.

19. Fig. 56. (SF 56) Iron hook. Context 146, Area A1/3, Phase C.

20. Fig. 56. (SF 54) Iron interconnecting hooks, possibly intended as a hinge or flexible joint between two wooden objects. Context 146, Area A1/3, Phase C.

ARROW-HEADS

Three arrow-heads were found in layers associated with the construction and use of the castle. They were all of the usual medieval type, shaped like a chilli-pepper with a tang for attaching them to the shaft. The two examples from Phase C differed from the one in Phase B by having rounded rather than rectangular cross-sections; with such a small sample, however, it is not possible to tell whether this change is chronologically significant. At Hama both rounded and rectangular types occur (Ploug

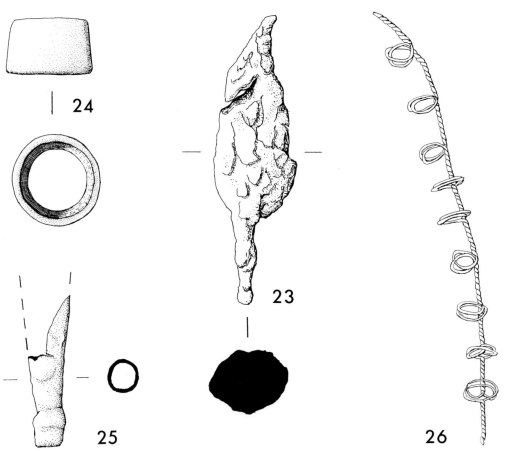

Fig. 57. Metalwork: Iron arrow-head (no. 23) and piece of bronze-work (nos. 24–26) (Scale 1 : 1).

et al. 1969, fig. 21, no. 1); at Corinth, 9th- to 12th-centuries (Davidson 1952, 200–201, nos. 1529–1530, 1532; pls. 91 and 93), and Montfort Castle, 13th-century (Dean 1927, 38n and p), they are rectangular and at ʿAtlit, 13th-century, they are rounded (Johns 1936, 48; fig. 15.3–4).

21. Fig. 56. (SF 85) Iron arrow-head of pyramidal shape, with tang (length 7·0 cm.). Context 132, Area C2, Phase B.

22. Fig. 56. (SF 73) Iron arrow-head, as no. 21 but with rounded cross-section (length 6·5 cm.). Context 146, Area A1/3, Phase C.

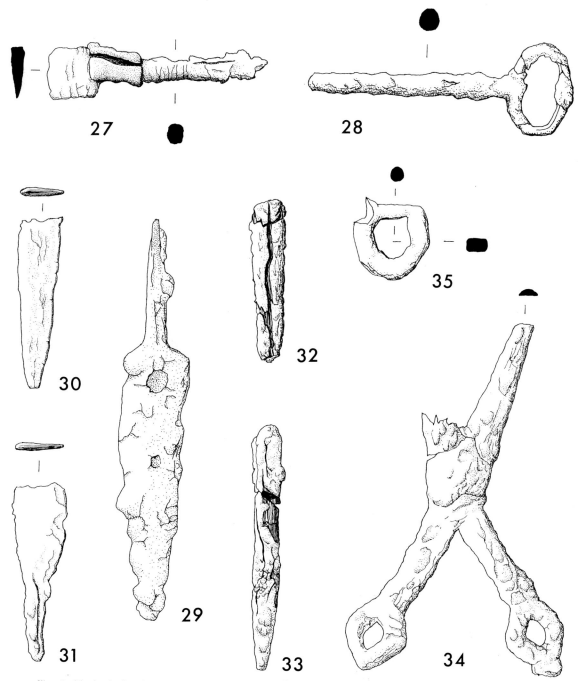

Fig. 58. Metalwork: Iron keys (nos. 27–28), knives (nos. 29–31), points (nos. 32–33) and scissors (nos. 34–35) (Scale 1:2).

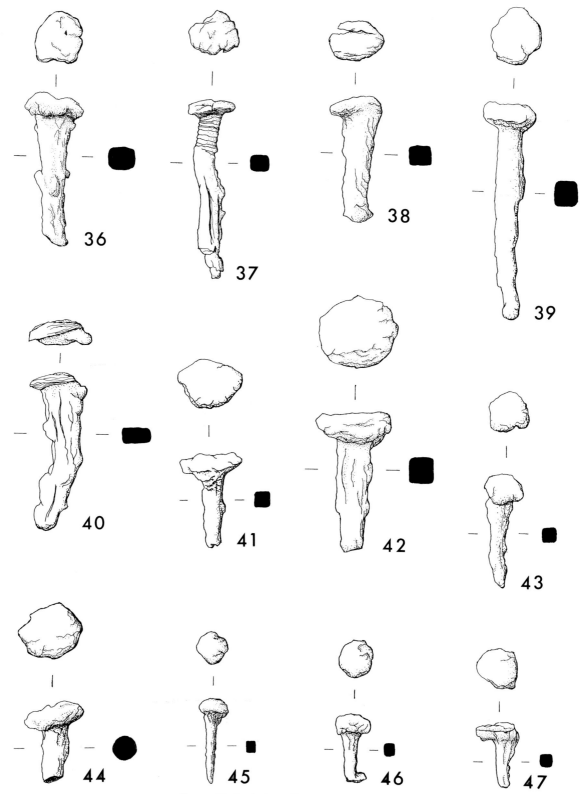

Fig. 59. Metalwork: iron nails (nos. 36-47) (Scale 1:2).

23. Fig. 57. (SF 53) Iron arrow-head, as no. 22 (length 7·5 cm.). Context 146, Area A1/3, Phase C.

MISCELLANEOUS BRONZE OBJECTS

24. Fig. 57. (SF 23) Bronze ring of uncertain function, possibly the capping for a stick (h. 1·3; d. 2·1–2·3; thickness 0·2–0·3 cm.). Context 133, Area A3, Phase D.

25. Fig. 57. (SF 99) Bronze chape ending with a rounded knob, from a scabbard such as no. 10. Cf. ʿAtlit Castle stables, 13th century (Johns 1936, 48; fig. 16.10). Context 46, Area A2, Phase E.

26. Fig. 57. (SF 60) Bronze braid, formerly wound around a long thin rounded object (d. 0·7 cm.) which has since perished (length 12 cm.). Context 146, Area A1/3, Phase C.

KEYS

The two medieval keys found at the Red Tower are of a very simple type in comparison, for example, with keys of the Roman or Byzantine periods. They may be compared with 10th- to 13th-century examples from Corinth (Davidson 1952, 139, nos. 1000–1002; pl. 71).

27. Fig. 58. (SF 55) Iron key with simple wards, lacking handle, fitting into bronze keyhole (length 11·5 cm.). Context 146, Area A1/3, Phase C.

28. Fig. 58. (SF 98) Iron key with ring handle, lacking wards (length 14·5 cm.). Context 34, Area B1, Phase E.

KNIVES AND OTHER IRON IMPLEMENTS

29. Fig. 58. (SF 8) Iron knife with double-edged blade (length of blade 15·5; total length 18; width of blade 3·2 cm.). Cf. Hama (Ploug et al. 1969, 61; fig. 23, no. 2),

Corinth, 9th century onwards (Davidson 1952, 203, nos. 1567–1569; pl. 93). Context 59, Area B1, Phase B.

30. Fig. 58. (SF 94) Iron knife, fragment of blade (length 8·5 cm.). Context 46, Area A2, Phase E.

31. Fig. 58. (SF 96) Iron knife, fragment of blade and tang (length 9·3 cm.). Possibly part of no. 30. This knife appears to have only a single sharp edge. Cf. Hama (Ploug et al., 1969, fig. 23, no. 3). Context 57, Area A1, Phase E.

32. Fig. 58. (SF 26) Iron point, fragment (length 8·0 cm.). Context 26, Area C, Phase E.

33. Fig. 58. (SF 20) Iron point (length 13 cm.). Context 98, Area A1, Phase D1.

34. Fig. 58. (SF 45) Iron scissors with rhomboid finger-grips, heavily corroded (length 20·5 cm.). Context 141, Area A1/3, Phase C.

35. Fig. 58. (SF 72) Iron D-shaped ring; possibly part of buckle, scissors or horse-harness. Context 146, Area A1/3, Phase C.

NAILS

Nails represented the commonest type of iron object recovered in the excavations. Though varying in length and size almost all the medieval nails conformed to a standard type, with rounded heads and square or rectangular shafts. At Corinth this also seems to have been the usual type of nail used from the 9th century onwards (Davidson 1952, 142, no. 1038; pl. 72). Some of the shorter nails may perhaps have been intended for shoeing horses (cf. Hama: Ploug et al. 1969, 61–62; fig. 23, no. 6). Any sort of recognizable horse equipment is singularly absent from the contexts excavated, however, and the fact that some small and large nails have bent ends suggest that most were used in carpentry which has not survived.

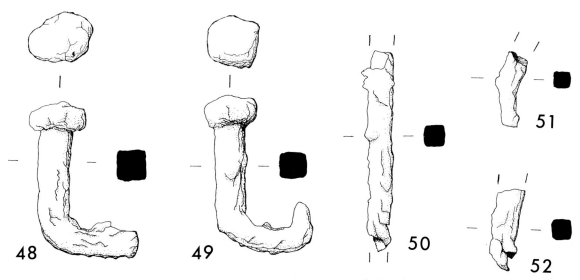

Fig. 60. Metalwork: iron nails (nos. 48–51) (Scale 1 : 2).

36. Fig. 59. (SF 59) Iron nail, broken (length 7·5 cm.). Context 121, Area A1, Phase C.

37. Fig. 59. (SF 78) Iron nail (length 9·5 cm.). Context 141, Area A1/3, Phase C.

38. Fig. 59. (SF 79) Iron nail, broken (length 6·5 cm.). Context 141, Area A1/3, Phase C.

39. Fig. 59. (SF 97) Iron nail, reconstructed (length 11·3 cm.). Context 46, Area A2, Phase E.

40. Fig. 59. (SF 70). Iron nail, squashed flat (length 8·5 cm.). Context 146, Area A1/3, Phase C.

41. Fig. 59. (SF 93) Iron nail, broken (length 5 cm.). Context 43, Area C1, Phase E.

42. Fig. 59. (SF 84) Iron nail, broken (length 7 cm.). Context 141, Area A1/3, Phase C.

43. Fig. 59. (SF 95) Iron nail (length 6 cm.). Context 59, Area B1, Phase B.

44. Fig. 59. (SF 69) Iron nail, broken (length 4·3 cm.). Context 146, Area A1/3, Phase C.

45. Fig. 59. (SF 77) Iron nail (length 4·5 cm.). Context 141, Area A1/3, Phase C.

46. Fig. 59. (SF 83) Iron nail, with bent end (length 4 cm.). Context 141, Area A1/3, Phase C.

47. Fig. 59. (SF 88) Iron nail (length 3·2 cm.). Context 131, Area A3, Phase D1.

48. Fig. 60. (SF 67) Iron nail with bent end (length *c.* 12 cm.), apparently at one time nailed through object(s) some 5 cm. thick. Context 146, Area A1/3, Phase C.

49. Fig. 60. (SF 71) Iron nail, bent as no. 48 and probably used for same purpose. Context 146, Area A1/3, Phase C.

50. Fig. 60. (SF 91) Iron nail, fragment (length 10·2 cm.). Context 141, Area A1/3, Phase C.

51–52. Fig. 60. (SF 90, 89). Iron nail fragments. Context 145, Area A1/3, Phase C.

IV. OBJECTS OF BONE, TERRACOTTA AND WOOD

1. Fig. 61. (SF 11) Spindle whorl of fine grey terracotta (h. 1·4; d. 3 cm.). Probably 5th- to 8th-century. Context 83, Area C1, Phase A.

2. Fig. 61. (SF 2) Terracotta bead of fine grey pipe-clay, broken (h. 1·6; d. 2·1 cm.). This perhaps represents a cheap imitation of a type of faience bead found at Hama (Ploug *et al.* 1969, 107; fig. 41, no. 6). Context 1, Area B, Phase F.

3. Fig. 61. (SF 48) Bone button or spindle whorl (h. 0·7; d. 1·6 cm.). The precise function of objects such as this is still a matter of dispute. In Greece they are already present in the Mycenaean period, but nine-tenths of those excavated at Corinth came from contexts of the 9th to 12th centuries (Davidson 1952, 296–304; pl. 123–125). They also occur at Hama (Ploug *et al.* 1969, 118–128; figs. 44–46). Context 146, Area A1/3, Phase C.

4. Fig. 61. (SF 87) Fine bone ring (d. 1·2–1·5 cm.). Context 146, Area A1/3, Phase C.

5. Not illustrated. (SF 47) Two small pieces from a wooden bowl (0·5 cm. thick), carbonized. Context 146, Area A1/3, Phase C.

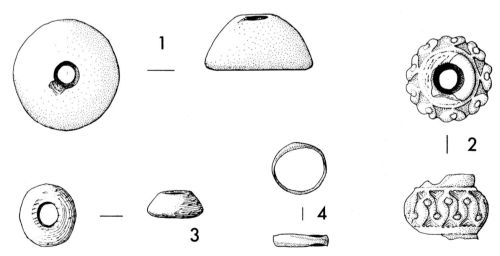

Fig. 61. Terracotta spindle whorl (no. 1) and bead (no. 2); bone button (no. 3) and ring (Scale 1:1).

V. STONE OBJECTS

by J. Hanbury-Tenison (Magdalen College, Oxford)

A small number of stone implements were found during the 1983 season at the Red Tower: hand tools chipped from the crude local chert and domestic objects, mainly of basalt. There were also numerous plain marble fragments, presumably used as floor coverings and reused in several phases. The material is very limited and a statistical or typological assessment is impossible.

CHIPPED STONE TOOLS

Fourteen flakes were found of the crude local chert, of which seven were natural, five had been used as stone tools and two were primary flakes discarded in the preparation of stone tools. Only two of the seven worked flakes are from the same chert, suggesting that no one local source was preferred. The five tools are roughly

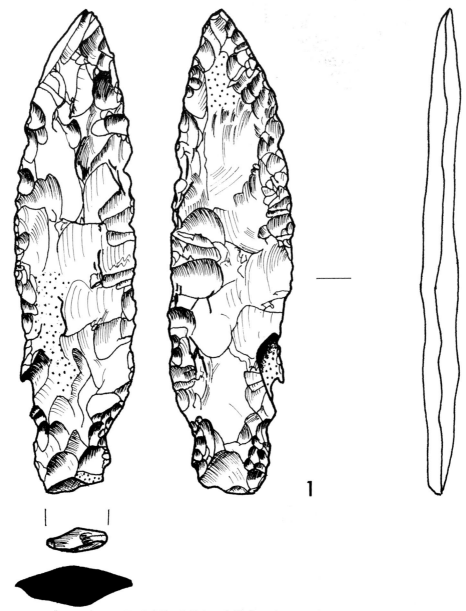

1

Fig. 62. Stone knife (no. 1) (Scale 1:1).

made and are clearly not part of a strong lithic tradition. This may be explained by the local chert rather than the date of the artefacts, for in areas with good raw material stone tools were being manufactured until very recently.

1. Fig. 62. Knife, mottled dark and pale brown chert, areas of cortex on both faces, latitudinal invasive retouch, with some micro-retouch along both edges, knotched hilt,

shows strong evidence of wear and resharpening, no striation marks on blade or hilt. Context 22, Area A2, Phase F.

2. Fig. 63. Chopping tool, lustrous pale brown and yellow chert, quite smooth, invasive retouch, proximal end dorsal face backed after removal from core. Context 17, Area C, Phase D.

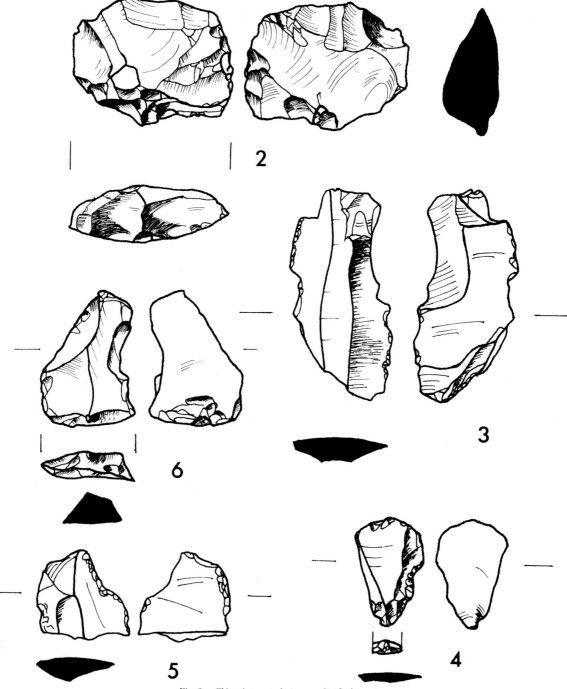

Fig. 63. Chipped stone tools (nos. 2–6) (Scale 1 : 1).

3. Fig. 63. Burin/blade (?), brown and pale grey chert, trapezoidal flake snapped at both ends, proximal end ventral face with steep backing, distal end ventral face with long flake removed on left (this seems to be natural and not a burin flaking), rough retouch along both edges, no bulb, no sheen on edges. Context 15, Area C, Phase E.

4. Fig. 63. Arrow-head (?), small brown flake, facetted platform, flaring blunted end, very fine pressure-flaking on right dorsal face, with small notch half-way up, left side of dorsal face snapped by blow from bulb, no sign of wear on sides. Context 56, Area A1, Phase E1.

5. Fig. 63, Flake, orange and pale brown chert (as no. 2), white flecks, blade segment, both ends snapped, midrib removed, trapezoidal flake with semi-truncated end, retouch on right dorsal and ventral faces, no sign of wear, coarse retouch. Context 7, Area B, Phase F.

6. Fig. 63. Flake, as no. 5. Context 46, Area A2, Phase E.

The functional designation is at best tentative and it is most likely that the assemblage represents an *ad hoc* tool kit whose function was as limited as its artistry. Given the almost total lack of debitage and the lack of uniformity among the five lithics with secondary working, there is no reason to suppose either that the material is all from the same site or that each object belongs to the stratified layer from which it came. Reuse of objects in later period is not only possible but probable; and while four of the tools are totally

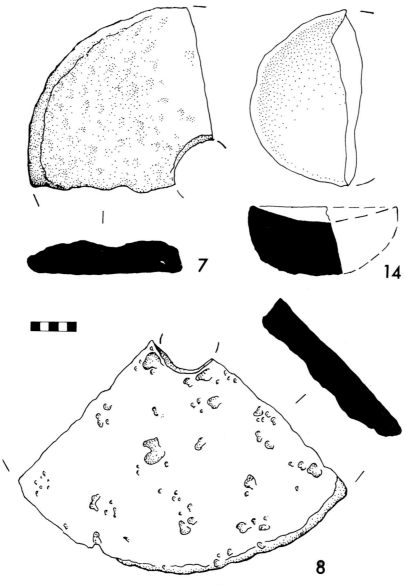

Fig. 64. Basalt quern-stones (nos. 7–8) and limestone mortar (no. 14) (Scale 1 : 4).

undiagnostic, there is a chance that the knife of tabular chert (no. 1) may be Chalcolithic.

BASALT OBJECTS

Pieces of basalt were found in all phases from Phase B onwards (viz., in contexts 8, 10, 22, 45, 108, 124, 129, 141). It appears therefore that basalt was being brought to the site, probably from north-eastern Galilee or the Jaulan, before the castle was built and perhaps already in Byzantine times. The stone would probably have been traded in the form of worked objects, of which various types of grinding tools predominate. The following tools were recognizable amongst the rather fragmentary collection of finds from the Red Tower:

7. Fig. 64. Circular quern-stone (r. 16·4; thickness 3·4 cm.). Context 10, Area A, Phase F.

8. Fig. 64. Circular quern-stone (r. 22.0; thickness 3·3 cm.). Context 129, Area A3, Phase E.

9. Not illustrated. Circular quern-stone of pinkish volcanic rock (r. uncertain; thickness 3·4 cm.). Context 22, Area A2, Phase F.

10. Not illustrated. Circular quern-stone (r. uncertain; thickness 3·2–3·7 cm.). Context 45, Area A2, Phase E1.

11. Not illustrated. Grinder for use in saddle-quern, with triangular cross-section and splaying base to be rocked back and forth, the top ridge gripped in the hand or socketed into a shaft (base 16 cm. wide; ht. 7 cm.). Context 10, Area A, Phase F.

12. Not illustrated. Grinder, as no. 11, with trapezoidal cross-section (base 9 cm.; ht. 11 cm.; surviving length 23 cm.). From ruined village house, unstratified.

13. Not illustrated. Fragment of large rotary quern (max. dims., 6 × 9 × 14 cm.). Context 141, Area A1/3, Phase C.

OBJECTS OF LIMESTONE AND MARBLE

Finer tools for grinding or rubbing were made in limestone or marble. The following three items came from the layers of destruction of the castle and probably belong to its last phase of occupation.

14. Fig. 64. Circular or oval-shaped mortar of white limestone, fragment (d. 18.6; max. thickness 5·5 cm.). Context 108, Area A1, Phase D.

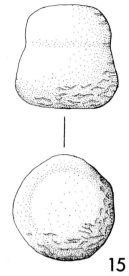

15

Fig. 65. Limestone pestle (no. 15) (Scale 1 : 2).

15. Fig. 65. (SF92) Truncated conical-shaped pestle of white marble (h. 5·5 cm.; max. d. 5·5 cm.). Context 133, Area A3, Phase D.

16. Fig. 66. Smooth rectangular piece of white grey-veined marble, with worn edges, evidently used as a rubbing stone of some kind (1·8 × 3·8 × 8·1 cm.). Context 133, Area A3, Phase D.

Fragments of marble, collapsed from the tower's first-floor paving, were found in almost all subsequent layers. None of the marble was decorated.

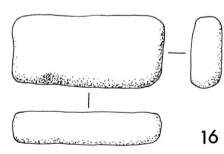

16

Fig. 66. Marble rubbing stone (no. 16) (Scale 1 : 2).

VI. COINS

by Yaakov Meshorer (Israel Museum, Jerusalem)

ROMAN AND BYZANTINE PERIODS

1. *Follis* of Diocletian (A.D. 306–308). Mint of Alexandria.
   Obv. Bust of Diocletian r., laureate, draped.
   Inscription obliterated.
   Rev. Providence standing r., extending r. hand to standing Quies l., holding branch, leaning on sceptre.
   PROVIDENTIA DEORVM; in exergue, ALE; in field, B
   Cf. *RIC*, 6, 675, no. 80.
   SF 6, Context 32, Area C, Phase C.

2. Constantine II (A.D. 337–340). Mint of Nicomedia.
   Obv. Veiled head r.
   DN CONS [TANTINVS P T AVG]
   Rev. Emperor in quadriga to r.
   Cf. *RIC*, 8, 472, no. 18
   SF 64, Context 146, Area A, Phase C.

3. *Aes IV* of Arcadius (?) (*c.* A.D. 384–387). Mint of Siscia (?).
   Obv. Head of emperor r.
   Incription obliterated.
   Rev. Victory advancing l., holding wreath and palm branch.
   Inscription obliterated.
   Cf. *RIC*. 9, 155, no. 39.
   SF 5, Context 8, Area B, Phase E.

4. Probably a Byzantine *nummus* of the 5th century A.D.
   SF 9, Context 71, Area B, Phase A.

THE CRUSADES

5. *Denier* of Amaury (1163–74). Mint of Jerusalem or Acre (1163–*c.*1219).
   Obv. Cross pattée.
   + AMALRICVS REX
   Rev. Church of the Holy Sepulchre (Resurrection)
   + DE IERVSALEM
   Cf. Metcalf 1983, no. 96.
   SF 27, Context 141, Area A, Phase C.

6. Same as no. 5.
   SF 62, Context 130, Area A, Phase E (derived from Phase C).

7. Same as no. 5.
   SF 63, Context 146, Area A, Phase C.

8. Same as no. 5 (broken).
   SF 9, Context 146, Area A, Phase C.

9. *Denier* of the Bishopric of Le Puy, Languedoc. Type imported into the Holy Land from the time of the Third Crusade onwards (*c.*1189–1291).
   Obv. Chrismon.
   Rev. Cross with knopped arms.
   Cf. Metcalf 1983, 49–51, no. 435.
   SF 28, Context 141, Area A, Phase C.

10. Same as no. 9.
    SF 29, Context 141, Area A, Phase C.

11. Same as no. 9.
    SF 30, Context 141, Area A, Phase C.

12. Same as no. 9.
    SF 31, Context 141, Area A, Phase C.

13. Same as no. 9.
    SF 32a, Context 141, Area A, Phase C.

14. Same as no. 9.
    SF 32b, Context 141, Area A, Phase C.

15. Same as no. 9.
    SF 33, Context 141, Area A, Phase C.

16. Same as no. 9.
    SF 34, Context 141, Area A, Phase C.

17. Same as no. 9.
    SF 35a, Context 141, Area A, Phase C.

18. Same as no. 9.
    SF 35b, Context 141, Area A, Phase C.

19. Same as no. 9.
    SF 36, Context 141, Area A, Phase C.

20. Same as no. 9.
    SF 37, Context 141, Area A, Phase C.

21. Same as no. 9.
    SF 38, Context 141, Area A, Phase C.

22. Fig. 67. Same as no. 9.
    SF 39a, Context 141, Area A, Phase C.

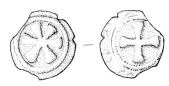

Fig. 67. Denier of the Bishopric of Le Puy (no. 22) (Scale 1:1).

23. Same as no. 9.
    SF 39b, Context 141, Area A, Phase C.

24. Same as no. 9.
    SF 39c, Context 141, Area A, Phase C.

25. Same as no. 9.
    SF 40, Context 141, Area A, Phase C.

26. Same as no. 9.
    SF 41a, Context 141, Area A, Phase C.

27. Same as no. 9.
    SF 41b, Context 141, Area A, Phase C.

28. Same as no. 9.
    SF 50, Context 146, Area A, Phase C.

THE MAMLUKS

29. Ismāʿil (A.D. 1342–45). Struck at Damascus (A.H. 744/A.D. 1343–44).
    Cf. Balog 1964, 173, no. 288.
    SF 13, Context 98, Area A, Phase D1.

30. Aʿli (A.D. 1377–81). Struck at Damascus (A.H. 782/A.D. 1380–81).
    Cf. Balog 1964, 235, no. 502b.
    SF 15, Context 114, Area C4, Phase F (surface of D).

31. Ḥājji II (A.D. 1381–82, 1389–90). Struck at Damascus (A.H. 791/A.D. 1388–89).
    Cf. Balog 1964, 246, no. 532.
    SF 4, Context 8, Area B, Phase E.

32. Shaʿbān II (A.D. 1363–77). Struck at Damascus.
    Cf. Balog 1964, 221, no. 458a.
    SF 14, Context 114, Area C4, Phase F (surface of D)

OTTOMANS

33. Anonymous (16th century A.D.).
    SF 18, Context 116, Area C4, Phase D.

34. *Five para* of Muḥammad v Rashād (A.D. 1909–18). Egyptian type (A.H. 1331/A.D. 1913).
    SF 10, Surface find.

VII. FAUNAL REMAINS

by Judith Cartledge (University of Sheffield)

The animal bones from the Red Tower (al-Burj al-Ahmar) are particularly interesting because they belong to a historical period. It was therefore possible to compare the faunal data with documentary evidence, notably during the time of Templar occupation. The bones from the Red Tower also demonstrate how the exploitation of the environment can be influenced not only by economic considerations, but also by religious and cultural preferences.

There was a total of 1387 fragments, of which 663 were unidentifiable. This is a very small sample, especially to cover such a time span. This limited the sort of quantitative and statistical analysis that I was able to do. Also the site had not been sieved, so that certain biases may be expected in the sample. First, there was probably a poor retrieval of the bones of smaller animals, which in any case will have been less likely to have survived the physical and chemical processes to which they would have been subjected after the animals had died. Secondly, there will also have been a bias against the retrieval of the smaller bones and the bones from younger members of the larger species, a bias which will vary according to the size of the species (Payne 1972).

The animal bones were studied at the British School of Archaeology in Jerusalem. Unfortunately no local comparative material was available, since I had unwittingly gone to Jerusalem in a month when the Hebrew University was closed. Thus I adopted the policy of sorting out any bones about which I was uncertain and these I brought back to Sheffield. In my analysis I am also at a disadvantage because of the lack of other published faunal material from medieval sites in the same area. As a result there were no data with which

to compare the few measurements that I was able to take.

ANALYSIS

I first divided the bones into three groups: (i) identifiable, (ii) unidentifiable, and (iii) to be taken away for further analysis. The ribs and vertebrae were counted amongst the unidentifiable fragments. This is because they are particularly friable and difficult to assign to species unless intact. I then recorded the animal- and bone-type of the identifiable fragments, whether they came from the left or right side of the skeleton and, if a fragment was a long bone, whether the distal or proximal epiphysis was present and, if so, whether these epiphyses were fused to the shaft or unfused.

Next I took measurements where possible. The measurement of animal bones can yield various sorts of information. It can indicate geographical and chronological variations in the size of species. Size-grouping can also indicate the presence of more than one population within a species on a particular site. Such groupings can be caused by sexual dimorphism, different planes of nutrition and/or the presence of more than one breed or type of a species. Certain measurements can also be used with special formulae to indicate withers-heights, sex-ratios, sheep/goat distinctions and other information.

I then recorded the developmental and wear stages of the mandibles. This is the most useful method for estimating the age at which an animal has died. Where possible I reconstructed the stages of the missing teeth in order to make an approximate age-estimate of the incomplete mandibles. Another method of ageing

Table 12 Total number of fragments

	A	B	C	D	D1	E	E1	F
Sheep/Goat	36	16	8	25	12	65	16	55
Pig			49	4				
Cattle	16	6		29	3	81	16	57
Equus		1		2		5		5
Fallow Deer	?1				?1			
Camel								1
Gazelle				1	2	4		4
Oryx leucoryx/Alcelaphas								?1
Cat			2	1		5		2
Dog			7	5		1		2
Honey Badger								1
Tortoise						2		2
Bird	6	5	118	10	7	9	3	10
Rodent (? Rat)			2					2
ribs	20	12	39	24	9	105	41	61
vertebrae	8	7	15	17	10	25	11	27
unidentifiable fragments	10	4	18	41	6	55	18	80
Total	97	51	258	159	50	357	105	310

Total = 1,387 fragments.

animals is to record the extent to which the long bones are fused, since each epiphysis fuses to the shaft at a particular age. However, there is considerable variation from the standard ages even within a single population of single sex on the same plane of nutrition, so that epiphyseal fusion should be used only as a back-up method when adequate mandibular evidence is available in the sample (Watson 1978). Other methods include the age at which the sutures of the cranium join up; but again there tends to be considerable variation from the given ages and the method also depends on the survival of the cranium, which tends to be retrieved only in little bits.

Table 13 Main mammalian species

	Sheep/goat		Pig		Cattle		Total
	No.	%	No.	%	No.	%	
Phase A	35	68·5	0	0·0	16	31·5	51
Phase B	16	72·5	0	0·0	6	27·5	22
Phase C	8	14·0	49	86·0	0	0·0	57
Phase D	25	43·0	4	7·0	29	50·0	58
Phase D1	13	81·25	0	0·0	3	18·75	16
Phase E	65	44·5	0	0·0	81	55·5	146
Phase E1	16	50·0	0	0·0	16	50·0	32
Phase F	55	49·0	0	0·0	57	51·0	112
Total	233	47·0	53	11·0	208	42·0	494

DISCUSSION

PHASES A–B (*c.*400–*c.*1150)

Main Mammalian Species (MMS)

The percentages of the main mammalian species (MMS) were as follows: sheep/goat, 70%; cattle, 30%; and no pigs (see Table 13). The absence of pigs might suggest Jewish rather than Christian or Samaritan occupation before the Muslim conquest. There are not enough bones from either sheep/goat or cattle, however, to be certain that pigs were never eaten, particularly

since pig bones tend to be more friable and more often gnawed that their ruminant counterparts. Secondly, only a small area was excavated and it would also be reasonable to expect pig carcasses to have been disposed of in another area. Moreover cattle and more especially sheep/goat are considerably commoner than pig in more recent prehistoric sites in Palestine (Davis 1982), so that the absence of pig need not be indicative of a deliberate taboo, religious or otherwise.

Only one measurement (from Phase B) was obtainable to apply the Boessneck method of distinguishing sheep from goat using the percentage relationship between two measurements taken from the distal medial condyle on the fused metacarpal. This produced a percentage of 56·9%. According to Boessneck (1969, 355), the dividing line is 63%, the percentages equal to or over this figure being sheep and those under being goat. This would indicate that this metacarpal came from a goat.

There were only two sheep/goat epiphyses unfused out of 10 possibles, suggesting that the animals were fairly mature at the point of death. The bones from more immature animals, however, may not have survived.

Other Species

Other mammal species present in these phases were limited to only one possible fallow deer pelvis and an equid calcaneum. The bird bones consisted mainly of domestic fowl (8) and goose (2). In addition, however, there was a distal humerus fragment from an imperial eagle. The imperial is a large eagle normally found in woody areas, steppes and marshes with scattered trees (Heinzel, Fitter and Parslow 1972, 78).

Phase C (c. 1191–c. 1265)

The bones from this phase were probably mostly from the Templar occupation of c. 1191–c. 1248.

Main Mammalian Species (MMS)

In this phase pig bones make a sudden appearance and form 86% of the MMS. Sheep/goat make up the remaining 14% and cattle are completely absent (see Fig. 13).

Certainly the occurrence of a relatively large number of pig bones in Phase C is a dramatic change both from the preceding and later phases. Moreover the total absence of cattle in this phase is at least as significant and perhaps more so. Because of the size and robustness of the bovine skeleton in relation to sheep/goat and pigs, post-mortem processes favour its survival. This absence of cattle bones may perhaps be related therefore to the dietary rules or preferences of the Templars, rather than to a significant change in the rural regime. The pig bones, however, could have come either from a very short temporal horizon or else from a very small geographical area, since the estimated minimum number of individuals (MIN) based on the number of pig mandibles in Phase C is only 3. They could therefore even have all been consumed at the same meal.

Very few of the pig bones were fused and it seems likely that most animals died under one year old; the meat would therefore have been tender and not very fatty. The similarity in the age-stages and appearance of most of the bones supports the theory that they derive

from a small number of animals. The small amount of mandibular evidence also confirms that the pigs died young, but it is not sufficient to be precise about ages. Because all the pig bones were very young, it was not possible to take any measurements from fused epiphyseal endings save from one radius. I therefore recorded some minimum shaft-measurements (Table 15). There was one pig canine, derived from a male mandible.

That bacon was imported into the Kingdom of Jerusalem along with other foodstuffs, such as tunny fish and cheeses, is indicated by a charter of King William II of Sicily, granting the Abbey of St. Mary Latin, in March 1168, freedom from tolls on certain specified exports from Messina to their house in Jerusalem. (Holtzmann, 70–71, no. 7; Sinopoli, nos. 29–30). At the Red Tower, however, all parts of the pig skeleton were present (Table 14), so that it seems likely that they were raised locally and not imported as bacon or ham. Indeed they may well have been bred in the oak forest on the edge of which the Red Tower at that time lay. Pigs thrive on acorns and the fruits of the forest. That pigs were being raised and eaten in Palestine before the Crusades, despite the prohibition on Muslims eating pork, is suggested by a tax (tuazo) levied on pig-butchers in Tyre, which was retained after the Frankish occupation (cf. Riley-Smith 1977, 13; Prawer 1980, 186).

In contrast with the pig the sheep/goat bones were comparatively mature.

It is noticeable in this horizon, in contrast with both the earlier and later phases, that there is an apparent absence of wild animals. The pigs seem unlikely to have been wild boar, both because of the consistent appearance of their bones, and because the Templars were forbidden by their Rule to consume wild animals that had been taken by hawking or hunting (see below).

Main Bird Species

There was a very large percentage of bird bones in Phase C, there being over twice as many bird fragments as there were MMS. Fifty percent of these bones are from geese and according to the measurements these are domestic geese, which tend to be stouter than their wild cousins. (The measurements were compared with those in Bucher 1967.) The other bird present is domestic fowl, bar one bone fragment. Many of the domestic fowl are juvenile, which makes them more difficult to identify with certainty, but there seemed to be no anomalies. Again we may note the domestic nature of the bird species and the absence of game birds. In contrast, a goose carpometacarpus from Phase E1, representing one of the few goose bones from this site which did not occur in Phase C, has measurements suggesting that it derived from a wild goose (Anser anser). Since there was a marsh surrounding the Nahr

Iskandaruna (River Alexander) near-by, it is possible that wild fowl would have been available for hunting had they been sought. This terrain would also have been very suitable for herding geese. Like the pig, the goose bones represented only a small number of individuals; in this case the estimated minimum is five. This confirms the possibility that many of these bones derive from birds that could have been consumed at a single feast or a few meals. It should also perhaps be noted that both pig and geese can be reared successfully in confined spaces and that geese can also be employed successfully as watch-dogs.

Other Species

Other species present in this phase were limited and confined to dog, cat and two rodent bones, probably from a rat. Most of the dog bones in this phase probably came from the same young animal. Again we see the mainly domestic nature of the animal bones in this phase.

PHASES D–D1 (c. 1265–c. 1390)

Main Mammalian Species (MMS)

The presence of the pig bones in the layers constituting these phases is probably due to material

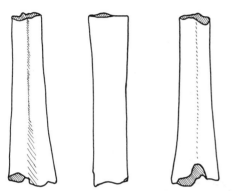

Fig. 68. Fragment of metatarsal: left, dorsal view; centre, lateral view; right, posterior view (Scale 1 : 2).

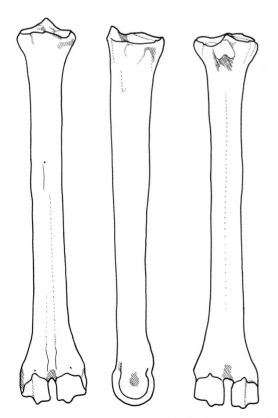

Fig. 69. Oryx leucoryx metatarsal (male): left, dorsal view; centre, lateral view; right, posterior view (Scale 1 : 2).

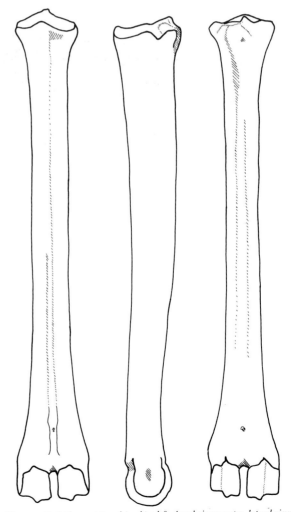

Fig. 70. Alcelaphus metatarsal (male): left, dorsal view; centre, lateral view; posterior view (Scale 1 : 2).

from the final Crusading occupation being mixed together with that from the subsequent village occupation. Thus there is not too much information to be derived from the MMS percentages. It is to be noted, however, that cattle have reappeared and form the majority percentage of the MMS.

More cattle bones were fused than not fused, most of the animals surviving at least till their fourth year. However, there were some young animals, probably mostly under 1½ years and possibly younger. Three unfused humeri, good cuts of meat, all come from Phase D and might suggest that the consumers were eating rather well.

As usual the cattle teeth evidence was scanty, but there is one complete mandible from Phase D from an animal of six months or less. This would tend to support the fusion evidence. Otherwise the teeth come mainly from mature animals, though of course this could be due at least in part to problems of preservation for immature bones.

Other Species

These included fallow deer, cat and several dog bones from Phase D. There were also three gazelle bones including a rather fine horn core from Phase D1.

There were 17 bird bones, 10 of which were domestic fowl, including 2 goose. There was also a wood pigeon radius and what was probably a merlin bone. This latter

Table 14 Total numbers of fragments—main mammalian species

	Sheep/Goat	Pig	Cattle
Mandible	21	12	25
Maxilla	5	1	2
Tooth	28	1	19
Skull	15	4	33
Horn	3	0	3
Scapula	15	0	20
Humerus	21	2	15
Radius	21	3	5
Ulna	4	3	3
Carpal/tarsal	0	0	4
Metacarpal	15	8	8
Pelvis	13	3	13
Femur	19	6	9
Patella	1	0	1
Tibia	26	5	16
Astragalus	3	0	3
Calcaneum	1	1	4
Navicular cuboid	0	0	1
Metatarsal	14	3	11
Phalange 1	5	1	7
Phalange 2	3	0	1
Phalange 3	0	0	3
Metapodial	1	0	2
Fibula	0	0	0
Splint	0	0	0
Total	233	53	208

Table 15 Measurements (in mm.)

Phase	Bone	PF	DF	1	2	3	4	5	6	7	L
1 SHEEP—GOAT											
A	Humerus		?					13·9			
D	Humerus		DF	25·8	28·2	17·7	28·5	12·2			
D1	Humerus		?					11·8			
E	Humerus		DF		30·9	18·9	31·5	12·4			
E	Humerus		?					13·8			
F	Humerus		DF	30·7	34·8	21·3	33·0				
F	Humerus		DF					16·8			
F	Radius	PF		37·1							
E	Radius	PF		34·3							
D	Radius	PF		35·7							
C	Radius	PF		30·5							
A	Metatarsal	PF	DF	21·8	20·0	25·9	14·8	25·3			119·5
B	Metatarsal	PF	DF	22·5	19·8	25·5	13·5	24·3	17·2	9·8	114·5
A	Metatarsal	PF		20·8	22·3						
B	Metatarsal	PF		21·0	19·2						
E	Metatarsal	PF		21·1	21·1						
D	Metatarsal	PF		20·8	19·4						
F	Metatarsal	PF			24·8						
E1	Metacarpal	PF		27·1	20·3						
F	Metacarpal	PF		25·6	19·1						

Table 15   *(cont.)*

Phase	Bone	PF	DF	1	2	3	4	5	6	7	L
E	Metacarpal	PF		24·3	17·1						
E	Metacarpal		DF			20·4	13·4		16·6	12·6	
F	Tibia		DF	28·9	19·9						
E	Tibia		DF	32·7	23·8						
A	Astragalus			30·1	15·5	27·4					
D	Astragalus			29·4	16·0	27·8					
E	Astragalus			26·4	13·8	24·7					
E	Calcaneum	PF		20·3	10·1	22·1	54·0				

2 PIG

Phase	Bone	PF	DF	1	2	3	4	5	6	7	L
C	Tibia		DNF			19·2					
C	Tibia	PNF	DNF			10·1					
C	Tibia		DNF			11·0					
C	Radius	PF		25·3		13·7					
D	Radius	PNF				14·0					

3 CATTLE

Phase	Bone	PF	DF	1	2	3	4	5	6	7	L
E	Humerus	PF	DF			34·9	26·0				
E	Humerus					32·5					
E	Tibia		DF	59·1	41·4						
E	Tibia		DF	61·1	42·6						
E	Astragalus					52·2					
E	Astragalus				34·5	59·3					
E	Calcaneum			24·9	27·3	50·2					
D	Metacarpal	PF	DF		32·7		27·6		31·7		
E	Metacarpal	PF		45·6	29·6						
F	Metacarpal	PF			29·0						
F	Metacarpal		DF				21·0		27·0		
E	Metatarsal		DF			44·9	26·4				
E	Metatarsal	PF	DF			46·4	27·8	49·2	30·7		
D	Metatarsal		DF			55·6	32·3	57·2	33·7		
A	Horncore			93·0	59·0						
E	Horncore frag.			73·0	> 184·0						
	(v. large—? Buffalo)										

4 EQUUS

Phase	Bone	PF	DF	1	2	3	4	5	6	7	L
E	Tibia		DF	57·0	35·0						
F	Metacarpal	PF	DF	52·6	33·2	47·3		49·5	37·5		

5 DOG

Phase	Bone	PF	DF	1	2	3	4	5	6	7	L
E	Radius	PF		18·7							

Other species:

GAZELLE
Phase D1, Horncore, Basal circumference = 77·0
Length of outer curvature = 135·0
(approximate—slight chip off end)
Phase D1, Scapula, Breadth of Fused Glenoid Cavity = 24·2
Phalange 1, PF, DF, Greatest Length: Phase D = 46·9
Phase F = 44·2
Phase F = 47·6

CAMEL
Phase F, Phalange 1, PF, DF, Greatest Length = 91·7

HONEY BADGER
Phase E, Humerus, PF, Proximal Width = 30·2

For Key to Table 15, see page 186 below

was the nearest I could come to the identification of a complete adult ulna. The bone was similar in appearance to the examples in the comparative collection at Tring Zoological Museum, but it was very slightly longer than the male and shorter than the female specimens.

PHASES E–F (*c.*1390–1983)

Main Mammalian Species (*MMS*)

In these latest phases, the numbers of cattle and sheep/goat bones are more equal and pig bones are no longer present.

Table 16 Summary of fusion data

Bone	Age of fusion	Phase A F	Phase A NF	Phase B F	Phase B NF	Phase C F	Phase C NF	Phase D F	Phase D NF	Phase D1 F	Phase D1 NF	Phase E F	Phase E NF	Phase E1 F	Phase E1 NF	Phase F F	Phase F NF
1 SHEEP/GOAT																	
Humerus (D)	10 months			1				2				2		1		2	
Radius (P)	10 months	1		1		1		1				2				1	
Phalange 1 (P)	13–16 months			1								1	1			1	1
Phalange 2 (P)	13–16 months											1				2	
Metacarpal (D)	2 years											1		1			
Metatarsal (D)	2¼ years	2	1	1							1		1				
Calcaneum (P)	2–2½ years											1					
Tibia (D)	1½–2 years							1				1		1			
Humerus (P)	3—3½ years				1												
Radius (D)	3 years													1			1
Femur (P)	2½–3 years							1	1								2
Femur (D)	3–3½ years	1				1											
Tibia (P)	3–3½ years					1					1						1
2 PIG																	
Humerus (D)	1 year						1										
Radius (P)	1 year					1	2										
Calcaneum (P)	2–2½ years						1										
Metacarpal (D)	2 years							1									
Metatarsal (D)	2½ years						8										
Phalange 1 (P)	2 years					1											
Tibia (D)	2 years						3										
Humerus (PF)	3½ years								1								
Radius (DF)	3½ years						1										
Femur (PF)	3½ years						2										
Femur (DF)	3½ years						1										
Tibia (PF)	3½ years					1	2										
Ulna (PF)	3–3½ years						1										
3 CATTLE																	
Humerus (D)	12–18 months							3				1					
Radius (P)	12–18 months									1				1			
Phalange 1 (P)	1½ years	2						1				3		1			
Phalange 2 (P)	1½ years	1															
Metacarpal (D)	2–2½ years							1								1	1
Metatarsal (D)	2 years				1			3				2	1				
Tibia (D)	2–2½ years											2	1	1			
Humerus (P)	3½–4 years											1					
Femur (P)	3½ years	1										1					
Calcaneum (P)	3–3½ years											2					

Key: D = Distal; P = Proximal; F = Epiphysis fused; NF = Epiphysis not fused. Age of fusion based on Silver 1969.

From Phase E there was a very large but incomplete horn. This is either from a long-horn cattle or else from a buffalo. The rearing water-buffalo by one of the nomadic tribes of the region, the *Jammāsin*, is recorded at the end of the 16th century (see above, p. 25).

The few sheep/goat measurements are large. Boessneck describes a method of distinguishing sheep from goat using the size of the articular surface of the calcaneum (1969, 353). The size of the articular surface of the calcaneum in Phase E is less than 50% of the

Table 17   Stages of mandibular wear, based on Grant's method (1975)

Phase	D2	D3	D4	P2	P3	P4	M1	M2	M3
1 SHEEP/GOAT									
Mandibles									
A					W			W*c. (e)	W(e) (*3rd cusp)
A					W	W(1)			
B								*	½W(b–c)
B	W	W	W(h)				½W(b)		
D1	P	W	W(f)				E		
E			W(k)				W(f)	W½	
E					slight abcess	W(j)	W*		
E			*so that P4 is visible	V	V	V	W*c. (g)	W(e)	
F									W(f) (*3rd cusp)
F				W	W				
F							M1/2 ½W(c)		
Teeth									
A							W(h)		
B									W(e) (*3rd cusp)
D							M1/2 ½W(c)		
F							M1/2 W(b) (*2nd cusp)		
2 PIG									
Mandible									
C									M3 *Wc. (c)
Loose teeth									
C								W(a)	
C							W(c)		
C—Canine, lower, masculine									
3 CATTLE									
Mandibles									
D			W(h–j)				½		
E			W(j–k)						
F							M1/2 W(d)		
Loose teeth									
B			W(h)						
E							M1/2 W(a)		
E							M1/2 W(k)		
E							M1/2 W(b)		
E							M1/2 W(k)		
F							M1/2 W(g)		
F							M1/2 W(k)		

Key: * = Broken; D = Milk Tooth; P = Premolar; M = Molar; V = Visible in crypt; E = Erupting above surface of bone; ½ = Half way up; W = Worn; (a) to (m) = wear stages; c. = about.

whole surface which means that it is more likely to be a goat. This measurement indicates that there are at least some goats in the sample and it may be the explanation for the large measurements. The fusion evidence suggests that they may have been dying about two to three years old, since none of the late-fusing epiphyses were fused and only one of the unfused epiphyses was from an early-fusing bone.

Other Mammalian Species

There are several equid bones. Most of these were of horse-size, but there was one metatarsal fragment in Phase E belonging to a small equid, probably a donkey. There were more gazelle bones, a tortoise leg-bone and some segments of its carapace, some cat, dog and rodent bones and a fused camel phalange I from Phase F. There was also a proximally-fused humerus fragment from a honey badger (*Mellivora capensis*). The honey badger, otherwise known as the ratel, is black below and white above and possesses stink-glands. It is known as the honey badger because of the taste that it has for bees, their grubs and their honey. It uses its stink-glands to "smoke" the bees out (Kingdom 1977).

The most perplexing bone from this phase was a fairly small shaft fragment of a right metatarsal (see Fig. 68). This I have drawn because I and those whom I consulted are unable to identify it with certainty. At first I thought that it was an *Oryx leucoryx* or North African antelope (Fig. 69). The fragment certainly resembles the *Oryx* most clearly in size. This is such a rare species, however, that the fragment could not simply be dismissed as unidentifiable. The vascular groove at the distal end, which in the red deer is so deep and sharply edged, seems in this bone to become shallow. However, the surface patina is that which often occurs on the bones of young animals. The fragment may therefore be that of a young hartebeest (*Alcelaphus*) (Fig. 70), it being denser than that of the *Oryx* and also lacking the slight irregularity and roughness that characterizes the surface of the *Oryx* metatarsal.

Birds

Another unusual fragment was the distal humerus of a vulture (*Trigonoceps occipitalis*). This is a large and mainly African species. There were also four bones from what was probably a young jackdaw.

ACKNOWLEDGEMENT

I am extremely grateful to the following people who offered valuable advice and aided me in the identification of the bird bones and the more exotic species: Dr. Juliet Clutton-Brock, Mr. G. Cowles, Dr. Caroline Grigson, Peter Rowley-Conwy and Sheila Sutherland.

Table 18 Bird numbers

	A	B	C	D	D1	E	E1	F
Goose	0	2	59	2	0	1	1	1
Domestic Fowl	4	2	30	4	2	4	2	2
Juvenile (?) Domestic Fowl	1	1	28	1	3	3	0	2
Others	1	0	0	2	2	1	0	4
Unidentifiable fragments			1	1				1
Total	6	5	118	10	7	9	3	10

Description of other birds

Phase	Number of fragments	Scientific name	Common name
A	1	*Aquila heliaca*	Imperial eagle
D	1	*Columba palumbus*	Wood pigeon
D	1	*?Falco columbarius*	Probably a merlin
D1	2	*Columba palumbus*	Wood pigeon
E	1	*Trigonoceps occipitalis*	Vulture
F	4	*?Corvus monedula*	Probably a juvenile jackdaw

Table 19 Bird measurements (in mm.)

Phase	1	2	3	4	Bb	BF	ML
DOMESTIC GOOSE (*Anser Anser Domesticus*)							
Coracoid							
C	72·8				31·4	30·2	64·4
C	72·8						
Humerus							
C				11·2			
C				11·0			
Carpometacarpus							
C	88·2						
C	96·3	21·9					
C		22·4					
Femur							
C	81·4						
C	79·8						
?WILD GOOSE (*Anser Anser*)							
Carpometacarpus							
E1	89·1	20·6					
DOMESTIC FOWL							
Humerus							
A				6·3			
C	62·1	17·5	13·9	6·5			
C			14·2	6·3			
C				6·6			
D			14·0				
F	66·0	18·4	13·5	6·3			
Femur							
A		14·8	14·2	6·0			
C		15·5	15·2	6·0			
C	74·7	14·9	15·2	6·7			
C				6·5			
C		15·9					
C			14·3	6·4			
C			15·7				
C		14·3					
D1		15·9	15·9	7·2			
E	77·0	16·3	15·2	6·6			
E1				7·5			
Ulna							
C	64·0			5·2			
C				4·8			
C				5·3			
C				5·5			
Coracoid							
C	52·0						

Table 19 (cont.)

Phase	1	2	3	4	Bb	BF	ML
OTHER BIRDS							
Imperial Eagle Humerus							
A		30·3					
Merlin Ulna							
D	54·7						
Wood Pigeon							
D1	54·7						

Key: 1 = Greatest Length; 2 = Proximal Width; 3 = Distal Width; 4 = Minimum Width of Shaft; ML = Medial Length; Bb = Greatest Basal Breadth; BF = Breadth of the Basal Articular Surface.

A NOTE ON THE TEMPLARS' DIET (*by* D.P.)

As explained above (pp. 127–128), it seems very possible that the material, including faunal remains, associated with Phase C represents for the most part rubbish left behind by the departing Templar garrison in *c.* 1248, subsequently tidied up by the incoming Hospitallers. The Rule of the Temple, which survives in manuscripts of the 13th and early 14th centuries and seems to have been compiled progressively between 1128 and *c.* 1265 (and certainly before 1304), provides a number of details about the diet of the Order's members.

Under the earliest version of the Rule, the brothers were commanded to be served meat three times a week, in order to remind them of the corruption of all flesh. The normal meat days were evidently Sunday, Tuesday and Thursday, and the Rule states that if a fast should fall on a Tuesday then meat should be served the following day instead (*Règle*, 35–36: cf. 26). Although the days for eating meat were restricted, the range of meats allowed on them was relatively broad. A regulation concerning the infirmary, for instance, states that lentils, beans, cabbage, beef, pork (sow), goat, mutton, veal or eels should be served there only when the rest of the convent was eating the same (*Règle*, 139: ch. 192). At the convent table itself, two or even three different kinds of meat could be served at once, so that those who did not care for one could have the other. Brothers could also send back to the kitchen meat that was under- or over-cooked or which smelled (*Règle*, 135–136: ch. 184–185). It was forbidden for a brother to receive food from anyone but the officer in charge of commissariat (*li Comandeor de la Viande*); an exception, however, was made for wild vegetables, fish so long as the brother caught them himself, and birds and wild animals so long as they were not taken by hawking or hunting (*Règle*, 56–57, 118, 208: chs, 55, 151, 369).

On days when meat was not allowed, two or three alternative dishes of legumes or *pulmentum* would be served or simply one main dish of eggs, cheese or fish. But during the two forty-day fasts of the year, brothers were given a choice of two or three dishes, with fresh or salted fish (or another *companagium*) on Sundays, Tuesdays and Thursdays (*Règle*, 36, 136: chs. 27, 186). On Friday, only one non-meat dish was served, followed by vegetables (*herbes*) or some other *companagium* (*Règle*, 37, 136: chs. 28, 187). All meals would of course have included bread, water and wine (cf. *Règle*, chs. 25, 29–30, 183, 193, 287, 291, 294, 320, 375, 519, 681).

The Rule and statutes of the Hospitallers provide less specific information about the types of food provided for the other major military order. The Rule of Raymond of Le Puy (1120–60), however, states that Hospitaller brethren should eat no more than twice a day, and have no meat on Wednesdays or Saturdays or between Septuagesima and Easter, the prescription of meat on Fridays being of course already understood (transl. King, 22–23, §8). Various other regulations concerned with the quality of the food suggest that, as in the Order of the Temple, it was recognized that fighting men needed to be properly nourished (cf. King, 47, 51, 89, 124, 168, 169–170).

KEY TO TABLE 15 (PAGES 180–181 ABOVE)

PF/NF = Proximal epiphysis fused/not fused; DF/NF = Distal epiphysis fused/not fused. 1–7 and L = Measurements in mm. as follows:

HORN (cattle)
1. basal circumference
2. length of the posterior-dorsal (outer) curvature (maximum length of the horncore)

HUMERUS
1. maximum width of distal humerus
2. maximum thickness of distal epiphysis
3. maximum height of distal articulation
4. maximum width of barrel
5. minimum width of shaft

RADIUS
1. maximum width of proximal epiphysis
2. minimum width of shaft (pig only)
L. Length

METAPODIALS (cattle and sheep/goat only)
1. maximum width of proximal epiphysis
2. maximum thickness of proximal epiphysis
3. maximum width at distal fusion point
4. maximum thickness at distal fusion point
5. maximum width of distal epiphysis
6. maximum thickness of distal epiphysis
7. maximum thicknesses of medial condyle (sheep/goat only)
L. Length

TIBIA
1. maximum width of distal epiphysis
2. maximum thickness of distal epiphysis
3. minimum width of shaft (pig only)

ASTRAGALUS
1. maximum length – lateral half
2. maximum thickness – lateral half
3. maximum length – medial half

CALCANEUM
1. length of the lateral process from the most proximal part of the articular surface to the most distal point of the bone
2. length of articular surface at the lateral process
3. length from most posterior point of bone to most anterior of articular surface

All long-bone measurements are from fused epiphyses except where other defined.

VIII. MEDIEVAL PLANT REMAINS

By R. N. L. B. Hubbard (North East London Polytechnic) and J. McKay (London University)

[Lack of time, personnel and above all water prevented any systematic attempt being made to recover samples of seeds and other organic remains from all phases of the excavation. A dense concentration of carbonized material, however, was excavated from the collapse of the medieval tower in Area C4, just south of the cross-wall in the western ground-floor chamber. From the context of this deposit (see Fig. 23), it appears probable that it had been lying on the first floor of the tower and fell into the position in which it was found when the vaulted floor was demolished c.1265. It probably belongs therefore to the final phase of the building's occupation; but whether those responsible for it were members of the Hospitaller establishment or squatters who had moved in after the Frankish abandonment of the site is uncertain. It is this deposit which forms the sample analysed in the following report (SF 19).]

Little is known about medieval agriculture from the archaeological point of view, whether in the Near East or Europe. The plant remains from the Red Tower are consequently simultaneously frustrating and valuable. They are frustrating because there is so little material with which then can be compared; and they are valuable because the study of the agriculture of historical periods by conventional archaeological methods might clarify a number of interpretational problems that plague the archaeological botanist concerned with prehistoric material.

THE PLANTS IDENTIFIED

The results of the macrobotanical analysis are given below and in Table 20. Where relevant, the measurements are given in the order: (minimum)—average—

Table 20. Carbonized seeds from the Red Tower

Name	Species		Number	Weight (mg)
A. CULTIVATED PLANTS				
Broad bean	*Vicia faba* L.	seeds	24	2,555·2
Chick pea	*Cicer arietinum* L.	seeds	28	1,688·5
Lentil	*Lens culinare* MEDIC.	seeds	9·5	115·9
Grass pea	*Lathyrus sativus* L.	seeds	2	39·2
Two-row hulled barley	*Hordeum distichon*	caryopses	2	5·9
	L. emend. LAM.	laterals	4	1·5
Bread wheat	*Triticum aestivum* L.	caryopses	9·5	95·9
		internode	1	0·75
		glume base	1	0·21
	Olea europaea L.	endocarp	1	236·1
B. WEEDS				
Darnel	*Lolium temulentum* L.	caryopses	29	112·7
	Phalaris minor RETZ.	caryopses	2	1·75
	Phalaris aff. *paradoxa*	caryopsis	1	0·45
	Sclerochloa dura L.	caryopsis	1	0·45
	Polypogon monspeliensis (L.) DESF.	caryopsis	1	0·07
	Gramineae aff. *Sphenopus*	caryopses	19	1·4
	Cichorium intybus L.	achenes	4	2·0
	Compositae sp. 1	achenes	2	0·30
	Compositae sp. 2	achenes	1	0·51
	Convolvulus cf. *arvensis*	seed	1	3·78
	Poterium sanguisorba L.	nutlet	1	0·42
	Caryophyllaceae	seed	1	0·09
	?*Hyoscyamus*	seed	1	0·09
C. MISCELLANEOUS				
Unidentifiable fragments	(mainly *Cicer* and charcoal)		c.4,000	

(maximum), coefficient of variation %, sk = skewness, ku = kurtosis, N = sum. The measurements are given in millimetres.

Vicia faba L. (Broad bean)

There were 22 complete and 3 non-matching halves of broad beans in the sample. One of the half-seeds appeared to have been severely attacked by grain-beetles, but all the others were quite untouched. The aberrant specimen may therefore have occurred as a weed in the chick pea crop, which was heavily infested with grain-beetles.

The measurements of the broad beans (excluding the insect-eaten specimen, which is likely to have come from another population) were as follows:

Length	(6·2)—	8·20	— (10·1)		
		12·6%			$N = 22$
Breadth	(4·6)—	5·91	— (8·0)		
		13·4%	sk = 0·86		$N = 23$
Thickness	(3·7)—	5·38	— (6·6)		
		14·7%			$N = 22$
100 × L/B	(112)—	140·6	— (156)		
		7·1%	sk = −0·90		$N = 22$
100 × T/B	(79)—	92·4	— (110)		
		7·8%			$N = 22$

The skewnesses of the breadth and the length/breadth index are statistically significant at the 89% and 90% levels of confidence respectively.

These measurements would seem to correspond to *V. faba minor*, the horse bean. Nowadays, the smaller-seeded cultivars are usually grown for animal fodder, but there is no reason to believe that these broad beans were not for human consumption.

Cicer arietinum L. (Chick pea)

Of the eleven complete chick peas and 17 non-matching halves, slightly under half were fat and rounded, and resembled very large peas, while the rest (with the exception of a single runt specimen) showed the coarsely rugulated surface typical of chick peas. Many of both groups showed signs of severe attack by the *Stegobium* beetles that were found in the sample.

Length	(3·8)—	5·10	— (6·6)		
		12·1%			$N = 24$
Breadth	(3·8)—	4·44	— (5·6)		
		9·7%	sk = 0·70		$N = 27$
Thickness	(3·3)—	4·72	— (6·1)		
		15·3%			$N = 27$
100 × L/B	(84)—	115·3	— (138)		
		9·4%			$N = 24$
100 × T/B	(78)—	106·2	— (127)		
		10·5%	sk = −0·60		$N = 27$

The skewness of the breadth is significant at the 85% confidence level, and that of the thickness/breadth ratio at the 79% level.

The length measurements exclude the projecting hilum, which is often missing, and which increases the length by about 7%.

Lens culinare MEDIC. (Lentil)

The lentils were uniformly well preserved and undistorted. Their size indicates that they were of the small-seeded race that originates with the wild ancestor of lentils, *L. orientalis*, whose seeds, like those of its prehistoric descendants, measure about 2·7 × 1·1 mm. The large-seeded lentils with which we are more familiar seem to have emerged in Bronze-Age times.

Breadth	(3·4)—	3·77	— (4·4)		
		9·8%			$N = 10$
Thickness	(2·2)—	2·46	— (2·7)		
		6·5%			$N = 9$
100 × B/T	(141)—	154·5	— (165)		
		4·9%			$N = 9$

Lathyrus sativus L. (Grass pea)

Lathyrus sativus seeds have a very characteristic shape that is best described as resembling the head of an axe. They are only likely to be confused with the seeds of their wild ancestor *L. cicera*, and with those of *Vicia ervilia*, which differ (amongst other things) in having the hilum flush with the top of the seed instead of slightly recessed. Two seeds were found, measuring 4·6 × 4·4 × 4·1 and 2·3 × 1·9 × 1·9 mm. respectively. The smaller is presumably a runt specimen rather than *L. cicera*, while the other is quite typical of the species.

Today *L. sativus* and *V. ervilia* are only grown as animal fodder; but in prehistoric times they were widely grown in the Mediterranean area for food. It is not clear when these crops were abandoned as food, but it may have been around two thousand years ago, probably at different times in different places. In this sample the usage is quite uncertain, as it seems likely that the specimens may have been from plants growing as weeds in one of the other pulse crops.

Triticum aestivum L. emend. SCHIEMANN (Bread wheat)

Of the nine and a half bread wheat grains, four had the steeply set radical typical of the terminal spikelets in an ear. There was also an internode fragment showing the deciduous glumes and non-disarticulating rhachis typical, according to G. Hillman, of *T. aestivum*, *T. compactum*, and *T. sphaerococcum*. The internode fragment was too short to show which of these very closely related wheats was involved, but the shape of the seeds (highly heterogeneous as they are) indicates that it was the first of them.

There was also an undiagnostic wheat glume base, measuring 0·81 mm. across the nerves.

Length	(3·6)—	4·52 — (5·3)		
		12·3%		$N = 9$
Breadth	(2·0)—	3·03 — (3·6)		
		15·2%	sk = −1·00	$N = 9$
Thickness	(1·9)—	2·44 — (2·9)		
		12·4%		$N = 9$
100 × L/B	(108)—	152·3 — (196)		
		19·3%		$N = 9$
100 × T/B	(74)—	81·1 — (92)		
		7·1%		$N = 9$

The skewness of the breadth is significant at the 75% level of confidence.

Hordeum distichon L. emend. LAM. (Two-row hulled barley)

Two fragmentary hulled barley seeds were recovered, and four bits of the sterile lateral florets that proved that it was two-row barley.

Olea europaea L. (Olive)

One almost complete olive stone, measuring 13·2 × 4·6 × 6·4 mm., was recovered, as well as fragments of a second pip. The olives were no doubt being eaten in the vicinity, and the seeds were spat out into a fireplace or hearth, leading to their preservation.

Lolium temulentum L. (Darnel)

Whether or not it can be identified with the tares mentioned in the Bible, darnel is one of the most well known crop weeds, and occurs in almost every archaeobotanical sample from the Levantine lowlands. Not merely do its seeds resemble small cereal grains, but they (or a fungus that usually infests them) are poisonous; consequently bread and beer made from darnel-polluted grain can be intoxicating or worse— whence darnel's French name, *ivraie*.

Length	(1·7)—	3·69 — (4·7)		
		19·7%	sk = −1·13	$N = 26$
Breadth	(1·1)—	1·81 — (2·4)		
		19·9%	ku = −1·16	$N = 28$
Thickness	(0·88)—	1·34 — (1·8)		
		16·7%		$N = 29$
100 × L/B	(151)—	201·7 — (250)		
		12·0%		$N = 26$
100 × T/B	(59)—	75·1 — (89)		
		9·7%		$N = 28$

The lop-sidedness of the length, with more short grains than a Normal distribution should have, is significant at the 79% level of confidence; and the un-normally flat distribution of the breadth measurements is significant at the 78% level.

Phalaris spp. (Canary grasses)

Phalaris caryopses look like tiny einkorn seeds, but are more stumpy, and instead of having a ventral furrow have an elliptical hilum just above the base of the ventral side. Two of the seeds, measuring 2·2 × 1·1 × 1·2 and 2·5 × 1·2 × 1·4 mm. repectively, matched *P. minor* RETZ.; but the third was much smaller (1·1 × 0·64 × 0·94 mm.), smaller than the seeds of *P. paradoxa*, the smallest seeded *Phalaris* in our reference collections.

Sclerochloa dura L. (Rigid dog's tail grass)

The seeds of this grass are somewhat like *Phalaris* caryopses, but the radical is positioned along the base of the dorsal side, and not obliquely between the dorsal side and the proximal end. The seed measured 1·9 × 0·74 × 0·94 mm.

Polypogon monspeliensis (L.) DESF. (Annual beard grass)

Polypogon semiverticillatus and *P. monspeliensis* are two of the commonest grasses of waste ground in the damper parts of the Near East. They have somewhat conical or drop-shaped seeds, with the embryo at the pointed end and a small elliptical hilum about a third of the way up the ventral side. The size of the seed found (1·08 × 0·47 × 0·45 mm.) is too big for *P. semiverticillatus*.

Gramineae (Gen. & sp. indeterminate)

Nineteen tiny grass seeds were found that could not be identified. Their size put *Sphenopus* in mind, but they lacked the ventral furrow, and had a long, narrow embryo that was 60% of the length of the seed and a basal hilum. They were far too slender to belong to any *Eragrostis* species. At present we are unable to make any guess at what group of grasses might be involved.

Length	(0·89)—	1·08 — (1·30)		
		9·6%		$N = 18$
Breadth	(0·35)—	0·454 — (0·56)		
		13·3%		$N = 18$
Thickness	(0·41)—	0·475 — (0·55)		
		9·8%		$N = 19$
100 × L/B	(189)—	240·9 — (284)		
		12·6%	ku = −1·39	$N = 17$
100 × T/B	(94)—	104·6 — (115)		
		5·3%		$N = 18$

The kurtosis of the length/breadth index is significant at the 74% level.

Scirpus fluitans L. (Floating scirpus)

Two smooth, biconvex sedge nutlets were found, whose average measurements were 1·5 × 1·0 × 0·88 mm. and could be matched by *Scirpus fluitans*.ecology to

?*Hyoscyamus* (?Henbane)

There was one small flat reticulated seed that could not be identified with certainty. It strongly resembled the seeds of the European henbane, but was about half the size (1·1 × 0·72 mm.). There are several common *Hyoscyamus* species in the Near East; but there are also common *Veronica*-like plants that might produce rather similar seeds.

Poterium sanguisorba L. (Salad burnet)

Half of one of the unmistakable tetragonal coarsely reticulated seeds of salad burnet was recovered. It was about 1·5 mm. in diameter. Salad burnet, as its name indicates, has leaves that are perfectly palatable; but it is also a common plant in damper places in the Near East, and there is no reason to believe that its presence here reflects anything more exciting than its existence as a weed.

Convolvulus cf. *arvensis* (Bindweed)

A single bindweed seed was found, measuring 3·0 × 2·4 × 2·2 mm. This is almost 25% smaller than the well-known and widespread *C. arvensis*, from which this seed also differs by its smooth and not verrucate seed-coat. There are many bindweeds in the Near East: no doubt this unidentified species, has similar habits and ecology to common bindweed, as G. Hillman tells us that he has also frequently encountered it in archaeological samples.

Compositae

Three groups of Compositae achenes were encountered in the analysis, only one of which could be identified precisely as *Cichorium intybus* L. (see below).

One seed looked like a small thistle achene, being smooth, longitudinally ribbed, 2·2 mm. long, and about 1mm. in diameter.

A second group of two seeds, measuring about 2·1 × 0·8 × 0·6 mm., resembled tiny, very elongated apple seeds. They did not appear to be *Artemisia* seeds, were too small to be attributable to *Micropus*, and could not be assigned to *Senecio* as they lacked hairs.

Cichorium intybus L. (Chicory)

Four chicory achenes were identified. They were plump, longitudinally ribbed seeds bearing fine transverse rugulations, averaging 2·01 × 1·13 × 0·74 mm.

Caryophyllaceae (Gen. & sp. indeterminate)

One tiny seed, resembling a mallow seed but half the size and quite smooth, was clearly the inner part of a seed of one of the carnation family that had lost its characteristically sculptured seed-coat. Without the seed-coat it was unidentifiable; but its small size suggests that it might be a *Silene*.

THE INSECTS
by K. D. Thomas

The fragmentary and charred insect remains associated with the burned chick peas were submitted to the Commonwealth Institute of Entomology for identification. Dr. R. Madge has kindly made the following identifications, which, because of the difficult nature of the material, cannot be regarded as absolutely certain:

Staphylinidae (?)

The remains of the possible staphylinid beetle are of no great significance. Some species of staphylinids may be associated with stored foodstuffs, but only as predators on other insects or as feeders on algae or fungi (Freeman 1980). Most species are free-living and are to be found in almost all terrestrial habitats. They are often abundant near human dwellings and, in the present case, may have become incidentally preserved in the archaeological record.

Anobiidae (?): *Stegobium paniceum* (Linnaeus)

Stegobium paniceum is often known as the "Bread beetle" or the "Drug store beetle". It is a common pest of stored foodstuffs. The adult does not feed, but the larva is known to attack a wide variety of foodstuffs including grains, flour, seeds, spices, and confectionary (Freeman 1980; Munro 1966). It has been recorded from food-offerings in the tomb of Tutankhamun (Alfieri 1931; Zacher 1937), and from fragments of desiccated bread from ancient Thebes (Chaddick and Leek 1972). Although perhaps most commonly reported from stores of grain or farinaceous products, the occurrence of *S. paniceum* with pulses should not occasion any great surprise.

DISCUSSION

In interpreting these results, it is necessary to remember that seeds of crops are meant to grow or to be eaten, and that any seed that gets charred is an economic or genetical failure. Whether seeds are carbonized intentionally or by accident, there is every reason to believe that the precise composition of a sample of carbonized plant remains is essentially meaningless from the economic point of view. We therefore cannot make deductions about the nature of 13th-century agricultural economics on the basis of this analysis alone. Given enough independent samples, however, it seems likely that an important crop plant will turn up in more samples than will a minor crop (Hubbard 1976; 1980).

Unfortunately, given the paucity of archaeobotanical information from the Near East—let alone Palestine—for the medieval period, putting the Red Tower plant remains into any general context is difficult. At Korucutepe, in Anatolia, W. van Zeist and J. A. H. Bakker-Heeres (1975) identified bread wheat and two-row barley in deposits of the 12th–14th centuries, while H. Helbaek (1961) found rye and what he thought might be *Triticum turgidum* (a derivative of emmer) in Byzantine contexts at Beycesultan. At Tell Bazmosian, Helbaek (1963) identified broad beans in a sample from early Islamic deposits. The cultivation of wheat, therefore, seems to have been ubiquitous (which is perhaps hardly surprising), with two-row hulled barley in second place. Whether this means that wheat and barley were of more economic importance than the pulses is not at all clear and, indeed, is one of the interpretational problems of prehistoric archaeobotany that investigations of historic material might elucidate. It is noteworthy that the suite of plants found at the Red Tower corresponds closely to the agricultural repertoires recorded for the area in later documents. It may well transpire that the rye found at Beycesultan is a crop that is restricted to the Anatolian plateau and the Iranian highlands, as this appears to be the pattern in prehistoric times in the Near East. In other respects, however, the extremely limited evidence available suggests that there may have been a considerable degree of uniformity in medieval agriculture in the Near Eastern lowlands.

The fact that the numerical composition of samples of carbonized seeds is largely meaningless does not mean that it is *entirely* meaningless. If enough is known about the sample before it got burnt, or enough can be deduced about its immediate history from internal evidence, then some useful information can sometimes be drawn from consideration of the sample's composition. In this case, the sample is dominated by pulses, and cereals are in a minority. The cereal remains, and at least part of the pulse component, are clearly the result of agricultural rubbish-disposal. The chick peas are insect-infested; the

darnel is a notorious and noxious field weed; and the wheat and barley are accompanied by small chaff fragments (suggesting that they got burned in disposal of some threshing refuse, or, as the excavator suggests, the use of threshing refuse for fuel). Only the lentils and the broad beans might be part of a clean crop that might have been burned in a cooking accident—and, as already noted, one of the broad beans was probably thrown out as rubbish. The sample can thus be identified as reflecting (overwhelmingly if not exclusively) the disposal of refuse from preparing crops for storage or consumption. The *Lathyrus sativus* seeds may have come from self-sown plants from a previous year's crop growing as a weed amongst one of the other pulse crops present, and might reflect the pattern of crop-rotation. The olive pip would have been spat out into a fire after the olive itself had been eaten. The darnel seeds are obviously from another crop-cleaning episode, presumably from a cereal crop. The darnel may be the result of hand-sorting, as it is difficult to remove by sieving, and the other weed seeds do not resemble sieving residues.

The small size of most of the remaining seeds suggests that they are winnowing refuse, and are therefore from the cereal crops. It is probably no accident that the biggest of them are Compositae achenes, which (apart from the chicory seeds) would originally have had a feathery pappus attached. The weeds and insects, where identifiable, are common and ubiquitous species, of which it only needs to be observed that the sedge nutlets presumably reflect irrigation of the fields. The darnel might have been burned in the same event as the winnowing rubbish, but it is perhaps more likely that the pulse remains record a number of separate episodes, in which case between two and five different burnings may have given rise to this single archaeological sample.

Whatever the precise history of events, the contents of the sample show, quite unequivocally, that not merely were broad beans, bread wheat, chick peas, two-row hulled barley, lentils, and grass pea being cultivated, but that they were being threshed and cleaned in the immediate vicinity.

APPENDIX 1

SUMMARY OF PHASES IDENTIFIED AT THE RED TOWER 1983

Phase	Description	Suggested date
Phase A	Layers predating the construction of the castle, mostly ploughsoil but including some traces of structures	*c.* 400–*c.* 1100/50
Phase B	Layers associated with the construction of the tower and its attendant buildings	*c.* 1100–*c.* 1150
Phase C	Templar occupation after the Third Crusade	*c.* 1191–*c.* 1248
	Refurbishment of the castle by the Hospitallers	*c.* 1248–*c.* 1265
Phase D	Destruction of the castle and levelling of the collapsed rubble	*c.* 1265–*c.* 1390
Phase D1	Upper layers of destruction (in Area A)	*c.* 1350–*c.* 1390
Phase E	Village occupation	*c.* 1390–*c.* 1920
Phase E1	Later village occupation	*c.* 1920–*c.* 1948
Phase F	Topsoil	1948–1983

APPENDIX 2

CONCORDANCE OF FINDS ASSEMBLAGES BY PHASE AND AREA

The numbers are those by which the pieces are identified in the reports in Part Three above.

PHASE A: AREA B–B1: Coin: 4 (5th-c.).
AREA C, 1, 4 and 6: Pottery: 22.
Glass: 3, 7, 12, 23.
Terracotta: 1.

PHASE B: AREA B–B1: Pottery: 71.
Glass: 8.
Metalwork: 2, 29, 43.
AREA C, 1, 4 and 6: Pottery: 16, 26–27, 78.
AREA C2–3, 5: Pottery 28.
Glass: 2, 6.
Metalwork: 3–4, 21.

PHASE C: AREA A–A3: Pottery: 7, 17–19, 23, 25, 42, 44, 55, 57–58, 61–62, 74.
Glass: 4, 11, 13–15, 17, 19.
Metalwork: 1, 8–16, 17a, 19–20, 22–23, 26–27, 34–38, 40, 42, 44–46, 48–51.
Bone: 3–4.
Wood: 5.
Stone: 13.
Coins: 2 (337–340); 5–8 (1163–*c.* 1219); 9–28 (*c.* 1189–*c.* 1291).
AREA C, 1, 4 and 6: Pottery: 7, 36, 38, 40–41, 63, 75.
Glass: 9, 18, 21.
Coin: 1 (306–308).

PHASE D: AREA A–A3: Pottery: 2–4, 6, 10, 24, 34, 69, 86.
Glass: 5.
Metalwork: 18, 24.
Stone: 14–16.
AREA C, 1, 4 and 6: Pottery 15, 20, 29, 32, 37, 39, 84.
Glass: 16.
Stone: 2.
Coin: 33 (16th-c.?).

PHASE DI :	AREA A–A3 :	Pottery: 9, 13, 43, 45–46, 52, 59, 65, 67–68, 72–73, 77.
		Metalwork: 5, 33, 47.
		Coin: 29 (1343/44).
PHASE E:	AREA A–A3 :	Pottery: 5, 8, 11–12, 21, 30–31, 35, 48–49, 53–54, 56, 77, 82–83, 87–90.
		Glass: 10, 22, 24.
		Metalwork: 6–7, 25, 30–31, 39.
		Stone: 6, 8.
	AREA B–BI :	Pottery: 64.
		Metalwork: 28.
		Coins: 3 (384–387); 31 (1388/89).
	AREA C, 1, 4 and 6:	Pottery: 50, 66.
		Glass: 25.
		Metalwork: 32, 41.
		Stone: 3.
	AREA C2–3, 5:	Pottery: 1, 33, 60, 81.
PHASE EI :	AREA A–A3 :	Pottery: 14.
		Stone: 4, 10.
PHASE F:	AREA A–A3 :	Pottery: 76, 79.
		Stone: 1, 7, 9, 11.
	AREA B:	Terracotta: 2.
		Stone: 5.
	AREA C, 1, 4 and 6:	Pottery: 47, 51, 80, 85.
		Glass: 1, 20.
		Metalwork: 17.
		Coins (both from surface of Phase D): 30 (1380/81); 32 (1363–77)
	AREA C2–3, 5:	Pottery: 70.
UNSTRATIFIED:		Coin: 34 (1913).

APPENDIX 3

CORRELATION OF CONTEXT NUMBERS WITH AREAS AND PHASES

Context	Area(s)	Phase	Context	Area(s)	Phase
1	B	F	25	B	D
2	C	F	26	C	E
3	C	F	27	C	F
4	C	F	28	B	B
5	B	F	29	B	D
6	B	F	30	B	B
7	B	F	31	B	B
8	B	E	32	C	C
9	C	F	33	C	B
10	A	F	34	BI	E
11	C	E	35	B	B
12	C	B	36	BI	D
13	C	E	37	BI	D
14	C	F	38	A2	EI
15	C	E	39	A2	EI
16	C	F	40	A2	EI
17	C	D	41	CI	F
18	A, C	B	42	CI	F
19	C	E	43	CI	E
20	B	D	44	AI, D	B
21	C	C	45	A2	EI
22	A2	F	46	A2	E
23	A2	EI	47	AI	EI
24	AI	F	48	AI	E

Context	Area(s)	Phase	Context	Area(s)	Phase
49	A1	E1	108	A1	D
50	A1	F	109	C3	B
51	A1	E1	110	C3	E
52	A	E1	111	C	A
53	A	F	112	C	Bedrock
54	A	E1	113	C1	A
55	A1	E	114	C4	F
56	A1	E1	115	C3	E
57	A1	E	116	C4	D
58	C1	D	117	C2	D
59	B1	B	118	C3	D
60	A2	E	119	C3	D
61	A1	E	120	C3	F
62	A2	E	121	A1	C
63	A2	E	122	A3	F
64	A2	E	123	C3	D
65	A1	E	124	C3	B
66	B	B	125	C3	B
67	B	A	126	A3	E1
68	B	A	127	C2	D
69	D	F	128	C3	A
70	Z	F(A)	129	A3	E
71	B	A	130	A3	E
72	C1	D	131	A3	D1
73	A2	E	132	C2	B
74	A2	E	133	A3	D
75	A2	E	134	C5	F
76	B	A	135	C2	A
77	A1	E	136	C2	A
78	A1	E	137	C2	B
79	C1	B	138	C2	A
80	C1	B	139	C5	B
81	C1	B	140	C5	E
82	C1	B	141	A1, A3	C
83	C1	A	142	A1, A3	C
84	C1	B	143	A1, A3	C
85	A2	E	144	A1, A3	B
86	A2	D1	145	A1, A3	C
87	B	A	146	A1, A3	C
88	B	A	147	C5	B
89	A2	D1	148	C5	B
90	A2	E	149	C5	B
91	A1	B	150	C5	E
92	C	B	151	C5	E
93	C	B	152	C5	E
94	C	A	153	C5	E
95	A2	E	154	A1, A3	B
96	A2	E	155	A1, A3	B
97	C1	B	156	A1, A3	A
98	A1	D1	157	A1	D1
99	C2	F	158	A1	E
100	A, C	B	159	C6	F
101	A2-3	B	160	A	F
102	C3	F	161	A3	B
103	C	A	162	C2	A
104	C2	E	163	B	E1
105	A1	D1	164	B	E1
106	A1	E	165	C3	A
107	A1	E			

BIBLIOGRAPHY

ABBREVIATIONS

AASOR   Annual of the American Schools of Oriental Research
ADAJ   *Annual of the Department of Antiquities of Jordan*
BAR-S   British Archaeological Reports, International Series
BASOR   *Bulletin of the American Schools of Oriental Research*
EAEHL   *Encyclopedia of Archaeological Excavations in the Holy Land*, ed. by M. Avi-Yonah and E. Stern, 4 vols. (Jerusalem 1975–78)
EHR   *English Historical Review*
IEJ   *Israel Exploration Journal*
JPOS   *Journal of the Palestine Oriental Society*
LA   *Liber Annuus Studii Biblici Franciscani* (Jerusalem)
Outremer   *Outremer: Studies in the History of the Crusading Kingdom of Jerusalem, Presented to Joshua Prawer*, ed. by B. Z. Kedar, H. E. Mayer and R. C. Smail (Jerusalem 1982)
PAM   Palestine Archaeological Museum, Archives of the Department of Antiquities of Palestine, 1918–1948
PE(F)Q(S)   *Palestine Exploration (Fund) Quarterly (Statement)*
PJb   *Palästinajahrbuch des deutschen evangelischen Instituts für Altertums-Wissenschaft des Heiligen Landes zu Jerusalem*
PPTS   *Palestine Pilgrims' Text Society Library*, 13 vols. (London 1890–97)
QDAP   *Quarterly of the Department of Antiquities of Palestine*
RB   *Revue biblique*
RHC   *Recueil des Historiens des Croisades*
—Occ   *—Historiens occidentaux*, 5 vols. (Paris 1844–95)
—Or   *—Historiens orientaux*, 5 vols. (Paris 1872–1906)
—Lois   *—Les Assises de Jérusalem*, 2 vols. (Paris 1841–43)
—Arm   *—Documents arméniens*, 2 vols. (Paris 1869–1906)
RIC   *Roman Imperial Coinage*, by H. Mattingly, E. A. Sydenham and others (London 1923–)
Rolls Series   Rerum Britanicarum medii aeui scriptores or Chronicles and Memorials of Great Britain and Ireland in the Middle Ages
ZDMG   *Zeitschrift der deutschen morganländischen Gesellschaft*
ZDPV   *Zeitschrift des deutschen Palästina-Vereins*

PRIMARY SOURCES

Amadi, *Chroniques d'Amadi et de Strambaldi*, ed. by R. de Mas Latrie, 1 (Paris 1891).

Ambroise, *L'Estoire de la Guerre Sainte (1190–1192)*, ed. and transl. by G. Paris (Paris 1897).

al-ʿAynī Badr al-Dīn, *Colliers de perles*, RHC Or, 2, 1 (Paris 1887), 181–250.

Bahā' al-Dīn Ibn Shaddād, *The Life of Saladin*, transl. by C. R. Conder, PPTS (London 1897).

Benjamin of Tudela, *The Itinerary of Benjamin of Tudela*, ed. and transl. by M. N. Adler (London 1907).

Burchard of Mount Sion, *Descriptio Terrae Sanctae*, ed. by J. C. M. Laurent, *Peregrinatores medii aeui quatuor* (Leipzig 1864), 1–100; transl. by A. Stewart, PPTS (London 1896).

Carmoly, E., *Itinéraires de la Terre Sainte des xiiie, xive, xve, xvie et xviie siècle, traduits de l'Hébreu* (Brussels 1847).

Cart. des Hosp. = *Cartulaire général de l'Ordre des Hospitaliers de Saint-Jean de Jérusalem (1100–1310)*, ed. by J. Delaville le Roulx, 4 vols. (Paris 1894–1906).

Cod. Dip. = *Codice diplomatico del Sacro Militare Ordine Gerosolimitano oggi di Malta*, ed. by S. Paoli, 2 vols. (Lucca 1733–37).

La Continuation de Guillaume de Tyr (1184–1197), ed. by M. R. Morgan (Documents relatifs à l'histoire des Croisades, 14: Paris 1982).

Delaborde, H. F., ed., *Chartes de la Terre Sainte provenant de l'abbaye de Notre-Dame de Josaphat* (Bibliothèque des Écoles françaises d'Athènes et de Rome, 19: Paris 1880).

Delaville le Roulx, J., ed., *Les Archives, la Bibliothèque et le Trésor de l'Ordre de St. Jean de Jérusalem à Malte* (Bibliothèque des Écoles françaises d'Athènes et de Rome, 32: Paris 1883).

Eracles = L'Estoire d'Eracles empereur et la conqueste de la Terre d'Outremer, RHC Occ, 1–2 (Paris 1844).

Ernoul, *Chronique d'Ernoul et de Bernard le Trésorier*, ed. by L. de Mas Latrie (Paris 1871).

Fulcher of Chartres, *Gesta peregrinantium francorum*, ed. by H. Hagenmeyer, *Historia Hierosolymitana (1095–1127)* (Heidelberg 1913); transl. by F. R. Ryan, *A History of the Expedition to Jerusalem 1095–1127* (Knoxville 1969).

Gesta Francorum expugnantium Hierusalem, RHC Occ, 3 (Paris 1866), 487–543.

Gesta Henrici II et Ricardi I, ed. by W. Stubbs, 2 vols. (Rolls Series, 49: London 1867).

Les Gestes des Chiprois, ed. by G. Raynaud (Société de l'Orient latin, Sér. hist., 5: Geneva 1887).

Holtzmann, W., ed., "Papst-, Kaiser- und Normannenurkunden aus Unteritalien", *Quellen und Forschungen aus italienischen Archiven und Bibliotheken*, 35 (1955), 46–85.

Ibn al-Furāt, *Tārīkh al-Duwal wa'l-Mulūk*, partly ed. and transl. by U. and M. C. Lyons, *Ayyubids, Mamlukes and Crusaders*, 2 vols. (Cambridge 1971).

Ibn Ḥajar al-ʿAsqalānī, *al-Durar al-Kāmina ...*, 3 (Dar al-Kutub al-Haditha: Cairo n.d.).

Itin. Ric. = *Itinerarium peregrinorum et gesta regis Ricardi*, ed. by W. Stubbs (Rolls Series, 38, 1: London 1864; repr. 1964).

John of Ibelin, *Livre de Jean d'Ibelin*, ed. by A. A. Beugnot, RHC Lois, 1 (Paris 1841), 7–432.

King, E. J., translator, *The Rule, Statutes and Customs of the Hospitallers 1099–1310* (London 1934).

Lambert of Hersfeld, *Annales*, ed. by C. L. F. Hesse, *Monumenta Germaniae Historica, Scriptores*, 5 (Hanover 1844; repr. Leipzig 1925), 134–263.

al-Maqrizi, *Histoire des Sultans mamlouks de l'Egypte*, transl. by M. Quatremère, 2 vols. (4 parts) (Paris 1837–45).

Marianus Scottus, *Chronicon*, ed. by C. Waitz, *Monumenta Germaniae Historica, Scriptores*, 5 (Hanover 1844; repr. Leipzig 1925), 481–568.

al-Muqaddasī, Muhammad Ibn Āhmad, *Description of Syria including Palestine*, transl. by G. Le Strange, PPTS (London 1886).

Nāsir-i Khusraw, *Diary of a Journey through Syria and Palestine*, transl. by G. Le Strange, PPTS (London 1888).

RCEA = *Répertoire chronologique d'épigraphie arabe*, ed. by E. Combé, J. Sauvaget and G. Wiet (Inst. français d'Archéologie orientale: Cairo 1931–).

La Règle du Temple, ed. by H. de Curzon (Société historique de France, 228: Paris 1886; repr. 1977).

Ricoldus de Monte Crucis, *Liber peregrinacionis*, ed. by J. C. M. Laurent, *Peregrinatores medii aeui quatuor* (Leipzig 1864), 101–141.

Röhricht, R., "Karten und Pläne zur Palästinakunde aus dem 7. bis 16. Jahrhundert", *ZDPV*, 14 (1891), 8–11, no. 1; 87–92, no. 2; 137–141, nos. 3–4; 15 (1892), 34–39. nos. 5–9; 185–188, nos. 10–14; 18 (1895), 173–182, nos. 15–17.

RRH = *Regesta Regni Hierosolymitani*, ed. by R. Röhricht (Innsbruck 1893); *Additamentum* (Innsbruck 1904).

Sanudo, Marino, *Liber secretorum fidelium crucis super Terrae Sanctae recuperatione et conseruatione*, ed. by J. Bongars (Hanau 1611; repr. Jerusalem 1972).

Sinopoli di Giunta, Sac. G. P., ed., "Tabulario di S. Maria di Agira", *Archivio storico per la Sicilia orientale*, 22 (1926), 135–190.

Templar of Tyre, in *Gestes des Chiprois*, p. 141f.

Theodoric, *Libellus de Locis Sanctis*, ed. by T. Tobler (St. Gall—Paris 1865); ed. by M. L. and W. Bulst (Heidelberg 1976); transl. by A. Stewart, *PPTS* (London 1891).

William of Tyre, *Historia rerum in partibus transmarinis gestarum*, *RHC Occ*, 1–2 (Paris 1844); transl. by E. A. Babcock and A. C. Krey, *A History of Deeds done beyond the Sea*, 2 vols. (Columbia University Press, Records of Civilization, 35: New York 1943).

SECONDARY LITERATURE

Abel, F. M., 1928, "Notes sur les environs de Bir-Zeit", *JPOS*, 8, 49–55.

Abel, F. M., 1933, *Géographie de la Palestine*, 2 vols. (Paris 1933–38).

Abel, F. M., 1940, "La liste des donations de Baïbars en Palestine d'après la charte de 663 h. (1265)", *JPOS*, 19, 39–44.

Abu Khalaf, M. F., 1983, "Khan Yunus and the khans of Palestine", *Levant*, 15, 178–186; pls. XXIII–XXVI.

Alfieri, A., 1931, "Les insectes de la tombe de Toutankhamon", *Bulletin de la Société entomologique d'Egypte*, 24, 188–189.

Alt, A., 1931, "Das Institut in den Jahren 1939 und 1930", *PJb*, 27, 5–50.

Amiran, D. H. K., 1953, "The pattern of settlement in Palestine", *IEJ*, 3, 65–78, 192–209, 250–260.

Andrews, D., and D. Pringle, 1977, "Lo scavo dell'area sud del convento di San Silvestro a Genova (1971–1976)", *Archeologia medievale*, 4, 47–99.

Ashtor, E., 1970a, "Quelques observations d'un orientaliste sur la thèse de Pirenne", *Journal of Economic and Social History of the Orient*, 13, 166–194 (= Ashtor 1978, ch. I).

Ashtor, E., 1970b, "Nouvelles reflexions sur la thèse de Pirenne", *Revue suisse d'Histoire*, 20, 601–607 (= Ashtor 1978, ch. II).

Ashtor, E., 1976, *A Social and Economic History of the Near East in the Middle Ages* (London).

Ashtor, E., 1978, *Studies on the Levantine Trade in the Middle Ages* (London).

Avi-Yonah, M., 1940, *Map of Roman Palestine*, 2nd edition (Jerusalem).

Avi-Yonah, M., 1958, "The economics of Byzantine Palestine", *IEJ*, 8, 39–51.

Avi-Yonah, M., 1970, "Palestine under the Mamluks and the Ottomans", *Atlas of Israel* (Jerusalem–Amsterdam), sheet IX/11.

Avi-Yonah, M., 1975, "Bahan", *EAEHL*, 1, 306.

Avi-Yonah, M., 1976, *Gazetteer of Roman Palestine* (Qedem, 5: Jerusalem).

Ayalon, D., 1965, "The Mamluks and naval power—A phase in the struggle between Islam and Christian Europe", *Proceedings of the Israel Academy of Sciences and Humanities*, 1, 8, 1–12; repr. in *Studies on the Mamluks of Egypt (1250–1517)* (London 1977), ch. VI.

Bagatti, B., 1979, *Antichi villaggi cristiani di Samaria* (Studium Biblicum Franciscanum, Collectio minor, 19: Jerusalem).

Balog, P., 1964, *The Coinage of the Mamluk Sultans of Egypt and Syria* (Numismatic Studies, 12: American Numismatic Society, New York).

Baramki, D. C., 1944, "The pottery from Kh. el Mefjer", *QDAP*, 10, 65–103; pls. XVI–XXI.

Ben-Tor, A., Y. Portugali and M. Avissàr, 1979, "The second season of excavations at Tel Yoqne'am, 1978: preliminary report", *IEJ*, 29, 65–83; pls. 9–11.

Ben-Tor, A., and R. Rosenthal, 1978, "The first season of excavations at Tel Yoqne'am, 1977", *IEJ*, 28, 57–82; pls. 16–18.

Benvenisti, M., 1970, *The Crusaders in the Holy Land* (Jerusalem).

Benvenisti, M., 1977, "Montfort", *EAEHL*, 3, 886–888.

Benvenisti, M., 1982, "*Bovaria—Babriyya*: a Frankish residue on the map of Palestine", in *Outremer*, 130–152.

Beyer, G., 1936, "Das Gebiet der Kreuzfahrerherrschaft Caesarea in Palästina", *ZDPV*, 59, 1–91.

Beyer, G., 1940, "Neapolis und sein Gebiet in der Kreuzfahrerzeit", *ZDPV*, 63, 155–209.

Beyer, G., 1942, "Die Kreuzfahrergebiete von Jerusalem und St. Abraham", *ZDPV*, 65, 165–211.

Beyer, G., 1951, "Die Kreuzfahrergebiete Südwestpalästinas", *ZDPV*, 68, 148–281.

Boessneck, J., 1969, "Osteological differences between sheep and goat", in *Science in Archaeology*, ed. by D. Brothwell and E. S. Higgs (London), 331–358.

de Bouard, M., 1974, "De l'*aula* au *donjon*: les fouilles de la motte de La Chapelle à Doué-la-Fontaine (X^e–XIe siècle)", *Archéologie médiévale*, 3–4 (1973–74), 5–110.

Brown, R. A., 1976, *English Castles*, revised edition (London).

Bucher, A., 1967, *Vergleichend morphlogische Untersuchungen an Einzelknochen des postkranalien Skeletts in Mitteleuropa vorkommender Schwäne und Gänse* (Munich).

Buckingham, J. S., 1822, *Travels in Palestine*, 2 vols. (London).

Bulst-Thiele, M. L., 1974, *Sacrae Domus Militiae Templi Hierosolymitani Magistri* (Abhandlungen der Akad. der Wissenschaften in Götingen, Phil.-hist. Klasse, 3s., 86: Götingen).

Cahen, C., 1951, "Le régime rural syrien au temps de la domination franque", *Bulletin de la Faculté des Lettres de Strasbourg*, 286–310.

Carswell, J., 1972a, *Kütahya Tiles and Pottery from the Armenian Cathedral of St. James, Jerusalem*, 2 vols. (Oxford).

Carswell, J., 1972b, *"Sīn in Syria"*, *Iran*, 17, 15–24.

Chaddick, P. R., and F. F. Leek, 1972, "Further specimens of stored product insects found in ancient Egyptian tombs", *Journal of Stored Products Research*, 8, 83–86.

Châtelain, A., 1973, *Donjons romans des Pays d'Ouest: Étude comparative sur les donjons romans quadrangulaires de la France de l'Ouest* (Paris).

Cherry, J. F., 1976, "Frogs round the pond: perspectives on current archaeological survey projects in the Mediterranean region", in Keller and Rupp (eds.) 1976, 375–416.

Clermont-Ganneau, C., 1888, *Recueil d'Archéologie orientale*, 8 vols. (Paris 1888–1924).

Clermont-Ganneau, C., 1896, *Archaeological Researches in Palestine during the Years 1873–1874*, 2 vols. (London 1896–99).

CNRS, 1979, *Géographie historique du village et de la maison rurale, Actes du colloque tenu à Bazas (Gironde) les 19–21 octobre 1978* (E.R.A., 443: Paris).

Comba, R., 1983, "Archeologia e storia delle campagne (secoli X–XV)", *Archeologia medievale*, 10, 89–110.

Conder, C. R., 1874, "Lieut. Claude R. Conder's reports, XVI–XXI", *PEFQS*, 11–24, 35–64, 178–187.

Conder, C. R., 1875, "The Survey of Western Palestine: Lieut. Claude R. Conder's reports, XXII–XXXV", *PEFQS*, 5–27, 63–94, 125–168, 188–195.

Conder, C. R., 1889a, "Norman Palestine", *PEFQS*, 195–201.

Conder, C. R., 1889b, "The Norman fiefs in Palestine", *PEFQS*, 201–202.

Conder, C. R., 1890, "Norman Palestine", *PEFQS*, 29–37.

Conder, C. R., and H. H. Kitchener, 1881, *The Survey of Western Palestine: Memoirs of the Topography, Orography, Hydrography and Archaeology*, 3 vols. (London 1881–83).

Dar, S., and S. Applebaum, 1973, "The Roman road from Antipatris to Caesarea", *PEQ*, 150, 91–99.

Davidson, G. R., 1952, *Corinth, XII: The Minor Objects* (Princeton).

Davis, S. J. M., 1982, "Climatic change and the advent of domestication," *Paléorient*, 8, 2, 5–16.

Dean, B., 1927, *A Crusaders' Fortress in Palestine: A Report of Excavations Made by the Museum, 1926* (Part II of the Bulletin of the Metropolitan Museum of Art: New York); repr. as *The Crusaders' Fortress of Montfort*, with introd. by M. Benvenisti (Jerusalem 1982).

Deschamps, P., 1934, *Les châteaux des Croisés en Terre Sainte, I: Le Crac des Chevaliers*, 2 vols. (Bibl. archéol. et hist., 19: Paris).

Deschamps, P., 1939, *Les châteaux des Croisés en Terre Sainte, II: La défense du royaume de Jérusalem*, 2 vols. (Bibl. archéol. et hist., 34: Paris).

Deschamps, P., 1973, *Les châteaux des Croisés en Terre-Sainte, III: La défense du comté de Tripoli et de la principauté d'Antioche*, 2 vols. (Bibl. archéol. et hist., 90: Paris).

Deyres, M., 1969, "Le donjon de Langeais", *Bulletin monumental*, 128, 177–193.

Dikigoropoulos, A. I., and A. H. S. Megaw, 1948, "Early glazed pottery from Polis", *Report of the Dept. of Antiquities, Cyprus* (1940–48), 77–93; pls. VIII–IX.

Edwards, R., 1984, "The Crusader donjon at Anavarza in Cilicia", *Tenth Annual Byzantine Studies Conference, Abstracts of Papers, November 1–4, 1984, The University of Cincinnati*, 53–55.

El'ad, A., 1982, "The coastal cities of Palestine during the early Middle Ages", *Jerusalem Cathedra*, 2, 146–167.

Enlart, C., 1925, *Les monuments des Croisés dans le Royaume de Jérusalem: Architecture religeuse et civile*, 2 vols. + albums (Bibl. archéol. et hist., 7–8: Paris 1925–28).

Finó, J.-F., 1970, *Forteresses de la France médiévale: Construction—attaque—défense* (Paris).

Fixot, M., 1974, "La construction de châteaux dans la campagne d'Apt et de Pélissanne du XIe au XIIIe siècle", *Archéologie médiévale*, 3–4 (1973–74), 245–296.

Fournier, G., 1978, *Le Château dans la France médiévale: Essai de sociologie monumentale* (Paris).

Franken, H. J., and J. Kalsbeek, 1975, *Potters of a Medieval Village in the Jordan Valley: Excavations at Tell deir ᶜAllā: A Medieval Tell, Tell Abu Gourdan, Jordan* (North Holland Ceramic Studies in Archaeology, 3: Amsterdam).

Freeman, P., ed. 1980, *Common Insect Pests of Stored Food Products: A Guide to their Identification* (British Museum, Natural History: London).

Frierman, J. D., 1975, *Medieval Ceramics VI to XIII Centuries* (Los Angeles).

Frova, A., M. Avi-Yonah and A. Negev, 1975, "Caesarea", *EAEHL*, 1, 270–285.

Gatt, G., 1885, "Industrielles aus Gaza", *ZDPV*, 8, 69–79.

Geva, H., 1983, "Excavations in the Citadel of Jerusalem, 1979–1980: preliminary report", *IEJ*, 33, 55–71; pls. 3–7.

Gophna, R., and M. Kokhavi, 1966, "An archaeological survey of the Plain of Sharon", *IEJ*, 16, 144.

Gophna, R., and Y. Porath, 1972, "The Land of Ephraim and Manasseh," in Kochavi (ed.) 1972, 196–241.

Grant, A., 1975, "The animal bones", in B. Cunliffe, *Excavations at Portchester Castle, I: Roman* (Reports of the Research Committee of the Society of Antiquaries of London, 32: London), 437–450.

Guérin, V., 1868, *Judée*, 3 vols. (Description géographique, historique et archéologique de la Palestine, 1: Paris 1868–69).

Guérin, V., 1874, *Samarie*, 2 vols. (Description géographique, historique et archéologique de la Palestine, 2: Paris 1874–75).

Guy, P. L. O. 1954, "Archaeological evidence of soil erosion and sedimentation in Wadi Musrara", *IEJ*, 4, 77–87; pls. 5–8.

Harding, G. J., 1951, "Excavations on the Citadel, Amman", *ADAJ*, 1, 7–16; pls. I–V.

Hartmann, R., 1910, "Die Strasse von Damaskus nach Kairo", *ZDMG*, 64, 665–702.

Hartmann, R., 1913, "Barīd", *Encyclopaedia of Islam*, 1 (Leiden-London), 658–659.

Haufani, I., 1977, *al-Qūds* (4 June).

Hazard, H. W., 1975, "Caesarea and the Crusades", in *Studies in the History of Caesarea Maritima*, ed. by C. T. Fritsch (BASOR, Supplemental Series, 19: Missoula, Montana), 79–114.

Heck, C., 1975, "Implantation religeuse et renouveau des campagnes en Provence du XIe au XIIIe siècle: la région de Lambese", *Archéologie médiévale*, 5, 45–72.

Heinzel, H., R. Fitter and J. Parslow, 1972, *The Birds of Britain and Europe* (London).

Helbaek, H., 1961, "Late Bronze Age and Byzantine crops at Beycesultan in Anatolia", *Anatolian Studies*, 11, 77–99.

Helbaek, H., 1963, "Isin-Larsan and Horian food plants at Tell Bazmosian in the Dokan valley", *Sumer*, 19, 27–35.

Héliot, P., 1969, "L'évolution du donjon dans le nord-ouest de la France et en Angleterre au XII⁰ siècle", *Bulletin archéologique du Comité des Travaux historiques et scientifiques*, ns., 5, 141–194.

Héliot, P., 1974, "Les origines du donjon résidentiel et les donjons-palais romans de France et d'Angleterre", *Cahiers de Civilization médiévale*, 17, 217–234.

Honigman, E., 1936, "al-Ramla", *Encyclopaedia of Islam*, 3 (Leiden-London), 1115–1117.

Hubbard, R. N. L. B., 1976, "Crops and climate in prehistoric Europe", *World Archaeology*, 8, 159–168.

Hubbard, R. N. L. B., 1980, "The development of agriculture in Europe and the Near East", *Economic Botany*, 34, 51–67.

Hütteroth, W., 1975, "The pattern of settlement in Palestine in the sixteenth century: geographical research on Turkish Defter-i Mufaṣṣel", in *Studies on Palestine during the Ottoman Period*, ed. by M. Maʿoz (Jerusalem), 3-10.

Hütteroth, A., and K. Abdulfattah, 1977, *Historical Geography of Palestine, Transjordan and Southern Syria in the Late 16th Century* (Erlanger Geographische Arbeiten, Sonderbuch, 5: Erlangen).

Irwin, R., 1977, "Iqṭāʿ and the end of the Crusader states", in *The Eastern Mediterranean Lands in the Period of the Crusades*, ed. by P. M. Holt (Warminster), 62–77.

Isings, C., 1957, *Roman Glass from Dated Finds* (Archaeologica Traiectina, 2: Groningen).

Israel (Govt. of), 1964, "Schedule of monuments and historical sites" [Hebrew], *Reshumot Yalqut ha-Pirsumium* (Official Gazette Announcements), 1091 (18 May), 1349–1561; i-xliii.

Jaussen, J. A., and F. M. Abel, 1923, "Trois inscriptions arabes, inédites, du Ḥaram d'Hébron", *RB*, 32, 80–96.

Jenkins, M., 1983, *Islamic Pottery: A Brief History* (Metropolitan Museum of Art: New York).

Jenkins, M., 1984, "Mamluk underglaze-painted pottery: foundations for future study", *Muqarnas*, 2, 95–114.

Johns, C. N., 1934, "Excavations at Pilgrims' Castle, ʿAtlit (1932); the ancient tell and the outer defences of the castle", *QDAP*, 3, 145–164; pls. XLVIII–LXV.

Johns, C. N., 1936, "Excavations at Pilgrims' Castle, ʿAtlit (1932–3); stables at the south-west of the suburb", *QDAP*, 5, 31–60; pls. XVIII–XXVIII.

Johns, C. N., 1937, *Palestine of the Crusaders: A Map of the Country on Scale 1:350,000 with Historical Introduction & Gazetteer* (Survey of Palestine: Jaffa).

Johns, C. N., 1939, "The abbey of St. Mary in the valley of Jehoshaphat, Jerusalem", *QDAP*, 8, 117–136.

Johns, C. N., 1947, *Guide to ʿAtlit* (Jerusalem).

Johns, C. N., 1975, "ʿAtlit", *EAEHL*, 1, 130–140.

Kallner-Amiran, D. H., 1951, "A revised earthquake-catalogue of Palestine", *IEJ*, 1 (1950–51), 223–246.

Karmon, Y., 1961, "Geographical influences on the historical routes in the Sharon plain", *PEQ*, 93, 43–60.

Kedar, B. Z., and R. D. Pringle, 1985, "La Fève: a Crusader castle in the Jezreel Valley", *IEJ*, 35, 164–179.

Keller, D. R., and D. W. Rupp, eds., 1983, *Archaeological Survey in the Mediterranean Area* (BAR-S, 155: Oxford).

Kennedy, H., 1985, "From *polis* to *madina*: urban change in late antique and early Islamic Syria", *Past and Present*, 106, 3–27.

Kingdom, J., 1977, *East African Mammals, IIIA: Carnivores* (London and New York).

Kloner, A., 1983, "Two Crusader sites in the south Judean foothills", *Israel—Land and Nature*, 8, 2 (Winter 1982–83), 58–60.

Kochavi, M., ed., 1972, *Judaea, Samaria and the Golan: Archaeological Survey 1967–68* (Archaeological Survey of Israel, 1: Jerusalem).

La Monte, J. L., 1947, "The lords of Caesarea in the period of the Crusades", *Speculum*, 22, 145–161.

La Monte, J. L., and N. Downs III, 1950, "The lords of Bethsan in the Kingdoms of Jerusalem and Cyprus", *Medievalia et Humanistica*, 6, 57–75.

Lane, A., 1937, "Medieval finds from al-Mina in North Syria", *Archaeologia*, 87, 19–78; pls. XVI–XXVII.

Lane, A., 1971, *Later Islamic Pottery: Persia, Syria, Egypt, Turkey*, 2nd edition revised by R. Pinder-Wilson (London).

Langé, S., 1965, *Architettura delle crociate in Palestina* (Como).

Lawlor, J., 1980, "The 1978 excavation of the Hesban north church", *ADAJ*, 24, 95–105.

Lawrence, T. E., 1936, *Crusader Castles*, 2 vols. (London).

Le Strange, G., 1890, *Palestine under the Muslims* (London).

Loffreda, S., 1983, "Nuovi contributi di Cafarnao per la ceramologia palestinese", *LA*, 33, 347–372; pls. 29–48.

NcNicoll, A., R. H. Smith and B. Hennessy, 1982, *Pella in Jordan, I: An Interim Report on the Joint University of Sydney and the College of Wooster Excavations at Pella 1979–1981*, 2 vols. (Canberra).

le Maho, J., 1976, "L'apparition des seigneuries châtelaines dans le Grand-Caux à l'époque ducale", *Archéologie médiévale*, 6, 5–148.

Mayer, H. E., 1977, *Bistümer, Klöster und Stifter im Königreich Jerusalem* (Schrifter der Monumenta Germaniae Historica, 26: Stuttgart).

Mayer, L. A., 1931, "Arabic inscriptions of Gaza, V", *JPOS*, 11, 144–151.

Mayer, L. A., 1932, "The name of Khān el Aḥmar, Beisān", *QDAP*, 1, 95–96.

Mayer, L. A., 1933, *Saracenic Heraldry: A Survey* (Oxford).

Mayer, L. A., and J. Pinkerfeld, 1950, *Some Principal Muslim Religious Buildings in Israel* (Ministry of Religious Affairs: Jerusalem).

Megaw, A. H. S., and R. E. Jones, 1983, "Byzantine and allied pottery: a contribution by chemical analysis to problems of origin and distribution", *Annual of the British School at Athens*, 78, 235–263; pls. 24–30.

Meistermann, B., 1936, *Guide de Terre Sainte*, 3rd edition (Paris).

Metcalf, D. M., 1983, *Coinage of the Crusades and the Latin East in the Ashmolean Museum, Oxford* (Royal Numismatic Society, Special Publication, 15: London).

Moaz, K., and S. Ory, 1977, *Inscriptions arabes de Damas: Les stèles funéraires, I: Cimetière d'al-Bab al-Saǧir* (Damascus).

Munro, J. W., 1966, *Pests of Stored Products* (London).

Neef, H.-D., 1981, "Die mutatio Betthar: eine römische Strassenstation zwischer Caesarea und Antipatris", *ZDPV*, 97, 74–80.

Neubauer, A., 1868, *La Géographie du Talmud* (Paris).

Oren, E. D., 1971, "Early Islamic material from Ganei-Hamat (Tiberias)", *Archaeology*, 24, 274–277.

Orfali, G., 1924, *Gethsémani, ou notice sur l'église de l'Agonie ou de la Prière, d'après les fouilles récentes accomplies par la Custodie franciscaine de Terre Sainte (1909–1920)* (Paris).

Orni, E., and E. Efrat, 1980, *Geography of Israel*, 4th edition (Jerusalem).

Ory, S., ed., 1975, *Archives Max Van Berchem conservées à la Bibliothèque publique et universitaire de Genève: Catalogue de la photothèque* (Beirut).

Ovadiah, A., 1970, *Corpus of the Byzantine Churches in the Holy Land* (Theophaneia, 22: Bonn).

Ovadiah, A., and C. Gomez de Silva, 1981–84, "Supplementum to the Corpus of the Byzantine Churches in the Holy Land", *Levant*, 13 (1981), 200–261; 14 (1982), 122–170; 16 (1984), 129–165.

Palestine (Govt. of), 1929, "Provisional schedule of historical sites and monuments", ed. by E. T. Richmond, *Palestine Gazette Extraordinary* (15 June).

Palestine (Govt. of), 1933, "Schedule of historical monuments and historical sites (Additions)", ed. by R. W. Hamilton, *Palestine Gazette Extraordinary*, 387 (7 Sept.).

Palestine (Govt. of), 1944, "Schedule of historical monuments and sites, Suppl. no. 2", ed. by R. W. Hamilton, *Palestine Gazette Extraordinary*, 1375 (25 Nov.).

Palestine (Govt. of), 1948, *Department of Antiquities: Geographical List of the Record Files, 1918–1948* (Israel Dept. of Antiquities: Jerusalem 1976).

Palestine Exploration Fund, 1881, *The Survey of Western Palestine: Special Papers* (London).

Paley, S. M., and Y. Porath, 1979, "The regional project in ʿEmeq Ḥefer, 1979", *IEJ*, 29, 236–239.

Paley, S. M., and Y. Porath, 1980, "The regional project in ʿEmeq Ḥefer 1980", *IEJ*, 30, 217–219.

Paley, S. M., and Y. Porath, 1982, "The ʿEmeq Ḥefer regional project, 1981", *IEJ*, 32, 66–67.

Paley, S. M., Y. Porath and R. R. Stieglitz, 1982, "The ʿEmeq Ḥefer archaeological research project, 1982", *IEJ*, 32, 259–261; pl. 43c.

Palmer, E. H., 1881, *The Survey of Western Palestine: Arabic and English Name Lists* (London).

Payne, S., 1972, "Partial recovery and sample bias: the results of some sieving experiments", in *Papers in Economic Prehistory*, ed. by E. S. Higgs (Cambridge), 49–64.

Ploug, G., et al., 1969, *Hama, fouilles et recherches 1931–1938, IV, 3: Les petits objets médiévaux sauf les verreries et poteries* (Nationalmuseets Skrifter, Storre Beretninger, 7: Copenhagen).

Porter, V., 1981, *Medieval Syrian Pottery (Raqqa Ware)* (Oxford).

Poulsen, V., 1957, "Les poteries", in *Hama, fouilles et recherches 1931–1938, IV, 2: Les verreries et poteries médiévales*, by P. J. Riis and V. Poulsen (Nationalmuseets Skrifter, Større Beretninger, 3: Copenhagen), 117–283.

Prawer, J., 1975, *Histoire du Royaume latin de Jérusalem*, 2nd edition, 2 vols. (Paris).

Prawer, J., 1980, *Crusader Institutions* (Oxford).

Prawer, J., and M. Benvenisti, 1970, "Palestine under the Crusaders", *Atlas of Israel* (Jerusalem–Amsterdam), sheet IX/10.

Pringle, R. D., 1977, "La ceramica dell'area sud del convento di S. Silvestro a Genova", *Archeologia medievale*, 4, 100–161.

Pringle, R. D., 1981, *The Defence of Byzantine Africa from Justinian to the Arab Conquest*, 2 vols. (BAR-S, 99: Oxford).

Pringle, R. D., 1983a, "Two medieval villages north of Jerusalem: archaeological investigations in al-Jib and ar-Ram", *Levant*, 15, 141–177; pls. XVI–XXIIa.

Pringle, R. D., 1983b, "Burj al-Aḥmar" [Hebrew], *Hadashot Arḥiologiot*, 83, 22–24.

Pringle, R. D., 1984a, "Thirteenth-century pottery from the monastery of St. Mary of Carmel", *Levant*, 16, 91–111.

Pringle, R. D., 1984b, 'Excavations at al-Burj al-Ahmar, July–August 1983: an interim report", *Notiziario di Archeologia medievale*, 37, 7; 38, 21–22; repr. *Bulletin of the Society for the Study of the Crusades and the Latin East*, 4, 16–19.

Pringle, R. D., 1984c, "El-Burj el-Aḥmar (Ḥ. Burgeta), 1983", *IEJ*, 34, 52–55; fig. 1; pl. 7b.

Pringle, R. D., 1984d, "El-Burj el-Aḥmar 1983", *RB*, 91, 267–271; fig. 11; pl. IXa–c.

Pringle, R. D., 1985a, "Magna Mahumeria (al-Bira): the archaeology of a Frankish new town in Palestine", in *Crusade and Settlement: Papers read at the First Conference of the Society for the Study of the Crusades and the Latin East and presented to R. C. Smail*, ed. by P. W. Edbury (Cardiff), 147–165.

Pringle, R. D., 1985b, "Medieval pottery from Caesarea: the Crusader period", *Levant*, 17, 171–202; pl. XVII.

Pringle, R. D., forthcoming, "ʿAkko 1974: the medieval pottery from Site D", in ʿ*Akko Excavations*, ed. by M. Dothan, 1 (Haifa).

Prutz, H., 1881, "Die Besitzungen des Johanniterordens in Palästina und Syrien", *ZDPV*, 4, 157–193.

Quatremère, M., 1837, *Histoire des Sultans mamlouks de l'Egypte*, 2 vols. (4 parts) (Paris 1837–45).

Reich, R., 1983, "Archaeological sites in the area of Nathanya" [Hebrew], in *Sepher Nethania* [Book of Nathanya], ed. by A. Shmuʿeli and M. Brawer (Tel Aviv-Nathanya n.d.), 101–114.

Reifenberg, A., 1951, "Caesarea: a study in the decline of a town', *IEJ*, 1 (1950–51), 20–32; pls. VIII–XVI.

Reifenberg, A., 1955, *The Struggle between the Desert and the Sown: Rise and Fall of Agriculture in the Levant* (Jerusalem).

Renn, D. F., 1968, *Norman Castles in Britain* (London).

Rey, E., 1871, *Étude sur les monuments de l'architecture militaire des Croisés en Syrie* (Paris).

Rey, E., 1883, *Les colonies franques de Syrie aux XIIme et XIIIme siècles* (Paris).

Riis, R. J., 1957, "Les verreries', in P. J. Riis and V. Poulsen, *Hama, fouilles et recherches 1931–1938, IV, 2: Les verreries et poteries médiévales* (Copenhagen), 30–116.

Riley-Smith, J. S. C., 1967, *The Knights of St. John in Jerusalem and Cyprus, c. 1050–1310* (History of the Order of the Hospital of St. John of Jerusalem, 1: London).

Riely-Smith, J. S. C., 1971, "Notes", in *Ayyubids, Mamlukes and Crusaders: Selections from . . . Ibn al-Furāt*, ed. and transl. by U. and M. C. Lyons, 2 (Cambridge).

Riley-Smith, J. S. C., 1972, "Some lesser officials in Latin Syria", *EHR*, 87, 1–26.

Riley-Smith, J. S. C., 1977, "The survival in Latin Palestine of Muslim administration", in *The Eastern Mediterranean Lands in the Period of the Crusades*, ed. by P. M. Holt (Warminster), 9–22.

Riley-Smith, J. S. C., 1983, "The motives of the earliest crusaders and the settlement of Latin Palestine, 1095–1100", *EHR*, 98, 721–736.

Rim, M., 1951, "Sand and soil in the coastal plain of Israel", *IEJ*, 1(1950–51), 33–48.

Robinson, R. C. W., 1985, "Tobacco pipes of Corinth and of the Athenian Agora", *Hesperia*, 54, 149–203; pls. 33–64.

Röhricht, R., 1887, "Studien zur mittelalterlichen Geographie und Topographie Syriens", *ZDPV*, 10, 195–344.

Roll, I., and E. Ayalon, 1981, "Two large wine presses in the red soil regions of Israel", *PEQ*, 113, 111–125; pls. IX–XII.

Roll, I., and E. Ayalon, 1982, "Apollonia/Arsur—A coastal town in the southern Sharon Plain" [Hebrew], *Qadmoniot*, 15, 16–22.

Runciman, S., 1954, *A History of the Crusades*, 3 vols. (Cambridge 1954–55).

Salamé-Sarkis, H., 1980, *Contribution à l'histoire de Tripoli et de sa région à l'époque des Croisades* (Bibl. archéol. et hist., 106: Paris).

Saller, S. J., 1957, *Excavations at Bethany (1949–1953)* (Studium Biblicum Franciscanum, Collectio maior, 12: Jerusalem).

Sauer, J. A., 1982, "The pottery of Jordan in the early Islamic periods", in *Studies in the History and Archaeology of Jordan*, 1, ed, by A. Hadidi (Amman), 329–337.

Sauvaget, J., 1941, *La poste aux chevaux dans l'empire des Mamelouks* (Paris).

Sawyer, P. H., ed., 1976, *Medieval Settlement: Continuity and Change* (London).

Schmidt, O. H., 1970, "Ortsnamen Palästinas in der Kreuzfahrerzeit: Ortsnamenregister zu den Aufsätzen von Prutz, Beyer und Kob in der ZDPV 4–83", *ZDPV*, 86, 117–164.

Shaw, S. A., and N. A. Pharaon, 1941, "Nablus-Tulkarm Valley", *Bulletin of the Government of Palestine Soil Conservation Board*, 1 (Jerusalem).

Silver, I. A., 1969, "The ageing of domestic animals", in *Science in Archaeology*, ed. by D. Brothwell and E. S. Higgs (London), 283–302.

Smail, R. C., 1956, *Crusading Warfare (1097–1193)* (Cambridge Studies in Medieval Life and Thought, ns., 3: Cambridge).

Smail, R. C., 1973, *The Crusaders in Syria and the Holy Land* (Ancient People and Places Series, 82: London).

Smith, R. H., *et al.*, 1980, "Preliminary report on the 1979 season of the Sydney–Wooster joint expedition to Pella", *ADAJ*, 24, 13–40; pls. I–XXXVII.

Steinfield, P., 1983, "Nahal Alexander regional survey", in Keller and Rupp (eds.) 1983, 357–360.

Stern, E., 1978, *Excavations at Tel Mevorakh (1973–1976), Part one: From the Iron Age to the Roman Period* (Qedem, 9: Jerusalem).

Thalmann, J. P., 1978, "Tell ʿArqa (Liban nord), Campagnes I–III (1972–1974), Chantier I, Rapport préliminaire", *Syria*, 55, 1–151.

Tsafrir, Y., 1984, "The Arab conquest and the gradual decline of the population of Eretz Israel" [Hebrew], *Cathedra*, 32 (Jerusalem), 69–78.

Turquety-Pariset, F., 1982, "Fouilles de la municipalité de Beyrouth (1977): les objets", *Syria*, 59, 27–76.

Tzaferis, 1983a, *The Excavations of Kursi-Gergesa* (ʿAtiqot, 16: Jerusalem).

Tzaferis, V., 1983b, "New archaeological evidence on ancient Capernaum", *Biblical Archaeologist*, 46, 198–204.

Van Berchem, M., 1922, *Matériaux pour un Corpus Inscriptionum Arabicarum, II: Syrie du Nord, 1: Jérusalem, Ville* (Mémoires de l'Institut français d'Archéologie orientale du Caire, 43: Cairo).

de Vaux, R., 1946, "Notes archéologiques et topographiques", *RB*, 53, 260–274.

de Vaux, R., and A. M. Steve, 1950, *Fouilles à Qaryet el-ʿEnab, Abū Ġôsh, Palestine* (Paris).

Vita-Finzi, C., 1969, *The Mediterranean Valleys: Geological Changes in Historical Times* (Cambridge).

Walls, A. G., 1974, "The Turbat Barakat Khān or Khalidi Library", *Levant*, 6, 25–50; pls. VII–XVII.

Watson, A. M., 1981, "A medieval green revolution: new crops and farming techniques in the early Islamic World", in *The Islamic Middle East, 700–1900: Studies in Economic and Social History*, ed. by A. L. Udovitch (Princeton), 29–58.

Watson, A. M., 1983, *Agricultural Innovation in the Early Islamic World: The Diffusion of Crops and Farming Techniques, 700–1100* (Cambridge Studies in Islamic Civilization: Cambridge).

Watson, J. P. N., 1978, "The interpretation of epiphyseal fusion data", in *Research Problems in Zooarchaeology*, ed. by D. R. Brothwell, K. D. Thomas and J. Clutton-Brock (University of London, Institute of Archaeology, Occasional Paper, 3: London), 97–101.

Weinberg, G. D., 1975, "A medieval mystery: Byzantine glass production", *Journal of Glass Studies*, 17, 127–141.

Wilson, C. W., 1880, *Picturesque Palestine, Sinai and Egypt*, 4 vols.(London n.d.).

Winnett, F. V., and W. L. Reed, 1964, *The Excavations at Dibon (Dhibân) in Moab* (AASOR, 36–37, for 1957–58: New Haven).

Yeivin, Z., 1955, "Chronique archéologique", *RB*, 65, 82–91.

Zacher, F., 1937, "Vorratsschädlinge und Vorratschutz ihre Bedeutung für Volksernährung und Weltwirtschaft", *Zeitschrift für hygienische Zoologie*, 29, 1–11.

van Zeist, W., and J. A. H. Bakker-Heeres, 1975, "Prehistoric and early historic plant husbandry in the Altinova Plain, southeastern Turkey", in *Korucutepe*, 1, ed. by M. N. van Loon (Oxford & Amsterdam).

Zertal, A., 1977, "A Samaritan ring and the identification of ʿAin-Kushi" [Hebrew], *Qadmoniot*, 10, 84–86.

Ziadeh, N., 1953, *Urban Life in Syria under the Early Mamluks* (American University of Beirut, Oriental Series, 24: Beirut).

INDEX OF PERSONAL NAMES

INDEX OF PLACE-NAMES

Note that names occurring in historical sources are distinguished by being printed in italics